The
Beginnings
of Critical
Realism
in
America

The Beginnings of Critical Realism in America

Main Currents in American Thought,
Volume III

Vernon Louis Parrington

With a new introduction by **Bruce Brown**

Transaction Publishers
New Brunswick (U.S.A.) and London (U.K.)

New material this edition copyright © 2013 by Transaction Publishers, New Brunswick, New Jersey. Originally published in 1927 by Harcourt, Brace and Company, Inc.

This book is printed on acid-free paper that meets the American National Standard for Permanence of Paper for Printed Library Materials.

Library of Congress Catalog Number: 2012028686
ISBN: 978-1-4128-5164-0
Printed in the United States of America

Library of Congress Cataloging-in-Publication Data

Parrington, Vernon Louis, 1871-1929.
    The beginnings of critical realism in America / Vernon Louis Parrington ; with a new introduction by Bruce Brown.
        p. cm. -- (Main currents in American thought ; v. 3)
    Includes bibliographical references and index.
    ISBN 978-1-4128-5164-0 (acid-free paper) 1. American literature--19th century--History and criticism. 2. Realism in literature. I. Title.
PS217.R4P37 2013
809'.912--dc23

                                    2012028686

VERNON LOUIS PARRINGTON

THE sudden death of Professor Vernon Louis Parrington in England, June 16, 1929, cut tragically short his labors on the last volume of *Main Currents in American Thought*. Of this third volume approximately the first half had been completed, which, together with the outline of the work and some scattered essays in sections otherwise undeveloped, constitutes all that the author left. Unfinished it is, yet no completion by another can be justified. That anyone could duplicate his felicity of style, so unobtrusively individual, so sensitively adjusted to the freighted thought, is hardly to be hoped for; and more important, that another scholar could accurately reproduce his interpretation is an assumption not to be warranted. The decision to publish the author's incomplete work is a tribute to his brilliance.

Nevertheless it is possible to know Professor Parrington's chief intentions, particularly when one understands, as his associates did, his principles for organizing materials and his standards of value. Students as well as associates first of all noticed beneath the richness and complexity of his thought a constancy of purpose as clear as the treatment of mass in a Gothic cathedral. Indeed it was through a delight in architecture pursued as a hobby for many years that Parrington expressed this desire for a unity, balanced, harmonious, and properly proportioned.

This architectonic feeling, abundantly illustrated in his writing habits, was carried over not only into his classroom procedure and conversation, but also into his varied interests. Painting as well as architecture had long intrigued him. Though few people knew it, he wrote poetry distinguished for restraint in expression and clarity of form; while in conversation he persistently sought the appropriate phrase, spiced it with wit, salted it with homely realism; for no gentleman of the eighteenth century was more conscious of the charms of good discourse.

Professor Parrington's classroom procedure had a reputation that attracted students not much interested in literature and which appealed to all ranges of intellect. The source of that popularity was the personality of the teacher, together with his gift for presenting ideas and evoking a response. By means of a Socratic cross-examination Parrington made the student discover his intellectual deficiencies; while the class, to its astonishment and delight, found the quest for truth both elusive and exciting. Surprise and satisfied expectation kept the easily bored from sinking into apathy, for there was no telling from day to day just what Professor Parrington was going to do. He paired every occasion with a fitting response; yet this flexibility did not degenerate into an aimless drifting, since he persistently simplified his main objectives and concentrated the material to be studied, while expressing its meaning through a significant symbol or a telling phrase. His classes in the eighteenth century, for example, were given the concept of harmony, balance, and proportion. They found it in architecture, they saw it in dress, they heard it in conversation, they watched it work out in the heroic couplet, they pursued it in Addison, Pope, and Swift; in short, they analyzed the whole social structure of the age and discovered it everywhere. A germinal idea, Parrington liked to call it, while he held it before the class like a many-faceted crystal, slowly turning it around and around so the student could see every face. As a result no student who had taken the course ever forgot the significance of this architectonic trilogy.

In writing habits there was a similar all-encompassing purpose. He habitually began with his thesis—a phrase, a sentence, or a revealing figure. This was examined and stripped of its implications as one would peel an onion layer by layer. So imperious was the habit of this procedure that his ability to write would be blocked until he had in mind a perfectly crystallized concept expressible at the maximum in one sentence. An example of this occurred shortly before he left on his trip to England. He had been working on the period that Mark Twain had labeled the "Gilded Age," but found the title inadequate to his idea, and, as a result, his writing did not get on. Another day some weeks later there was an obvious satisfaction expressed in his bearing and an exceptionally pronounced twinkle in his eye. "I have found the phrase," he said; "I will call it The Great Barbecue." Similarly, the three volumes of this work began in a single paragraph which by progressive unfoldings he expanded to its present scope.

After having made a provisional outline, with each section condensed into a single sentence, he began writing, completing a unit here or there as circumstance and mood directed. When it was completed the process of readjustment began. Each portion was inspected for its length, which had to be fitted to its relative importance; an emphasis here was shifted to balance an emphasis there; the mood of one part was altered to make it harmonize with the mood of its neighbor. As many as twelve times he rewrote a single section in this complex and delicate effort for harmonious adjustment. Finally, he made from this his finished outline.

Knowing Professor Parrington's methods one can now understand the problem he faced and the solution he found when bent on the task of writing a history of American literature. Although he was by nature partial to the claims of aesthetics, yet it was obvious to him that such an approach was foredoomed to failure. All too few of the American writers would deserve treatment on any aesthetic test, while many who were undeniably significant could not possibly be left out even though inferior artistically. Moreover, one only had to look at the numerous attempts already made to see the failure of the belletristic interpretation. What were these histories of American literature? Sprawling lists of names arranged in a fashion that gave little save conventionalized data and some dubious evaluations. Already there was a widespread demand for a new interpretation growing out of these past failures.

Professor Parrington found the first step to a solution when he remembered the day he opened Taine's *Histoire de la littérature anglaise*. It had come as a new and inspiring discovery to find a method that envisaged the literature of a people as the inevitable outgrowth of their racial peculiarities, environment, and epoch. It is true that the claim set up by Taine, that his method was scientific and could account for every phenomenon, proved to be unfounded; but nevertheless his work was epoch-making; it gave a unity and a significance never before attained, and this was what attracted Parrington. Nothing less unifying than Taine's method was thinkable.

A second source of inspiration came from a close friend and colleague, J. Allen Smith, another pioneer figure, who applied to the abstract theorizings of political science the economic realities that underlie and determine them. The method was so fruitful of results that it quickly spread to a group of American political scientists, from whose findings much of Parrington's significant work received its first flattering confirmation. Under such a stimulus Parrington was quick to realize the fruitfulness of economic determinism when applied even to literature.

A third idea completed the synthesis. When he envisaged American literature as American thought, the trammel of the belletristic was broken and he was free to reëvaluate American writers, to follow the trail of their work wherever it led; for at last he had found a method true to facts, yet one which would satisfy his insatiable demand for a significant unity, balanced, harmonious, and properly proportioned. The economic forces imprint their mark upon political, social, and religious institutions; literature expresses the result in its thought content.

But a technique, though vitally necessary, is not the end of the story. There still remains, even for the most impartial scholar, the final and, be it admitted, inescapable evaluation. Parrington was too honest with himself to dodge the issue; he made his choice and abided the result. In the foreword to the first volume he made his confession: "The point of view from which I have endeavored to evaluate the materials is liberal rather than conservative, Jeffersonian rather than Federalistic; and very likely in my search I have found what I went forth to find, as others have discovered what they were seeking. Unfortunately the *mens aequa et clara* is the rarest of attributes, and dead partisanships have a disconcerting way of coming to life again in the pages of their historians. That the vigorous passions and prejudices of the time I have dealt with may have found an echo in my judgments is, perhaps, to be expected; whether they have distorted my interpretation and vitiated my analysis is not for me to determine."

Professor Parrington's *Main Currents in American Thought* has, then, for its subject the adventures of American liberalism. To anyone alive to the issue an adventurous story it is, as becomes more apparent when the author's own liberalism is completely understood. Those sections where his sympathies are kindled, where he stamps his seal of enthusiastic admiration, provide the clue which his treatment of Roger Williams, Benjamin Franklin, Tom Paine, Jefferson, Emerson, Thoreau, Channing, and Theodore Parker assuredly verifies. All of his latent enthusiasms burst into bloom until, as in his essay on Roger Williams, nothing less than the cadence and passion of the Song of Solomon would express it. "Running through his writings is a recurrent echo of the Hebrew love-song that Puritan thought suffused with glowing mysticism:

'I am my beloved's and my beloved is mine: he feedeth among the lilies. . . . I will arise now, and go about the city in the streets, and in the broad ways I will seek him whom my soul loveth.' But when he went into the broad ways of Carolinian England, seeking the rose of Sharon and the lily of the valley, he discovered only abominations. The lover was tempted by false kisses; the Golden Image was set up in the high places, and the voice of authority commanded to bow down to it. And so as a Christian mystic Roger Williams became a Separatist, and set his mind upon the new world where the lover might dwell with his bride."[1]

The liberalism of Parrington had this great virtue, which all too many creeds lack: it was built on an obligation first to examine and understand all points of view before exercising the right to condemn them. Although he disliked the personalities and groaned at the dreary pages of men like Cotton Mather, yet he was not satisfied until he got at their marrow. And again there was an abiding sense of the humane in Parrington before which all abstractions, generalizations, and logical systems had to pass in review. He feared above all, as did the sensitive Jefferson, the cancer of power. "Man," he used to say, "has never proved himself worthy of an unrestrained control of his fellows, nor has any special group of men ever been dominant without injustice to others." Combined with this love of freedom was an urbanity and a sense of personal integrity not subject to the interference of outside forces in convention or mob—an integrity which so impressed everyone having contact with the man, that he has been often called an aristocrat. Parrington would not have objected to the label, nor have seen it as contradictory to the principles of liberalism, since in his opinion only liberalism expressing itself in a democratic society provides for the free exercise of personal rights. Elevating oneself by riding on the shoulders of others, a common device of the pseudo-aristocrat, was to him but a vulgar gymnastic performance.

When he described Jefferson "with his aristocratic head set on a plebeian frame"[2] he was unconsciously describing himself, for there was a deep love of the soil in Parrington. One saw it, surprisingly, in his hands. They were thick and sturdy, blunted at the ends as if from too much delving into the black loam of his flower garden, where roses, peonies, and crocuses were cherished companions, and the delight of his leisure hours. He secretly suspected

---

[1] Vol. I, p. 65. [2] *Ibid.*, p. 343.

the apartment dweller as any true farmer would; and though there
was a twinkle in his eye when he called New York a Babylon or
spoke of its corrupting influence on scholar and artist, yet there was
a meaning implied more serious than the jest.

It was Parrington's hope to vindicate this liberalism "stemming," as he said, "from the fruitful loins of the eighteenth century." As he diagnosed it, that era had two creative currents of
thought: a hopeful, vigorous liberalism, together with a sturdy
realism which did not balk at men's selfishness or deny the economic basis of social forces. Unfortunately the nineteenth-century
liberal attended only to hopes and neglected the realism, while the
swelling forces of industrialism accepted the economic realities
but cynically brutalized them. Failure was the inevitable result;
the liberals despair while Babbitt, regnant, infests the country with
his blustering agents. In the unfinished section of this last volume
it was Parrington's purpose to show this parlous state of twentieth-
century America, to discern the hopeful gleam in the darkness, and
to uncover the hidden forces working for a more stable and just
society. Parrington's point of view then, was that of a staunch
and kindly liberalism, the motif in the three volumes, the theme
never absent from a page of the whole composition. It is a liberalism not to be found. in any program yet formulated by political
party or economic sect; it is rather a generous idealism that can
envisage a future richer in values, more humane in distribution of
favors than any known past. Wise to the ways of man, such a liberalism refuses confinement in the strait-jacket of any set formula,
yet escapes the emasculation awaiting mere enthusiasm; for it can
separate foes from friends and recognize the point where compromise means surrender.

If my analysis thus far is to any purpose it will suggest what
these main objectives that Parrington never completed were to
have been. The unfinished Book Two was to chronicle three parties
of revolt against the plutocracy born of the Gilded Age. Of these
rebellions the first was engendered on the Middle Border, where
the farmers, beset by hard times, struck out against the source of
their ills. As the agrarians diagnosed the situation, these economic
maladjustments were brought on by a currency manipulated for
the benefit of creditors, and further enhanced by capitalistic control of the political machine. One of the last of Parrington's completed units deals with the economic phase of the revolt; the next

section was to record the farmer's effort to democratize the government. Through pressure of third-party movements the farmers tried to inject such reforms as the initiative and referendum, the recall, the direct primary, and the income tax; until, seduced by Bryan's oratory, they joined with the Democrats in an attack upon the intrenchments of capitalism. As Parrington saw it, these agrarian descendants of Jefferson, lacking the intellectual leadership which the South had contributed in earlier days, at a tactical disadvantage, and already a minority economic group, were fated to lose their last great uprising.

Also out of the valley of the Mississippi came a literature of the Middle Border. Such writers as Edward Eggleston and E. W. Howe had already initiated a realism that revealed the drabness of frontier life and suggested its smoldering discontent, although the pastoral note fathered by the genial and romantic James Whitcomb Riley did not lack its prose children. Notably did Meredith Nicholson, William Allen White, and Booth Tarkington[3] portray the village neighborliness, its wholesomeness, its spirit of democracy, until they cast such a fog of sentiment over the scene as to blur all the realities. But the true spirit of Populism is represented in the impassioned work of Hamlin Garland, whose "admirable realism and passionate democracy" Parrington depicts in a chapter that he completed.

The second chorus of dissent came from the very citadels of plutocracy, for the wage-earners, unable to escape slavery by flight to an unshackled frontier that no longer existed, were brought to bay. The doctrine of class war, which had been ignored since the eighteenth century, was revived by the German socialists and given an added plausibility by the employers' unscrupulous use of injunction, black list, and lockout. T. V. Powderly, who found a solution to the labor problem in syndicalism, organized the Knights of Labor. Although this union had a promising inception, it was soon wrecked, while the craft unionism recommended by Samuel Gompers forged to the front because of its middle-class ideology and spirit of compromise. On the other hand the left wing of the labor cause embraced various brands of socialism. The tragic flare-up of the Haymarket riot, which resulted in a "red" scare and persecution of the humane Governor Altgeld, served Parrington as a dramatic illustration of the obloquy that descended upon the

[3] See Addenda for notes on these men.

leaders of socialism, Daniel De Leon, Eugene V. Debs, and Victor
Berger. Needless to say, Parrington had planned a vindication of
them born of his desire to see more justice in the world.

There were echoes of this proletarian strife manifested in the
world of letters. Certain writers following Edward Bellamy joined
the quest for a socialistic Utopia. Parrington had completed his
passage on Bellamy, but of the party formed to agitate for principles advanced in *Looking Backward* and of the other writers of Utopian novels, such as Tourgee, he left no treatment. A second set of
writers were grouped together by reason of their common concern
over the darkening future of American civilization. Edwin Markham, his humanitarian sympathies aroused, penned an indictment
of wage exploitation in his "The Man with the Hoe" that caused
no little concern in its day and spurred defenders of the existing
economic system to offer liberal prizes for an equally convincing
reply. The emergence of naturalism, seen in Stephen Crane[4] and
Frank Norris,[4] was also a response to the darkening social outlook.
Parrington defined naturalism as "a pessimistic realism that sets
man in a mechanical world." He traced this pessimistic determinism to the machine industrialism so overwhelming in its power as
to impress man with his own impotence, to the centralization of
wealth, which causes a caste regimentation of society, and finally
to the great city, which reduces the inhabitant to an infinitesimal
unit of a vast beehive. Other writers, equally oppressed by this
state of affairs, concentrated on the phenomena of the city. It was
here that Parrington intended to discuss Henry B. Fuller, Harold
Frederic, Robert Grant, and Edith Wharton.[5]

The third party of revolt was a hesitant one—the South, still
convalescing from the Civil War and further weakened by divisions
in its counsels. Though burdened by parochial creeds, weakened
by lack of intellectual leadership, the agrarian South, largely plebeian, joined the Middle Border in its uprising. The middle-class
South, represented by Henry W. Grady, proposed a surrender to
the Yankee principle of industrial exploitation, while the remnant
of the old aristocracy resisted the new and clung to the traditions
of the past. Thomas Nelson Page, Joel Chandler Harris, Mary
Murfree, and George Washington Cable attended to these romantic traditions of the plantation, the negro, the mountaineer, and

---

[4] See Addenda for lecture notes on these writers.
[5] See Addenda for brief notes on these writers.

the creole; while Sidney Lanier [5] became the poet of southern landscape and sunrise. Far more significant in Parrington's eye was the rebirth of a southern intelligentsia represented in letters by Ellen Glasgow, W. W. Woodward, the debunker, and James Branch Cabell,[6] the ironic romanticist. Professor Parrington, who had been among the first to appreciate Cabell, admired the competence of his style and the effectiveness of his ironic commentary on American civilization.

Book Three was to present the movement of liberalism from 1903 to 1917, and the reaction to it following the war. Parrington called this period of liberalism the "great stock-taking venture." These liberals announced that the democratic hopes of earlier days had not been fulfilled, that the Constitution is not a democratic instrument nor was it intended to be, and that while Americans were professing to create a democracy, they had been creating in fact a plutocracy. They then determined upon a new program based on their discovery of the relations between economics and politics. Such relations made necessary the control of property by the collective will, and to that end they endeavored to squeeze the Hamiltonian state into a Jeffersonian mold.[7]

The muckrakers of 1903 to 1910 attacked the plutocracy where its joints creaked. In effect this group of writers from Henry D. Lloyd to Charles Edward Russell, Gustavus Meyers, and A. M. Simons popularized economics and made the liberals conscious of what was going on behind the closed doors of the directors' meetings. On the other hand, the movement of Progressivism, engaged in the hopeless task of directing the political machinery to democratic ends, was typified by Robert LaFollette, Theodore Roosevelt, and Woodrow Wilson. Only one, LaFollette, remained true to the colors; the other two compromised, then surrendered, and the hopes of liberalism went down in a tragic débâcle.

In the realm of letters this liberalism found expression in three major groups of writers. A set of intellectuals turned critical began to scrutinize the economic, political, and social institutions of America. Of these critics Parrington considered Randolph Bourne and Charles A. Beard [8] the most important. Another set turned

[5] See Addenda for brief notes on these writers.
[6] See Addenda for magazine article on Cabell.
[7] "A Chapter in American Liberalism," which is included in the Addenda, deals with this subject, with the muckraking movement, and with post-war realism.
[8] See Addenda, "A Chapter in American Liberalism."

to fiction, shifting their point of view from liberalism to radicalism, from politics to economics. Winston Churchill [9] had discovered the emptiness of the profit motive with its resultant destruction of beauty, freedom, and creative craftsmanship. Similarly Robert Herrick [9] became a pathologist of the city, investigated its ethics, and then rebelled at the predatory egoism which ruled its life to the destruction of all ethical integrity. At his best Jack London [10] wrote of the revolution, though later selling out to bigger and better royalties; while Upton Sinclair became the revolutionary sleuth spying upon the indecencies of the capitalist system. Perhaps these novelists were too seriously engaged in social criticism and reform propaganda to become great craftsmen, yet they were to Parrington important writers, because they were in touch with deep currents of American thought.

Still a third set of writers turned to a realistic technique appropriate to the times, yet avoided the weakness inherent in direct propaganda. The poets Masters, [11] Sandburg, Frost, and Robinson, Parrington chose for consideration as realists with an art, an underlying criticism of conditions, and a philosophy that set them above the other poets of the time. For the same reasons he had planned a section on Huneker. Theodore Dreiser, [12] because of his massive documentation, his deterministic philosophy, and his sense of the inevitable tragedy inherent in life, Parrington labeled a modern, meaning by this that Dreiser most adequately and most thoroughly represented modern America.

The last section of the book was to be a consideration of the post-war reaction to the liberalism of the preceding period. The economic democracy which liberals had marked for their goal was now attacked by the younger intellectuals. H. L. Mencken turned to farce and burlesque for methods adequate to express his contempt of American democracy. Biologists pointed to the inescapable laws of heredity as a refutation of the liberals' hopes for social improvement; while some psychologists, discovering morons, ruled out all equalitarian Utopias. Parrington could find little sympathy in his heart for a return to the spirit of aristocracy. This narrow, doctrinaire biology, denied by the more careful biologists and

[9] See "The Problem Novel and the Diversion from Naturalism," in the Addenda.
[10] See Addenda for notes on London.
[11] See Addenda, "Ole Rölvaag's *Giants in the Earth.*"
[12] See Addenda for lecture notes on Dreiser.

the behaviorists who assert that environment is determining, cannot rule out all environmental changes. As long as the *milieu* is an effective force in molding the organism, room is left for social betterment by social readjustments. A disputed psychology dealing in primitive sex drives, gland secretions, and intelligence scores is no more conclusive on the subject.

The attack on industrialism is nearer to the heart of Parrington's ideals, because it proved to him that liberalism is not by any means dead. Such a comprehensive movement enlisting first-class minds —intellectuals, poets, novelists, dramatists—revealed clearly to him the increasing criticism of a dehumanized economics, and such criticism proceeds from an implicit liberalism.

The attack on the middle class is seen best in Zona Gale,[13] Evelyn Scott, and particularly in Sinclair Lewis,[14] whom Parrington rated the chief of our younger satirists. This satire is a searching criticism of the *bourgeois* ideals and habitat, its tyrannical herd-mind, its povery-stricken materialism. By its nature this satire clearly suggests a set of new ideals which grow out of a free individualism rather than a political or economic socialism. The emphasis is shifted by implication from externalities to things of the spirit. This is more clearly seen in the new philosophies just now arising, which deny the finality of economic law, turn in politics to the ideal of a decentralized state, and in science to new syntheses emphasizing the pragmatic and relative aspects of scientific law.

The latest literary fashions that Parrington intended to consider embody a psychological emphasis seen in the impressionism of biography, in the brutal but frank pacifism of war novels,[13] and most significantly of all in the impressionism and expressionism of Sherwood Anderson.[14] Parrington felt that there were rich potentialities latent in these new methods although the writers of the new school were themselves painfully at sea. In technique as well as in direct statement there was to be seen, though obscurely, a renewed emphasis upon individual integrity, the necessity for creative expression, and the reaffirmation of what some may choose to call spiritual values.

In effect he believed that all is not lost. Through the influence of science we are recovering the neglected realism of the past; we

[13] See Addenda for brief notes.
[14] See Addenda, "Sherwood Anderson: a Psychological Naturalist."

are not only reaffirming it but making its acquaintance more intimately than ever before. Weld that science to enlightened and
humane aspirations (Parrington believed that there was nothing
in the findings of science that prevented the union) and a revivified
liberalism will make the world a fit place to live in. It is by no
means an easy program, for it requires knowledge of fact, and
ability to carry knowledge into the sphere of effective action. It is
made doubly difficult by the untimely death of one of its chief pro-
ponents, yet in the young men and women whom he liked to have
around him there must be, however obscurely, a feeling and a
groping for the way out. They will be guided and inspired by such
utterance as Parrington's diagnosis of Sinclair Lewis, where he
quarries out a vein of his own enduring liberalism.

"Some lingering faith in our poor human nature he still clings
to. In the great American mass that human nature is certainly
foolish and unlovely enough. It is too often blown up with flatulence, corroded with lust, on familiar terms with chicanery and
lying; it openly delights in hocus pocus and discovers its miracle-
workers in Comstocks and Aimee Semple McPhersons. But for all
its pitiful flabbiness human nature is not wholly bad, nor is man
so helpless a creature of circumstance as the cynics would have us
believe. There are other and greater gods than Mumbo Jumbo
worshiped in America, worthier things than hocus pocus; and in
rare moments even Babbitt dimly perceives that the feet of his
idol are clay. There are Martin Arrowsmiths as well as Elmer
Gantrys, and human nature, if it will, can pull itself out of the trap.
Bad social machinery makes bad men. Put the banker in the scullery instead of the drawing-room; exalt the test-tube and deflate
the cash register; rid society of the dictatorship of the middle class;
and the artist and the scientist will erect in America a civilization
that may become, what civilization was in earlier days, a thing to
be respected. For all his modernity and disillusion learned from
Pullman-car philosophers, Sinclair Lewis is still an echo of Jean
Jacques and the golden hopes of the Enlightenment—thin and
far-off, no doubt, but still an authentic echo."

"Thin and far-off, no doubt," is this contemporary liberalism,
yet Parrington found hints of it in the midst of the war fiasco that
culminated in reaction and despair. Death did not grant him the
opportunity to show what he found, but the young men who learned
from him the love of sound craftsmanship, who were inspired by

his enlightened dreams, will some day complete the monument. In the meantime Vernon Louis Parrington would like to be held in memory as he held his friend, J. Allen Smith—as a "scholar, teacher, democrat, gentleman."

E. H. EBY

University of Washington
Seattle, Washington
March, 1930

FOREWORD

WITH the present volume I bring to a close my studies in the main currents in American thought. The broad drifts of American opinion, as I interpret that opinion, should now be sufficiently clear. The volume immediately preceding the present one dealt with the romantic revolution in America—one of the most stimulating experiences the American mind has undergone—which was traced to twin forces: the influence upon an expansive generation of French romantic thought, and the spirit of robust individualism resulting from a fluid economics; and the creative result was the spontaneous emergence in America of a buoyant spirit of hopefulness that expressed itself in democratic programs and faith in a benevolent progress. The present volume deals with the slow decay of this romantic optimism in more thoughtful minds, and the cause of that decay is traced to three sources: the stratifying of economics under the pressure of centralization; the rise of a mechanistic science; and the emergence of a spirit of skepticism which, under the pressure of industrialism, the teachings of the physical sciences, and the lessons of European intellectuals, is resulting in the questioning of the ideal of democracy as it has been commonly held hitherto, and the spread of a spirit of pessimism. The custodianship of America by the middle class has brought unsuspected consequences in its train.

Thus after three hundred years' experience we have returned, intellectually, to the point from which we set out, and the old philosophy brought to the new world from the compact societies of Europe, with its doctrine of determinism and its mood of pessimism, has come back in changed form to color the thinking of our generation. Emersonian optimism, that was the fullest expression of the romantic faith, is giving way to Dreiserian pessimism, and the traditional doctrine of progress is being subjected to analysis by a growing skepticism. Our intellectual history thus conceived falls into three broad phases: Calvinistic pessimism, romantic optimism, and mechanistic pessimism. Between the first and the last lies the America of yesterday that shaped the American mind

and American institutions; and with the submergence of that
native world we are in the way of repeating here the familiar history of Europe, with its coercive regimentations reproduced on a
larger scale and in more mechanical fashion. Once more a gloomy
philosophy stands on the threshold of the American mind. Whether
it will enter and take possession of the household, no one can predict as yet. This much nevertheless is clear: an industrialized society is reshaping the psychology fashioned by an agrarian world;
the passion for liberty is lessening and the individual, in the presence of creature comforts, is being dwarfed; the drift of centralization is shaping its inevitable tyrannies to bind us with. Whether
the quick concern for human rights, that was the noble bequest of
our fathers who had drunk of the waters of French romantic faith,
will be carried over into the future, to unhorse the machine that
now rides men and to leaven the sodden mass that is industrial
America, is a question to which the gods as yet have given no
answer. Yet it is not without hope that intelligent America is in
revolt. The artist is in revolt, the intellectual is in revolt, the conscience of America is in revolt.

.   .   .   .   .   .

It ought not to be necessary to add that in these volumes I have
not essayed to write a history of American literature—that rather
difficult task for which no scholar is as yet equipped. But I have
suffered so many gentle reproofs for failing to do what I did not set
out to do, that it may be well to repeat what I said in the Foreword
to Volume I, that I have been concerned in the present study with
the total pattern of American thought—the broad drift of major
ideas—and not with vagrant currents or casual variations. In particular I have been repeatedly taken to task for a seeming slight
put upon certain of our artists, and it has been inferred that I
slighted them because I chose to ignore whatever did not fit into
a rigid scheme of economic determinism. Let me say in rebuttal
that I hold no brief for a rigid scheme of economic determinism.
I recognize the rich culture potentialities that inhere in individual
variation from type, and I realize that the arts are likely to receive
their noblest gifts from men who should be classed biologically as
cultural sports or variations from the cultural type. But in such
a study as I have undertaken, individual variation is significant
not for its own sake, but rather for the help it may offer in deter-

mining the type. After due consideration I see no cause to apologize for my treatment of Poe, for example, if indeed I have done so. I am content to have placed him historically and culturally in relation to the whole, leaving the fascinating problem of his variation from type to those who deal with such problems.

V. L. P.

INTRODUCTION *

In the second volume of my studies I laid down the thesis that at the beginning of our national existence two rival philosophies contended for supremacy in America: the humanitarian philosophy of the French Enlightenment, based on the conception of human perfectibility and postulating as its objective an equalitarian democracy in which the political state should function as the servant to the common well-being; and the English philosophy of *laissez faire*, based on the assumed universality of the acquisitive instinct and postulating a social order answering the needs of an abstract "economic man," in which the state should function in the interests of trade. And I pointed out further, with adequate backing up, I hope, that the first of these antagonistic philosophies was accepted by the agrarian leaders of America and found issue in the Jeffersonian program; that the second came to dominate the thinking of the mercantile, capitalistic America and took form in Hamiltonian Federalism. Unfortunately this logical alignment of diverse economic groups was obscured by the needs of practical politics, and in passing through the explosive Jacksonian revolution both philosophies underwent subtle changes. Jacksonianism imposed upon America the ideal of democracy to which all must thereafter do lip service, but it lost its realistic basis in a Physiocratic economics and wandered in a fog of political equalitarianism; and the Whiggery that issued from Federalism turned to the work of converting the democratic state into the servant of property interests. Both political parties contented themselves with an egoistic individualism that took no account of social ends, forgetful of the humanitarian spirit that underlay the earlier democratic program. The finer spirit of the Enlightenment was lost, and in consequence the major parties chose to follow the economic interests of master groups, heedless of all humanitarian issues.

* The Introduction, as will be readily seen by the reader, is not complete, yet it undoubtedly contains the gist of what Professor Parrington intended to include in it. He wrote several forms of some parts, from which the Introduction as it stands has been pieced together in logical order. It is probable that the last words he wrote were the significant closing words here—" to summon forth the potential intelligence of the younger generation."—*Publisher*.

But the spirit awakened by the earlier democratic enthusiasm could not be kept in political strait-jackets. The Jacksonian revolution overflowed all narrow party dikes, expressing itself in diverse humanitarian and reform movements and quickening the minds of ardent Americans with larger democratic aspirations. The noble idealism of successive third parties that have sprung up reasserted the democratic principles flouted by the major parties. The Locofoco movement, the Free-soil Party, the early Republican Party, the Greenback Party, the Populist Party, the Progressive Party, have had a common objective, namely to carry further the movement inaugurated by the Jeffersonians to make of America a land of democratic equality and opportunity—to make government in America serve man rather than property. The third-party movements have always been democratic movements, and though they have failed in their immediate objectives they have served the purpose of reminding the major parties—oftentimes rudely—that America presumes to be a democratic country. Thus interpreted the history of the political struggle in America since 1790 falls into three broad phases: the Jeffersonian movement that asserted the ideal of political democracy; the Jacksonian movement that established it crudely in practice; and the successive third-party movements that attempted to regain such ground as had been lost, to extend the field, and to perfect the machinery of democratic government.

As a result of the long struggle the abstract principle of democracy—during the period under consideration—was firmly established in the popular mind; but as it fell under the successive custodianship of different economic groups it came to receive strangely diverse interpretations. Interpreted by the coonskin Jacksonians it meant political equalitarianism; by the slave economy it meant a Greek democracy; by the industrial economy it meant the right of exploitation. It has changed service with each new master. Always the principles of Jeffersonianism—of democracy as a humane social order, serving the common well-being—have been lost out of the reckoning, and except in so far as the tendency has been checked by the third-party threat, democratic professions have been only a thin cover under which the old class warfare has gone forward vigorously. In the decades immediately following the Civil War democracy passed under the custodianship of the middle class, who were busily engaged in creating a plutocracy, and the major ideas of the earlier movement took on a characteristic middle-class coloring. The idea of a beneficent progress, which was the flower of the doctrine of human perfectibility, came to be interpreted as material expansion with constantly augmenting profits; and the idea of democracy came to be interpreted as the right to use the government of the whole for the benefit of the few.

. . . .

Considered historically perhaps the chief contribution of the Progressive movement to the democratic cause is to be found in its discovery of the fundamentally undemocratic nature of the federal Constitution. That so obvious a fact so long escaped recognition was due to political causes easily understood. For a century the Constitution had been a symbol of national unity, a cohesive force amidst ·the drift of expansion, a counter influence to the disintegrations of states-rights particularisms; and as such it had appealed to the national loyalties of men in every commonwealth. To criticize it was reckoned disloyal. The long process of interpretation had remained in the hands of the lawyers and had been wholly legalistic and antiquarian. In all this earlier commentary—except for a small group of left-wing Abolitionists who repudiated the entire instrument—no question as to the democratic spirit of the Constitution was raised, no doubts as to its sufficiency as a fundamental democratic law were suggested. The class divisions that presided at its making were ignored, and the aristocratic spirit of its creators was forgotten. But with the rising revolt against the custodianship of government by financial and industrial interests came a new critical interest in the fundamental law. Discovering that its hands were tied the democracy began to question the reason for the bonds that constrained its movements. The latent distrust was quickened by what was regarded by many as judicial usurpations of power, such as the act of the Supreme Court in declaring unconstitutional the federal income-tax law, and the question of the desirability of an eighteenth-century document that by its complexity unduly impeded the functioning of the democratic will, was thrust into the foreground of political debate. It was the struggle of 1789 over again.

The new school of criticism was historical rather than legalistic. It was concerned primarily with origins—and it must take into account the political theories and class interests of the eighteenth-century gentlemen who framed the document. It refused to look upon the Fathers as supermen, devoted unselfishly to high patriotic duty, but chose to regard them as capable statesmen, saturated with aristocratic prejudices, who fearful of losing control of the new venture in republicanism, took care to shape an instrument that threw sharp restrictions about the majority will.

. . . .

The theme of the present volume is the industrialization of America under the leadership of the middle class, and the consequent rise of a critical attitude towards the ideals and handiwork of that class. It concerns itself primarily with the spirit of realism that under the constrictions of industrialism and with the spread of scientific modes of thought emerged to question the ardent romanticisms of an earlier age, and bring under doubt the excellence of a social order created by the Industrial Revolution.

The field to be traversed is thus predetermined. The interpretation of our literature since 1860 must be fitted into the broad lines of our national experience and will follow the main divisions of development.

I. The conquest of America by the middle class and its custodianship of democracy. The philosophy of the middle class.

II. The challenge of that overlordship by:
 1. The older democratic agrarianism as expressed chiefly in the third-party movements.
 2. The new proletarian philosophy that came likewise out of the ferment of the French Revolution, but that traveled a different course—through Europe and the earlier continental Industrial Revolution, and thence to America.

III. The intellectual revolution brought about by science with the results:
 1. The recovery of a spirit of realism.
 2. The appropriation of science by the middle class.

IV. The rise of a detached criticism by the younger intellectuals.

In dealing with this material it will be necessary to follow sectional lines in the earlier decades until the encompassing movement of centralization finally obliterated them and produced a common national spirit and purpose.

In the welter that is present-day America militant philosophies with their clear-cut programs and assured faiths are wanting, and many feel, as Matthew Arnold felt fourscore years ago, that they are dwelling between worlds, one dead, the other powerless to be born. The old buoyant psychology is gone and in the breakdown and disintegration of the traditional individualism no new philosophies are rising. Builders of Utopias are out of a job. Political and economic theory is in charge of paymasters and is content with the drab rim of the familiar landscape. Retainer-fees have blotted out for it the lovelier horizons that earlier thinkers contemplated. Academic political scientists and economists have largely joined the Swiss guards, and abdicated the high prerogative of speculative thought. It is the men of letters—poets and essayists and novelists and dramatists, the eager young intellectuals of a drab generation—who embody the mind of present-day America; not the professional custodians of official views. They at least decline to block the path to the Promised Land with retainer-fees; they at least are free souls, and in the measure of their abilities, free thinkers. It is to them therefore that one must turn to discover the intellectual currents of later America—to their aspirations as well as to their criticisms. Literature at last has become the authentic voice of this great shapeless America that means so much to western civilization. Not theologians any longer, nor political philosophers, nor industrial masters, nor bankers, are the spokesmen of this vibrant life of a continent, but the intellectuals, the dreamers, the critics, the historians, the men of letters, in short; and to them one may turn hopefully for a revelation of American life.

The period dealt with in the present study marks the complete triumph of the middle class and the final defeat of the traditional agrarianism. The disintegration of the earlier romanticisms, both native and imported, has run its course. The philosophy of Jefferson and John Taylor, with its physiocratic bias, its antipathy to a money economy, its love of local autonomy, has been buried in the potter's field.

· · · · · · ·

Amidst all the turmoil and vague subconscious tendencies, certain ideas slowly clarified: first, that the earlier democratic aspirations had somehow failed, that an equalitarian philosophy adapted to frontier conditions could not easily be carried over into a centralizing and stratifying America and was doomed to eventual defeat; second, that even in the supposed heyday of our democracy, we had never achieved a democracy, but rather a careless individualism that left society at the mercy of a rapacious middle class; third, that we must take our bearings afresh and set forth on a different path to the goal. As these convictions slowly rose into consciousness, a quick suspicion of our earlier philosophies arose to trouble us. With the growing realism of the times came a belief that our French romantic theories were mainly at fault and we must somehow go back to the rationalistic eighteenth century and start once more to recreate a democratic philosophy. The crux of the matter seemed to lie in the romantic conception of human nature. Rousseau and Godwin were the false prophets who led us astray, and we must return to the solid realism of John Locke. In the light of a realistic psychology, with its discovery of morons, and its study of mob tendencies, it was no longer possible to take seriously that attractive figment of the romantic imagination—man in the state of nature, perfectible by following the light of reason, seeking justice. Morons do not fit nicely into the older theory—they jar one's faith in human perfectibility. In the light of intelligence tests perhaps the whole romantic theory of democracy was only a will-o'-the-wisp. With the very foundations of our traditional philosophy turning to quicksand under our feet, no wonder we are bedeviled by doubts and uncertainties. Utopias no longer seem so near at hand as they did; plans and specifications of the ideal commonwealth no longer seem simple matters to be drawn by any competent social carpenter. Our jauntiness is gone, speculation is less important than investigation, and in the spirit of sober realism we are setting about the serious business of thinking.

In this thinking two major forces are at hand: economics and psychology. In our economic realism we are returning to the spirit of the eighteenth century, and adapting the determinism that marked political thought from Harrington and John Adams to Webster and Calhoun; but we are equipped with a psychological knowledge that those earlier thinkers lacked. Wedding the new psychology to the older economic determinism, we may hope in a spirit of sober realism to make some progress in our thinking.

Yet not too hastily should we abandon our earlier faith: the eighteenth-century conception of environment as a creative influence in determining character is a vital idea not yet adequately explored. Even morons may be traced back to adenoids or diets of salt pork and whisky or to later machine labor, and aristocracies are still seen to be economic. And aristocratic albinos may well breed mobs and morons. Jefferson was not as foolish as many of his disciples have been, and Jeffersonian democracy still offers hope. Education begins to fail—except education to individualize and to summon forth the potential intelligence of the younger generation.

INTRODUCTION TO THE TRANSACTION EDITION
VERNON LOUIS PARRINGTON

Bruce Brown

> *"Ideas are not godlings that spring perfect-winged from the head of Jove; they are not flowers that bloom in a walled garden; they are weapons hammered out on the anvil of human needs."*
> —*Vernon Louis Parrington*

THE FIELD AT THE FAIRGROUNDS in Guthrie, the capital of the Oklahoma Territory, was frozen but free of snow for the kickoff of the big college football game on New Year's Eve 1897. The contest, which was actually the prelude to the day's main event, the Territorial Intercollegiate Oratorical Contest, pitted the University of Oklahoma against another Oklahoma school, Kingfisher College.

It was the fledgling University of Oklahoma football team's first game that far from home, and during the early part of the contest they had some tough sledding. Oklahoma end Bill McCutcheon was being punished particularly hard by a heavy-set Kingfisher tackle. "He hurt me every time he hit me," McCutcheon recalled later. Closer inspection revealed that McCutcheon's opponent was wearing armor: Beneath his jersey he had concealed an elbow of stovepipe over each shoulder and arm.

Although McCutcheon's opponent was forced to shed his extra gear, Kingfisher continued to dominate Oklahoma, and carried an 8-6 lead to the bench at halftime. There is no record of what the Oklahoma coach told his beleaguered team as they warmed themselves during the break, but its results were evident during the second half in classic college football fashion. The Oklahoma offense came alive, eating up the field with plays that called for the tackles and ends to cross-block their opposite numbers while the ball carrier swung through the gap boosted by supporting backs, for in those days, football offenses relied as much on pushing from behind as blocking in front.

Midway through the second half, the game was interrupted by the Logan County sheriff, who had never seen a football game before, and supposed the action on the gridiron to be a brawl in progress. It took the appeals of several notables present, including University of Oklahoma President David Ross Boyd (Oklahoma was by then leading), before the sheriff would let the game be completed. Finally relenting, he gave the affair a Wild West touch by firing his gun over his head to restart the contest, prompting the spectators to respond with the appropriate rodeo cries: "Hold that steer!" "Ride 'em cowboy!" "E-yip-eeeeeeee!"

Out on the playing field, the flavor was not so much Red River as Crimson Wave. Although Oklahoma's young Harvard-educated football coach had chosen not to play in this game himself, the Sooners still bore the strong mark of Harvard football, that rough rugby/soccer amalgam which won first the Ivy League colleges and ultimately all of America away from traditional soccer. Striding the sidelines in a tweed suit and tie, the Oklahoma coach exhorted his men. They were an odd crew, composed of a professional baseball player, a Chickasaw Indian, some local farmers and a smattering of University of Oklahoma students, but now the drilling he had put them through paid off and they won handily by the score of 17 to 8.

This was the first of many hurrahs for both University of Oklahoma football and its tweedy coach and English professor, Vernon Louis Parrington. During the four years he coached the Sooners, Parrington, then a darkly handsome young man in the Robert Louis Stevenson mold, only lost twice, and one of those games turned on what was later revealed to be an illegal drop kick by the University of Arkansas Razorbacks, according to Harold Keith's *Oklahoma Kickoff.* After shutting out the last four opponents Oklahoma faced at the close of the 1900 season, Parrington retired forever from football coaching with what is at this writing still the second highest winning percentage in the history of Sooner football after Bud Wilkinson.

Parrington's explanation for the move was that he wanted to devote more energy to the teaching of English, but his motives, like everything else about him, were far from simple. A voracious reader who actually hated Harvard and the old Brahmin-dominated culture it represented, Parrington also wanted more time for personal questing. As William Allen White recalled in his Pulitzer Prize winning autobiography, Parrington was part of a crowd of young fellows "too proud for pool, too wicked for prayer meetings, too lazy for baseball—although Vernon Parrington pitched a mean outcurve for the Emporia Browns—too sophisticated for the local poker game, and too young and full of vision to let the world go by without trying to understand it."

Parrington's real passion of the moment was poetry, which he wrote and published in the local newspapers. He also spent several years in intense Bible study while at Oklahoma, as a recent article by Lark Hall in the *Pacific Northwest Quarterly* shows. In time, the wide ranging intellectual curiosity that was a life-long characteristic carried him from Victorian poets to the arts and architecture to English and American literature to political science and the history of ideas, and finally landed him on shores far removed from the close-drawn world of his early Presbyterian schooling.

Although the glory he achieved on the gridiron and the diamond would be considered crowning achievements for many fondly remembering their careers, they are for Parrington a mere footnote compared to his later accomplishments in the arena of intellectual history. Long recognized as one of the brilliant teachers of his generation, Vernon Louis Parrington reached the apex of his career in 1928 when the first two volumes of his epic study of the development of American culture, *Main Currents in American Thought*, were awarded the Pulitzer Prize for history.

He was felled by a heart attack the next year, but his influence continued to grow posthumously. By 1940, even Lionel Trilling, who was highly critical of Parrington, acknowledged that "his book now stands at the center of our thought about America." Parrington's reputation has fallen so drastically during the intervening decades, however, that younger students of American literature may be surprised to learn that his writings were once thought of comparable importance to those of Oswald Spengler, Alfred North Whitehead, and Vladimir Lenin.

The same cycle of style that made Parrington seem so hopelessly old-fashioned a few years ago may now be bringing him back, though, for our own time bears more than a passing resemblance in terms of the interests and the excesses of the high 1920s, an era which both produced Parrington his greatest work and gave him his first global acclaim.

VERNON LOUIS PARRINGTON was six years old in the spring of 1877 when his father decided to give up the law and office work for farming. A restless idealist of a sort more common to the previous century than our own, John Parrington had already been a high school principal, commanded black troops in battle as a captain in the Union Army, been elected to county office, herded sheep, and practiced law.

Now he concluded that physical and mental health demanded an agrarian life, and so he moved the family from Aurora, Illinois, to the town of Americus, Kansas, and then on to the 160 acre homestead he proved up outside town. The farm's improvements amounted to a 50-foot well which "yielded an abundance of slippery-tasting, alkaline water," as Vernon later recalled, a four room house (with blue clay from the well in the walls for insulation), and a rude stable. The land itself was almost perfectly flat with only one wild tree, a broken-crowned cottonwood that stood a half mile from the house.

In an unpublished autobiographical reminiscence he wrote for members of his family in 1918, Parrington said Hamlin Garland's classic agrarian novel, *Son of the Middle Border*, accurately pictured every "detail of ugliness and discomfort" of the years he spent on the farm outside Americus, but added that for him the life was not an entirely drab or hopeless existence. "It was filled with poignant emotions," he recalled. "To go to bed with … the wild fascination of a prairie fire in the soft darkness of a spring night … and then wake in the morning to the call of the prairie cock from a low ridge half a mile away—a call that was compact of the dawns and freedoms of the untamed places—was that not to sleep and wake in the very Land of Desire?"

Although he left the farm for good by the time he was twenty, Parrington credited it with making a lasting contribution to his intellectual makeup. "[F]rom the vantage point of our farm, two and one half miles north of the village, I saw the border move beyond us and the countryside change from a wild, unploughed prairie, to a well-tilled farming region. Of the diverse experiences of my life I value none more than this. In the most receptive years of my life I came under the influence of … the frontier with its democratic sympathies and democratic economies. From that influence I have never been able to escape, nor have I wished to escape. To it and the spirit of agrarian revolt I grew out of, I owe much of my understanding of American history and much of my political philosophy."

When the Parringtons moved again in 1877 to Emporia, the largest town in the vicinity, with a population of about 8,000, it was partly to enable John Parrington to better carry out his new duties as probate judge, and partly to give the Parrington boys a chance for a better education than was available at the one-room school house at Pumpkin Ridge. Both Vernon and his brother John were promptly enrolled in Emporia College, a small Presbyterian academy which Parrington described as "provincial—quite wholesomely I now think." Although academically minimal in many respects, Emporia College did Vernon the great service of introducing him to two ideals that were to play important parts in his life: the curveball and art.

"I was fifteen when I first saw an out-curve thrown," Parrington wrote in February 1918 when he was forty-seven years old. "Time, place, circumstance, the way the great Pack twisted the ball in his palm and delivered it with a full arm sweep, the lucid explanation of the theory—these things are still fresh in my memory … for these are among the golden experiences of youth. In that moment new fields, fresh interests were opened to me, and thereafter I was assiduous in practice until I could throw a curve that the most skeptical must acknowledge." More than that, he quickly developed into one of Kansas' better players, touring the area at age nineteen as part of an all-star battery that local baseball teams hired to come in for important games.

Meanwhile, other interests were already competing for his time, particularly painting, which he studied for several years at Emporia. "When I was 16 I had definitely determined to be a painter," he wrote. "By the time I was 18 … an increasing realization of economic demands had driven this idea out of my mind; but not before some realization of the significance of art in the life of men had come to me—a realization which later was to make such writers as William Morris my intellectual masters. The love of beauty rather than the love of truth was to dominate me and turn me aside from the stream of scientific learning which bore away so many of my generation."

By the time he graduated from Emporia with a bachelor of arts degree in 1891, Parrington had begun to cut a swath outside Emporia and Kansas. An essay of his, "History and God," was published in *College Life* magazine, and that fall he went away to Harvard on a full academic scholarship. Although he graduated two years later with Oswald Garrison Villard and William Vaughn Moody in the class of `93, Parrington largely loathed his time in Cambridge. "I was too inexperienced to know the ropes," he wrote, "and I got an appalling percentage of shiftless and stupid instructors."

While in Emporia, Parrington had begun a habit of heavy reading in the public library with an emphasis on Victorian novelists such as

Dickens, Thackeray, George Eliot, Trollope, and Reade. At Harvard, he continued the practice on a broader scale. Like Hamlin Garland, who "took his degree" in the Boston Public Library, Parrington made self-directed study a major part of his education. Later, he would observe with an ironic glimmer that it was the "library and not the college that opened my mind to English literature, preparing me for the work I was to take up."

Parrington had never consciously decided to be a teacher, but upon his graduation from Harvard he was offered a position as an English instructor back at Emporia College, and he accepted. He also played baseball professionally during the summers, pitching, catching and managing for the Emporia Browns in the Kansas League. He seemed to have considered professional baseball as a career (despite the poor pay and low social status the game enjoyed during those days), but the heat of the summer, the six game a week schedule, and the responsibility for keeping his players out of the bars finally took the bloom off the sport for him. Then, too, he was discovering at Emporia College that his gift for teaching might be greater than his one with the small white sphere.

The four years he spent at Emporia as an instructor were probably the busiest of his life, combining teaching English and French, earning his masters degree, playing baseball, courting an occasional young lady, handling a raft of his students' extra-curricular activities, and seeing friends like William Allen White, the editor of the *Emporia Gazette* and author of the influential essay, "What's the Matter with Kansas?" which helped swing the tide against populist William Jennings Bryan and elect Republican William McKinley president in 1896. Parrington himself was headed in the opposite direction politically. He voted for Bryan in 1896 (his first break with the staunch Republicanism of his father), and was soon borne farther to the left by the general distress that afflicted American agriculture during this period, and specifically by the decline in the Parrington family fortunes.

John Parrington had lost his judgeship some years before, and by 1897, after a decade of low corn prices and unrealized schemes, he was about to lose the only thing he and Vernon's mother had left—the farm. In his family reminiscence, Parrington recalled warming himself by the stove on his parents farm during the winter of 1897 and listening as full big ears of corn burned "briskly, popping and crackling in the jolliest fashion. And if while we sat around such a fire watching the year's crop go up the chimney, the talk sometimes became bitter about railroads and middlemen, who will wonder? We were in a fitting mood to respond to Mary Ellen Lease and her doctrine of raising less corn and more hell."

Assuming financial responsibility, Vernon asked Emporia College for a raise to save the family farm from foreclosure. The president would not grant it, but a short time later Vernon obtained the needed money by taking a job teaching English at the University of Oklahoma in Norman. Despite the good times he was to find in Norman, the experience was in some ways an ordeal, as is immediately apparent from Parrington's description of his introduction to the town and campus. "A searing wind blew great dust clouds from the southwest as I stepped off the train and started for the University. I passed through a stretch of burnt-up, slovenly village, and out along a quarter mile of plank walk—the very nails of which were partly drawn out by the heat—and at last came to the University grounds, a small patch of brown prairie with a single red brick building topped off with a wartlike cupola."

Parrington's response was to throw himself into his labors, both academic and otherwise. "He would lay out for himself a given amount of work, and he was unhappy if he didn't get it all done," recalled his wife, the former Julia Williams, whom he married in 1901 when he was a professor at Oklahoma. "After his coaching and teaching came his evenings of work on his chief love, the writing of poetry. Always his great desire was to have more time to write. He felt that the true fullness of life came only through the imagination. Facts were dead lumber to him and he must reconstruct in his own imagination." By his own estimation, he was then "still the bookman, drawing my nourishment from *belle lettres*."

Although certainly not a pedant, he was nonetheless undistinguished in his thinking, and might have remained so had not great good fortune come to him in the form of personal disaster. The bad news was that in 1908 Parrington was fired from his position at the University of Oklahoma, which had by then come to include responsibility for directing the English and Athletic departments as well as teaching. Although in no way personal (Parrington was one of 23 people refused new contracts, including the president of the university, in the political turmoil that accompanied Oklahoma's statehood), the loss of his livelihood was nonetheless distressing on a number of scores, among them the fact that it meant that he would have to give up the new house he had just designed and had built in Emporia.

The good news came a few weeks later when University of Washington President Thomas Kane made a special trip to Emporia on the recommendation of outgoing Oklahoma President Boyd to talk with Vernon Louis Parrington. Kane offered him a job before he got on the train out of town that night, and Parrington followed Kane to Seattle almost immediately. The verdant forests, island-strewn expanses of water, and volcanic peaks of the Pacific Northwest were as refreshing to him as the burnt prairie of Norman was oppressive. He already had friends and relatives in Seattle (he and Julia had been married there), and soon added more from the faculty of the University of Washington, among them Edward McMahon, William Savery, Frederic Morgan Padelford, and most important of all from an intellectual standpoint, J. Allen Smith, whose seminal Progressive history, *The Spirit of American Government*, had appeared the year before.

Although Smith was eleven years Parrington's senior and a member of the History rather than the English department, the two were remarkably similar in background and interests. Both had grown up in the Midwest, attended college, taught, and been fired by institutions of higher learning there. Both shared a fondness for Herbert Spencer and William Morris, and a perhaps not unconnected belief in Progressive ideals. The two became close friends, freely sharing their intellectual impulses, and in the process, the older man helped crystallize the younger man's thinking in several areas, among them the use of economics as a tool for cultural analysis. "When I quitted Norman the economic interpretation of history had not yet risen for me," Parrington wrote, "but it lay just below the horizon and was soon to become the chief luminary in my intellectual sky."

One obvious manifestation of Vernon Louis Parrington's deepening command of English and American literature was the tremendous popularity his classes attained. Still fit and handsome, with a full head of dramatically white hair, he had a powerful classroom presence that kindled a spark that still burns in his surviving students. "He was the best classroom teacher I ever saw or heard," declared Gladys Savage, eighty-two, a former student who later taught English herself at U.C.L.A. By the early 1920s, a course with Parrington became the *sine qua non* of liberal education at the University of Washington.

E. H. Eby, a former student and colleague of Parrington's at the University of Washington, reflected that "the source of that popularity was the personality of the teacher, together with his gift for presenting ideas and provoking a response. By means of a Socratic cross-examination, Parrington made the student discover his intellectual deficiencies; while the class, to its astonishment and delight, found the quest for truth both elusive and exciting."

All during this time Parrington was also quietly working on a book. As far back as his Oklahoma days, Parrington had been thinking about a study of American literature. Finally in 1913, five years after he came to Washington, he began to write *The Democratic Spirit in American Letters, 1620-1870*. The book was finished in 1918, but lack of interest by publishers forced him to put it on the shelf. Returning to it during the 1920s, Parrington continued to expand, strengthen, and polish it, until finally in 1927, seventeen years after he began it, the book appeared as *Main Currents in American Thought, vol. I and II*.

NINETEEN TWENTY-EIGHT was a vintage year for Pulitzer Prize recipients. The drama award that year went to Eugene O'Neill's *Strange Interlude*, while the novel award was won by Thornton Wilder's *The Bridge of San Luis Rey*, and the poetry award was claimed by Edward Arlington Robinson's *Tristram*.

However, for sheer originality and force of imagination—to say nothing of depth of study—none of these works could compare with that year's winner of the Pulitzer for history, Vernon Louis Parrington's *Main Currents in American Thought*.

Parrington's opus was not only the first comprehensive history of American letters and thought to appear in this country, it was the first major work to consider American literature as an expression of American culture, rather than some academic aesthetic schema. We now take both of these perceptions so much for granted that it is easy to forget the bedrock contribution Parrington made to both literary criticism and intellectual history in America.

Working alone in Seattle, Parrington realized that much of American literature was crude by refined critical standards. Furthermore, if the reader was restricted to those dainty morsels fit for the period's contemporary aesthetics, most of the best American writing would be thrown out. Parrington therefore seized on the idea of treating American literature and letters as an expression of the central American cultural value, democracy.

"And indeed in this country, with its long history of democratic aspiration, why should there not be a grand history of thought and letters celebrating the democratic theme?" Richard Hofstadter wrote of Parrington in *The Progressive Historians*. "Why should not someone, at last, use the history of letters to illuminate national life and thought, and discuss literature, in the tradition of Sainte-Beuve and Taine, as an index of culture?"

There had previously been a couple of minor efforts at American literary history by writers like Barrett Wendell, but none had come close to the breadth of Parrington's study, nor exhibited the felicitous quality of his prose. Similarly, a few efforts at American intellectual history had been attempted by writers like Moses Coit Tyler, but the subject had been almost entirely ignored by conventional academic historians, giving the old Sooner footballer an open field.

In Parrington's hands, American literature, which had been a ragtag poor relative of the literatures of England and the Continent, was suddenly transformed, almost before the reader's eyes, into a noble creature worthy of all the world's attention, since it embodied so compellingly one of history's great social experiments. While it is not entirely true that Parrington created the study of American literature in the nation's colleges, it is fair to say that he did more than any other critic to hasten its initial acceptance, and thus paved the way, with the subsequent contribution of the great American novelists and critics of the 1930s and 1940s, for the unquestioned acceptance it enjoys today.

In developing the concept for what would become *Main Currents*, Parrington drew on intellectual sources as diverse as his rich fare of study. From Hippolyte Taine's *History of English Literature*, which made a big impression on him during his college days, he absorbed three important lessons: the idea of using literature as a means of portraying national culture; the idea of organizing a grand literary history around a series of biographical and critical portraits; and lastly, the idea that environment plays at least some role in forming the art of a given era or nation, From William Morris and John Ruskin, Parrington picked up elements of the Victorian tradition of moral-aesthetic criticism, as well as something of their refined 19th century style. Thomas Jefferson gave him the marrow of democracy, while George Santayana provided germinal phrases like "winds of doctrine," and J. Allen Smith, the pioneering Progressive historian, impressed upon him the importance of economics as a cultural determinant, and fostered his reading of Karl Marx.

Out of this and much more, Parrington wove a clear and consistent picture of the development of democracy in America during the 300 years between 1620 and approximately the beginning of the twentieth century. He saw in this nation's literature the record of the tremendous struggle between the forces of majority and minority rule that spanned generations and even centuries to link writers as diverse as John Winthrop, J. Hector St. John de Crevecoeur, Theodore Parker, and Theodore Dresser in a grand and continuing debate about the very nature of America. For Parrington, the crux of this debate was embodied in the clash between Thomas Jefferson and Alexander Hamilton, the former representing the best of America's indigenous agrarian democratic tradition, and the later representing the rising power of the business oligarchy issuing from the marriage of the unearned increment to the centralized state.

Journalists, essayists, historians, propagandists, and satirists were all given consideration in *Main Currents*, along with the more traditionally literary writers such as novelists and poets. Parrington was primarily interested in tracing the development of "certain germinal ideas that have come to be reckoned traditionally American," but this did not deaden him to aesthetic concerns when they were warranted. He was one of the first influential twentieth century critics to champion both Walt Whitman and Herman Melville, and his own writing immediately reveals a distinctive aesthetic sense. Parrington was a master of the apt quote, the illuminating image, and the epigrammatic expression.

As a mature critic, Parrington demanded only one thing: that art have some bearing on the real world that produced it. He no longer had any patience with the idea of beauty for beauty's sake, and little more for the belle lettristic critics. "Do they understand the origin and significance of those ideas which they study so lovingly?" he asked in a 1917 essay, "Economics and Criticism."

Ideas are not godlings that spring perfect-winged from the head of Jove; they are not flowers that bloom in a walled garden; they are weapons hammered out on the anvil of human needs. Freedom to think is bought with a price; and to ignore the price is to lose all sense of values. To love ideas is excellent, but to understand how ideas themselves are conditioned by social forces, is better still. To desire culture, to enjoy commerce with the best that has been known and thought in the world is excellent also; but to understand the dynamics which lies back of all culture signifies more. Men who will be free, struggle to be free, fashion themselves ideas for swords to fight with. To consider the sword apart from the struggle is to turn dilettante and a frequenter of museums.

Regarding his partisanship on the larger social and political issues, Parrington was equally straightforward, writing in the foreword to volume I of *Main Currents*, "the point of view from which I have endeavored to evaluate the materials, is liberal rather than conservative, Jeffersonian rather than Federalist ..." This bias provided the values which lay behind Parrington's judgments, but did not prevent him from memorably portraying figures he did not particularly admire. Regarding Hamilton, for instance, Parrington conveys the considerable magnitude of the first Treasury Secretary's genius ("Certainly no other man in America saw so clearly the significance of the change that was taking place in English industrialism, and what tremendous reservoir of wealth the new order laid open to the country that tapped them"), as well as what might be called the moral blindness that led him to advocate child factory labor and the rule of the wealthy.

A self-taught architect who loved the balance and proportion of Gothic cathedrals, Parrington strove to impart a similar balance to his recounting the great American debate concerning democracy, as is evident in his pointed pairings of opposing views on essential questions. Thus Fisher Ames ("The essence and almost quintessence of good government is to protect property and its rights") is set against James Fenimore Cooper ("A government founded on the representation of property ... is radically vicious. It is the business of government to resist the corruption of money, not to depend on them"), John Dickinson is set against John Adams, Robert Treat Paine against Horace Greeley, and so forth. Parrington was the rarest of all partisans in that his biases were honed, not in the darkness, but rather against the brightest intellects that divergent thought could provide.

Main Currents bears the mark of Parrington's intellectual openness throughout. He was more than willing to follow the logic of situations and history wherever they might lead, even when they ran counter to his deepest assumptions and conditioning. It was Vernon Louis Parrington, the son of a Union Army officer and an abolitionist, who kindled in twentieth century America an appreciation of Southern writers like John Pendleton Kennedy (author of *Swallow Barn*), and who traced the history of a regional literature that has continued to grow in stature and importance since his death with the work of William Faulkner, Carson McCullers, Alice Walker, and many others. Similarly, Parrington, who devoted the final twenty years of his life to celebrating the theme of democracy in America, was all too aware of the problems at the heart of American democracy.

From his own youth, Parrington knew that the spirit of American democracy was rooted in the freedom of the frontier, but also realized from first-hand experience that the frontier ethos carried within it the seed of its own destruction. "In the presence of vast, unpreempted resources, the right of every man to preempt and exploit what he would [became] synonymous with individual liberty," he wrote, "and if the small man were free to enjoy his petty privilege, the greater interests might preempt unchallenged … Where the policy of preemption has run its course, the function of government is seduced from its social purpose to perpetuate the inequalities which spring from the progressive monopolization of natural resources, with the augmenting corruption and injustice."

Parrington's sudden death in 1929 at the age of fifty-eight, while seemingly in the peak of health and at the height of his powers, prevented him from finishing volume III of *Main Currents*, but from what he left of the last volume, it is clear he believed the hour was late for the America he loved. "In the welter that is present day America," Parrington wrote in a passage which has a distinctly contemporary ring, "militant philosophies with their clear-cut programs and assured faiths are wanting. The old buoyant psychology is gone and in the breakdown and disintegration of the traditional individualism no new philosophies are rising. Builders of Utopias are out of a job. Political and economic theory is in the charge of the paymasters and is content with the drab rim of the familiar landscape."

Vernon Louis Parrington never lost the agrarian faith of his youth, nor the hope of Jeffersonian democracy it entailed. A realist to the end, however, he clearly saw the fate of that aspect of the American tradition, and described it in characteristically memorable fashion. "The philosophy of Jefferson and John Taylor," he wrote in the introduction to volume III, "with its physiocratic bias, its antipathy to a money economy, its love of local autonomy, has been buried in the potter's field."

Although he died before the Great Depression, the election of Franklin Roosevelt, and the New Deal, he could see that liberalism must embrace the centralized state, but that the risk in such an enterprise was great. Writing to a friend, Parrington succinctly described the dilemma that subsequently has eaten America alive: "We must have a political state strong enough to deal with corporate wealth, but how are we going to keep the state with its augmenting power from being captured by the force we want to control?"

THE INITIAL CRITICAL reaction to *Main Currents in American Thought* was overwhelmingly positive. Henry Steele Commager called it "the finest piece of creative criticism in our literature," while the *Saturday Review* found it as "accurate as sound scholarship should be," and Howard Mumford Jones noted how it compelled "all other histories of literature ... to pale their fires ... Here was a useable past, adult, reasonable, coherent."

During the 1930s, *Main Currents* became one of those rare popular books that galvanizes minds and changes lives. My mother recalls how the many volumes at the Library of Congress were continually worn out and replaced, and in Malcolm Cowley and Bernard Smith's *Books That Changed Our Minds* (1938), Parrington ranked roughly on par with such seminal authors as Spengler, Whitehead, Lenin, and I. A. Richards in terms of frequency of mention by those nominating books for inclusion.

In fact, the only serious initial critical reservations about *Main Currents* arose, not from its specific treatment of American literature and letters, but from the originality of its conception, especially to the field of history. "There was so little regard for this kind of history, as history," noted Hofstadter, "that Main Currents, even though it received the Pulitzer Prize in the field, was not at first taken by most historians as a historical work ..."

By 1940, however, critical assessment of *Main Currents* had begun to shift, partly because of the new material that continuing historical and literary research had brought to light, and partly because certain original aspects of Parrington's analysis challenged academic convention. Perry Miller at Harvard was one of several New England scholars who questioned Parrington's interpretation of Roger Williams, and Clifford K. Shipton contested Parrington's treatment of the Mathers.

More damaging to Parrington's overall reputation was the emergence of a new group of literary critics who were primarily interested in detailed textual analysis and wished to avoid the contamination of literature with base concerns such as politics—in short, a group of critics in the very belletristic tradition that Parrington had stung so bitterly. Lionel Trilling led the charge of the "New Critics" against Parrington with a scathing reassessment of *Main Currents* that originally appeared in the *Partisan Review* in 1940, and was later collected in *The Liberal Imagination*.

Parrington was not a great mind; he was not a precise thinker or, except when measured by the low eminences that were about him, an impressive one. … Separate Parrington from his informing idea of the economic and social determination of thought and what is left is a simple intelligence, notable for its generosity and enthusiasm but certainly not for its accuracy or originality. Take him even with his idea and he is, once its direction has been established, rather too predictable to be continuously interesting. It does not occur to Parrington that there is any other relation possible between the artist and reality than this passage of reality through the transparent artist; he meets evidence of imagination and creativeness with a settled hostility the expression of which suggests that he regards them as the natural enemies of democracy.

Trilling even suggested that some of Parrington's alleged critical gaucheries were due to what Trilling imagined to be sexual repression, while in *The Anatomy of Nonsense* (1942), Yvor Winters accused Parrington of "brutally crude thinking" and "vulgar floridity," pronouncing *Main Currents* "obsolete before it was written." Of all the critics who turned against Parrington during the 1940s, Alfred Kazin was among the more tempered in his judgement. In *On American Grounds* (1942), recently reissued in a 40th anniversary edition, Kazin faulted Parrington's "simplicity of judgment" which led him to see "his own image in the rebels of every generation," as well as "the indifference to literary values which his book displayed" in the treatment of literature. And yet Kazin also recognized that Parrington himself was an excellent writer and perhaps the outstanding Progressive intellectual.

Some of the criticisms of Parrington's *Main Currents in American Thought* were certainly warranted, for he could in fact be prolix and repetitive, and in his effort to single-handedly span the width and breadth of American letters, he sometimes spread himself thin. It is hardly fair to blame Parrington for developments that have occurred since, but one can not help wish he had been acquainted with certain writers available during his own time. For instance, Lewis Henry Morgan, who in 1851 first outlined the Native American contribution to the concept of democracy made by the Great Law of the Iroquois, could have greatly enriched Parrington's concept of democracy, and perhaps made him see America as something more than a seedbed for the flowers and weeds of Europe to multiply. On at least a few of the nearly 1,500 pages of *Main Currents* it is clear that Parrington did not really have a complete grasp of the beast he was wrestling.

Yet as critic Roger Sale observed in 1976, "it is a vastly better work than its subsequent detractors have tried to realize, one that people

who share none of Parrington's bias can read with admiration and pleasure." One reflection of this, perhaps, has been the steady sales *Main
Currents* has enjoyed over the years. Harcourt Brace Jovanovich has
had the book in continuous print for fifty-eight years with total sales
through 1985 of 380,000 copies in combined hardcover and paperback
editions. Moreover, it has continued to sell: According to Harcourt,
nearly 70,000 copies of the paperback editions have been sold in the
fifteen years since 1970.

And so, Vernon Louis Parrington remains a great Ozymandian figure
of American literature and letters, nearly buried and forgotten in the
drifting sands of aesthetic fashion, but still in touch with the American bedrock of which he was also a part. His visage has been defaced by
vandals as well as those wishing to build monuments to other causes, but
what remains today is still powerful enough to impress the unsuspecting
sojourner with the wonder of a great heart and mind, and the America
that made them.

CONTENTS *

BOOK I: CHANGING AMERICA

Part I

The Gilded Age

* This is given in full, as Professor Parrington left it, with those parts not completed by him in brackets. Some revision has been made for the parts he completed,
but notes have been added to the text to show his original intention. For some of the
bracketed headings after Part II of Book II some material is given in the Addenda
from other work of Parrington's.—*Publisher.*

BOOK TWO: THE OLD AND THE NEW: STORM CLOUDS

PART I

The Middle Border Rises

PART II

Proletarian Hopes   PAGE

[1] See "Naturalism in American Fiction," in the Addenda—lecture notes including Crane and Norris.

[2] See Addenda for lecture notes on Lanier.
[3] See Addenda for magazine article on Cabell.
[4] See "A Chapter in American Liberalism," the last of the Addenda.

[5] See *Ibid.*
[6] See Addenda, "The Problem Novel and the Diversion from Naturalism."
[7] See Addenda for brief notes.
[8] See Addenda for notes of lecture on Dreiser.

Part III

Reaction

[9] See Addenda for reprint of pamphlet on Lewis.
[10] See Addenda for brief notes.

BOOK ONE: CHANGING AMERICA

BOOK ONE

CHANGING AMERICA

When America laid aside its arms after Appomattox and turned back to the pursuits of peace it was well advanced toward the goal set by Alexander Hamilton three-quarters of a century before. The great obstacle that had withheld its feet hitherto had been swept from its path. A slave economy could never again thwart the ambitions of the capitalistic economy. The jealous particularism that for a generation had obstructed the inevitable drift toward a coalescing national unity had gone down in defeat. The agrarian South was no longer master in the councils of government; the shaping of the future had fallen to other hands and the unfolding of the new order could go forward without southern let or hindrance.

Other obstacles were falling away of themselves. North as well as South, the traditional domestic economy was already a thing of the past. An easier way to wealth, and one enormously more profitable, had been discovered. The future lay in the hands of the machine that was already dispossessing the tool. In the hurry of the war years the potentialities of the factory system had been explored and the ready resources of liquid capital had been greatly augmented. From the smoke of the great conflict an America had emerged unlike any the earlier generations had known. An ambitious industrialism stood on the threshold of a continental expansion that was to transfer sovereignty in America from a landed and mercantile aristocracy to the capable hands of a new race of captains of industry. Only the western farmers, newly settled in the Middle Border and spreading the psychology of the frontier through the vast prairie spaces of a greater Inland Empire, remained as a last stumbling-block. Other battles with agrarianism must be fought before capitalism assumed undisputed mastery of America; but with the eventual overthrow of the agrarian hosts in their last stronghold the path would lie broad and straight to the goal of an encompassing industrialism, with politicians and political parties its willing servants. There would be no more dissensions in the household. With southern Jeffersonians and western agra-

3

rians no longer sitting as watch dogs to the Constitution, the political state would be refashioned to serve a new age, and the old dream of a coalescing national economy become a reality. The American System was in the way of complete establishment.

Other changes impended, and greater. The enthronement of the machine was only the outward and visible sign of the revolution in thought that came with the rise of science. As a new cosmos unfolded before the inquisitive eyes of scientists the old metaphysical speculations became as obsolete as the old household economy. A new spirit of realism was abroad, probing and questioning the material world, pushing the realm of exact knowledge into the earlier regions of faith. The conquest of nature was the great business of the day, and as that conquest went forward triumphantly the solid fruits of the new mastery were gathered by industrialism. Science and the machine were the twin instruments for creating a new civilization, of which the technologist and the industrialist were the high priests. The transcendental theologian was soon to be as extinct as the passenger pigeon.

With the substitution of the captain of industry for the plantation master as the custodian of society, the age of aristocracy was at an end and the age of the middle class was established. A new culture, created by the machine and answering the needs of capitalism, was to dispossess the old culture with its lingering concern for distinction and its love of standards—a culture that should eventually suffice the needs of a brisk city world of machine activities. But that would take time. In the meanwhile—in the confused interregnum between reigns—America would be little more than a welter of crude energy, a raw unlovely society where the strife of competition with its prodigal waste testified to the shortcomings of an age in process of transition. The spirit of the frontier was to flare up in a huge buccaneering orgy. Having swept across the continent to the Pacific coast like a visitation of locusts, the frontier spirit turned back upon its course to conquer the East, infecting the new industrialism with a crude individualism, fouling the halls of Congress, despoiling the public domain, and indulging in a huge national barbecue. It submerged the arts and created a new literature. For a time it carried all things before it, until running full tilt into science and the machine, its triumphant progress was stopped and America, rejecting individualism, began the work of standardization and mechanization. It is this world in transition from an aristocratic to a middle-class order, turmoiled by the last flare-up of the frontier spirit, shifting from a robust individualism to a colorless standardization, which the chapters that follow must deal with. A confused and turbulent scene, but not without its fascination to the American who would understand his special heritage—perhaps the most characteristically native, the most American, in our total history.

PART ONE: THE GILDED AGE

CHAPTER I

THE AMERICAN SCENE

I

FREE AMERICA

THE pot was boiling briskly in America in the tumultuous post-war years. The country had definitely entered upon its freedom and was settling its disordered household to suit its democratic taste. Everywhere new ways were feverishly at work transforming the countryside. In the South another order was rising uncertainly on the ruins of the plantation system; in the East an expanding factory economy was weaving a different pattern of industrial life; in the Middle Border a recrudescent agriculture was arising from the application of the machine to the rich prairie soil. All over the land a spider web of iron rails was being spun that was to draw the remotest outposts into the common whole and bind the nation together with steel bands. Nevertheless two diverse worlds lay on the map of continental America. Facing in opposite directions and holding different faiths, they would not travel together easily or take comfort from the yoke that joined them. Agricultural America, behind which lay two and a half centuries of experience, was a decentralized world, democratic, individualistic, suspicious; industrial America, behind which lay only half a dozen decades of bustling experiment, was a centralizing world, capitalistic, feudal, ambitious. The one was a decaying order, the other a rising, and between them would be friction till one or the other had become master.

Continental America was still half frontier and half settled country. A thin line of homesteads had been thrust westward till the outposts reached well into the Middle Border—an uncertain thread running through eastern Minnesota, Nebraska, Kansas, overleaping the Indian Territory and then running west into Texas —approximately halfway between the Atlantic and the Pacific. Behind these outposts was still much unoccupied land, and beyond stretched the unfenced prairies till they merged in the sagebrush plains, gray and waste, that stretched to the foothills of the Rocky Mountains. Beyond the mountains were other stretches of plains and deserts, vast and forbidding in their alkali blight, to the wooded coast ranges and the Pacific Ocean. In all this immense territory were only scattered settlements—at Denver, Salt Lake City, Sacramento, San Francisco, Portland, Seattle, and elsewhere— tiny outposts in the wilderness, with scattered hamlets, mining camps, and isolated homesteads lost in the great expanse. On the prairies from Mexico to Canada—across which rumbled great herds of buffalo—roved powerful tribes of hostile Indians who fretted against the forward thrust of settlement and disputed the right of possession. The urgent business of the times was the subduing of this wild region, wresting it from Indians and buffalo and wilderness; and the forty years that lay between the California Gold Rush of '49 and the Oklahoma Land Rush of '89 saw the greatest wave of pioneer expansion—the swiftest and most reckless—in all our pioneer experience. Expansion on so vast a scale necessitated building, and the seventies became the railway age, bonding the future to break down present barriers of isolation, and opening new territories for later exploitation. The reflux of the great movement swept back upon the Atlantic coast and gave to life there a fresh note of spontaneous vigor, of which the Gilded Age was the inevitable expression.

It was this energetic East, with its accumulations of liquid capital awaiting investment and its factories turning out the materials needed to push the settlements westward, that profited most from the conquest of the far West. The impulsion from the frontier did much to drive forward the industrial revolution. The war that brought devastation to the South had been more friendly to northern interests. In gathering the scattered rills of capital into central reservoirs at Philadelphia and New York, and in expanding the factory system to supply the needs of the armies, it had opened to capitalism its first clear view of the Promised Land. The bankers had come into control of the liquid wealth of the nation, and the industrialists had learned to use the machine for production; the time was ripe for exploitation on a scale undreamed-of a generation before. Up till then the potential resources of the continent had not even been surveyed. Earlier pioneers had only scratched the surface—felling trees, making crops, building pygmy watermills, smelting a little iron. Mineral wealth had been scarcely touched. Tools had been lacking to develop it, capital had been lacking, transportation lacking, technical methods lacking, markets lacking.

In the years following the war, exploitation for the first time was provided with adequate resources and a competent technique, and busy prospectors were daily uncovering new sources of wealth. The coal and oil of Pennsylvania and Ohio, the copper and iron ore of upper Michigan, the gold and silver, lumber and fisheries, of the Pacific Coast, provided limitless raw materials for the rising industrialism. The Bessemer process quickly turned an age of iron into an age of steel and created the great rolling mills of Pittsburgh from which issued the rails for expanding railways. The reaper and binder, the sulky plow and the threshing machine, created a large-scale agriculture on the fertile prairies. Wild grass-lands provided grazing for immense herds of cattle and sheep; the development of the corn-belt enormously increased the supply of hogs; and with railways at hand the Middle Border poured into Omaha and Kansas City and Chicago an endless stream of produce. As the line of the frontier pushed westward new towns were built, thousands of homesteads were filed on, and the speculator and promoter hovered over the prairies like buzzards seeking their carrion. With rising land-values money was to be made out of unearned increment, and the creation of booms was a profitable industry. The times were stirring and it was a shiftless fellow who did not make his pile. If he had been too late to file on desirable acres he had only to find a careless homesteader who had failed in some legal technicality and "jump his claim." Good bottom land could be had even by late-comers if they were sharp at the game.

This bustling America of 1870 accounted itself a democratic world. A free people had put away all aristocratic privileges and conscious of its power went forth to possess the last frontier. Its social philosophy, which it found adequate to its needs, was summed up in three words—preëmption, exploitation, progress. Its immediate and pressing business was to dispossess the government of its rich holdings. Lands in the possession of the government were so much idle waste, untaxed and profitless; in private hands they would be developed. They would provide work, pay taxes, support schools, enrich the community. Preëmption meant exploitation and exploitation meant progress. It was a simple philosophy and it suited the simple individualism of the times. The Gilded Age knew nothing of the Enlightenment; it recognized only the acquisitive instinct. That much at least the frontier had taught the great American democracy; and in applying to the resources of a continent the lesson it had been so well taught the Gilded Age wrote a profoundly characteristic chapter of American history.

II

FIGURES OF EARTH

In a moment of special irritation Edwin Lawrence Godkin called the civilization of the seventies a chromo civilization. Mark Twain, with his slack western standards, was equally severe. As he contemplated the slovenly reality beneath the gaudy exterior he dubbed it the Gilded Age. Other critics with a gift for pungent phrase have flung their gibes at the ways of a picturesque and uncouth generation. There is reason in plenty for such caustic comment. Heedless, irreverent, unlovely, cultivating huge beards, shod in polished top-boots—the last refinement of the farmer's cowhides —wearing linen dickeys over hickory shirts, moving through pools of tobacco juice, erupting in shoddy and grotesque architecture, cluttering its homes with ungainly walnut chairs and marble-topped tables and heavy lambrequins, the decade of the seventies was only too plainly mired and floundering in a bog of bad taste. A world of triumphant and unabashed vulgarity without its like in our history, it was not aware of its plight, but accounted its manners genteel and boasted of ways that were a parody on sober good sense.

Yet just as such comments are, they do not reach quite to the heart of the age. They emphasize rather the excrescences, the casual lapses, of a generation that underneath its crudities and vulgarities was boldly adventurous and creative—a generation in which the democratic freedoms of America, as those freedoms had taken shape during a drab frontier experience, came at last to spontaneous and vivid expression. If its cultural wealth was less than it thought, if in its exuberance it was engaged somewhat too boisterously in stamping its own plebeian image on the work of its hands, it was only natural to a society that for the first time found its opportunities equal to its desires, a youthful society that accounted the world its oyster and wanted no restrictions laid on its will. It was the ripe fruit of Jacksonian leveling, and if it ran to a grotesque individualism—if in its self-confidence it was heedless of the smiles of older societies—it was nevertheless by reason of its uncouthness the most picturesque generation in our history; and for those who love to watch human nature disporting itself with naïve abandon, running amuck through all the conventions, no other age provides so fascinating a spectacle.

When the cannon at last had ceased their destruction it was a strange new America that looked out confidently on the scene. Something had been released by the upheavals of half a century, something strong and assertive that was prepared to take possession of the continent. It did not issue from the loins of war. Its origins must be sought elsewhere, further back in time. It had been cradled in the vast changes that since 1815 had been reshaping America: in the break-up of the old domestic economy that kept life mean and drab, in the noisy enthusiasms of the new coonskin democracy, in the romanticisms of the California gold rush, in the boisterous freedoms discovered by the forties and fifties. It had come to manhood in the battles of a tremendous war, and as it now surveyed the continent, discovering potential wealth before unknown, it demanded only freedom and opportunity—a fair race and no favors. Everywhere was a welling-up of primitive pagan desires after long repressions—to grow rich, to grasp power, to be strong and masterful and lay the world at its feet. It was a violent reaction from the narrow poverty of frontier life and the narrow inhibitions of backwoods religion. It had had enough of skimpy, meager ways, of scrubbing along hoping for something to turn up. It would go out and turn it up. It was consumed with a great hunger for abundance, for the good things of life, for wealth. It was frankly materialistic and if material goods could be wrested from society it would lay its hands heartily to the work. Freedom and opportunity, to acquire, to possess, to enjoy—for that it would sell its soul.

Society of a sudden was become fluid. With the sweeping-away of the last aristocratic restraints the potentialities of the common man found release for self-assertion. Strange figures, sprung from obscure origins, thrust themselves everywhere upon the scene. In the reaction from the mean and skimpy, a passionate will to power was issuing from unexpected sources, undisciplined, confused in ethical values, but endowed with immense vitality. Individualism was being simplified to the acquisitive instinct. These new Americans were primitive souls, ruthless, predatory, capable; single-minded men; rogues and rascals often, but never feeble, never hindered by petty scruple, never given to puling or whining—the raw materials of a race of capitalistic buccaneers. Out of the drab mass of common plebeian life had come this vital energy that erupted in amazing abundance and in strange forms. The new freedoms meant diverse things to different men and each like Jurgen followed after his own wishes and his own desires. Pirate and priest issued from the common source and played their parts with the same picturesqueness. The romantic age of Captain Kidd was come again, and the black flag and the gospel banner were both in lockers to be flown as the needs of the cruise determined. With all coercive restrictions put away the democratic genius of America was setting out on the road of manifest destiny.

Analyze the most talked-of men of the age and one is likely to find a splendid audacity coupled with an immense wastefulness. A note of tough-mindedness marks them. They had stout nippers. They fought their way encased in rhinoceros hides. There was the Wall Street crowd—Daniel Drew, Commodore Vanderbilt, Jim Fisk, Jay Gould, Russell Sage—blackguards for the most part, railway wreckers, cheaters and swindlers, but picturesque in their rascality. There was the numerous tribe of politicians—Boss Tweed, Fernando Wood, G. Oakey Hall, Senator Pomeroy, Senator Cameron, Roscoe Conkling, James G. Blaine—blackguards also for the most part, looting city treasuries, buying and selling legislative votes like railway stock, but picturesque in their audacity. There were the professional keepers of the public morals—Anthony Comstock, John B. Gough, Dwight L. Moody, Henry Ward Beecher, T. De Witt Talmage—ardent proselytizers, unintellectual, men of one idea, but fiery in zeal and eloquent in description of the particular heaven each wanted to people with his fellow Americans. And springing up like mushrooms after a rain was the goodly company of cranks—Virginia Woodhull and Tennessee Claflin, "Citizen" George Francis Train, Henry Bergh, Ben Butler, Ignatius Donnelly, Bob Ingersoll, Henry George—picturesque figures with a flair for publicity who tilled their special fields with splendid gestures. And finally there was Barnum the Showman, growing rich on the profession of humbuggery, a vulgar greasy genius, pure brass without any gilding, yet in picturesque and capable effrontery the very embodiment of the age. A marvelous company, vital with the untamed energy of a new land. In the presence of such men one begins to understand what Walt Whitman meant by his talk of the elemental.

Created by a primitive world that knew not the machine, they were marked by the rough homeliness of their origins. Whether wizened or fat they were never insignificant or commonplace. On the whole one prefers them fat, and for solid bulk what generation has outdone them? There was Revivalist Moody, bearded and neckless, with his two hundred and eighty pounds of Adam's flesh, every ounce of which "belonged to God." There was the lyric Sankey, afflicted with two hundred and twenty-five pounds of human frailty, yet looking as smug as a banker and singing "There were ninety and nine" divinely through mutton-chop whiskers. There was Boss Tweed, phlegmatic and mighty, overawing rebellious gangsters at the City Hall with his two hundred and forty pounds of pugnacious rascality. There was John Fiske, a philosophic hippopotamus, warming the chill waters of Spencerian science with his prodigious bulk. There was Ben Butler, oily and puffy and wheezy, like Falstaff larding the lean earth as he walked along, who yearly added more flesh to the scant ninety-seven pounds he carried away from Waterville College. And there was Jim Fisk, dressed like a bartender, huge in nerve as in bulk, driving with the dashing Josie Mansfield down Broadway—prince of vulgarians, who jovially proclaimed, "I worship in the Synagogue of the Libertines," and who on the failure of the Erie coup announced cheerfully, "Nothing is lost save honor!"

Impressive as are the fat kine of Egypt, the lean kine scarcely suffer by contrast. There were giants of puny physique in those days. There was Uncle Dan'l Drew, thin as a dried herring, yet a builder of churches and founder of Drew Theological Seminary, who pilfered and cheated his way to wealth with tobacco juice drooling from his mouth. There was Jay Gould, a lone-hand gambler, a dynamo in a tubercular body, who openly invested in the devil's tenements as likely to pay better dividends, and went home to potter lovingly amongst his exotic flowers. And there was Oakey Hall, clubman and playwright, small, elegant, and unscrupulous; and Victoria Woodhull who stirred up the Beecher case, a wisp of a woman who enraged all the frumpy blue-stockings by the smartness of her toilet and the perfection of her manners; and little Libby Tilton with her tiny wistful face and great eyes that looked out wonderingly at the world—eyes that were to go blind with weeping before the candle of her life went out. It was such men and women, individual and colorful, that Whitman and Mark Twain mingled with, and that Herman Melville—colossal and dynamic beyond them all—looked out upon sardonically from his tomb in the Custom House where he was consuming his own heart.

They were thrown up as it were casually out of the huge caldron of energy that was America. All over the land were thousands like them, self-made men quick to lay hands on opportunity if it knocked at the door, ready to seek it out if it were slow in knocking, recognizing no limitations to their powers, discouraged by no shortcomings in their training. When Moody set out to bring the world to his Protestant God he was an illiterate shoe salesman who stumbled over the hard words of his King James Bible. Anthony Comstock, the roundsman of the Lord, was a salesman in a dry-goods shop, and as careless of his spelling as he was careful of his neighbors' morals. Commodore Vanderbilt, who built up the greatest fortune of the time, was a Brooklyn ferryman, hard-fisted and tough as a burr-oak, who in a lifetime of over eighty years read only one book, *Pilgrim's Progress*, and that after he was seventy. Daniel Drew was a shyster cattle-drover, whose arid emotions found outlet in periodic conversions and backslidings, and who got on in this vale of tears by salting his cattle and increasing his—and the Lord's—wealth with every pound of water in their bellies— from which cleverness is said to have come the Wall Street phrase, "stock-watering." Jim Fisk was the son of a Yankee peddler, who, disdaining the unambitious ways of his father, set up for himself in a cart gilded like a circus-wagon and drove about the country-side with jingling bells. After he had made his pile in Wall Street he set up his own opera house and proposed to rival the Medici as a patron of the arts—and especially of the artists if they were of the right sex. A surprising number of them—Moody, Beecher, Bar-num, Fisk, Comstock, Ben Butler—came from New England; Jay Gould was of Connecticut ancestry; but Oakey Hall was a southern gentleman; Fernando Wood, with the face of an Apollo and the wit of an Irishman, was the son of a Philadelphia cigar-maker and much of his early income was drawn from sailors' groggeries along the waterfront; Tweed was a stolid New Yorker, and Drew was a York State country boy.

What was happening in New York was symptomatic of the

nation. If the temple of Plutus was building in Wall Street, his devotees were everywhere. In Chicago, rising higgledy-piggledy from the ashes of the great fire, Phil Armour and Nelson Morris were laying out stockyards and drawing the cattle and sheep and hogs from remote prairie farms to their slaughter-houses. In Cleveland, Mark Hanna was erecting his smelters and turning the iron ore of Michigan into dollars, while John D. Rockefeller was squeezing the small fry out of the petroleum business and creating the Standard Oil monopoly. In Pittsburgh, Andrew Carnegie was applying the Bessemer process to steel-making and laying the foundations of the later steel trust. In Minneapolis, C. C. Washburn and Charles A. Pillsbury were applying new methods to milling and turning the northern wheat into flour to ship to the ends of the earth. In San Francisco, Leland Stanford and Collis P. Huntington were amassing huge fortunes out of the Southern Pacific Railway and bringing the commonwealth of California to their feet. Everywhere were boom-town and real-estate promoters, the lust of speculation, the hankering after quick and easy wealth.

In the great spaces from Kansas City to Sacramento the frontier spirit was in the gaudiest bloom. The experiences of three centuries of expansion were being crowded into as many decades. In the fifties the highway of the frontier had run up and down the Mississippi River and the golden age of steamboating had brought a motley life to Saint Louis; in the seventies the frontier had passed far beyond and was pushing through the Rocky Mountains, repeating as it went the old frontier story of swagger and slovenliness, of boundless hope and heroic endurance—a story deeply marked with violence and crime and heart-breaking failure. Thousands of veterans from the disbanded armies, northern and southern alike, flocked to the West to seek their fortunes, and daily life there soon took on a drab note from the alkali of the plains; yet through the drabness ran a boisterous humor that exalted lying to a fine art—a humor that goes back to Davy Crockett and the Ohio flatboatmen. Mark Twain's *Roughing It* is the epic of this frontier of the Pony Express, as *Life on the Mississippi* is the epic of the preceding generation.

The huge wastefulness of the frontier was everywhere, East and West. The Gilded Age heeded somewhat too literally the Biblical injunction to take no thought for the morrow, but was busily intent on squandering the resources of the continent. All things were held cheap, and human life cheapest of all. Wild Bill Hickok with forty notches on his gun and a row of graves to his credit in Boot Hill Cemetery, and Jesse James, most picturesque of desperadoes, levying toll with his six-shooter on the bankers who were desecrating the free spirit of the plains with their two per cent. a month, are familiar heroes in Wild West tales; but the real plainsman of the Gilded Age, the picturesque embodiment of the last frontier, was Captain Carver, the faultless horseman and faultless shot, engaged in his celebrated buffalo hunt for the championship of the prairies. Wagering that he could kill more buffalo in a day than any rival hero of the chase, he rode forth with his Indian marker and dropping the miles behind him he left an endless trail of dead beasts properly tagged, winning handsomely when his rival's horse fell dead from exhaustion. It was magnificent. Davy Crockett's hundred and five bears in a season was but 'prentice work compared with Captain Carver's professional skill. It is small wonder that he became a hero of the day and his rifle, turned now to the circus business of breaking glass balls thrown from his running horse, achieved a fame far greater than Davy's Betsy. With his bold mustaches, his long black hair flying in the wind, his sombrero and chaps and top-boots, he was a figure matched only by Buffalo Bill, the last of the great plainsmen.

Captain Carver was picturesque, but what shall be said of the thousands of lesser Carvers engaged in the same slaughter, market-hunters who discovered a new industry in buffalo-killing? At the close of the Civil War the number on the western plains was estimated at fifteen millions. With the building of the Union Pacific Railroad they were cut asunder into two vast herds, and upon these herds fell the hunters with the new breech-loading rifles, shooting for the hide market that paid sixty-five cents for a bull's hide and a dollar and fifteen cents for a cow's. During the four years from 1871 to 1874 nearly a million head a year were slain from the southern herd alone, their skins ripped off and the carcasses left for the coyotes and buzzards. By the end of the hunting-season of 1875 the vast southern herd had been wiped out, and with the building of the Northern Pacific in 1880 the smaller northern herd soon suffered the same fate. The buffalo were gone with the hostile Indians —Sioux and Blackfeet and Cheyennes and a dozen other tribes.[1]

[1] See Allan Nevins, "The Taming of the West," in *The Emergence of Modern America.*

It was the last dramatic episode of the American frontier, and it wrote a fitting climax to three centuries of wasteful conquest. But the prairies were tamed, and Wild Bill Hickok and Captain Carver and Buffalo Bill Cody had become romantic figures to enthrall the imagination of later generations.[2]

It was an abundant harvest of those freedoms that America had long been struggling to achieve, and it was making ready the ground for later harvests that would be less to its liking. Freedom had become individualism, and individualism had become the inalienable right to preëmpt, to exploit, to squander. Gone were the old ideals along with the old restraints. The idealism of the forties, the romanticism of the fifties—all the heritage of Jeffersonianism and the French Enlightenment—were put thoughtlessly away, and with no social conscience, no concern for civilization, no heed for the future of the democracy it talked so much about, the Gilded Age threw itself into the business of money-getting. From the sober restraints of aristocracy, the old inhibitions of Puritanism, the niggardliness of an exacting domestic economy, it swung far back in reaction, and with the discovery of limitless opportunities for exploitation it allowed itself to get drunk. Figures of earth, they followed after their own dreams. Some were builders with grandiose plans in their pockets; others were wreckers with no plans at all. It was an anarchistic world of strong, capable men, selfish, unenlightened, amoral—an excellent example of what human nature will do with undisciplined freedom. In the Gilded Age freedom was the freedom of buccaneers preying on the argosies of Spain.

III

POLITICS AND THE FAIRY GODMOTHER

Certainly the Gilded Age would have resented such an interpretation of its brisk activities. In the welter of change that resulted from the application of the machine to the raw materials of a continent, it chose rather to see the spirit of progress to which the temper of the American people was so responsive. Freedom, it was

[2] It is the same story in the matter of the passenger pigeon. In early days the flights of these birds ran to untold millions. The last great nesting was at Petoskey, Michigan, in 1878, covering a strip forty miles long and from three to ten miles wide. Upon the nests fell the market-hunters and a million and a half squabs were shipped to New York by rail, besides the thousands wasted. Within a generation the passenger pigeon had become extinct. See W. B. Mershon, *Outdoor Life and Recreation,* February, 1929, p. 26 ff.

convinced, was justifying itself by its works. The eighteenth
century had been static, the nineteenth century was progressive.
It was adaptable, quick to change its ways and its tools, ready to
accept whatever proved advantageous—pragmatic, opportunist.
It was not stifled by the dead hand of custom but was free to adapt
means to ends. It accepted progress as it accepted democracy,
without questioning the sufficiency of either. The conception
accorded naturally with a frontier psychology. Complete opportu-
nism is possible only amongst a people that is shallow-rooted, that
lives in a fluid society, scantily institutionalized, with few vested
interests. In a young society it is easy, in a maturing society it
becomes increasingly difficult.

Dazzled by the results of the new technique of exploitation
applied on a grand scale to unpreëmpted opportunities, it is no
wonder the Gilded Age thought well of its labors and confused the
pattern of life it was weaving with the pattern of a rational civilization. It had drunk in the idea of progress with its mother's milk.
It was an inevitable frontier interpretation of the swift changes
resulting from a fluid economics and a fluid society in process of
settling into static ways. It served conveniently to describe the
changes from the simplicities of social beginnings to the complexities of a later order. It was made use of following the War of 1812
to explain the stir resulting from the westward expansion and the
great increase in immigration; but it was given vastly greater
significance by the social unsettlements that came with the industrial revolution. With the realization of the dramatic changes
in manner of living—the added conveniences of life, release from
the laborious round of the domestic economy, ease of transportation—that resulted from the machine order, it was inevitable that
the idea of progress should have been on every man's tongue. The
increase of wealth visible to all was in itself a sufficient sign of
progress, and as the novelty of the industrial change wore off and
the economy of America was more completely industrialized, it
was this augmenting wealth that symbolized it.

In such fashion the excellent ideal of progress that issued from
the social enthusiasms of the Enlightenment was taken in charge
by the Gilded Age and transformed into a handmaid of capitalism.
Its duties were narrowed to the single end of serving profits and its
accomplishments came to be exactly measured by bank clearings.
It was unfortunate but inevitable. The idea was too seductive to

the American mentality not to be seized upon and made to serve a rising order. Exploitation was the business of the times and how better could exploitation throw about its activities the sanction of idealism than by wedding them to progress? It is a misfortune that America has never subjected the abstract idea of progress to critical examination. Content with the frontier and capitalistic interpretations it has confused change with betterment, and when a great idealist of the Gilded Age demonstrated to America that it was misled and pointed out that the path of progress it was following was the highway to poverty, he was hooted from the market-place.

Having thus thrown the mantle of progress about the Gold Dust twins, the Gilded Age was ready to bring the political forces of America into harmony with the program of preëmption and exploitation. The situation could hardly have been more to its liking. Post-war America was wholly lacking in political philosophies, wholly opportunist. The old party cleavage between agriculture and industry had been obscured and the logic of party alignment destroyed by the struggle over slavery. Democrat and Whig no longer faced each other conscious of the different ends they sought. The great party of Jefferson and Jackson was prostrate, borne down by the odium of slavery and secession. In the North elements of both had been drawn into a motley war party, momentarily fused by the bitterness of conflict, but lacking any common program, certain indeed to split on fundamental economic issues. The Whig Republican was still Hamiltonian paternalistic, and the Democrat Republican was still Jeffersonian *laissez faire*, and until it was determined which wing should control the party councils there would be only confusion. The politicians were fertile in compromises, but in nominating Lincoln and Johnson the party ventured to get astride two horses that would not run together. To attempt to make yoke-fellows of democratic leveling and capitalistic paternalism was prophetic of rifts and schisms that only the passions of Reconstruction days could hold in check.

In 1865 the Republican party was no other than a war machine that had accomplished its purpose. It was a political mongrel, without logical cohesion, and it seemed doomed to break up as the Whig party had broken up and the Federalist party had broken up. But fate was now on the side of the Whigs as it had not been earlier. The democratic forces had lost strength from the war, and democratic principles were in ill repute. The drift to centralization, the enormous development of capitalism, the spirit of exploitation, were prophetic of a changing temper that was preparing to exalt the doctrine of manifest destiny which the Whig party stood sponsor for. The middle class was in the saddle and it was time to bring the political state under its control. The practical problem of the moment was to transform the mongrel Republican party into a strong cohesive instrument, and to accomplish that it was necessary to hold the loyalty of its Democratic voters amongst the farmers and working-classes whilst putting into effect its Whig program.

Under normal conditions the thing would have been impossible, but the times were wrought up and blindly passionate and the politicians skillful. The revolt of Andrew Johnson came near to bringing the party on the rocks; but the undisciplined Jacksonians were overthrown by the appeal to the Bloody Flag and put to flight by the nomination of General Grant for the presidency. The rebellion of the Independent Republicans under Horace Greeley in 1872 was brought to nothing by the skillful use of Grant's military prestige, and the party passed definitely under the control of capitalism, and became such an instrument for exploitation as Henry Clay dreamed of but could not perfect. Under the nominal leadership of the easy-going Grant a loose rein was given to Whiggish ambitions and the Republican party became a political instrument worthy of the Gilded Age.

The triumph of Whiggery was possible because the spirit of the Gilded Age was Whiggish. The picturesque embodiment of the multitude of voters who hurrahed for Grant and the Grand Old Party was a figure who had grown his first beard in the ebullient days before Secession. Colonel Beriah Sellers, with his genial optimism and easy political ethics, was an epitome of the political hopes of the Gilded Age. With a Micawber-like faith in his country and his government, eager to realize on his expansive dreams and looking to the national treasury to scatter its fructifying millions in the neighborhood of his speculative holdings, he was no other than Uncle Sam in the boisterous days following Appomattox. The hopes that floated up out of his dreams were the hopes of millions who cast their votes for Republican Congressmen who in return were expected to cast their votes for huge governmental appropriations that would insure prosperity's reaching certain post-office addresses. Citizens had saved the government in the trying days that were past; it was only fair in return that government should aid the patriotic citizen in the necessary work of developing national resources. It was paternalism as understood by speculators and subsidy-hunters, but was it not a part of the great American System that was to make the country rich and self-sufficient? The American System had been talked of for forty years; it had slowly got on its feet in pre-war days despite the stubborn planter opposition; now at last it had fairly come into its own. The time was ripe for the Republican party to become a fairy godmother to the millions of Beriah Sellerses throughout the North and West.

It is plain as a pikestaff why the spirit of Whiggery should have taken riotous possession of the Gilded Age. With its booming industrial cities America in 1870 was fast becoming capitalistic, and in every capitalistic society Whiggery springs up as naturally as pigweed in a garden. However attractive the disguises it may assume, it is in essence the logical creed of the profit philosophy. It is the expression in politics of the acquisitive instinct and it assumes as the greatest good the shaping of public policy to promote private interests. It asserts that it is a duty of the state to help its citizens to make money, and it conceives of the political state as a useful instrument for effective exploitation. How otherwise? The public good cannot be served apart from business interests, for business interests are the public good and in serving business the state is serving society. Everybody's eggs are in the basket and they must not be broken. For a capitalistic society Whiggery is the only rational politics, for it exalts the profit-motive as the sole object of parliamentary concern. Government has only to wave its wand and fairy gifts descend upon business like the golden sands of Pactolus. It graciously bestows its tariffs and subsidies, and streams of wealth flow into private wells.

But unhappily there is a fly in the Whiggish honey. In a competitive order, government is forced to make its choices. It cannot serve both Peter and Paul. If it gives with one hand it must take away with the other. And so the persuasive ideal of paternalism in the common interest degenerates in practice into legalized favoritism. Governmental gifts go to the largest investments. Lesser interests are sacrificed to greater interests and Whiggery comes finally to serve the lords of the earth without whose good will the wheels of business will not turn. To him that hath shall be given. If the few do not prosper the many will starve, and if the many have bread who would begrudge the few their abundance? In Whiggery is the fulfillment of the Scriptures.

Henry Clay had been a prophetic figure pointing the way America was to travel; but he came a generation too soon. A son of the Gilded Age, he was doomed to live in a world of Jacksonian democracy. But the spirit of Henry Clay survived his death and his followers were everywhere in the land. The plain citizen who wanted a slice of the rich prairie land of Iowa or Kansas, with a railway convenient to his homestead, had learned to look to the government for a gift, and if he got his quarter-section and his transportation he was careless about what the other fellow got. A little more or less could make no difference to a country inexhaustible in resources. America belonged to the American people and not to the government, and resources in private hands paid taxes and increased the national wealth. In his favorite newspaper, the *New York Tribune*, he read daily appeals for the adoption of a patriotic national economy, by means of which an infant industrialism, made prosperous by a protective tariff, would provide a home market for the produce of the farmer and render the country self-sufficient. Money would thus be put in everybody's pocket. Protection was not robbing Peter to pay Paul, but paying both Peter and Paul out of the augmented wealth of the whole.

The seductive arguments that Horace Greeley disseminated amongst the plain people, Henry Carey purveyed to more intelligent ears. The most distinguished American economist of the time, Carey had abandoned his earlier *laissez-faire* position, and having convinced himself that only through a close-knit national economy could the country develop a well-rounded economic program, he had become the most ardent of protectionists. During the fifties and later he was tireless in popularizing the doctrine of a natural harmony of interests between agriculture and manufacturing, and to a generation expanding rapidly in both fields his able presentation made great appeal. It was but a step from protectionism to governmental subsidies. Beriah Sellers and Henry Clay had come to be justified by the political economists. (Note that amongst Carey's converts were such different idealists as Wendell Phillips and Peter Cooper.)

IV

THE GREAT BARBECUE

Horace Greeley and Henry Carey were only straws in the wind that during the Gilded Age was blowing the doctrine of paternalism about the land. A Colonel Sellers was to be found at every fireside talking the same blowsy doctrine. Infectious in their optimism, naïve in their faith that something would be turned up for them by the government if they made known their wants, they were hoping for dollars to be put in their pockets by a generous administration at Washington. Congress had rich gifts to bestow—in lands, tariffs, subsidies, favors of all sorts; and when influential citizens made their wishes known to the reigning statesmen, the sympathetic politicians were quick to turn the government into the fairy godmother the voters wanted it to be. A huge barbecue was spread to which all presumably were invited. Not quite all, to be sure; inconspicuous persons, those who were at home on the farm or at work in the mills and offices, were overlooked; a good many indeed out of the total number of the American people. But all the important persons, leading bankers and promoters and business men, received invitations. There wasn't room for everybody and these were presumed to represent the whole. It was a splendid feast. If the waiters saw to it that the choicest portions were served to favored guests, they were not unmindful of their numerous homespun constituency and they loudly proclaimed the fine democratic principle that what belongs to the people should be enjoyed by the people—not with petty bureaucratic restrictions, not as a social body, but as individuals, each free citizen using what came to hand for his own private ends, with no questions asked.

It was sound Gilded Age doctrine. To a frontier people what was more democratic than a barbecue, and to a paternalistic age what was more fitting than that the state should provide the beeves for roasting. Let all come and help themselves. As a result the feast was Gargantuan in its rough plenty. The abundance was what was to be expected of a generous people. More food, to be sure, was spoiled than was eaten, and the revelry was a bit unseemly; but it was a fine spree in the name of the people, and the invitations had been written years before by Henry Clay. But unfortunately what was intended to be jovially democratic was marred by displays of plebeian temper. Suspicious commoners with better eyes than

manners discovered the favoritism of the waiters and drew attention to the difference between their own meager helpings and the
heaped-up plates of more favored guests. It appeared indeed that
there was gross discrimination in the service; that the farmers'
pickings from the Homestead Act were scanty in comparison with
the speculators' pickings from the railway land-grants. The *Crédit
Mobilier* scandal and the Whisky Ring scandal and divers other
scandals came near to breaking up the feast, and the genial host—
who was no other than the hero of Appomattox—came in for some
sharp criticism. But after the more careless ones who were caught
with their fingers where they didn't belong, had been thrust from
the table, the eating and drinking went on again till only the great
carcasses were left. Then at last came the reckoning. When the
bill was sent in to the American people the farmers discovered that
they had been put off with the giblets while the capitalists were
consuming the turkey. They learned that they were no match at a
barbecue for more voracious guests, and as they went home unsatisfied, a sullen anger burned in their hearts that was to express
itself later in fierce agrarian revolts.

What reason there was for such anger, how differently rich and
poor fared at the democratic feast, is suggested by the contrast
between the Homestead Act and the Union Pacific land-grant.
Both were war-time measures and both had emerged from the
agitations of earlier decades. By the terms of the former the homesteader got his hundred and sixty acres at the price of $1.25 an
acre; by the terms of the latter the promoters got a vast empire for
nothing. It was absurd, of course, but what would you have? The
people wanted the railway built and Collis P. Huntington was
willing to build it on his own terms. The government was too
generous to haggle with public-spirited citizens, and too Whiggish
to want to discourage individual enterprise. Ever since the cession
of California there had been much talk of a continental railway
to tie the country together. In the first years the talk in Congress
had all been of a great national venture; the road must be built by
the nation to serve the common interests of the American people.
But unfortunately sectional jealousies prevented any agreement as
to the route the survey lines were to run, and the rising capitalism
was becoming powerful enough to bring into disfavor any engagement of the government in a work that promised great rewards.
Under its guidance political opinion was skillfully turned into the

channel of private enterprise. The public domain backed by the public credit, it was agreed, must pay for the road, but the government must not seek to control the enterprise or look to profit from it directly; the national reward would come indirectly from the opening-up of vast new territories.

The definite shift in policy came about the year 1855. In 1837 Stephen A. Douglas had been the driving force behind the state enterprise of building the Illinois Central Railway. In 1853 he proposed that the Pacific Railroad should be built by private enterprise. With the change promptly came a request for a patriotic land-grant. The government was expected to provide the road, it appeared, but private enterprise was to own it and manage it in the interest of speculators rather than the public. For old-fashioned souls like Thomas A. Benton, who still remembered the Jeffersonian concern for the common well-being, it was a bitter mess to swallow.

I would have preferred [he said] that Congress should have made the road, as a national work, on a scale commensurate with its grandeur and let out the use of it to companies, who would fetch and carry on the best terms for the people and the government. But that hope has vanished . . . a private company has become the resource and the preference. I embrace it as such, utterly scouting all plans for making private roads at national expense, of paying for the use of roads built with our land and money, of bargaining with corporations or individuals for the use of what we give them.[3]

With this speech the old Jeffersonianism pulled down its flag and the new Whiggery ran up its black banner. The Gilded Age had begun and Old Bullion Benton had outlived his time. In the tumultuous decades that followed there was to be no bargaining with corporations for the use of what the public gave; they took what they wanted and no impertinent questions were asked. The hungriest will get the most at the barbecue. A careless wastefulness when the supply is unlimited is perhaps natural enough. There were hard-headed men in the world of Beriah Sellers who knew how easy it was to overreach the simple, and it was they who got most from the common pot. We may call them buccaneers if we choose, and speak of the great barbecue as a democratic debauch. But why single out a few, when all were drunk? Whisky was plentiful at barbecues, and if too liberal potations brought the

[3] Quoted in J. P. Davis, *The Union Pacific Railway*, pp. 67–68.

Gilded Age to the grossest extravagancies, if when it cast up accounts it found its patrimony gone, it was only repeating the experience of a certain man who went down to Jericho. To create a social civilization requires sober heads, and in this carousal of economic romanticism sober heads were few—the good Samaritan was busy elsewhere.

The doctrine of preëmption and exploitation was reaping its harvest. The frontier spirit was having its splurge, and progress was already turning its face in another direction. Within the next half-century this picturesque America with its heritage of crude energy —greedy, lawless, capable—was to be transformed into a vast uniform middle-class land, dedicated to capitalism and creating the greatest machine-order known to history. A scattered agricultural people, steeped in particularistic jealousies and suspicious of centralization, was to be transformed into an urbanized factory people, rootless, migratory, drawn to the job as by a magnet. It was to come about the more easily because the American farmer had never been a land-loving peasant, rooted to the soil and thriving only in daily contact with familiar acres. He had long been half middle-class, accounting unearned increment the most profitable crop, and buying and selling land as if it were calico. And in consequence the vigorous individualism that had sprung from frontier conditions decayed with the passing of the frontier, and those who had lost in the gamble of preëmption and exploitation were added to the growing multitude of the proletariat. It was from such materials, supplemented by a vast influx of immigrants, that was fashioned the America we know today with its standardized life, its machine culture, its mass psychology—an America to which Jefferson and Jackson and Lincoln would be strangers.

v

FOLK HEROES

Perhaps one cannot penetrate more directly to the heart of the Gilded Age than in taking account of certain of its heroes, figures of earth whom it accounted great in its generation, and to whom its admiration flowed out in unstinted measure. It is our own secret desires we attribute to our gods, and if from the muck of the times a queer lot of heroes was singled out, if an undisciplined generation rioting in its new freedoms chose to honor men who had scrambled upward in uncouth ways, it only suggests that such figures were a composite picture of the secret desires of an age vastly concerned with getting on. From a host of striking personalities two must suffice to suggest the spirit of the times, authentic folk-heroes of the Gilded Age, fashioned out of the commonest stuff and realizing such greatness as multitudes of Americans were then dreaming of; and over against them a third figure, a mordant intellectual, who sardonically swam with the stream of tendency and in serving all the gods of the Gilded Age gained for himself a brilliant career.

I

GENERAL GRANT

Greatest of all the heroes of the age was the victor of Appomattox. His fame was in all men's mouths, and his reputation was substantial enough to withstand the attacks of enemies and the gross shortcomings of his own character. It was not for any singular or remarkable qualities of mind or personality that General Grant was taken to the heart of his generation, but rather because he was so completely a product of the times, so strikingly an embodiment of its virtues and weaknesses. In his spectacular career were the sharp contrasts that appealed to a plebeian people wanting in fine and discriminating standards of appraisal. He had come up from the people and the marks of his origins—the slovenly manners and uncritical force of frontier folk-ways—were stamped on him as indelibly as they were stamped on his fellow soldiers who proclaimed his greatness. To a later generation he seems an odd and unaccountable figure for the high rôle of national hero, yet he was as native and homespun as Lincoln, like him sprung from the common stock and learning his lessons from harsh experience, a figure blown to huge dimensions by the passions of civil war. A generation that discovered something praiseworthy in the "smartness" of Jim Fisk, in the burly acquisitiveness of Commodore Vanderbilt, or in the clever humbuggery of Barnum the Showman, certainly would judge with no very critical eyes the claims to greatness of a grim leader of armies who succeeded where so many before had failed.

General Grant was no conventional military hero. It was not the gold stars on his epaulets that dazzled his generation. The people of the North had seen too many gold stars rise and set on the military horizon, they had been stricken too sorely by the bitter struggle, to be caught by military popinjays. They had gone through the fire and any hero of theirs must himself have passed through the fire. It was something veracious in the man, something solid and unyielding in the soldier, something plain as an old shoe in the field marshal of bloody battles, that caught the imagination of the North and made Grant a hero—this together with a certain gift of pungent phrase, befitting the leader of democratic hosts, that served to spread his fame amongst the common people. Vicksburg did much for his reputation, but the demand for "unconditional surrender," sent to a Confederate leader, did far more. The words fixed his character in the popular mind. Here at last was a fighting man who instead of planning how to fall back, as other generals did, thought only of going ahead; so the popular judgment shut its eyes to his dull plebeian character and set a wreath on his brows. It rested there somewhat grotesquely. In spite of a deep unconscious integrity and a stubborn will that drove him forward along whatever path his feet were set on, he was the least imposing of military heroes. Short, stooped, lumpish in mind and body, unintellectual and unimaginative, devoid of ideas and with no tongue to express the incoherent emotions that surged dully in his heart, he was a commonplace fellow that no gold braid could set off. He hated war and disliked soldiering, yet accepting life with a stolid fatalism he fought his bloody way to ultimate victory.

Graduated from West Point after four sterile years of drill, quite uneducated and unread even in his profession, he served for a time at different army posts, went through the Mexican War—which he looked upon as a stupid imperialistic debauch—as quartermaster without gaining distinction, and eventually, oppressed by the eventless routine of garrison life, he fell into the habit of solitary drinking and was dismissed from the service. Misfortune that it seemed, it was his making. Only as a volunteer could he have risen so quickly to high command; as a captain or major in the regular army he would have been detailed as drill-master to the raw troops and have had no chance. Nevertheless hard times came with his dismissal. Indolent by nature and inclined to drift, he was as incompetent a man in practical affairs as one could find in a frontier township. But with a wife and children to support he must turn his hand to something, so he tried his luck at farming, selling real estate, and various odd jobs, yet all the time growing poorer and seedier, till the war came and picking him up flung him to mountain heights of popularity and reputation. Thereafter till his death he was accounted the greatest American of his generation. No accumulating evidence of his well-meaning but witless incapacity in civic and political affairs could pluck from his brows the wreath that had been thrust upon him.

In his spectacular career Grant was an embodiment of the dreams of all the Beriah Sellerses of the Gilded Age. He was a materialistic hero of a materialistic generation. He was dazzled by wealth and power, and after years of bitter poverty he sat down in the lap of luxury with huge content. He took what the gods sent, and if houses and fast horses and wines and cigars were showered upon him he accepted them as a child would accept gifts from a fairy godmother. He had had enough of skimping meanness; with his generation he wanted to slough off the drabness of the frontier; he wanted the good things of life that had so long been denied him, and he was not scrupulous about looking a gift horse in the mouth. He sought out the company of rich men. He was never happier than when enjoying the luxury of Jay Cooke's mansion in Philadelphia or riding with A. T. Stewart in Central Park. As he grew fat and stodgy the vulgar side of his plebeian nature was thrown into sharper relief. He accepted gifts with both hands, and he seems never to have suspected the price that would be exacted of the President for the presents to the General. He never realized how great a bill was sent to the American people for the wine he drank or the cigars he smoked with his wealthy hosts; yet if the wine had been molten gold and the cigars platinum they would have been far cheaper. In return for a few boxes of choice Havanas, Jay Cooke laid his hands on millions of western lands for the Northern Pacific Railway. It was the way of the Gilded Age, and Grant was only doing what all his friends and associates were doing. If he accepted a fifty-thousand-dollar house in Philadelphia, his comrade General Sherman accepted a hundred-thousand-dollar house at Washington. Such gifts were not bribes; they were open and aboveboard; it was the free and easy way of the times. What the age was careless about is the fact that it is hard to refuse a reasonable request from one's fairy godmother, and what the General never understood is that if one is President such a godmother is certain to be a very dangerous member of the family.

There was far too much of that sort of thing all about him for Grant to serve as President with credit to himself or profit to the country. Honest himself, he was the source of more dishonesty in others than any other American President. His eight years in the White House marked the lowest depths—in domestic affairs at least—to which any American administration has fallen. They were little better than a national disgrace. All the festering evils of post-war times came to a head and pock-marked the body politic from head to foot. Scandal and corruption whispered all about him, the hands of his closest advisers were dirty; yet he stubbornly refused to hear the whispers or see the dirt. In judging men and policies he was no more than a child. He could never distinguish between an honest man and a rascal. He was loyal to his friends and open-handedness he regarded as a mark of friendship. In the end it turned out that like the thieves of Jericho his blatant followers despoiled him of pretty nearly everything.

In what must pass for his political views Grant was as naïvely uninformed as a Wyoming cowboy. Utterly wanting in knowledge of political principles, he was a fit leader for the organized mob that called itself the Republican party, whose chief objective was the raiding of the treasure-box of which it was the responsible guardian. He had been nominally a Democrat and the first vote he cast for President he cast for Buchanan. After Lincoln's death he turned naturally to President Johnson and was one of his supporters till the wily Radical group got his ear and carried him over to the rival camp. They wanted his reputation to hide under, and they took possession of it with no great credit to the General's reputation. Thereafter he was a Republican of the Whig wing. It was where he belonged. He was swayed politically by his emotional reactions and it was natural for him to drift into the opulent camp of money and power. His frontier democracy sloughed away and with his generation he went over easily to a buccaneer capitalism. No social conscience obtruded itself to give him trouble. His millionaire friends were Whig Republicans and with his respect for rich men, his admiration for material success, he found himself in congenial company amongst the Whig group. About the only political policy he ever interested himself in was the policy of a protective tariff, and his Whig associates took care that his interest did not wane. Yet so completely did the naïve General reflect the spirit of the Gilded Age that his noisy followers, conspiring to confuse in the public mind southern reconstruction and capitalistic expansion, and hiding a precious set of rascals in the folds of the bloody flag, came near to making him President for a third term. The General was bitterly disappointed at their failure, and the General's wife, who liked to live in the White House, was even more disappointed. To millions of Americans Grant was an authentic hero, to Mark Twain he was a very great man, and to Jay Cooke he was a pawn to be used in the noble strategy of fortune-seeking. What a comedy it all seems now—yet one that leaves an unpleasant taste in the mouth.

Yet to dismiss the stolid General thus is scarcely to do justice to the substantial core of the man. There remains the work written in pain during his last days, the two volumes of *Memoirs* that in their plain directness—as uninspired, says a late biographer, as "a bale of hay"— laid bare his honest simplicity and rugged meagerness. No blackguard and no charlatan could have written such pages. If General Grant was not the great man so many thought, he was a native growth from American soil, endowed like his age with a dogged will and a plodding energy, and he gave his country what he had. Though the branches of the tree were ungainly and offered too hospitable shelter to unseemly birds of the night, the gnarly trunk was sound at the heart.

2

JAY COOKE

Another hero of the times likewise was flung up as it were casually out of obscurity and reaped an amazing harvest from the gigantic struggle. In those difficult years the name of Jay Cooke— "the financier of the Civil War," as his biographer calls him— became as familiar to the people of the North as the names of Grant and Lincoln, and was often joined with theirs as that of one of the saviors of the Union. He was the first great American banker, and good fortune sent him into the world at a moment when his skill in brokerage found opportunity for free play. The war was as great a godsend to Jay Cooke as it was to Grant, for alone amongst our money-lenders he realized the problems and foresaw the profits in a popular system of war financing. He was a pioneer in exploring all the potentialities of the banker's trade, and in his dramatic exploitation of salesmanship and his skillful manipulation of money and credit he marked out the highway our later financiers have traveled. Jay Cooke occupies too significant a place in the history of American capitalism to be overlooked in casting up the accounts of the Gilded Age.

Of Yankee-Puritan stock, he was born in the frontier hamlet of Sandusky, Ohio, when the Western Reserve was at the beginning of its development. His father was a country lawyer of Federalist-Whig affinities, proficient in high-flown western oratory, who liked to be much in the neighborhood eye. He was a pushing, self-confident fellow, highly patriotic, soberly moral, fearing God and loving his country, who felt that the government he supported so heartily should serve him and his town with equal heartiness. His readiness in florid speech won him a single term in Congress, and he used his position as a heaven-sent opportunity to promote a government road from Sandusky—which it seems was not prospering as its inhabitants had expected it would—deep into the Indian country. It was a good Clay-Whig scheme of internal improvement; it would open up a rich timber country, and be highly profitable to the real-estate promoters of Sandusky. Cradled thus in speculation and faith in a benevolent government, his three sons grew up native Whigs, with vigorous Puritan-Yankee minds, who found no difficulty in reconciling the interests of God and Mammon. Eager to get on "the right side of fortune," they went into the three professions of banking, journalism, and the law. The eldest, Pitt, found the law little to his liking; the youngest, Henry, labored diligently at journalism, at Sandusky and later at Columbus, where he was part owner of the *Ohio State Journal* and "boss" of young William Dean Howells, who was likewise seeking to rise through the medium of journalism. It was the family itch for politics that took him to Columbus, and although the venture was financially unsuccessful it brought him influential connections. He was useful to Governor Salmon P. Chase, afterwards to be Lincoln's Secretary of the Treasury, and to John Sherman, who was later to become a great influence on financial policies at Washington. His reward came in the shape of an appointment to do the government binding, reputed to be worth $25,000—a commission that allowed him to unload his paper on some investors who speedily lost the $20,000 they put into it.

Henry Cooke's Whiggery was justifying itself, yet to both Pitt and Henry it soon became clear that Jay had hit upon the true road to wealth. At twelve years of age he had begun his career in his father's store at Sandusky, and with characteristic enterprise he put in some side lines and became "quite a capitalist." At fourteen he ventured so far as St. Louis to help in a general store, and at the age of seventeen he went to Philadelphia and took a place in a broker-banker's office. That was in 1839, a golden time for brokers, when every business man must keep a sharp eye on the table of banknote discounts and see to it that bad paper was worked off. Into this world of discounts and premiums the young clerk plunged with immense zest. "The business I am engaged in is of the most respectable kind and the house is the first in the city," [4] he wrote to Pitt Cooke. "He was ambitious, industrious, and faithful to each day's duties," his biographer reports of him. His quick mind ran to calculations and his slender sensitive fingers seemed made for telling money. He was soon the admiration of the office, an expert in detecting counterfeits, a walking table of "wild-cat" currency, with a genius for smelling out possible commissions. Every art of extracting profits from note-shaving, gold-juggling, delayed payments, and other devices known to the world of brokerage, he speedily made himself master of. When he reached his majority he was entered a member of the firm, and before he was thirty he aided his partners—"noble" fellows he called them, of honest Puritan extraction—in squeezing huge commissions out of the financing of the Mexican War. "It was a grand time for brokers and private banking," he remarked; and late in life he wrote glowingly of his cleverness in twice overreaching the Secretary of the Treasury. It was quite legal and the patriotic banker was vastly pleased to report, "So we victimized him again." [5] He was the brains of the company and under his guidance the business piled up profits at an astonishing rate. During the panic of 1854 he wrote: "We use our money at 1 1/2 to 3 per cent. per month from day to day and frequently it pays 1/8 to 1/4 a day. We have done a noble business since 1st of January; profits up to 1st July $135,000." [6] On the reorganization of the firm in 1858 he withdrew, and three years later, on January 1, 1861, he opened the doors of what was soon to become the greatest banking-house in America, Jay Cooke and Company of Philadelphia.

He was then in his fortieth year and his private fortune he reckoned at $150,000. But with the breaking-out of the war, oppor-

[4] E. P. Oberholtzer, *Jay Cooke, Financier of the Civil War*, Vol. I, p. 52.
[5] *Ibid.*, Vol. I, pp. 81 and 83.
[6] *Ibid.*, Vol. I, p. 85.

tunity knocked at the door of the new bank. Ardently patriotic, Jay Cooke was anxious to do his bit for the cause, but he seems never to have thought of going to the front. He came of fighting Revolutionary stock, but love of the battlefield had died out of the family. His father had been drafted for the War of 1812, but hired a substitute who was unfortunate enough to be killed, and none of the three sons got nearer the front than the Treasury Department at Washington. It was there that the battles of the Cooke brothers were fought. Henry Cooke went to Washington to attend the inauguration of the new administration, and twenty-one days later Jay Cooke modestly proposed a plan for mobilizing the resources of the firm in defense of the country. On March 25, he wrote to his brother:

> What we wish to do with the Treasury is to have the Department allow us to make the frequent transfers that are made from point to point instead of giving the business to Adams and Company [Express]. We can make those transfers and the Department when flush can give us 30, 60, 90 or 120 days time, as it is no loss to them, and the interest in the meantime would be clear profit and to be divided.[7]

When the magnitude of the task in which the country was engaged became clear to him he was no longer content with a single banking-house at Philadelphia. A branch at Washington under the shadow of the Treasury was highly desirable, and Henry Cooke was the man for the business. A born lobbyist, a close friend of John Sherman—who was looking out for a profitable opening in some war business for a brother—and of Secretary of the Treasury Chase, he let no grass grow under his feet. The war loans had not been taken freely and in July, Jay Cooke wrote to Chase suggesting a close alliance between the Treasury and two Philadelphia firms, Jay Cooke and Company and Drexel and Company.

> We would wish to make our business mostly out of the Treasury operations and we feel sure that we could by having a proper understanding with yourself greatly help you in the management of your vast negotiations. . . . We could not be expected to leave our comfortable homes and positions here without some great inducement and we state frankly that we would, if we succeeded, expect a fair commission from the Treasury in some shape for our labor and talent. If you feel disposed to say to us . . . that you will give us the management of the loans to be issued by the government during the war, allowing us a fair commission on them, . . . we are ready to throw ourselves into the matter heartily. . . .[8]

[7] *Ibid.*, Vol. I, pp. 132–133.   [8] See *Ibid.*, Vol. I, pp. 143–144.

It was quite an amazing proposal and one that Secretary Chase dared not accept. Bankers and brokers in New York and Boston would scarcely approve a monopoly of loan-commissions granted to two Philadelphia houses. But Jay Cooke would not acknowledge defeat. He cultivated the acquaintance of the Secretary, lent him money, entertained his family, presented him with gifts, and gave him sound advice. He took the harassed servant of the people to his warm and generous heart and was vigilant in keeping him out of the clutches of Copperhead profiteers. His opportunity came in October, 1861, when in competition with other brokers he undertook the sale of a new bond-series. His success was so great that he won the complete confidence of Secretary Chase, and it was only a matter of time when he should secure his coveted monopoly. In February, 1862, he opened the branch house at Washington, immediately opposite the Treasury building, and Henry Cooke soon made its offices an indispensable club for Congressmen and government employees. He was charmingly cordial and during the next ten years he knew everybody and every political move at the Capital. With the same bland and deacon-like appearance as his brother, he was master of the art of ingratiating himself into the confidence of influential men, and successive Secretaries of the Treasury—Chase and Fessenden and McCulloch—were easily induced to look with partial eye upon the firm of Jay Cooke and Company. When Grant returned to Washington after the war he was soon like a brother to Henry Cooke, and when the General had tasted the quality of cigars kept for his use at Jay Cooke's Philadelphia home, his heart warmed to the kindly banker.

Meanwhile the firm was discovering innumerable ways to help win the war; amongst others Henry Cooke put through a congressional franchise for a street railway at Washington, and the new cars were soon carrying citizens and soldiers to and fro, to their great content and the company's great profit. He was hourly in and out of the Treasury and he knew as much about the government business as the Secretary. The interests of the firm extended with amazing rapidity; other banks came under their control and their agents were everywhere. Their later successes in selling bonds were a revelation to older-fashioned brokers. On the day that Richmond fell the "financier of the Civil War" marked out the lines of a pretentious country house that was to cost a million dollars and to become a show place of America, where Secretaries of the Treasury,

Presidents, and great men from every walk of life were to find a welcome release from their cares. "As rich as Jay Cooke" had become a common saying from the Atlantic to the Pacific. The gigantic war had been no ill wind to the money-teller of 1861.

In certain aspects Jay Cooke may be reckoned the first modern American. He was the first to understand the psychology of mass salesmanship. It was his fertile brain that created the syndicate and conceived and executed the modern American "drive." Under his bland deacon-like exterior was the mind of a realist. He assumed that every man has his price, but he knew that few men like to acknowledge the fact even to themselves; so he was at immense pains to cover our poor human nakedness with generous professions. If he were to lure dollars from old stockings in remote chimney-corners he must "sell" patriotism to his fellow Americans; and to do that successfully he must manufacture a militant public opinion. The soldier at the front, he announced in a flood of advertisements, must be supported at the rear. It was every loyal American's war, and patriotism demanded that idle dollars—in greenbacks—should be lent to the boys in blue, and a grateful government would return them, both principal and interest, in gold. To induce slacker dollars to become fighting dollars he placed his agents in every neighborhood, in newspaper offices, in banks, in pulpits—patriotic forerunners of the "one-minute men" of later drives. They also served their country, he pointed out, who sold government bonds on commission. He subsidized the press with a lavish hand, not only the metropolitan dailies but the obscurest country weeklies. He employed an army of hack-writers to prepare syndicated matter and he scattered paying copy broadcast. His "hired friends" were everywhere. In a hundred delicate ways he showed his appreciation of patriotic coöperation in the bond-sales—gifts of trout caught with his own hand, baskets of fruit from his own garden. He bought the pressings of whole vineyards and cases of wine flowed in an endless stream to strategic publicity-points. Rival brokers hinted that he was debauching the press, but the army of greenbacks marching to the front was his reply. It all cost a pretty penny, but the government was liberal with commissions and when all expenses were deducted perhaps two millions of profits remained in the vaults of the firm, to be added to the many other millions which the prestige of the government agency with its free advertising brought in its train.

With such prestige and with the greatest fluid resources as yet accumulated by any American, it was inevitable that the Rothschild of the North should play a bold part in the speculations of the Gilded Age. Jay Cooke vastly enjoyed the game and it was idle to expect him to sit back quietly when others were playing for high stakes. In those halcyon days promoters were as thick as flies about a dead carcass; wild-cat railroads had succeeded wild-cat banks as short-cuts to wealth; and in an unlucky moment Jay Cooke was tempted. He had expected to be made Secretary of the Treasury by President Grant, but failing of appointment in spite of countless boxes of twenty-five-cent cigars provided for the General's pleasure, he determined to back the Northern Pacific Railway enterprise. The company had been chartered in July, 1864, receiving a congressional grant of 12,800 acres of public land for every mile of track laid in the states, and double that amount in the territories. As the proposed line would run almost entirely through territories the grand total was reckoned at 47,360,000 acres.[9] Early land-sales were at the rate of $6 an acre. At such valuation the prospective value of the grant through the territories was $153,600 for every mile of track, yet in portions of an earlier line absorbed by the company the road had been built for $8,225 a mile, and a stretch of 112 miles at the rate of $9,500.[10] To be sure there were great stretches of unsalable land, but in compensation the company was free to run its surveys so as to embrace choice mineral deposits, virgin timber, water-power, and town sites.

As Jay Cooke contemplated the possibilities his buoyant temperament took fire, and he dreamed of empire-building. He quickly rationalized the project into a great patriotic undertaking that would carry the blessings of civilization to the farthest Northwest. He would lay open to the poor man the rich wheat lands of the Dakotas, the mineral wealth of the Rockies, the vast timber resources of the Puget Sound territory. He would annex western Canada by benevolent absorption. It was a dream worthy of the Gilded Age and Jay Cooke was chief amongst the Beriah Sellerses of the day. He threw himself into the project with boundless optimism, and proved again his right to be called a great financier. He proposed to sell the Northern Pacific as he had sold govern-

[9] See *Ibid.*, Vol. II, pp. 97–98.
[10] C. E. Russell, *Stories of Great Railroads*, p. 19.

ment bonds. He had learned that to catch the little fish he must first catch the big fish, for the shilling is timid till the pound shows the way. He must create confidence, cost what it would, and to that end he opened a huge pool and created a special syndicate. Stocks, jobs, cash, influence, were distributed judiciously where they would do good. In the language of stock-jobbing much "sweetening" was used.[11] And there was need of much "sweetening," for the times were inauspicious. Jay Cooke drove the publicity work with his old vigor, but sales were slow, and as the great patriotic venture showed signs of lagging he turned for help to a sympathetic government.

His engineer had made a careful estimate of the prospective cost of the road, which including rolling-stock, terminals, a branch line to Portland, and interest on bonds during the construction, came to $42,638 a mile for the entire line.[12] But the financier was not satisfied "with the magnificent property the government has given us," and made ready to buy from Congress a revision of the terms of the charter, which amongst other things would widen the land-grant belt through the territories to 120 miles, convey a second right-of-way zone from the Rocky Mountains to the Pacific, and permit the company to hypothecate the whole before the terms of the contract were fulfilled. It was an audacious proposal even to a generation used to audacious proposals. There was bitter opposition, for the rumblings of the *Crédit Mobilier* scandal were already disturbing the halls of Congress; but his lobbyists used "the company's money freely" to bring in the common breed of Congressmen, and the Cooke brothers employed their well-practiced skill to take care of such important persons as Speaker Blaine of the House, Vice-President Colfax of the Senate, and President Grant. The matter was handled with great delicacy in the case of the latter—"the glorious honest man," the banker called him. "He sent a fishing-rod and creel to the President's little son Jesse, for which he was duly thanked in a childish hand." He invited

[11] The list of his "beneficiaries," some of whom were drawn in delicately and some realistically, included, according to his biographer, Vice-President Colfax, Speaker Blaine and James A. Garfield of the House, Governor Rutherford B. Hayes of Ohio and Governor Geary of Pennsylvania, General Horace Porter, President Grant's private secretary, Senators John Sherman, William Windom, and Ben Wade, Delegate Garfielde of Washington Territory, Bayard Taylor. Amongst the papers were Henry Ward Beecher's *Christian Union*, Greeley's *Tribune*, the *Philadelphia Press*, the *Washington Chronicle*, the *London Times*.

[12] See Oberholtzer, Vol. II, p. 154.

the General to a day's fishing-trip, and together the heroes whipped the trout stream in the most charming comradeship. "It may be thought," remarks his biographer, "that such machinations were unbecoming in a man of Mr. Cooke's moral dimensions." [13] But surely delicate "machinations" were not unbecoming to such "moral dimensions." "We let the other side do most of the talking," wrote the deacon-like Henry Cooke, who kept the Sabbath as strictly as his brother, "and we do the voting." The President's cabinet was bitterly divided on the issue, but wheels turn on well-greased axles and delicate attentions have their reward. The bill was signed and the building of the Northwest empire could go forward.

Unfortunately, however, black days were pressing hard on the great success. The money of the company ran in fructifying streams through Europe and America but the expected crop was short. Thirty papers were subsidized in Germany; agents lived in ducal palaces; commissions, stocks, bonuses, were plowed in for manure; but the crop of bond-sales was still scanty. Ugly rumors were abroad. There was talk of a congressional investigation, and when General Banks offered a resolution of inquiry Jay Cooke was hurt to the quick. An investigation he regarded as no other than persecution of legitimate business, and he wrote to his brother: "He ought to be expelled from Congress for such outrageous attacks upon the great interests of the country. . . . If I get at him I will give him a piece of my mind, and no mistake, for his impertinence and foolishness." [14] Then the *Crédit Mobilier* scandal broke and in a panic he wrote to Henry Cooke denouncing the proposal to stop payment on the interest-coupons of the Union Pacific.

Now I want you to go to the Attorney General at once and tell him how wrong this whole procedure is. This whole persecution of the Union Pacific is nonsense, and is damaging our credit abroad. If the government sets the example of enjoining the payment of interest coupons, who will buy a bond abroad? The whole thing is wrong, ill advised and scandalous. . . . Williams ought to make a public apology for such an attack and instruct the lawyers to desist from anything of the kind. The bonds are long since in the hands of innocent holders, and, if they were not, they could never reach them in this way. Some wily speculators have put the idea into the heads of the government lawyers and they, without knowing anything of its effect upon business, have made this attack. It will damage us hundreds of millions unless withdrawn at once. No man of sense

[13] *Ibid.*, Vol. II, p. 176.　　　　　[14] *Ibid.*, Vol. II, p. 322.

would buy a railroad bond or anything else in this country if such legal proceedings are to be permitted under the sanction of the highest officer of the government.[15]

Jay Cooke's ethics were simple. Whatever helped bond-sales was patriotic and right; whatever hurt them was wicked and immoral. Let government take care of business and business will take care of the country. That the newspapers could not see this great truth, but often indulged in wild demagoguery, was painful to one who had been generous to them. "It is too bad," he wrote of a certain attack, "that these newspapers are permitted by the law thus to interfere with great public works."[16] But the black days were at hand. The *Crédit Mobilier* scandal was a whirlwind reaped from the sowings of the Gilded Age. With the outbreak of the Franco-Prussian war bond-sales stopped short in Europe and the firm of Jay Cooke and Company was broken. September 18, 1873, the New York house suspended payment; the house of cards tumbled to pieces; and a panic swept the country. The crash was as spectacular as the rise; it had been built on credit and when credit was shaken it fell.

Because he had amassed a great fortune Jay Cooke was regarded by his fellow Americans as an intelligent man whose opinions were entitled to heedful consideration. A national figure in finance must become a national figure in the public councils; and this added function he assumed with the utmost seriousness. As the power behind the United States Treasury he regarded himself as responsible for the program of the Treasury; and he made use of his immense publicity-machine to shape public opinion in regard to taxation, funding, and the currency. His "views" of those questions were as simple as a child's primer. In brief they were: no taxes for the extinction of the debt; consolidate the debt and fund it in a form attractive to capital; retire the greenbacks and return at once to specie payments. Like others who had made money out of the war he did not take kindly to the idea of returning a part of it in taxes to pay off a debt that was highly profitable to him as a broker and banker. The men of '65 had fought and suffered to secure the blessings of liberty to their posterity, and it was only fair that posterity should help pay the bills. To popularize this pregnant thought he subsidized a pamphlet contributed by one of his hack-writers, entitled *Our National Debt a National Blessing;*

[15] *Ibid.*, Vol. II, p. 409.   [16] *Ibid.*, Vol. II, p. 411.

but the Hamiltonian argument overshot the mark and aroused bitter opposition. In this as in his attitude towards currency-contraction and funding he was thinking exclusively in terms of the money-lender. Very likely he was probably not so much self-seeking as ignorant. Intellectually he was poverty-stricken and outside the narrow realm of brokerage and banking he was only a child. He read nothing, thought little and was unconcerned with social or economic principles. His business life was regulated by a set of ready-made formulas, in which ideas played no part. William Cullen Bryant rightly judged him in the following comment:

We counsel Mr. Jay Cooke in all good will, not to abandon his proper vocation of dealing in stocks and government securities, for the sake of giving lectures on political economy—a subject which he does not understand. We do not say that he might not understand it if he had given it his attention, but that he has evidently never done, and knows no more of the matter than Red Jacket knew of Greek. We advise all who have any money to invest to take Mr. Jay Cooke's seven-thirty bonds, and eschew his political economy. His seven-thirties are first rate, his political economy is a tissue of mistakes.[17]

Any program that lay outside the bounds of his formulas he regarded as dangerous radicalism, and any policy that threatened to reduce his commissions he regarded as unchristian. He bitterly disliked Secretary Boutwell of the Treasury, who rejected his guidance, and he wrote to his brother:

I observe . . . that Boutwell is to leave the Treasury. I think that if he does not propose to do any better than he has in the past it will be a grand move for Grant to put some more practical person in his place. A man who has no more breadth of thought . . . and no more spunk than to let the country drift along without even an attempt at funding the debt, and who insists upon keeping up an enormous taxation for the foolish object of paying off rapidly a debt that no one wants paid off, excepting gradually, it will be a great benefit to have replaced by some one who will take an opposite course.[18]

A month later one of the causes of the hostility was suggested by a member of the firm:

All of our transactions with Boutwell have shown conclusively that he will never permit one dollar to be made out of the business of the Treasury, if he can possibly prevent it. With all his friendly feelings I cannot remember a single dollar that we have made directly or indirectly out of his administration of the Treasury, . . .[19]

[17] *Ibid.*, Vol. I, pp. 643–644.   [18] *Ibid.*, Vol. II, pp. 267–268.
[19] *Ibid.*, Vol. II, p. 269.

Against the Greenback movement his hostility was bitter. He regarded it as an attempt to repudiate the "plighted faith" of the nation, and in 1867 he issued a pamphlet, written to order, aimed at combating the movement. In the opinion of a subsidized admirer it was "able, unanswerable and timely," calculated to do immense good in a country where universal suffrage encourages the "attempts of demagogues to excite the poor against the rich, labor against capital, and all who haven't money against the banks who have it." [20] How deeply the members of the firm felt in presence of any threat to the money interests is suggested in a letter from Henry Cooke of October 12, 1867.

> You know how I have felt for a long time past in regard to the course of the ultra infidelic radicals like Wade, Sumner, Stevens, *et id omne genus*. They were dragging the Republican party into all sorts of isms and extremes. Their policy was one of bitterness, hate, and wild agrarianism without a single Christian principle to give it consistency, except the sole idea of universal suffrage. . . . These reckless demagogues have had their day and the time has come for wiser counsels. With Wade uttering agrarian doctrines in Kansas and fanning the flame of vulgar prejudices, trying to array labor against capital and pandering to the basest passions; with Butler urging wholesale conscription throughout the South and wholesale repudiation throughout the North so far as the national debt is concerned; with Stevens joining hands with the traitor Vallandigham and advocating the idea of a flood of irredeemable paper money sufficient in volume to drown the whole country; with Pomeroy and Wade and Sprague and a host of others clamoring for the unsexing of woman and putting the ballot in her hand . . . what wonder it is that the accumulated load was too heavy for any party to carry and that it broke down under it? [21]

There can be little doubt that the spectacular career of Jay Cooke quite dazzled his contemporary fellow citizens. Nothing like it had before appeared in America. The greatest salesman that the rising middle class had yet produced, a financier who understood the psychology of mass appeal, a propagandist of truly heroic proportions, he was reckoned no other than a magician by all the lesser money-grabbers of the Gilded Age. From nothing he built up a vast fortune. Scrupulous in all religious duties, a kind husband, a generous friend, benevolent in all worthy charities, simple and democratic in his tastes, ardently patriotic, uncreative and unintellectual, he exemplified all the substantial middle-class virtues of a people newly given to the worship of a sterile money economy.

[20] *Ibid.*, Vol. II, p. 56 note.   [21] *Ibid.*, Vol. II, p. 28.

To call him a vulgarian and the chronicle of his life nauseous would scarcely be charitable. The record of his days has been laid before us, naked and mean, by his biographer, who has done his best to construct a hero from the poor materials. No doubt he was a hero of his generation—and perhaps of ours also.

3

CHARLES A. DANA

If General Grant and Jay Cooke were naïve heroes, ignorant as the generation that delighted to honor them, Charles A. Dana, the journalist of the Gilded Age, was a disillusioned intellectual who after immersing himself in the golden dreams of the forties, put away all Utopian hopes and made use of his brains to serve himself. Disappointed with idealism, he turned materialist and dedicated to capitalistic exploitation the abilities that before had been given to a venture in coöperative living. A brilliant fellow, playing the new game in Gilded Age fashion and winning a brilliant success, he was a conspicuous victim of the bankruptcy of idealism that is the price of all wars, and his later triumph as editor of the *New York Sun* only served to measure the greatness of his fall. The career of Dana is a cynical commentary on the changing spirit of America from the days of Brook Farm to the days of Mark Hanna.

A child of the Puritan frontier, Dana early crossed over into New York State and became a shop-boy in the backwoods village of Buffalo at a time when the Indian trade was important enough to justify him in learning Algonquin. In these early manhood days he was living in the midst of the coonskin democracy, and falling in with the frontier spirit he became an ardent Jacksonian. He was eager for an education and quitting Buffalo he went to Harvard, but his eyes failing him after two years, he joined the Brook Farm community where he speedily became one of the chief counselors, and was deeply concerned for the success of the experiment. In those generous years he was a militant idealist, widely read in socialist literature and warmly espousing associationism as a cure for the evils of competition. Upon quitting Brook Farm after the burning of the Phalanstery he joined Greeley and for fifteen years was one of the directing minds on the *Tribune*. In 1848 he went abroad as foreign correspondent, saw much of the revolutions of that great year, studied the temper of the French and German people, analyzed the popular leaders and programs with singular acuteness, and found his sympathies warmly enlisted in the cause of the lower classes. He was then thirty-nine, and his active mind had gathered up all the diverse radicalisms—Jacksonian, Utopian, European proletarian—of his revolutionary generation. Shrewdly observant and with a sensitive social conscience, he was amply equipped to become such another critic of the Industrial Revolution as England had bred from its bitter experience.

But the war intervened, and after the war a dun twilight gathered about the hopes of the forties. Few generous enthusiasms survived those years of struggle and Dana in his editorial rooms underwent successive changes of heart. The realist slowly dispossessed the idealist and then the cynic swallowed up the realist. The last forty years of his life were spent undoing the work of his earlier years. His political philosophy went to pieces and the policy of the *Sun* became a mere hodge-podge of jingo programs, an irrational bundle of personal prejudices and private interests. His reaction from associationism carried him over to a stark and ruthless individualism. He saw all about him the strong and capable as the masters of the earth, with social justice an outcast and mendicant begging from house to house. The millennium to which belongs the ideal of social democracy which he had earlier served, he could no longer make out from any present bend in the road, and putting away his faith he went with the masters. The reaction began during the *Tribune* days with his espousal of the American System—the first outcropping of the middle-class qualities of his mind—and thereafter he drifted steadily to the right and the Dismal Swamp of exploitation. With augmenting wealth and the sense of power that came from the great success of the *Sun* he became the apologist and defender of capitalism, phrasing with clever vivacity all the sophistries of Gilded Age argument. Professing to be a Democrat, he made much of states rights and governmental *laissez faire*. He would countenance no interference with the principle of free competition, but would reduce the government to the rôle of policeman to keep the peace. He professed to believe that the dry bones of Manchesterism were a living democratic faith. He ridiculed the proposal for pure-food legislation, civil service reform, the control of monopolies, professing to see in every such move the insidious beginnings of an un-American bureaucracy. No social pretext justified in his eyes the regulation of business enterprise. Centralization of economic power he accepted as in the nature of things, and the popular denunciation of trusts he called "the greatest humbug of the hour." His argument was simple and to the Gilded Age wholly satisfactory.

The objects of trade being to buy as cheap as possible, to sell as dear as possible, and to get control of the market as far as possible, the formation for these purposes of these gigantic and widely extended partnerships is just as natural and regular as the partnership of two shoemakers or of two blacksmiths.[22]

Thus far Dana must be reckoned a belated disciple of the Manchester school. The days of transcendental and Utopian idealism were past and he knew it. The Gilded Age had traveled far from such naïve enthusiasms and it was time to face reality. But his realism was only a gesture to cover his surrender to capitalism. It was not honest. When his principle of individualism trod on his own toes he threw it aside with no compunctions. He was a *laissez-faire* Democrat only when a free field favored business, but when business desired government assistance he made no scruple to turn Whig. Accepting the principle of private exploitation under the drive of the acquisitive instinct, and content with the social ethics of Captain Kidd, he would weaken government or strengthen government as business profits dictated. In these later years he became cynically class-conscious, while professing to deny the existence of classes. He would disarm the government as against the capitalist, but he would triple-arm it against the farmer and workingman. He was shrill in his demands for a high protective tariff for the manufacturers, huge grants of public lands for speculative railway companies, and a monetary system in the control of the bankers. But for the economic demands of the western farmers he had only contempt—the agrarians were flying in the face of economic law as economic law was understood by the high priests of capitalism. When he talked about "honest money" he laid his brains on the shelf. He would have no other money than the gold standard, and to achieve that object he never suffered candor to weaken his plea. He bitterly opposed the income tax and when the Democratic platform of 1896 suggested the reorganization of the Supreme Court to reverse the decision on its con-

[22] See James Harrison Wilson, *The Life of Charles A. Dana*, p. 479.

stitutionality, he turned demagogue and indulged in talk about "the destruction of the independence of the judiciary." When it was proposed that the railways be nationalized he protested that he could not "imagine anything more absurd, unpatriotic, and dangerous"—on the assumption no doubt that railways existed to pay dividends on their stock. "Still more alarming" to him was the "clearly implied approval of lawless violence contained in the denunciation of what is denominated in the [Democratic] platform 'government by injunction.' Veiled in the language of moderation, the wild light of anarchy shines through." [23] He urged upon government the necessity of holding the labor unions in strict control, he was eloquent in defense of the individual laborer's sacred right of "free contract," and he was loud in applause of President Cleveland's lawless suppression of the Pullman strike. When it came to Bryan and Populism he lost his head and became quite maudlin.

Dana was no fool to be deceived by his own insincerity. On the contrary he was highly intelligent and knew perfectly well what he was about. Having gone over to capitalism, he would fight its battles with whatever weapons came to hand, and like a son of New England he would cover his breast with a shield of morality. He became the chief journalistic exponent of the "lawless violence" he was fond of attributing to other social classes. He turned into a flaming jingo imperialist, talked patriotically about "adequate" coast defenses, demanded a great navy, and was the loudest spokesman of the blowsy doctrine of "Manifest Destiny." He was always peering through his glasses to discover some fresh territory to annex—Haiti, Cuba, Mexico—and so late as 1887 he was still calling for the annexation of Canada. Naturally he approved President Cleveland's Venezuelan proclamation and he probably would have enjoyed a tussle with the British lion. In his morality he was quite as truculent as in his patriotism and in his advocacy of capitalism. Perhaps it was a salve to a conscience that could not have been easy. He hated political corruption and he attacked the sordid looting that marked President Grant's administration with gusto. He took sardonic delight in giving the widest publicity to the classic corruptionist phrase of the day— "He understands addition, division, and silence." He erected into a fetish the cry "Turn the rascals out!" yet while helping to pry

[23] See *Ibid.*, p. 491.

loose one set of rascals from their spoils he was busily providing another set with his demand for subsidies and tariffs. It was a situation that must have amused the cynical Dana. He had long since left off worrying about the damned human race. It was more sensible to pile up one's plate at the barbecue and send the bill to the American people. He had made a huge success and what mattered it if his old Brook Farm associates, Ripley and Curtis, no longer spoke to him when they met?

CHAPTER II

THE CULTURE OF THE SEVENTIES

It was in the seventies that good taste reached its lowest ebb. Not only in America, but in England as well, where rebels like William Morris were contemptuously rejecting a machine civilization. A veritable *débâcle* of the arts was in process, the lesser as well as the greater, in New York and Boston as well as in Chicago and San Francisco, from which literature could not wholly escape; and that *débâcle* was an expression of profound changes taking place at the bases of society. The dignified culture of the eighteenth century, that hitherto had been a conserving and creative influence throughout the Jeffersonian revolution, was at last breaking up. The disruptive forces that swept out of the great West, bringing the frontier spirit to every threshold, and the factory economy that displaced the wares of the craftsman with the products of the machine, were destroying that earlier culture and providing no adequate substitute. Distinction of manners and dress was gone, dignity and repose were gone, traditional standards were gone; and in their stead a bumptious restlessness, a straining for originality and individuality that exuded in a shoddy and meaningless grotesque. It was not without justification that Godkin contemptuously applied the phrase, "a chromo civilization," to the works of that singular generation dwelling between worlds, the one dead, the other seeming powerless to be born.

How much was lost in the break-up of the excellent culture of the eighteenth century the children of the seventies neither knew nor cared. Generations of growth had gone to its shaping. It had been formed by the needs of men and women conscious of the ties that linked them with the past. It was bound back upon the rich cultural life of medieval times, and in the aristocratic eighteenth century it had come to flower in forms of fine distinction and dignity. Touch that century on any side—dress, architecture, furniture, manners, letters—and the same note of refinement, of grace, of balanced harmonious form, is everywhere evident. The culture of the times of the Coffee House Wits was all of a piece, held to-

48

gether by an inner pervasive unity. The formality of the wig and the heroic couplet was symbolic of a generation that loved dignity, and the refinement of the Chippendale sideboard, wrought in slender Honduras mahogany, was the expression of a society that cultivated the graces of life. But when the tie-wig and smallclothes disappeared before the social revolutions of the end of the century, when the gentleman was pushed from his place by the banker and manufacturer, and broadcloth gave way to tweeds, the culture of the eighteenth century was doomed; and until another culture should impose its standards upon society and reëstablish an inner spiritual unity, there would be only the welter of an unlovely transition.

In no other field is the sprawling formlessness of the seventies more grotesquely suggested than in its architecture and in interior decoration, which is a lesser form of architecture. Upon the buildings of the times the hallmark of the Gilded Age is stamped in gaudy colors. By the end of the thirties the fine traditions of colonial craftsmanship were gone and the builders set forth on a foolish quest for historical styles. Revivals followed on each other's heels. The Greek revival and the Gothic revival marked the successive decline of the noble art of building, until at last, turning away from the past, architecture erupted in what it conceived to be a new American style, the expression of a free democratic people, but which later generations reckon a sign and proof of cultural bankruptcy. It was the golden age of the jig saw, of the brownstone front, of the veranda that ran about the house like a spider web, of the mansard roof, the cupola, the house of stilts. Flamboyant lines and meaningless detail destroyed the structural unity of the whole; tawdry decoration supplanted beauty of materials and a fine balance of masses. A stuffy and fussy riot of fancy, restrained by no feeling for structural lines, supplied the lack of creative imagination, and architecture sank to the level of the jerry-builder. Bad taste could go no further.

With this decay of aristocratic culture and the attendant disintegration of the earlier cultural unity, three diverse strands of cultural impulse remained, each of an individual fabric that could not easily be woven into a harmonious pattern: a decadent Federalistic culture that occupied the seats of authority in New England and wherever New England opinion was respected; the body of social aspiration that had come from the French Enlightenment, from which individual dreamers still drew nourishment; and the vigorous individualism of the frontier that bit so deeply into the psychology of the age. Behind these diverse impulses lay still another that would eventually shoulder them aside and provide the pattern for the America that was rising—the culture of an urbanized and mechanized society that in its vast warrens of business was creating the psychology and manners of a standardized, middle-class world of salesmanship.

I

NEW ENGLAND IN DECAY

In one spot in America, at least, the disruption of the fine old aristocratic culture would not be suffered without a protest. Brahmin New England would cling to its traditional standards though all the rest of America should go whoring after strange gods. The welter of the seventies it looked upon with undisguised contempt. It would not follow the way that other portions of the country were hastening. It would have nothing to do with a bumptious frontier spirit that recognized no obligations to the past—for the excellent reason that it had no past. It had had its fill of the visionary Enlightenment that had come to logical fruit in the vagaries of Thoreau and the grotesque vaporings of Alcott. It had had more than its fill of the strident causes that spawned like mushrooms in the rank soil of French romanticism. Emerson it could forgive, for Emerson was a Brahmin, but it quietly ignored his philosophic anarchism and chose to dwell on pleasanter aspects of his teaching. Wendell Phillips it regarded as a common nuisance, but Edmund Quincy it forgave, for after a season of vagrant wanderings he returned to the placid ways of his ancestral Brahminism. Of all these things, whether frontier or Utopian or what not, it had had enough, and so it turned back lovingly to the culture of earlier times and drew comfort from a dignified Federalism—enriched now by a mellow Harvard scholarship that was on intimate terms with Dante and Chaucer and Cervantes and Shakespeare—a Federalism that fitted the dignified Brahmin genius as comfortably as an old shoe.

It was an excellent heritage—that old culture. Never richly creative, never endowed with a fleshly paganism, it possessed nevertheless a solidity got from long wrestling with the eternities, a pleasantly acrid flavor got from crotchety old books, and a sober morality got from much contemplation of the sinfulness of the children of Adam. It was as native to New England as Boston brown bread, and it issued in self-respecting and dignified character. Underneath all transcendental and other eruptions it had lain unmoved like the granite foundations of the New England fields; and now after those eruptions had subsided it provided the solid footing on which the later culture might rear its chaste temples. But unhappily the building days of New England were over. Matters were going ill there. Emigration to the West was draining the vitality from farm and village, and in Boston disastrous changes were under way. The familiar places where Sam Adams and Josiah Quincy had dwelt with their fellows were being invaded by immigrants who brought with them another faith and discordant manners. The Roman Catholic church grew strong as the Old North declined; the Irish brogue displaced the Yankee on Boston Common; Faneuil Hall was given over to alien fishmongers. The Brahmin remnant was absorbed in banking and brokerage and railway investments. It still held the Boston purse but it was fast losing the Boston vote. The capital of the Puritan fathers was being destroyed by the Industrial Revolution that their descendants had set on foot. New England was visibly falling into decay and the years of its intellectual leadership in America were numbered.

The days of high thinking were over and the familiar home of humanitarian causes was inhabited by other tenants. All that remained of the golden forties was the quiet atmosphere of good breeding. Unitarianism, that Theodore Parker had kept openminded and militant, settled into a staid and respectable orthodoxy, its pale negations sufficing to soothe its placid congregations. Transcendentalism, that had thrown a lovely mist about the lean New England character, was evaporating in the rising sun of science; and the ardor of reform, that had burned fiercely in the Puritan heart, subsided into a well-bred interest in negro schools and foreign missions. The Abolition leaders laid aside their pens, convinced that the last injustice had been removed from American society. Their work was done and they turned unwilling ears to calls for new crusades. The New England conscience was tired. It had borne the burden and heat of a long day and was glad to be released from its cares to set up monuments to its sacred dead and to write the chronicles of its past. New England lost interest in ideas and turned away from creative intellectual life to catalogue its libraries and revere the men who had written those libraries. The Enlightenment was over in Boston and the stir of reform passed to New York and the West, where Amelia Bloomer and Elizabeth Cady Stanton carried forward the great crusades for temperance and women's rights, and Henry George was preaching the gospel of a new social economics. Whatever militants existed in New England were not likely to be Brahmins and their labors did not roil the quiet waters. Clamorous distractions no longer disturbed the calm of Federalistic culture, and Cambridge and the Back Bay quietly appropriated the literary earnings of Concord' and lived pleasantly on its revenues.

The inevitable fruit of such thin soil was the genteel tradition, the excellence of which in the seventies New England maintained in the face of all frontier leveling and romantic liberalisms—a timid and uncreative culture that lays its inhibitions on every generation that is content to live upon the past. It was a penalty for backsliding. The men of the preceding generation had got their cheeses made—and excellent cheeses they were, with a fine native flavor. But the transcendental cow had gone dry and with no fresh cows coming in the Brahmins of the seventies were hard put to it to live an adequate intellectual life. Translations and medieval scholarship were no better than remainder biscuit after voyage. Ever since Lowell put away his youthful radicalisms and turned bookman, Brahmin culture had been undernourished. The story of intellectual New England after 1870 is little more than a repetition of the story of New England after 1790—a resurgence of the traditional Toryism that assumed an unquestioned custodianship of all matters intellectual.

That was her own business, of course, and it would have been of no great concern to the rest of the country if New England had not set up a cultural dictatorship over American letters. It was not content to follow its own path to sterility, but was bent on dragging the country with it. Boston taste determined American literary standards, and Boston taste rejected most of the new movements then getting under way. Stoddard and Stedman in New York, Boker in Philadelphia, and Aldrich in Boston, stoutly upheld the genteel tradition, of which the *Atlantic Monthly* was the authoritative spokesman. Great figures from the past—Emerson, Longfellow, Lowell, Whittier, Holmes, Motley, Parkman—

still walked the streets of Boston, and their extraordinary reputations were little less than tyrannous in the inhibitions they laid
on younger men. It is incomprehensible today, the authority of
these great reputations. Young William Winter walking twenty
miles to stand in the moonlight at Craigie House gate and view
reverently the silent walls within which the great Longfellow was
sleeping; Mark Twain in the fullness of his powers abashed and
put out of countenance at his temerity in speaking humorously of
Emerson and Longfellow and Holmes at the *Atlantic* dinner—one
understands such things with difficulty now that those reputations
have so much bated and dwindled. Yet to the generation of the
seventies the inhibitions of the genteel tradition were all-powerful,
and the little Boston group set themselves up as a court of final
jurisdiction over American letters. New England parochialism had
become a nation-wide nuisance.

The genteel tradition, as Professor Santayana has pointed out,
had long been a disease in New England. Some of the finest minds
of the Renaissance—Emerson and Hawthorne in particular—had
suffered from it; their mental processes "had all a certain starved
and abstract quality," a lack of the rich paganism that endows life
and art with sensuous beauty.

They could not retail the genteel tradition [he goes on]; they were too
keen, too perceptive, and too independent for that. But life offered
them little digestible material, nor were they naturally voracious. They
were fastidious, and under the circumstances they were starved. . . .
Therefore the genius of . . . Hawthorne, and even of Emerson, was employed in a sort of inner play, or digestion of vacancy. It was a refined
labor, but was in danger of being morbid, or tinkling, or self-indulgent.
It was a play of intra-mental rhymes. Their mind was like an old music-
box, full of tender echoes and quaint fancies. These fancies expressed
their personal genius sincerely, as dreams may; but they were arbitrary
fancies in comparison with what a real observer would have said in the
premises. Their manner, in a word, was subjective. In their own persons
they escaped the mediocrity of the genteel tradition, but they supplied
nothing to supplant it in other minds.[1]

If the thin pale atmosphere in which the genteel tradition throve
starved the minds of greater men in a more vigorous age, it would
play havoc with smaller men in an imitative age. After Emerson
and Hawthorne came Stedman and Stoddard and Aldrich, upon

[1] *The Genteel Tradition in American Philosophy, University of California Chronicle*, Vol. XIII, Number 4.

whose studiously correct pages the genteel tradition laid a hand of death. In the seventies it had become the refuge of a stale mentality, emptied of all ideals save beauty, and that beauty become cold and anemic. Its taboos were no more than cushions for tired or lazy minds. The idea of morality—with its corollary of reticence—and the idea of excellence were well enough in the abstract, but become empty conventions, cut off from reality, they were little more than a refuge for respectability, a barricade against the intrusion of the unpleasant. In compressing literature within the rigid bounds of a genteel morality and a genteel excellence, New England was in a way of falsifying it. Highways are easy traveling, but the artist who will not venture from them misses much. In the seventies and eighties the incurious Boston mentality missed pretty much everything vital and significant in American life, and the more daring children of Boston—men like Henry Adams and, shall we add, Henry James—sought congenial atmosphere elsewhere.

I

THOMAS BAILEY ALDRICH AND THE GENTEEL

In the expansive days of Walt Whitman and Mark Twain the official custodian of the genteel in letters was Thomas Bailey Aldrich, who as editor of the *Atlantic* from 1881 to 1890 sturdily combated all literary leveling. Sitting in the high seat of Boston authority he would countenance none of the "Josh Billingsgate" corruptions of the English language that he professed to believe were sullying the purity of American literary taste. A Portsmouth, New Hampshire, boy, early transplanted to New York City, he lisped in numbers before he learned to think. At the age of nineteen he published a volume of poems entitled *The Bells, A Collection of Chimes*, the tintillations of which were little more than faint echoes of Keats, Chatterton, Tennyson, Poe, Bryant, Willis, and Longfellow; and to the end of his life his state of ideal felicity was to be "loaded to the muzzle with lyrics and sonnets" wherewith to do execution on all purveyors of realism with its "miasmatic breath blown from the slums." Transplanted to Boston from the Bohemian world of Pfaff's restaurant where Willis held court, he settled down into the staid atmosphere of the Back Bay with immense content. Though he was fond of calling himself only Boston-plated he was soon as completely Bostonian as the Autocrat himself. Intellectually and esthetically he had been Cambridge

bred, and the influence of Longfellow, Lowell, and Holmes determined his every literary endeavor. Like the returned prodigal he
wandered no more but was satisfied to feast on the dainties of
Back Bay culture. He immersed himself in the genteel. His one
ambition as editor of the *Atlantic* was to keep it as Lowell wished
it kept. To the end of his life he remained completely insulated
against the creative forces of the times, and in the year that
Stephen Crane was writing *Maggie* he published *The Sisters'
Tragedy*. He would have been shocked by *Maggie*, if he had read
it, as a later generation wonders at *The Sisters' Tragedy*.

It is easy to see why Aldrich should have been taken to Boston's
heart. His refined and delicate technique more than compensated
for an intellectual sterility that seems never to have been apparent
to his ardent admirers. Witty, charming in manners, in love with
art and devoted to a painstaking craftsmanship, he was a hollow
reed through which blew into flawless form the refinements of his
world and group. Good taste found nothing to offend in his scanty
pages. If he worshiped at the altar of beauty, beauty to him was
always a chaste goddess, severe and pale and slight. A blowsy goddess like Whitman's, or a slattern like Mark Twain's, he would have
none of. As a youthful poet, to be sure, he sometimes hinted that
she had red cheeks and plump breasts and rounded limbs, but on his
removal to Boston he discovered that she was quite Beacon Street
with her slender form and modest reserve—no Greek but a lovely
Puritan maiden; and the mature Aldrich came to prefer her chaste
reticence to the freer ways the younger generation liked. They were
destroying beauty—this younger generation—with their vulgar realism, besmirching the goddess with their vulgarities. In an interlude
entitled "Realism" he gave voice to the following pastoral lament:

> Romance beside his unstrung lute
>   Lies stricken mute.
> The old-time fire, the antique grace,
> You will not find them anywhere.
> To-day we breathe a commonplace,
> Polemic, scientific air:
> We strip Illusion of her veil;
> We vivisect the nightingale
> To probe the secret of his note.
> The Muse in alien ways remote
>   Goes wandering.[2]

[2] *Poetical Works*, Vol. I, p. 45.

And in a dramatic monologue, quite evidently suggested by
The Grammarian's Funeral, he voiced the following protest against
an age enslaved to realism:

> A twilight poet, groping quite alone,
> Belated, in a sphere where every nest
> Is emptied of its music and its wings.
> Not great his gift; yet we can poorly spare
> Even his slight perfection in an age
> Of limping triolets and tame rondeaux.
> He had at least ideals, though unreached,
> And heard, far off, immortal harmonies,
> Such as fall coldly on our ear to-day.
> The mighty Zolaistic Movement now
> Engrosses us—a miasmatic breath
> Blown from the slums. We paint life as it is,
> The hideous side of it, with careful pains,
> Making a god of the dull Commonplace.
> For have we not the old gods overthrown
> And set up strangest idols? We would clip
> Imagination's wing and kill delight,
> Our sole art being to leave nothing out
> That renders art offensive. Not for us
> Madonnas leaning from their starry thrones
> Ineffable, nor any heaven-wrought dream
> Of sculptor or of poet; we prefer
> Such nightmare visions as in morbid brains
> Take form and substance, thoughts that taint the air
> And make all life unlovely. Will it last?
> Beauty alone endures from age to age,
> From age to age endures, handmaid of God.[3]

It was not the realists alone, he thought, who were fouling their
own nests, but all who turned aside from the narrow path of
Victorianism to explore new ways. Whitman he regarded as a
charlatan whose mannerisms were a "hollow affectation" representing "neither the man nor the time." Riley's formal verse
he preferred to his dialect poems—"The English language is
too rich and sacred a thing to be mutilated and vulgarized," he
wrote, overlooking the *Biglow Papers*. He held Kipling's cockney-
isms in contempt and said he would not have opened the pages of
the *Atlantic* even to the "Recessional." Lanier he thought a less
significant figure than Fitz-Greene Halleck, and of Poe he remarked that if he "had been an exemplary, conventional, tax-

---

[3] "At the Funeral of a Minor Poet," *Ibid.*, Vol. II, p. 94.

oppressed citizen, like Longfellow, his few poems, as striking as they are, would not have made so great a stir."[4] In such literary judgments the arch-conservative is engaged in defending the genteel tradition against every assault, convinced that the portals of creative literature open into the past and that in following in the footsteps of the dead we shall come upon a living world. The sterility of his own refined craftsmanship is perhaps sufficient commentary upon his faith.

When in later years he turned to prose his work revealed the same negative qualities. His prose style is finished, clean, and thin, wanting in homely idiom and a rich suggestiveness. The water trickled gently from the spring of his invention, cool and unroiled, but never abundant. The dignity that results from a strong nature held in restraint, he never achieved. There were no depths in him. He waited patiently for his vessel to fill and measured it out carefully. As a short-story writer he gained a surprising repute, and admirers like Sarah Orne Jewett were never tired of praising the sprightliness of his humor. Nevertheless his most celebrated story scarcely explains today the immense stir it made. *Marjorie Daw* is a clever *jeu d'esprit* but a bit thin and artificial, too consciously written backwards from its surprise ending. Other distillings of his wit and wisdom, done in the sententious manner and gathered up in *Ponkapog Papers*, are slight in content, and the effervescence is long since gone out of them. *The Story of a Bad Boy*, with its pleasant recollections of his Portsmouth youth, remains his most important work in prose and deserves much of the praise that has been lavished upon it; but set over against *Huckleberry Finn* its shortcomings are evident.

It is absurd, of course, to expect an aesthete to concern himself with ideas, or to care greatly about what goes on outside his ivory tower. The rumblings of the vulgar world beat ineffectually against the gate behind which he sits and dreams. For years the editor of the *Atlantic* was scarcely conscious of his complete aloofness from the world of reality, and he wrote in some surprise to Hamilton Wright Mabie, in 1897:

I like to have you say that I have always cared more for the integrity of my work than for any chance popularity. And what you say of my "aloofness" as being "due in part to a lack of quick sympathies with contemporary experience" (though I had never before thought of it) shows

[4] Ferris Greenslet, *Life of Thomas Bailey Aldrich*, p. 215.

true insight. To be sure, such verse as "Elmwood," "Wendell Phillips," "Unguarded Gates" and the "Shaw Memorial Ode" would seem somewhat to condition the statement; but the mood of these poems is not habitual with me, not characteristic. They did, however, grow out of strong conviction.[5]

Yet though he spoke rarely on social themes, during the long years in Boston most of the Back Bay prejudices seemed to have seeped into his mind and when the "strong convictions," to which he refers, found utterance they proved to be Brahmin convictions. In the vigorous poem "Unguarded Gates"—a poem tense, outspoken, almost unique in its deliberate declamation—he sallied forth from his ivory tower to speak to the American people on the dangers of uncontrolled immigration, a subject that Boston Brahmins had been talking about since the days of Harrison Gray Otis.

> Wide open and unguarded stand our gates,
> And through them presses a wild motley throng—
> Men from the Volga and the Tartar steppes,
> Featureless figures from the Hoang-Ho,
> Malayan, Scythian, Teuton, Kelt, and Slav,
> Flying the Old World's poverty and scorn;
> These bringing with them unknown gods and rites,
> Those, tiger passions, here to stretch their claws.
> In street and alley what strange tongues are loud,
> Accents of menace alien to our air,
> Voices that once the Tower of Babel knew!
>
> O Liberty, white Goddess! is it well
> To leave the gates unguarded? On thy breast
> Fold Sorrow's children, soothe the hurts of fate,
> Lift the down-trodden, but with hand of steel
> Stay those who to thy sacred portals come
> To waste the gifts of freedom. Have a care
> Lest from thy brow the clustered stars be torn
> And trampled in the dust. For so of old
> The thronging Goth and Vandal trampled Rome,
> And where the temples of the Caesars stood
> The lean wolf unmolested made her lair.[6]

What emotions lay back of the measured words of the poem, and how deeply they were colored by the social passions of the times, he tells in a letter to George E. Woodberry, written May 14, 1892:

I went home and wrote a misanthropic poem called "Unguarded Gates" , . . in which I mildly protest against America becoming the cesspool of

5 Ibid., p. 200.   6 Poetical Works, Vol. II, p. 72.

Europe. I'm much too late, however. I looked in on an anarchist meeting the other night . . . and heard such things spoken by our "feller citizens" as made my cheek burn. These brutes are the spawn and natural result of the French Revolution; they don't want any government at all, they "want the earth" . . . and chaos. My Americanism goes clean beyond yours. I believe in America for the Americans; I believe in the widest freedom and the narrowest license, and I hold that jail-birds, professional murderers, amateur lepers . . . and human gorillas generally should be closely questioned at our Gates. Or the "sifting" that was done of old will have to be done over again. . . . A certain Arabian writer, called Rudyard Kipling, described exactly the government of every city and town in the . . . United States when he described that of New York as being "a despotism of the alien, by the alien, for the alien, tempered with occasional insurrections of decent folk!" [7]

Two years later he again gave private expression to one of his rare judgments on matters political and social:

When not otherwise engaged I sit and smoke, and smile at the present administration [President Cleveland's]. . . . The best kind of Democracy (as per sample) is no better than the worst kind of Republicanism. The Income Tax is the deformed child of Coxey and his brother scalawags. I vote for McKinley. We shall have bloody work in this country some of these days, when the lazy *canaille* get organized. They are the spawn of Santerre and Fouquier-Tinville. In about twenty years we shall bring out an American edition (illustrated with cuts) of the beautiful French Revolution.[8]

And again in 1899:

Personally I must confess that I have never been very deeply impressed by the administrative abilities of what we call the lower classes. The Reign of Terror in France is a fair illustration of the kind of government · which the masses give us when they get the happy opportunity.[9]

The literary conservative, it appears, was no better than a social and political Tory. He has traveled back a hundred years and speaks again the very language of Robert Treat Paine. *Canaille* is not a nice word to apply to American workingmen, and the French Revolution has never been well thought of by the children of the *ancien régime*. Thomas Bailey Aldrich was a cultivated gentleman, on the pleasantest terms with the Muse of Beacon Street. Twice he traveled around the world; innumerable summers he spent in Europe; yet of many things that concern men greatly he was very, very ignorant. Of the American people beyond the

[7] Ferris Greenslet, *Life of Thomas Bailey Aldrich*, pp. 168–169.
[8] *Ibid.*, p. 176.   [9] *Ibid.*, p. 205.

Hudson River, he knew nothing. Of social economics he knew nothing. Fearful lest his art should get a smutch from the streets, he withdrew within his tower, where perhaps it is well to leave him. Yet it is odd to recall that he was once regarded as a significant literary figure and that intelligent people listened to him seriously.

2

THE NEW ENGLAND SCENE

In fields less distinguished than poetry and the essay the sway of the genteel was neither so magisterial nor so repressive. As fiction somewhat tardily encroached upon the older literary preserves of New England it brought with it a fresher and more realistic spirit that was eventually to deny the validity of the traditional standards. The group of fiction writers that arose in the seventies and eighties to chronicle the life of New England, was greatly concerned with the decay of the old New England world, and with the causes of that decay. As it set down with loving fidelity the characteristics of an earlier order it could not fail to consider the unloveliness of the new world that was rising on the decay of the old—the alien industrial towns with their polyglot workers that were flourishing as the native villages and quiet countryside declined. New England fiction, therefore, came to embody two main features, chronicle and criticism. It gathered up such picturesque bits of the past as time and change had left, and it questioned with some anxiety the ways of an industrialism that was destroying what it loved. It was not Boston fiction, but up-country fiction, given to exploring quiet villages and decaying towns; and in both its chronicles and its criticisms the spirit of realism became more searching as the years passed.

In its own fashion such fiction would finally be brought into service to the social conscience and issue as sociological studies. As the evils of sweated labor under the factory system were brought home to the common knowledge, one would suppose that New England would have been the first to conscript the novel to arouse the public conscience. There had been anxious discussion amongst the Concord intellectuals on the evils of industrialism, and in the early forties the talk had turned upon associationism as the likeliest cure; but though from such discussions came Brook Farm and other Utopian ventures, no fiction resulted. It was elsewhere, in the Pennsylvania iron district where exploitation was harsher and more brutal than in the textile mills, that fiction first turned to consider the ways of industrialism. In 1861 Rebecca Harding contributed to the *Atlantic* a story entitled "Life in the Iron Mills," that was stark and fierce in its drab realism.[10] Nevertheless ten years were to pass before Elizabeth Stuart Phelps published *The Silent Partner* (1871), a dithyrambic plea for justice for the mill-hands.

If this was not the first New England novel of industrialism it was certainly one of the earliest. In conception, temper, and technique it belongs to the emotional fifties, and is almost primitive in comparison with Rebecca Harding's work. Underlain with religion, it is sticky with sentiment. Although Miss Phelps professed to base her work on the Reports of the Massachusetts Bureau of Statistics of Labor, to which she says she was "deeply in debt for the ribs" of her story, the result is more a tract than a study. There is no realistic grasp of the materials. She was grieved that the mill-masters should reveal so little Christian understanding of the hard lot of the hands and so little sympathy with their poverty. "I believe," she said, "that a wide-spread ignorance exists among us regarding the abuses of our factory system, more especially, but not exclusively, as exhibited in many of the country mills." "Had Christian ingenuity been generally synonymous with the conduct of manufacturing corporations, I should have found no occasion for the writing of this book."[11] It was to lessen such ignorance and encourage Christian sympathy between the classes that she offered her study.

The book is a closet study done with more unction than skill. It is the work of an emotional woman who lived in a world of sentiment rather than reality. Miss Phelps was an Andover Brahmin, highly sensitive, whose deeply religious nature was ruffled by every vagrant wind. She was tremulous in her eager desire to lessen the injustice of men. *The Silent Partner* is a story of a young woman brought up in luxury, daughter of a manufacturer, who on her father's death wishes to join in the management of the factory, but on being politely rejected by her partners she engages in personnel work amongst her employees. There she comes upon

[10] Fred Lewis Pattee, *The Development of the American Short Story*, pp. 171-172. See the entire chapter for a discussion of early realism in the *Atlantic*.
[11] Preface, p. 5.

poverty as a sordid fact, and that discovery works a moral change in her life. She is overwhelmed by it and cannot understand why the conscience of the world is not overwhelmed. "Sometimes I do not see," she exclaimed, "what else there can *be* to talk about in such a world as this! I've stepped into it, as we have stepped out into this storm. It has wrapped me in. . . ." [12] Of the complexity of the problem she is wholly ignorant. Surely there must be some road that leads to justice—justice based on understanding and Christian kindliness; and the working girl whom she singles out for heroine becomes in the end a street preacher to the textile workers, after refusing to marry and bring children into a world of factory toil. *The Silent Partner* is an emotional Puritan document that was out of date when it came from the press.

While Miss Phelps was thus summoning the New England conscience to cleanse the textile mills, her Brahmin sisters were little inclined to engage in such thankless labors, but preferred to gather up and preserve such fragments of the homely traditional New England as had not been swept away in the engulfing stream of industrialism. Female writers, from the days of Mrs. Sarah Wentworth Morton, had long been busy in New England but never had they written so well or so understandingly as in the days of the New England decline. Harriet Beecher Stowe, Elizabeth Stuart Phelps, Harriet Prescott Spofford, Rose Terry Cooke, Mary Wilkins Freeman, and Alice Brown were not great writers, but they essayed to be faithful recorders of what came under their eyes. It was the earlier New England that quickened their imaginations, the rugged Yankee character that had taken form under a homely domestic economy. They had no liking for the New England that was rising in the shadow of the mills; the cleavages of race and religion that were sundering the old homogeneous society were bitterly distasteful to them. The Irish, the French-Canadians, the masses of raw immigrants that were swept into the hoppers of the mills, were unwelcome gobbets to the Brahmin stomach. And so these recorders of the New England decline turned away from the sordid industrial scene, and it was not till thirty years later that Mary Wilkins Freeman, in *The Portion of Labor* (1901), essayed to do more adequately what Elizabeth Stuart Phelps had first sketched.

From Catherine Sedgwick to Mrs. Freeman the note shifted

[12] Chapter VIII, p. 183.

from the moralistic to the sentimental, then to the idyllic, then to the realistic; and the successive changes are sufficiently marked by three writers, Harriet Beecher Stowe, Sarah Orne Jewett, and Mary Wilkins Freeman.   Seeking their materials remote from Boston, amidst the old native stock pottering through the traditional round of life, they discovered a world of angular figures that had grown knotty and gnarly from a harsh climate and a meager soil. The stoic repressions that were a heritage from Puritan ancestors had bred a hard race that any twist of circumstance was likely to turn into grotesques. Calvinists have always at hand a providential justification of any freakish outcome to men's struggles, and in piously denying freedom of the will they often put the seal of God's approval on their own willfulness. Mrs. Freeman's *Pembroke* is not unlike *Winesburg, Ohio*, as a record of abortive lives; and Sarah Orne Jewett, in spite of a Brahmin temperament that chose to see the idyllic rather than the grotesque, could not overlook what New England provided so abundantly. In *A Country Doctor* a visitor in the village of Oldsfield thus analyzed the New England character:

> . . . for intense, self-centred, smouldering volcanoes of humanity, New England cannot be matched the world over. It's like the regions in Iceland that are full of geysers. I don't know whether it is the inheritance from those people who broke away from the old countries, and who ought to be matched to tremendous circumstances of life, but now and then there comes an amazingly explosive and uncontrollable temperament that goes all to pieces from its own conservation and accumulation of force. By and by you will all be blown up,—you quiet descendants of the Pilgrims and Puritans, and have let off your superfluous wickedness like blizzards; and when the blizzards of each family have spent themselves you will grow dull and sober, and all on a level, and be free from the troubles of a transition state. Now, you're neither a new country nor an old one. You ought to see something of the older civilizations to understand what peace of mind is. Unless some importation of explosive material from the westward stirs them up, one century is made the pattern for the next.[13]

They deal wholly with the past—these chronicles of a decaying New England—concerning themselves with a "primitive and Biblical people" who dwelt in quiet inland towns or about the lonely shores of the Maine coast; yet always under the shadow of the meeting-house, with few defenses betwixt them and the eter-

[13] Chapter IX, p. 100.

nities. The age had traveled far beyond them and they were left pottering about in their narrow Hebraic world, unaware that science and industrialism were undermining the foundations on which village and meeting-house rested. "In that handful of houses," said old Captain Littlepage in *The Country of the Pointed Firs*, "they fancy that they comprehend the universe." But if they understood God's plan of redemption they knew nothing of the ways of capitalism. A certain romantic quaintness colors the realism of these country tales and imparts a note of the idyllic. Harriet Beecher Stowe first discovered the literary possibilities of decaying New England, and in *Old-Town Folks*, *Poganuc People*, and *The Minister's Wooing*, she turned back to the days of its prime and sketched the scene with a loving hand. But it was rather in *The Pearl of Orr's Island*, especially the first part before the heavy moralism that was always entrapping her art had closed upon the tale, that she revealed its possibilities to later writers. In a letter of July 5, 1889, Sarah Orne Jewett suggests the source of her own more finished work:

> I have been reading the beginning of *The Pearl of Orr's Island* and finding it just as clear and perfectly original and strong as it seemed to me in my thirteenth or fourteenth year, when I read it first. I never shall forget the exquisite flavor and reality that it gave me. . . . It is classical—historical—anything you like to say, if you can give it high praise enough.[14]

But Miss Jewett desired a more adequate realism and so she turned curiously to consider the technique of the great continental realists of the eighties. She read Zola and Flaubert, Tolstoi and Turgenev, and oddly enough was persuaded that she had long been trying to do what Tolstoi was doing. In a letter of 1888 she wrote:

> That story of Tolstoi's was such an excitement that I did not sleep until almost morning. What a wonderful thing it is! . . . It startled me because I was dimly feeling the same kind of motive (not the same plan) in writing the "Gray Man.". . . I have felt something of what Tolstoi has been doing all the way along. I can tell you half a dozen stories where I tried to say it, "Lady Terry," "Beyond the Toll-Gate," and this "Gray Man." Now and then it came clearer to me. I never felt the soul of Tolstoi's work until last night . . . but now I know what he means, and I know that I can dare to keep at the work I sometimes have despaired about. . . .[15]

[14] *Letters of Sarah Orne Jewett*, pp. 46–47. [15] *Ibid.*, pp. 38–39.

Yet to later readers the tie that drew her to Tolstoi seems the thinnest of gossamers. The roots of her character—and of her art—went down too deep into Brahmin soil, she was too completely under the critical sway of Lowell and Fields and Aldrich, for her to turn naturalist. Her realism—if one may use the word—was as dainty and refined as her own manners—bleached out to a fine maidenly purity. In *The Country of the Pointed Firs*—a story that Willa Cather would destine for immortality in the select company of *Huckleberry Finn* and *The Scarlet Letter*—she discovers an innate gentility, or at least gentleness, in the simple fisherfolk of the Maine village, and she suggests as its source a primitive environment supplemented by an encompassing religion. Nowhere does she paint in the smutch of vulgarity, for in these eddies of New England life she discovers no vulgarity either of mind or manners. But in the cities it is different. There she found evidence in plenty of what she called the "cheap side of life," and she attributed it to the increasing material well-being of the country. Of the new middle class she held a low opinion—

> Their grandparents or even their own parents went hungry and ill clothed, and it will take some time for these people to have their fling, to eat all they want and to wear fine raiment, and flaunt authority. They must get to a state, and by slow stages too, where there is going to be something fit for education. . . . The trouble is to us old-fashioned New Englanders that "the cheap streak" so often spoils what there is of good inheritance, and the wrong side of our great material prosperity is seen almost everywhere.[16]

There spoke the Brahmin. That this "cheap streak" should have spread so far through American life, that the vulgar middle class should have taken over the rule of the country, gave her concern. To one brought up on Carlyle and Lowell and Arnold the ways of the plutocracy were abhorrent, and she clung the more tenaciously to the land of her memories, where the gentry ruled, where the plain people respected themselves and their betters, and where vulgar display was unknown. "I think as Mr. Arnold does," she wrote in 1884, "and as Mr. Lowell did, that the mistake of our time is in being governed by the ignorant mass of opinion, instead of by thinkers and men who know something."[17] Though she disliked and distrusted the America that was submerging the old landmarks, she was as ignorant as her Maine fisherfolk of the

[16] *Ibid.*, pp. 186–187.　　　　　　　　　　[17] *Ibid.*, p. 23.

social forces that were blotting out the world of her fathers, and she clung with pathetic futility to such fragments of the old order as remained. Like Lowell in his later years her heart was given to a Brahmin democracy where gentlemen ruled and where "the best traditions of culture and manners, from some divine inborn instinct toward what is simplest and purest," were held in universal respect.

What Miss Jewett with her love of the idyllic did not see—the grim and stark ugliness that resulted from the long Puritan repression—Mary Wilkins Freeman was to make the very warp of her work. She did not come of Brahmin stock. Bred up in the narrow village world of New England, she was a part of that world and she knew it as Miss Jewett could not. The decay of a social order was all about her in her youth. The more ambitious were drifting to the cities or to the new West, and those who remained were deeply marked by the constricting round of duties. Catastrophe seems always to be lying in wait for the characters that fill her meager pages. They are either timid and querulous, or fiercely "sot," yet in either case happiness has a way of slipping through their fingers. There was too little of the wine of paganism in their veins for them to enjoy what life offers. They held themselves in with too tight a rein. The New England conventions were always building higher the dams of their emotions until they broke and the roily waters rushed out in a wasting flood. Potential disaster peeps out of every page of her stories. *Pembroke* is an extraordinary collection of mean and petty and tragic lives, besotted with stubborn willfulness, without grace or comeliness, extracting no pleasant flavors from the crushed grapes of life. In that narrow world daily existence demands an unending struggle and the pinching meanness breeds miserly instincts and dour ways. *A Humble Romance* is a stark bit of sordid futility, and in many another of her short stories Mrs. Freeman etched in the familiar scene with a mordant pen. Drawn with realistic strokes the picture of New England in decay is not so lovely as Miss Jewett found it to be.

Realizing poignantly what was happening in the home of Puritanism, Mrs. Freeman turned eventually to deal with the problem of industrialism that was subduing New England to its will. *The Portion of Labor* picks up the theme where it had been dropped a generation before by Miss Phelps, and attempts in realistic manner to portray the life of the New England villager in the shoe factory. It is a tract rather than a story, and it finds no difficulty in reconciling industrialism with morality. It revives the old Puritan ethics of work—preached by Richard Baxter to his Kidderminster weavers two hundred and fifty years before; it discovers in discipline of character the great end of life; and it accepts the factory as a necessary instrument of civilization. It is the Cinderella story of a village girl who, refusing a chance to be sent to Vassar, enters a shoe factory, becomes a proletarian leader, engineers a strike, gains a wider vision of the function of labor, accepts the principle of exploitation, and is rewarded by marriage into the exploiting class. In her girlhood she was a radical in an untaught way, and from her valedictory essay at the High School Commencement to her organization of the factory workers she boldly attacked the factory owners. With the machine itself she had no quarrel. This is how she felt when she took her place for the first time in the mill:

Scared she was not; she was fairly exultant. All at once she entered a vast room in which eager men were already at the machines with frantic zeal, as if they were driving labor herself. When she felt the vibration of the floor under her feet, when she saw people spring to their stations of toil, as if springing to guns in a battle, she realized the might and grandeur of it all. Suddenly it seemed to her that the greatest thing in the whole world was work and that this was one of the greatest forms of work—to cover the feet of progress of the travellers of the earth from the cradle to the grave. She saw that these great factories, and the strength of this army of the sons and daughters of toil, made possible the advance of civilization itself, which cannot go barefoot. She realized all at once and forever the dignity of labor, this girl of the people, with a brain which enabled her to overlook the heads of the rank and file of which she herself formed a part. She never again, whatever her regret might have been for another life for which she was better fitted, which her taste preferred, had any sense of ignominy in this. She never again felt that she was too good for her labor, for labor had revealed itself to her like a goddess behind a sordid veil.[18]

Nevertheless she is ready to fight for control of the machine—for a return to the workers of a larger share of their earnings; but when the strike fails and she contemplates the misery that it has spread amongst the workers, she recants:

Her youthful enthusiasm carried her like a leaping-pole to conclusions beyond her years. "I wonder," she said to herself, "if, after all, this
[18] Chapter XXXV, p. 350.

inequality of possessions is not a part of the system of creation, if the righting of them is not beyond the flaming sword of the Garden of Eden? I wonder if the one who tries to right them forcibly is not meddling, and usurping the part of the Creator, and bringing down wrath and confusion not only upon his own head, but upon the heads of others? I wonder if it is wise, in order to establish a principle, to make those who have no voice in the matter suffer for it—the helpless women and children?" . . . She reflected, as she had so many times before, that the world was very old— thousands of years old—and inequality was as old as the world. Might it not even be a condition of its existence, the shifting of weights which kept it to its path in the scheme of the universe? [19]

Mrs. Freeman wisely chose a girl in her teens as the leader in a fierce labor battle, for Mrs. Freeman's own thinking on social questions was still in its teens. She had the warmest sympathy for the exploited poor; her conscience was as tender as Miss Phelps's; but her inadequate knowledge of economics served her ill. If economic inequality is necessary to keep the world from flying from its orbit, it serves the purpose likewise of character development. When an old factory-hand looks back upon a long life of futile labor he thus philosophizes:

Andrew quoted again from the old King of Wisdom—"I withheld not my heart from any joy, for my heart rejoices in all my labor, and that was my portion of labor." Then Andrew thought . . . of all the toilsome lives of those beside him, of all the work which they had done with their poor, knotted hands, of the tracks which they had worn on the earth to- wards their graves, with their weary feet, and suddenly he seemed to grasp a new and further meaning for that verse of Ecclesiastes.

He seemed to see that labor is not alone for itself, nor for what it ac- complishes of the tasks of the world, not for its equivalent in silver and gold, not even for the end of human happiness and love, but for the growth in character of the laborer.

"That is the portion of labor," he said.[20]

So the book ends on a Hebraic note. In 1901 when Mrs. Free- man wrote *The Portion of Labor* the psychology of work had been pretty well explored. For years William Morris had been preaching a very different doctrine, pagan rather than Hebraic, yet Mrs. Freeman seems to have been acquainted with Morris no more than was Ellen Brewster, her girlish heroine. Even the starkest New England realism was not very critical of the industrialism that was destroying the traditional New England. A cynical reader

[19] Chapter LVII, pp. 519-520.   [20] *Ibid.*, p. 563.

might perhaps suggest that the explanation is to be found in the fact that the Yankee was profiting enormously from this fouling of the Puritan nest.

II

THE AFTERGLOW OF THE ENLIGHTENMENT— WALT WHITMAN

If the philosophy of the Enlightenment was fast disintegrating in the America of 1870, it still numbered its picturesque followers who sought to leaven the age with the social spirit of an earlier generation. It was a noble bequest—this gift of the French thinkers—with its passion for liberty, its faith in man, its democratic program. From that great reservoir had come pretty much all that was generously idealistic and humanitarian in the life of the two preceding generations. Its persuasive idealism had woven itself so closely into the fabric of national thought that our fathers had come to believe that America was dedicated in a very special sense to the principles of a free society. The democratic movement returned to it constantly to refresh its strength and take new bearings. At every great crisis the familiar pronouncement of the Declaration of Independence had been confidently appealed to in furtherance of social justice. And now in the days of an acquisitive individualism, when idealism was begging alms in the market-place, it still threw flashes of romantic splendor on the crude American scene. Old Peter Cooper still dreamed his dreams of social justice after eighty years had passed over his head; and Thaddeus Stevens, grown crabbed and surly from bitter struggles, mutely testified to his passionate equalitarianism on the day of his burial. But it was Walt Whitman in his den at Camden— culturally and in the things of the spirit countless leagues removed from Boston—who was the completest embodiment of the Enlightenment—the poet and prophet of a democracy that the America of the Gilded Age was daily betraying.

In his somewhat truculent pose of democratic undress Whitman was a singular figure for a poet, and especially an American poet. The amplitude and frankness and sincerity of his rich nature were an affront to every polite convention of the day. Endowed with abundant sensuousness and catholic sympathies, he took impressions as sharply as wax from the etcher's hand; and those impressions he transcribed with the careful impartiality of the modern expressionist. His sensitive reactions to experience were emotional rather than intellectual. A pagan, a romantic, a transcendentalist, a mystic—a child of the Enlightenment yet heeding the lessons of science and regarding himself as a realist who honored the physical as the repository of the spiritual—to an amazing degree he was an unconscious embodiment of American aspiration in the days when the romantic revolution was at flood tide. His buoyant nature floated easily on the turbulent stream of national being, and his songs were defiant chants in praise of life—strong, abundant, procreative—flowing through the veins of America.

Oracular and discursive, Whitman lived and moved in a world of sensuous imagery. His imagination was Gothic in its vast reaches. Thronging troops of pictures passed before him, vivid, vital, transcripts of reality, the sharp impress of some experience or fleeting observation—his own and no one's else, and therefore authentic. Delighting in the cosmos he saw reflecting its myriad phases in the mirror of his own ego, he sank into experience joyously like a strong swimmer idling in the salt waves. Borne up by the caressing waters, repressing nothing, rejecting nothing, he found life good in all its manifestations. As an Emersonian he was content to receive his sanctions from within, and as he yielded to the stimulus of the environing present his imagination expanded, his spirits rose to earth's jubilee, his speech fell into lyric cadences, and from the exalted abandon of egoistic experience there issued a strong rich note of the universal. His like had not before appeared in our literature for the reason that the childlike pagan had not before appeared. Emerson with his serene intelligence almost disencumbered of the flesh, and Hawthorne with his dessicating skepticisms that left him afraid of sex, were the fruits of a Hebraized culture that Puritan America understood; but Walt Whitman the caresser of life, the lover who found no sweeter fat than stuck to his own bones, was incomprehensible, and not being understood, it was inevitable that he should be inexorably damned. The most deeply religious soul that American literature knows, the friend and lover of all the world, the poet of the democratic ideal to which, presumably, America was dedicated, Whitman was flung into outer darkness by the moral custodians of an age that knew morality only from the precepts of the fathers.

The early stages of Whitman's intellectual development are obscure, but that in his twenties he caught most of the infections of the times, literary, political, and social, is clear enough. The young printer-editor in frock coat and tall hat, with cane and boutonnière, who often joined the Bohemian society at Pfaff's restaurant, was a callow romantic, practicing the conventional literary arts of the time, writing formal verse, spinning romantic tales,[21] and seeking to approve himself a reputable littérateur. But the passion of reform was already stirring within him and a succession of causes—temperance, anti-capital-punishment, abolitionism—recruited his pen. As a child of Manhattan and of the Jacksonian revolution it was inevitable that his first great passion should have been political, and when in the late forties he found a suitable vehicle of expression in the *Brooklyn Eagle*, his native Jeffersonianism took stock of current political programs. His political master was the radical equalitarian William Leggett—whose praises in after life he never stinted—and from Leggett and the *Evening Post*, supplemented by Fanny Wright and Tom Paine and other disreputable influences, he seems to have got the first clear expression of the sweeping democratic postulates on which later he was to erect his philosophy. The times were stirring everywhere with revolution and on Manhattan Island Locofocoism, with the newfangled matches, ten years before had started its little local bonfire by way of preparation for a general conflagration that should consume the accumulated mass of wrong and injustice. The ardent young Whitman was deeply infected with Locofoco enthusiasm and his editorials for the *Eagle* were the pronouncements of an extreme left-wing Democrat, as became a disciple of Leggett.

In this early phase of his democracy he fixed his hopes on the great West where, he believed, a freer and more democratic America was taking shape. He was an expansionist, full of ardent hopes, an apostle of "manifest destiny." In such lesser matters as finance and governmental subsidies he was a good Jacksonian, following Old Bullion Benton in his preference for hard money and dislike of shin-plasters. He was opposed to the bankers and monopolists. He called himself a "free-trader by instinct," and so late as 1888 he said, "I object to the tariff primarily because it is not humanitarian—because it is a damnable imposition upon the masses."[22] But these lesser things were inconsequential in comparison with the

---

[21] See Mabbott, *Short Stories by Walt Whitman*, Columbia University Press, 1927.
[22] For his late views see Horace Traubel, *With Walt Whitman in Camden*, Vol. I, p. 99, and elsewhere.

great objective towards which America was moving—the ever-widening freedom of men in society. "There must be," he wrote in those early years, "continual additions to our great experiment of how much liberty society will bear."[23] On that grand theme he was never tired of speaking. With Tom Paine he believed that just government was a simple thing, fitted to the capacity of many heads; it is made complex to hide its dishonesty. After commenting on the "once derided, but now widely worshipped doctrines which Jefferson and the glorious Leggett promulgated," he went on:

. . . this one single rule, rationally construed and applied, is enough to form the starting point of all that is necessary in government: *to make no more laws than those useful for preventing a man or body of men from infringing on the rights of other men.*

And again:

There is not a greater fallacy on earth than the doctrine of *force*, as applied in government. . . . Sensible men have long seen that the best government is that which governs least.[24]

Such comments, of course, are only familiar echoes of the Enlightenment—echoes that run through all the thinking of the naturistic school, from Godwin and Paine to Channing and Emerson and Thoreau. In the minds of the children of the Enlightenment the creative ideal of individualism was always pointing toward the ultimate end of philosophic anarchism, and Whitman with his assured faith in the average man accepted the Godwinian political theory as naturally as did Thoreau. What other politics, indeed, was possible for those who built upon the postulates of the innate excellence of human nature and the measureless potentialities of men when vicious social codes have been swept away and the plastic clay is molded by a kindly environment? The perfectibility of man was no romantic dream to the disciples of the French school, but a sober statement of sociological fact, based on a rationalistic psychology; and Whitman was convinced that he was a competent realist in thus envisaging the social problem. If man's instincts are trustworthy, what justification is there for narrow repressions laid on his freedom? Hitherto those repressions have only maimed and distorted him, encouraging his baser rather than his better impulses; and before he can realize his potentialities he

[23] Cleveland Rogers and John Black, *The Gathering of the Forces*, Vol. I, p. 12.
[24] *Ibid.*, Vol. I, pp. 53, 54, 57.

must put away all external compulsions and learn to rely solely upon himself. Hence the immediate objective of the democratic revolution was individual freedom, the breaking of all chains, to the end that free men may create a society worthy of them.

So it was as a revolutionary that Whitman began his work; and a revolutionary he remained to the end, although in his last years he chose to call himself an evolutionist. A born rebel, he was always preaching the gospel of rebellion. "I am a radical of radicals," he said late in life, "but I don't belong to any school." [25] It was this revolutionary spirit that made him the friend of all rebellious souls past and present. "My heart is with all you rebels—all of you, today, always, wherever: your flag is my flag," [26] he said to a Russian anarchist; and it was this sympathy that enabled him to understand Fanny Wright and Tom Paine and Priestley, who "have never had justice done them." [27] "The future belongs to the radical," and so Leaves of Grass—he says in "Starting from Paumanok"—"beat the gong of revolt." Conventional law and order he frankly despised and those individuals who sought their own law and followed it awoke his admiration. Thoreau's "lawlessness" delighted him—"his going his own absolute road let hell blaze all it chooses." It is a coward and a poltroon who accepts his law from others—as true of communities as it is true of individuals. He was a good Jeffersonian in his fear of Federalistic consolidation that must put an end to local rights and freedoms.

> To the States or any one of them, or any city of the States,
> *Resist much, obey little,*
> Once unquestioning obedience, once fully enslaved,
> . . . no nation, state, city of this earth, ever afterward resumes
>   its liberty.[28]
> I am for those that have never been master'd,
> For men and women whose tempers have never been master'd,
> For those whom laws, theories, conventions can never master.[29]

This is the spirit of the radical forties when men were prone to repudiate their allegiance to the political state; when left-wing Abolitionists were dissolving the Union by resolutions; and tran-

[25] Traubel, *op. cit.*, Vol. I, p. 215.
[26] *Ibid.*, Vol. I, p. 65.
[27] *Ibid.*, Vol. I, pp. 79–80.
[28] *Leaves of Grass*, inclusive edition ed. by Emory Halloway, Garden City, N. Y., 1927. Hereafter called *Leaves*. "To the States," p. 8.
[29] *Ibid.*, "By Blue Ontario's Shore," p. 297, ll. 21–23.

scendentalists were proclaiming the doctrine of nullification of unrighteous law. It had come out of the Jacksonian upheaval, but it was daily discovering fresh sanctions as the anarchistic premises of the Enlightenment were more adequately explored and the revolutionary spirit of Europe broke in upon America. During these turbulent years Whitman's great plan was in gestation, but before *Leaves of Grass* came to print in the first slender edition of 1855 other influences had been at work, confirming his earlier views, endowing them with lyric passion and expanding them into a grandiose whole. Those influences would seem to have been the fervid emotionalism of the fifties, the monistic idealism of the transcendental school, and the emerging scientific movement. On the whole perhaps it was the first, with its vague and expansive Utopianism, that bit most deeply, stimulating his rich pagan nature to unconventional frankness and encouraging him to throw off the inhibitions of a Puritan ethicism that held American thought in narrow bondage. The rude and ample liberalisms that so shocked his early readers were in no sense peculiar to Whitman, despite common opinion, but the expression of the surging emotionalism of the times, and *Leaves of Grass*, can best be understood by setting its frank paganism against the background of the lush fifties.

With its Calvinistic antecedents—Scotch-Irish and Huguenot as well as New England Puritan—America had always been unfriendly to a pagan evaluation of man's duties and destiny, and the revolutionary movement of the forties had been kept within sober ethical bounds. John Humphrey Noyes was probably the most radical American of the times, yet the Perfectionism of his earlier years, with its ascetic religiosity, bore little resemblance to the later communism of the Oneida Community. But the liberalism of the fifties was casting off all Hebraic restraints and running wild, proclaiming a new heaven about to appear on the free continent of America, and bidding the youth of the land live joyously as children of the earth. Paganism for the first time lifted up its head and surveyed the American scene—a youthful paganism, lusty and vigorous, that suggested amazing applications of the respectable doctrines of freedom and individuality, to the scandal of older-fashioned folk. From the free spaces of the West, carried on the tide of the Gold Rush, had come a spontaneous

reaction from the earlier repressions. Liberalism was passing from
the political to the social—a free welling-up of repressed desires,
a vast expansiveness. Too long had the natural human emotions
been under the ban of asceticism; too long had a God of wrath
dispossessed a God of love. Life is good in the measure that it is
lived fully, and to live fully is to live in the flesh as well as the
spirit. Emerson the prophet of the earlier decade had suffered
from an extreme unfleshliness; Whitman the prophet of the fifties
would recover the balance. As the current of emotionalism gathered force a frank *joie de vivre* submerged the old reticences; candor,
frankness, a very lust of self-expression, was the new law for free
men and women—a glorification of the physical that put to rout
the traditional Hebraisms. A riotous sentimentalism ran about
the land until it seemed to timid souls as if liberty were quite
running away with decency. Freedom for black slaves was one
thing, but freedom for women—the loosening of social convention—suggested terrifying eventualities like free love and the disruption of the family. They would countenance no such immoral
freedom and under the leadership of young Anthony Comstock
the forces of reticence and respectability made ready to do battle
with the new liberalisms.

It was not alone Walt Whitman who threw down the gage to
the Comstockian watchmen in the gates. The apostle of the new
freedom, the high priest of emotional liberalism, was Henry Ward
Beecher, lately come out of the West, who from the pulpit of
Plymouth Church swept his thousands of idolizing followers along
the path of Utopian emotionalism. With a rich amplitude and
golden vagueness of metaphor he preached the new gospel. From
his lips flowed a lyric chant, a vast paean, a very shout in praise
of liberty and love, of godlike man and a manlike God. "Life—
affirmative, immediate, in a highly ornamented Mayday world—
he acknowledged and commemorated life!" [30] He bathed in a
"perpetual tropical luxuriance of blessed love." "I never knew
how to worship until I knew how to love," he cried; "and to love
I must have something . . . that touching my heart, shall not
leave the chill of ice but the warmth of summer." Like a good
Emersonian he discarded reason—the discipline of the ancestral
Calvinism—to follow the "secret chords of feeling," the "heart's
instincts, whose channels you may appoint but whose flowing is

[30] Constance Mayfield Rourke, *Trumpets of Jubliee*, p. 171.

beyond control." A "magnificent pagan"—so Thoreau called him—he reveled in sensuous beauty. His emotions mounted as he contemplated this new land, this new people, the golden future that beckoned—with all shackles broken, dedicated to freedom, warm and palpitating from abundant life—a radiant world of lovely women and manly men. He dwelt on Pisgah and from the heights looked out on a divine democracy. "The life of the common people is the best part of the world's life," he exclaimed; "the life of the common people is the life of God." And to his congregation intoxicated with his rhetoric he shouted, "Ye are gods! You are crystalline, your faces are radiant!" [31] And the end and outcome envisaged by this prophet of the American Idea was a vaguely grandiose fellowship, not of the Saints alone, but of all the thronging children of men, for of such is God's kingdom of this world.

As such lyric chants fell on Whitman's ears, they must have quickened the ferment of thought that was eventually to clarify for him the ideal of democracy, exalting it by making it warm and human and social. The old Jacksonian leveling had been negative; its freedoms had been individual, its anarchism selfish and unsocial. The great ideal of the fellowship had been lost in the scramble for rights. Even transcendental democracy had narrowed its contacts. The hermit Thoreau in his cabin at Walden Pond was no symbol of a generous democratic future. In the struggle for liberty and equality the conception of fraternity had been denied and the golden trinity of the Enlightenment dismembered. It was this idea of fraternity, made human and hearty by his warm love of men and women, that Whitman got from the expansive fifties and built into his thinking. The conception of solidarity, then entering the realm of proletarian thought through the labors of Friedrich Engels and Karl Marx, was his response to the new times—a response that infused his democratic faith with a glowing humanism. Democracy spiritualized by Channing and Emerson and Parker had suffered limitations from their lingering Hebraisms—the Puritan passion for righteousness had imposed strict ethical bounds on the democratic will. In Thoreau it had been subjected to caustic skepticisms—the transcendental individualist quizzically asked, "What *is* your people?" and refused to subject himself to the mass. But in Whitman all limitations and skepticisms were swept away by the feeling of comrade-

[31] *Ibid.*, p. 172.

ship. Flesh is kin to flesh, and out of the great reserves of life is born the average man "with his excellent good manliness." Not in distinction but in oneness with the whole is found the good life, for in fellowship is love and in the whole is freedom; and love and freedom are the law and the prophets. The disintegrations of the earlier individualism must be succeeded by a new integration; fear and hate and jealousy and pride have held men apart hitherto, but love will draw them together. After all solidarity—the children of America merging in the fellowship, sympathetic, responsive, manlike yet divine, of which the poet should be the prophet and literature provide the sermons.

It was a noble conception—washing away all the meanness that befouled Jacksonian individualism—and it somewhat slowly found its way to parity with his first master conception, the universal ego, and settled into place in those later opening lines of *Leaves of Grass:*

> One's-self I sing, a simple separate person,
> Yet utter the word Democratic, the word En-Masse.[32]

Then came the war to strengthen his faith in the common man. As he watched the soldiers marching, fighting, suffering, he was deeply impressed with their courage, patience, kindness, manliness, and came to reverence the deep wellspring of national being from which issued such inexhaustible waters. It was not the few but the many that gave him hope. "I never before so realized the majesty and reality of the American people *en masse*," he wrote of some regiments returning from the front. "It fell upon me like a great awe." [33] And as he contemplated this fecund people, with its sons and daughters issuing strong and wholesome from every part of the land, there came to him a new conception of unity— the Union that Lincoln loved—the drawing together into an indissoluble whole of the far-flung commonwealths—a realization of the perfect State where reign liberty, equality, fraternity. Solidarity had taken on a political complexion but its life-blood was in the veins of a free people.

But pagan though he was in his deeper nature, a child of the emotional fifties, he was a transcendentalist also and his democratic philosophy, as it took shape, bears unmistakable marks of the New England school, supplemented perhaps by Quakerism. His well-

---

[32] *Leaves,* "One's-Self I Sing," p. 1, ll. 1–2.
[33] *Autobiographia,* p. 73. See also *Democratic Vistas,* p. 74.

known comment, "I was simmering and simmering; it was Emerson brought me to boil," suggests much, and in particular that the Enlightenment as it had come to him through the Jeffersonian heritage was supplemented and spiritualized by the Enlightenment as it had taken special form in passing through the transcendental mind. To this latter source must be traced the philosophic monism that served to draw his speculations together—a mystic sense of the divine oneness of life that took his major postulates in golden hands and fused them into a single spiritual whole. Thus instructed the "great Idea, the idea of perfect and free individuals," became curiously Emersonian in all its amplifications. There is the same glorification of consciousness and will, the same exaltation of the soul, the same trust in the buried life that men call instinct, the same imperious call to heed the voice of innate Godhood; and round and about this "perfect and free individual" is a mystical egocentric universe wherein the children of men may luxuriate in their divinity. The body is excellent as the soul is excellent; away, therefore, with all shamefacedness—the mean secretiveness, the putting of fingers to the lips in presence of the naked, the lies in presence of open palpable fact! For if this be indeed God's universe, and He is in and through it all, the children of Adam may stand in His presence unafraid—nay, rather with pride in their own excellence. "I exist as I am, that is enough," for "Divine am I inside and out, and I make holy whatever I touch or am touch'd from."

Whitman not only accepted Emerson with ungrudging loyalty but he dwelt much with Hegel and the German idealists, and with their help he penetrated curiously to the core of things, discovering there an inner spiritual reality that is the abiding substance behind the external manifestation. He had come upon food to sustain his faith in presence of the mean and base that compassed him about, and the puzzling contradictions of life no longer troubled him. If man be perfectible, if he be indeed a child of God though still in his infancy, how glorious must be the future toward which he is pressing! The evil will pass and the good remain.

Roaming in thought over the Universe, I saw the little that is Good
    steadily hastening towards immortality,
And the vast all that is call'd Evil I saw hastening to merge itself and
    become lost and dead.[34]

        [34] *Leaves*, "Roaming in Thought," p. 233.

When he turned from the oracular utterance of *Leaves of Grass* to sober exposition, he phrased it thus:

There is, apart from mere intellect . . . a wondrous something that realises without argument . . . an intuition of the absolute balance, in time and space, of the whole of this multifarious, mad chaos of fraud, frivolity, hoggishness—this revel of fools, and incredible make-believe and general unsettledness, we call the *world;* a soul-sight of that divine clue and unseen thread which holds the whole congeries of things, all history and time, and all events however trivial, however momentous, like a leash'd dog in the hands of the hunter.[35]

To discover this divine clue and be drawn by the unseen thread into the orbit of things, to suffer the Me—the "human identity of understanding, emotions, spirit"—to fuse with the Not Me—"the whole of the material, objective universe and laws, with what is behind them in time and space"—became therefore for Whitman the grand objective of man's life and effort. This for him was the sum and substance of religion, which was no other than the binding of the individual back upon the whole. "A vast similitude interlocks all." And so from his conception of social solidarity he went forward to the conception of spiritual solidarity, and discovered religion to be the crown and glory of the "American Idea." Walt Whitman and America were to be the prophets of religion. "Easily at home in a natural world of prodigious brightness and scale, he . . . saw 'the most splendid race the sun ever shone upon,' and was urging the life of instinct and impulse. Love was the key—taking form and in 'Starting from Paumanok' he asserted his Love, Democracy, Religion—a new religion." [36] His message was purpose.

The soul,
Forever and forever—longer than soil is brown and solid—longer than water ebbs and flows.

I will make the poems of materials, for I think they are to be the most spiritual poems,
And I will make the poems of my body and of mortality,
For I think I shall then supply myself with the poems of my soul and of immortality.

I will make a song for these States that no one State may under any circumstances be subjected to another State,

.   .   .   .

[35] "Carlyle from the American Point of View," in *Specimen Days, Prose Works,* pp. 174–175.   [36] Rourke, *op. cit.,* p. 173.

I will sing the song of companionship,

. . . .

I will write the evangel-poem of comrades and of love,

. . . .

I am the credulous man of qualities, ages, races,
I advance from the people in their own spirit,

. . . .

I, too, following many and follow'd by many, inaugurate a religion, . . .

. . . .

Each is not for its own sake,
I say the whole earth and all the stars in the sky are for religion's sake.

I say no man has ever yet been half devout enough,
None has ever yet adored or worship'd half enough,
None has begun to think how divine he himself is, and how certain the
  future is.

I say that the real and permanent grandeur of these States must be their
  religion,
Otherwise there is no real and permanent grandeur;

. . . .

My comrade!
For you to share with me two greatnesses, and a third one rising inclusive
  and more resplendent,
The greatness of Love and Democracy, and the greatness of Religion.[37]

But this new religion of the mystical Whitman, in harmony
with post-transcendental thought, was deeply impregnated with
the spirit of science. He was in the very fullness of his powers when
the conception of evolution came to him and he greeted it gladly,
weaving it into all his thinking and discovering in it a confirmation
of his idealistic philosophy. It was the evolution of Herbert
Spencer, it must be remembered, that Whitman accepted—teleological, buoyantly optimistic, dominated by the conception of
progress, shot through with the spirit of the Enlightenment; and
such an evolution was a confirmation and not a denial of his
transcendental premises. It supplemented rather than contra-
dicted the tenets of his faith. Like Emerson as he saw the bounds
of the material universe slowly pushed back by science he discovered amidst the constant change the presence of growth,
development, the natural passage from the simple to the complex;

[37] *Leaves*, "Starting from Paumanok," p. 14, ll. 22–26; p. 15, ll. 1, 13, 19, 22–23;
p. 16, ll. 2, 5–11; p. 17, ll. 7–10.

and like Theodore Parker he felt that this slow unfolding was no other than the unfolding of God, making Himself evident and unmistakable to man. Evolution was God's great plan. "The law over all, the law of laws, is the law of successions," he was persuaded; "for what is the present after all but a growth out of the past?" But noble as is the evidence of God's work discoverable by science, the soul is not content to rest with such evidence; it must seek out the reality behind the manifestation; and for this work the poet alone is fitted. The poet must complete the work of the scientist. The noble "Passage to India" is a lovely chant of human progress, the adventurous soul conquering the earth; but it must not pause there; it must seek God through the universe until it finds Him, and "Nature and Man shall be disjoin'd and diffused no more," and "All these hearts as of fretted children shall be sooth'd."

> Bathe me O God in thee, mounting to thee,
> I and my soul to range in range of thee.[38]

It was in this profoundly religious spirit that Whitman accepted science, built it into his poetry, rested confidently upon it; and it is this spirit that explains his formal statement in the "Song of Myself."

I accept Reality and dare not question it,
Materialism first and last imbuing.

Hurrah for positive science! long live exact demonstration!
Fetch stonecrop mixt with cedar and branches of lilac,
This is the lexicographer, this the chemist, this made a grammar of the
    old cartouches,
These mariners put the ship through dangerous unknown seas,
This the geologist, this works with the scalpel, and this is the mathema-
    tician.

Gentlemen, to you the first honors always!
Your facts are useful, and yet they are not my dwelling,
I but enter by them to an area of my dwelling.[39]

Equipped with such a philosophy and supported by such a faith Whitman accepted the twin duties laid upon him: to make clear to America her present failure in the great adventure—how far she had fallen short hitherto of any adequate democratic

[38] *Leaves*, p. 349, ll. 18-19.   [39] *Leaves*, p. 43, ll. 9-17.

reality; and to mark out afresh the path to the Canaan of democratic hopes—reviving the early hopes of the Enlightenment and
drawing in lovelier colors the democratic Utopia dreamed of for a
hundred years. To be both critic and prophet—that he conceived
to be his mission, a mission that he was faithful to for upwards of
forty years. For the first duty he was admirably equipped. No
other knew this America so intimately or so broadly—had penetrated so lovingly to the common heart and read so clearly its
secret hopes and fears. That America was not yet a democracy—
was very far indeed from a democracy—that it was a somewhat
shoddy *bourgeois* capitalistic society shot through with cant and
hypocrisy and every meanness, he saw with calm, searching eyes.
No contemporary critic, not Godkin, not Emerson, saw more
clearly the unlovely reality or dealt with it more scathingly, not
only in *Leaves of Grass* but especially in his prose writings and in
casual talk. Amongst scores of such passages a single one must
serve for illustration.

I say that our New World democracy, however great a success in uplifting the masses out of their sloughs, in materialistic development,
products, and in a certain highly-deceptive superficial popular intellectu-
ality, is, so far, an almost complete failure in its social aspects, and in really
grand religious, moral, literary, and esthetic results. . . . Shift and turn
the combinations of the statement as we may, the problem of the future
of America is in certain respects as dark as it is vast. Pride, competition,
segregation, vicious wilfulness, and license beyond example, brood already
upon us. Unwieldy and immense, who shall hold in behemoth? who bridle
leviathan? Flaunt it as we choose, athwart and over the roads of our
progress loom huge uncertainty, and dreadful threatening gloom. It is
useless to deny it: Democracy grows rankly up the thickest, noxious, dead-
liest plants and fruits of all—brings worse and worse invaders—needs
newer, larger, stronger, keener compensations and compellers. Our lands
embracing so much . . . hold in the breast that flame also, capable of consuming themselves, consuming us all. . . . Even today, amid these whirls,
incredible flippancy, and blind fury of parties, infidelity, entire lack of
first-rate captains and leaders, added to the plentiful meanness and vulgarity of the ostensible masses—that problem, the labor question, beginning to open like a yawning gulf, rapidly widening every year—what
prospect have we? We sail a dangerous sea of seething currents, cross and
under-currents, vortices,—all so dark and untried.[40]

As a realist Whitman granted the worst charges of the critics of
democracy, but he probed deeper and brought other facts to light
that modified the equation. It was the difficult question the old

[40] *Democratic Vistas, Prose Works,* pp. 254–255.

Federalists had posed and that Carlyle had lately revived—the question, is not this meanness inseparable from democracy? is not your people in fact a great beast, requiring the lash and the curb? It was the crux of the long debate over democracy and to it Whitman gave anxious and frequent consideration. In fighting the battle of 1790 over again, like Jefferson he rested his case on the native integrity and measureless potentiality of the "bulk-people"—they are the deep soil from which spring the abundant fruits and flowers of civilization. Gentle-nurtured folk do not understand this—they do not like the rank qualities of vital being. Matthew Arnold "always gives you the notion that he hates to touch the dirt—the dirt is so dirty! But everything comes out of the dirt—everything: everything comes out of the people . . . not university people, not F.F.V. people: people, people, just people!" In the rude, vital, natural man is the inexhaustible wellspring of good and evil; "He's got it all . . . not only the cruel, beastly, hoggish, cheating, bedbug qualities, but also the spiritual—the noble—the high-born"; [41] in "some ways" he is a "devil of a fellow," but he is not "all devil or even chiefly devil." [42] And because he is not chiefly devil such love and beauty and justice and comradeship as there is in the world, such progress in civilization as has been made hitherto, have been possible—how otherwise? If he has journeyed thus far out of the primeval slime, what bounds shall be set to his eventual journeyings? Why put out one's eyes with a mere handful of years?

So Whitman projected his democratic commonwealth far into the future; he would not have us believe that it had been realized here in America. Political democracy, the struggle for political rights that had engaged America hitherto, was only negative, a necessary preliminary to the ultimate reality. "I submit," he said, "that the fruition of democracy, on aught like a grand scale, resides altogether in the future," and its realization depends upon the use to which the people put their freedom. If from it emerges a proud and self-conscious individualism—"the quality of Being, in the object's self, according to its own central idea and purpose, and of growing therefrom and thereto—not criticism by other standards, and adjustments thereto"—then democracy on a grand scale will be possible and the self-reliant citizen will take his place in a free creative society. The ideal of the growing man, and the

[41] Traubel, *op. cit.*, Vol. I, p. 174.   [42] *Ibid.*, Vol. I, p. 285.

ideal of the perfect State—broadly social rather than narrowly political—these were his twin ideals; and the tie that is to bind men together in spontaneous solidarity is love. How characteristic is his sketch of the perfect city, and how deeply saturated with the Enlightenment! There is wanting only a physiocratic economics to make it perfect.

A great city is that which has the greatest men and women,

. . . .

Where the city stands with the brawniest breed of orators and bards,
Where the city stands that is belov'd by these, and loves them in return
and understands them,
Where no monuments exist to heroes but in the common words and deeds,
Where thrift is in its place, and prudence is in its place,
Where the men and women think lightly of the laws,
Where the slave ceases and the master of slaves ceases,
Where the populace rise at once against the never-ending audacity of
elected persons,

. . . .

Where outside authority enters always after the precedence of inside
authority,
Where the citizen is always the head and ideal, and President, Mayor,
Governor and what not, are agents for pay,
Where children are taught to be laws to themselves, and to depend on
themselves,
Where equanimity is illustrated in affairs,

. . . .

Where the city of faithfulest friends stands,
Where the city of the cleanliness of the sexes stands,

. . . .

There the great city stands.[43]

Individualism, solidarity—on such strong bases he erected his ideal democracy, and the heaven-reaching temple will be overlaid with the rich arts and graces of a civilization worthy at last of the name. Such was the Enlightenment as it came to flower in the passionate idealism of Walt Whitman—a dream that was mocked and flouted and nullified by the Drews and Fisks and Goulds— the "hoggish, cheating, bedbug qualities" of a generation that scorned him for a beast. Even his stout faith was shaken at times

[43] *Leaves*, "Song of the Broad Axe," p. 160, ll. 7, 14-20, 21-22; p. 161, ll. 1-2, 6-7, 10.

by the infidelities of the Gilded Age. He was troubled by the gap that opened between the free individual and the perfect State. "I seem to be reaching for a new politics—for a new economy," he confessed in 1888; "I don't quite know what, but for something." [44] Although he protested, "The older I grow . . . the more I am confirmed in my optimism, my democracy," he projected his hopes farther into the future. He sympathized with the socialists but he was not one of them. His revolutionary ardor abated and he preferred in later years to call himself an evolutionist. [45] "Be radical—be radical," he said to Traubel, "be not too damned radical." [46] With his catholic sympathies that refused all bitterness he could not be a partisan—"after the best the partisan will say something better will be said by the man." [47]

So in the twilight of the romantic revolution Whitman quietly slipped away. The great hopes on which he fed have been belied by after events—so his critics say;[48] as the great hopes of the Enlightenment have been belied. Certainly in this welter of today, with science become the drab and slut of war and industrialism, with sterile money-slaves instead of men, Whitman's expansive hopes seem grotesque enough. Democracy may indeed be only a euphemism for the rulership of fools. Yet in a time of huge infidelities, in the dun breakdown and disintegration of all faiths, it is not wholly useless to recall the large proportions of Walt Whitman, his tenderness, his heartiness, his faith, his hope. There was in him no weak evasion, no sniveling over the shards of the goodly vessel broken at the well, but even when "old, alone, sick, weak-down, melted-worn with sweat," a free and joyous acceptance of life.

Thanks in old age—thanks ere I go,
For health, the midday sun, the impalpable air—for life, mere life,
     .   .   .   .   .   .

For all my days—not those of peace alone—the days of war the same,
For gentle words, caresses, gifts from foreign lands,
For shelter, wine and meat—for sweet appreciation,
     .   .   .   .   .   .

[44] Traubel, *op. cit.*, Vol. I, p. 101.
[45] *Ibid.*, Vol. I, pp. 193, 215.
[46] *Ibid.*, Vol. I, p. 223.
[47] *Ibid.*, Vol. I, p. 363.
[48] See Norman Foerster, *American Criticism*, pp. 211–222; Lucy Lockwood Hazard, *The Frontier in American Literature*, pp. 170–177.

For beings, groups, love, deeds, words, books—for colors, forms,
For all the brave strong men—devoted, hardy, men—who've forward
    sprung in freedom's help, all years, all lands,
For braver, stronger, more devoted men—(a special laurel ere I go, to
    life's war's chosen ones,
The cannoneers of song and thought—the great artillerists—the foremost
    leaders, captains of the soul:)
As soldier from an ended war return'd—As traveler out of myriads, to the
    long procession retrospective,
Thanks—joyful thanks!—a soldier's, traveler's thanks.[49]

A great figure, the greatest assuredly in our literature—yet perhaps only a great child—summing up and transmitting into poetry
all the passionate aspirations of an America that had passed through
the romantic revolution, the poet of selfhood and the prophet of
brotherhood, the virile man and the catholic lover—how shall
Walt Whitman become dumb or cease to speak to men unless the
children of those who are now half-devil and half-God shall prove to
be wholly devil—or wholly moron?

III

THE BACKWASH OF THE FRONTIER—MARK TWAIN

As Whitman contemplated the feeble literature purveyed by the
worshipers of the genteel he asked with some irritation: "What is
the reason in our time, our lands, that we see no fresh local courage,
sanity, of our own—the Mississippi, stalwart Western men, real
mental and physical facts, Southerners, etc., in the body of our
literature?" That was in 1870 and the answer was at hand in the
person of Mark Twain. Here at last was an authentic American—
a native writer thinking his own thoughts, using his own eyes,
speaking his own dialect—everything European fallen away, the
last shred of feudal culture gone, local and western yet continental.
A strange and uncouth figure in the eyes of Thomas Bailey Aldrich,
yet the very embodiment of the turbulent frontier that had long
been shaping a native psychology, and that now at last was turning
eastward to Americanize the Atlantic seaboard. Yet in spite of a
rare vein of humor, the outcropping of a rich and whimsical imagination, he made his way slowly to polite recognition. For years he
was regarded by authoritative critics as little more than a buffoon,
an extravagant fun-maker with a broad streak of western coarseness; and it was not till near the end, when he had long been an in-

[49] *Leaves,* "Thanks in Old Age," p. 435.

ternational figure, that the culture of the East accepted him. It was Howells then who pronounced him "the sole, the incomparable, the Lincoln of our literature . . . the very marrow of Americanism."

Just as that judgment was at the time, it needs qualification now. The marrow of Americanism is not the same substance from generation to generation. The outer environing life of a people works itself slowly into the bones and brings about subtle changes. Mark Twain was indubitably an embodiment of three centuries of American experience—frontier centuries, decentralized, leveling, individualistic; but the Americanism that issued from them came to its flower and was quickly succeeded by another kind as the fields of experience were re-plowed by industrialism and sowed to a different grain. Mark Twain was the child of a frontier past—as Lincoln was, as the Gilded Age was—and the America of today could no more breed him than it could breed Lincoln, or Greeley, or Whitman; his Americanism was the reflection of an environment that is no longer ours, in the slack folk-ways of the frontier that we have outgrown. Child of the Southwest in its early boom days, he was cradled in profitless schemes and nourished on dreams of vast potential wealth. The frontier spirit was an effervescence in his blood and golden expectations flung their mirage over the drab reality. As a boy he took impress from a kindly, ignorant, slave-holding, Calvinistic village world, and he quitted the slattern village life to plunge into the picturesque traffic of the Mississippi in the boom days when every river pilot drove his boat full steam ahead. Then the Far West of silver mines and the Golden Gate took him in hand—a gambling, romantic, optimistic frontier, feverish with flush times, "a beggar's revel of potential millionaires without the price of a square meal." [50]   And finally this buoyant, irreverent adolescent was taken in hand by the Far East: by New England respectability in the persons of Olivia Langdon of Elmira, William Dean Howells of Cambridge, Twitchell and Warner of Hartford; and by New York in the persons of Carnegie and Gilder and Whitelaw Reid and Henry H. Rogers, to be made over into a man of the world.

Such were his origins and his schooling. All his life he remained a boy, with the imitativeness of youth, and yet with something deep within him that cherished its own integrity. Quick to take color from his environment and at home in crowds, he lived nevertheless in the solitude of his own heart. Acutely conscious of his

[50] Lucy Lockwood Hazard, *The Frontier in American Literature*, p. 223.

rough western ways, he admired the culture of the Langdons and the refined art of Howells, and he wanted to be approved by them. A kinsman of Beriah Sellers, he delighted in the great barbecue and wanted to carve great portions for himself, to heap up his plate as others were doing. His reactions to experience were always emotional. He was not a Walt Whitman to penetrate curiously to the core of his own being and grow thence outwardly, content to wait till the world came round to him. He loved to make a splurge, to be talked of, to be in the public eye, to live on an ample scale; he accepted the world's standards and wished to be measured by them. It was characteristic of the frontier. Wanting other standards, the frontier measured success by obvious material standards. Its aggressive individualism was never spiritual or intellectual or cultural. So with all his heritage of generations of frontier individualism he never achieved an intellectual or spiritual unity, an untroubled conscious integrity, as Emerson did and Whitman did. He never was at home in the world of catholic thought, but all his life he suffered from the petty inhibitions of his origins. He could not throw off the frontier—its psychology and its morality were too deeply intertwined with his primitive self; and the result was a harassing inner conflict that left him maimed.

Yet with all his shortcomings—because of them indeed—Mark Twain is an immensely significant American document. He is a mirror reflecting the muddy cross-currents of American life as the frontier spirit washed in, submerging the old aristocratic landmarks. To know Mark Twain is to know the strange and puzzling contradictions of the Gilded Age. With unconscious fidelity he reveals its crudity, its want of knowledge, discipline, historical perspective; its intellectual incapacity to deal with the complexities of a world passing through the twin revolutions of industrialism and science. And he reflects with equal fidelity certain other qualities that go far to redeem the meanness: a great creative power; an eager idealism, somewhat vague but still fine; a generous sympathy; a manly independence that strove to think honestly; a passionate hatred of wrong and injustice and an honest democratic respect for men as men. A significant if not an unsoiled or heroic document!

That in his later years an impassable gulf opened between Mark Twain and his generation, that the buoyant humorist of the seventies ripened into the bitter satirist of the nineties, is a matter that has been much remarked upon. The fact is clear enough but the explanation is not so clear. In part no doubt—as Van Wyck Brooks has pointed out—the change resulted from a thwarting of the creative artist by a disastrous surrender to the ideals of the Gilded Age; in part, also, it was the inevitable toll exacted by the passing years. A humane and generous spirit cannot long watch with indifference the motley human caravan hastening to eternity—cannot find food for laughter alone in the incredible meanness and folly of men cheating and quarreling in a wilderness of graves. Tenderness, chivalry, love of justice, are poor bucklers to withstand the blows of fate, and Mark Twain had little skill in defense. The humorist like the poet is sensitively responsive to life and the scars multiply fast. Endowed with a nature not unlike Swift's in its fierce rage at inhumanity, not unlike Sir Philip Sidney's in its romantic chivalry, he was not a stoic to endure with equanimity. He was foredoomed to suffer vicariously. The comment he wrote Howells in 1899 throws a white light on the man. "I have been reading the morning paper," he said. "I do it every morning—well knowing that I shall find in it the usual depravities and basenesses and hypocrisies and cruelties that make up civilization, and cause me to put in the rest of the day pleading for the damnation of the human race."

Yet granting so much, and granting also a morbid conscience that harassed him with self-condemnation—"What a man sees in the human race is merely himself in the deep and honest privacy of his own heart"—it still remains true that the bleakness of his later years was due in part, at least, to the insubstantial dwelling he chose to live in. The architects of the Gilded Age were jerry-builders, and Mark Twain found his jerry-built house a poor protection against the winter winds. It was perhaps not greatly his fault that he built so flimsily. He was too willing to be caught in the web of material things. He could not reach out for companionship with the great earth. Hamlin Garland in a bleak Dakota shack found help and comfort in the philosophy of Taine, but Mark Twain could not get outside his own skin. He could not break a path through the provincialism of his environment. He was held prisoner to his own thoughts and his only release was through the window of imagination. When harassed beyond endurance he sought release in writing that hid the evidence of his rebellion.

What would Livy say, what would the American public say, if they knew he had come to deny all the tribal gods!

There is no more pathetic figure in American literature than Mark Twain, alone and solitary amid the blatant American crowd, living in a dreary wash of speeches and banquets, spinning the threads of a rebellious philosophy out of his own bowels, unaware of what others were spinning, regarding himself as a dangerous fellow and stowing away in his strong-box intellectual bombs that he thought too explosive for the Gilded Age to play with. In his intellectual isolation he could not take the measure of his speculations and he did not realize how common were such conclusions— that his own generation indeed, under the tutelage of the physical sciences, was fast drifting in the same direction, and that the clouds of pessimism were obscuring for many the brighter horizons of an earlier day. If he had known Henry Adams as intimately as he knew Henry H. Rogers, very likely his eyes would have been opened to many things that would have done him good. As it was he knew only that his speculations ran counter to the formal creed of his middle-class neighbors and friends. To deny the dogmas of the conventional orthodoxy and in the face of a smug optimism to assert a mechanistic pessimism, was an unpleasant business that he would have avoided if he could.

But he couldn't avoid it wholly, and in that fact is to be found the thread that runs through his later life, giving to it such unity and coherence as it possessed. It is this: here was a thoroughly honest mind, that hated all sham and quackery and humbug, and a singularly warm heart, that hated all wrong and cruelty and injustice; and this honest mind and chivalrous heart, deceived and led astray by the mass *mores*, espoused and defended such fragments of ideals, such bits of truth, as he came upon in his solitary brooding, until driven from one stronghold after another he came to doubt the adequacy of all strongholds and took refuge in a black pessimism—God is a malignant being, the universe is a machine; and man is a creature of determinism. It was a fierce and stark reaction from the emotionalism of the fifties—from Beecher's God of love and Whitman's religion of democracy. His earlier loyalty to half-gods had brought him at last to deny all the gods. And so a maimed giant, stumbling and uncertain, he made such way as he could; and his journeyings wrung from him many a fierce comment that his generation did not understand.

When the milk of western humor curdled in his veins, a Mark Twain emerged who was a puzzle to the Gilded Age. A humorist who was a good Republican and business man, the Gilded Age could understand; but a satirist who launched his shafts at sacred things —at evangelical religion, the Republican party, the government at Washington, the damned human race itself—it could not understand. The professional fun-maker had outgrown his audience. Expecting the familiar exaggeration, they accounted his bitterest sally a characteristic whimsy, and laughed when he commented bitterly on "this plodding sad pilgrimage, this pathetic drift between the eternities," or when he exclaimed, "Everything human is pathetic. The secret source of Humor is not joy but sorrow. There is no humor in heaven." But the significant thing is that in the end the tyrannizing *mores* did not conquer, they did not destroy him wholly; but such convictions as he had hewn from puzzling experience, however bleak or repellent they might be, he clung to firmly, desperately, and at last flung them in the face of the Gilded Age that had kept him prisoner.

The slow drift of Mark Twain's thought from humor to satire— it smacks of Philistinism to call it progress with its many false alarums and excursions and its huge frontier wastefulness—is plain enough to anyone who will take the trouble to chart his course. Roughly it falls into definite stages: the swaggering gayety of western youth in *Innocents Abroad* and *Roughing It*—the mood of flush times, down-grade with the brakes off; then a gay plunge into satire in *The Gilded Age;* then the West recalled in middle life—*Tom Sawyer, Life on the Mississippi, Huckleberry Finn*— living over again a youth that is gone; then an excursion into the Middle Ages—*The Prince and the Pauper* and *A Connecticut Yankee in King Arthur's Court*—a romantic flare-up of the democratic passions of the Enlightenment; then the search for the ideal in *Joan of Arc*—the dream of the perfect woman, the Domnei of James Branch Cabell; and finally *The Mysterious Stranger* and *What is Man?*—a fierce satire of disillusion, the cry of an idealist who realizes at last how greatly he has been cheated by his dreams.

That he should have begun by burlesquing life was itself a broad sign of his frontier origins. Since the first crossing of the Allegheny Mountains a swaggering extravagance of speech had been a hallmark of the Westerner. In part this swagger was an unconscious defense-mechanism against the drabness of frontier life; and in part it was the spontaneous expression of new experiences in an untrammeled world, the spirit of wilderness-leveling. Its procreative source would seem to have been the Ohio River where the rough flatboatmen bequeathed the Mike Fink legend to literature; and it expanded in the huge Davy Crockett hoax—a hoax that would have tickled the ribs of Mark Twain had he traced its genesis and progress, as a colossal example of how the damned human race loves to be humbugged. It developed further in Gus Longstreet's *Georgia Scenes* with its grotesque Ransy Sniffle —sorriest of backwoods heroes, too mean-spirited to ruffle like Canebrake Davy; and in Joseph Baldwin's *Flush Times of Alabama and Mississippi*, with its greasy frontier blackguard, Colonel Simon Suggs.

This earliest backwoods humor had been done in realistic colors and bears the impress of authenticity. But the school that succeeded—John Phoenix, Artemus Ward, Petroleum V. Nasby— quickly conventionalized its technique, relying on burlesque, tall lying, distorted spelling, genial philosophy. The picaresque strain was softened and perverted by deliberate human-interest touches— a better case must be made out for the untutored children of nature. It was this humor that Mark Twain inherited, and he enriched it with a wealth dug from his own large and generous nature. An incorrigible idealist, as all great humorists must be, he recreated some of the earlier types, translating Colonel Simon Suggs into Colonel Sellers, and Ransy Sniffle into Huck Finn. It was a glorious transformation, but the result lacked something of the soiled reality of the earlier blackguards. Yet underneath his idealism was a generous deposit of the common mud of life. The spirit of Mike Fink was never far from Mark Twain. It haunted him like an evil genius, refusing to be exorcised by Olivia Clemens, and it found vent in sly literary sprees that begot offspring to be handed about furtively and chuckled over by the sons of Adam; but for the most part it was kept in strict subjection to the proprieties of Elmira and Hartford.

Roughing It and *The Gilded Age* are brilliant complementary pictures of the gaudy frontier spirit that was washing in upon the staid realm of the genteel, to the vast concern of such genteelists as Thomas Bailey Aldrich. The former is a buoyant chronicle of the West of Captain Carver and Wild Bill Hickok, the West of the Pony Express, the Comstock lode, the bad man and the lynch law; a land of young men in red flannel shirts, heavy boots, and six-shooters, who feared neither God nor the devil. Bret Harte in San Francisco first realized the literary possibilities of this picturesque world, and his tales of life in the mining-camps were received with a shout of approval. But Bret Harte had never been a miner. He was not realist enough, nor honest enough, to portray the West in its stark, grotesque reality. He was only a literary middleman who skillfully purveyed such wares as his eastern readers wanted. In consequence he coated his tales with a senti-mental picaresque—pandered to the common taste by discovering nuggets of pure gold in the dregs and outcasts of the mining-camps. But Mark Twain was too honest for that. He had been a part of the flush times and had seen the economic process work itself out. He had seen the grub-stake prospector succeeded by the wild-cat speculator, and him in turn followed by the eastern capitalist. He had seen the mining frontier become a thing of the past in a single decade, with the Comstock lode in the hands of competent exploiters and the pick-and-shovel miners plunging deeper into the mountains to pursue their feverish hopes. From that experience he had learned a lesson he was to carry East with him. "Because we judged that we had learned," he said, "the real secret of success in silver mining, which was, not to mine the silver ourselves by the sweat of our brows and the labor of our hands, but to *sell* the ledges to the dull slaves of toil and let them do the mining." [51]

It was the great lesson of his generation, and thus instructed he proposed to sell his brains in the best market. Exploitation was the royal road to wealth and he was eager to exploit both himself and his fellows. Yet not all of Mark Twain was thus eager. Deep in his heart was another Mark Twain, the artist, the chivalrous lover of justice, the simple child puzzled at life—and this Mark Twain was already plotting treason against the exploiting Mark Twain. For the first time this deeper self got out of hand in *The Gilded Age*. As he contemplated the common scoundrelism at Washington and elsewhere, his anger exuded in scathing satire. He hated the dirty thing, yet he seems never to have realized that such scoundrelism was only the backwash of the spirit of exploitation and that he himself was riding on its waves. With the soap-bubble dreams of Colonel Sellers he dealt lovingly, for he was sketching his own

[51] Vol. I, Chapter XXXIII, p. 237.

origins; the Colonel and the Hawkinses were his own flesh and blood and the Tennessee lands were an old investment about which the family dreams of wealth had been woven for years. He delighted in the Colonel's childlike faith that prosperity only awaited a vote of Congress—with adequate appropriations, of course. He asked no questions about unearned increment; to question that would have been treason to the frontier philosophy. So into Colonel Sellers he put all that was naïve and lovable in the Gilded Age. But Senator Dillworthy was another matter. Hypocrite and corruptionist, he was laying obscene hands on sacred things, betraying his high trust for sordid ends. Mark Twain hated graft—the word had not been coined but the ugly thing was there—and with the innocence of his generation he damned the agent and overlooked the principal. It was not his fault. The economics of history was a closed book to Americans of the seventies, and even Henry Adams in his analysis of the current corruption in his novel *Democracy* was no better than a mole nosing blindly underground.

He had opened another door to his genius and discovered the satirist. There lay the real Mark Twain. But the wares of the satirist were not in demand at the barbecue, so he closed the door and fell to purveying what the public wanted. *Tom Sawyer* was in part a malicious thrust at the Sunday School tale, and in part a whimsical pronouncement of the natural rights of the small boy. But it is in *Huckleberry Finn*—the one great picaresque tale of the frontier—that the western philosophy of Mark Twain, a philosophy that derives straight from the old naturistic school, crops out most sharply. It is a drama of the struggle between the individual and the village *mores*, set in a loose picturesque framework, and exemplifying the familiar thesis that the stuff of life springs strong and wholesome from the great common stock. Huck Finn is a child of nature who has lived close to the simple facts of life, unperverted by the tyrannies of the village that would make a good boy of him. He had got his schooling from the unfenced woods, from the great river that swept past him as he idly fished, from the folk-tales of negroes and poor whites, from queer adventures with Tom Sawyer; and from such experiences he had got a code of natural ethics. Then he found himself on the raft with Jim the runaway nigger, and his little pagan soul felt the stirrings of the problem of right and wrong. The village code and the natural code clashed and the conflict was terrifying. The village code warned him that hell yawned for one who helped a slave escape, and the human code warned him that betrayal was a blackguardly thing. With the fear of hell upon him he wrote to Miss Watson, and then his sense of the kindliness of Jim, the honest humanity under the black skin, rose up in fierce protest.

It was a close place. I took [the letter] up, and held it in my hands. I was a-trembling, because I'd got to decide, forever, betwixt two things, and I knowed it. I studied for a minute, sort of holding my breath, and then says to myself:
"All right, then, I'll *go* to hell"—and tore it up.
It was awful thoughts and awful words, but they was said. And I let them stay said; and never thought no more about reforming.[52]

It was a triumph over the sacred tribal law of conformity—the assertion of the individual will in opposition to society—and it reveals the heart of Mark Twain's philosophy. The rebel Huck is no other than the rebel Mark Twain whose wrath was quick to flame up against the unrighteous customs and laws of caste. If men were only honest realists—that is, if they were men and not credulous fools—how quickly the stables might be cleansed and life become decent and humane. If only the good brains could be segregated and trained in a real "man-factory," the history of civilization might become something the angels need not weep over as they read it. It all comes back to an honest realism that in accepting fact will clear away the superstitious fogs in which men have floundered and suffered hitherto. The one sacred duty laid on every rational being is the duty of rebellion against sham—to deny the divinity of clothes, to thrust out quack kings and priests and lords, to refuse a witless loyalty to things. This creed of the rebel is written all through Mark Twain's later work, edging his satire and lending an Emersonian note to his individualism. In such a passage as this it emerges sharply:

You see my kind of loyalty was loyalty to one's country, not to its institutions or its office-holders. The country is the real thing, the substantial thing, the eternal thing; it is the thing to watch over, and care for, and be loyal to; institutions are extraneous, they are its mere clothing, and clothing can wear out, become ragged, cease to be comfortable, cease to protect the body from winter, disease, death. To be loyal to rags, to shout for rags, to worship rags—that is a loyalty to unreason, it is pure animal; it belongs to monarchy, was invented by monarchy; let monarchy keep it. I was from Connecticut, whose Constitution declares "that all

[52] Chapter 31.

political power is inherent in the people, and all free governments are founded on their authority and instituted for their benefit; and that they have *at all times* an undeniable and indefeasible right to *alter their form of government* in such manner as they may think expedient."

Under that gospel, the citizen who thinks he sees that the commonwealth's political clothes are worn out, and yet holds his peace and does not agitate for a new suit, is disloyal; he is a traitor. That he may be the only one who thinks he sees this decay, does not excuse him; it is his duty to agitate anyway, and it is the duty of others to vote him down if they do not see the matter as he does.[53]

In the Middle Ages clothes-worship had been exalted to a religion, he believed, and he turned with gusto to reply to the aristocratic romanticism of Sir Walter, who, delighting in the picturesque company gathered in the great hall, forgot to penetrate to the *oubliettes*—is not the word commentary enough on the ways of the seigneur?—where nameless wretches were rotting under the walls of the castle. He had small patience with the cult of medievalism that was turning such men as Henry Adams and William Morris back to the Middle Ages as to their lost home. He had the frontier contempt for medieval ways, and for the *ancien régime* that was the last rags of the Middle Ages. The French Revolution had thrust the abomination away forever, and he thanked God for that "ever memorable and blessed Revolution, which swept a thousand years of . . . villainy away in one swift tidal wave of blood." He had no tears for Marie Antoinette. What was the Terror but "a settlement of that hoary debt in the proportion of half a drop of blood for each hogshead of it that had been pressed by slow tortures out of that people in the weary stretch of ten centuries of wrong and shame and misery the like of which was not to be mated but in hell . . . that unspeakably bitter and awful Terror which none of us has been taught to see in its vastness or pity as it deserves."[54] The past that had been consumed in that fierce conflagration had been a brutal, tyrannical, superstitious past, and not till king and priest had been flung out on the dungheap did the people walk their native soil as free men. The whole king business was preposterous to him; with Freneau he cried, "Kings are the choicest curse that man e'er knew." The battle against medievalism had been fought and won and why go maundering back over past battlefields, when other battles await?[55]

[53] *The Connecticut Yankee*, N. Y., 1917, p. 107.
[54] *Ibid.*, Chapter XIII, pp. 105–106.
[55] Cf. Whitman's view, *The Gathering of the Forces*, Vol. II, pp. 284–286.

Mark Twain's passionate republicanism was a product of the Enlightenment as it had passed into the psychology of western Americans, and it retained the militant idealism of Jeffersonian times. It is shot through with the nature philosophy. In *The Prince and the Pauper*, the heir of Offal Court and the heir of the Tudors are both children of nature, endowed with warm hearts, generous sympathies, and clever wits. Put rags on the prince and robes on the pauper and their own kin cannot tell them apart. The latter, indeed, promises to make the better king, for he has suffered the lot of the subject, and not till the prince has put on rags does he come to know his people. It is caste that breeds cruelty and wrong; the brutalities of the English criminal code were deviltries devised by king and nobles to safeguard their stealings. Only when the laws spring from the people are they just. "The world is made wrong," cried the young king when he was brought out of prison to watch the burning at the stake of two women who had befriended him—women whose only crime was that of being Baptists—"the world is made wrong, kings should go to school to their own laws, at times, and so learn mercy." And this great lesson of mercy is exemplified in the acts of the pauper king, who during his brief reign tempers the harshness of the law with a sense of justice learned, like Huck Finn's, from sharp contact with reality.

It is in *A Connecticut Yankee in King Arthur's Court*—a curious medley, half philippic and half farce—that Mark Twain's passion for justice rises to white heat. The book has been grossly misunderstood. It is not an attack on chivalry—at least not primarily; it is rather an attack on thirteen centuries of reputed Christian civilization that under pretense of serving God has enslaved and despoiled the children of God. The keen satire is given point and edge by the long tragic perspective. Thirteen centuries heavy with sorrow and misery and frustrated hopes—a meaningless succession of foolish and futile generations, wandering in fogs of their own brewing, hagridden by superstitions, deceived and exploited by priest and noble, with no will to be free—here is a perspective to correct our callow enthusiasms, our revolutionary hopes! Why indeed should we expect men to possess the will to freedom, seeing that each generation is molded after the likeness of the past and none has been free? There is change, advance and recession, but the story of the generations is no more than a "sad drift between

the eternities," without purpose or meaning. In the brain of the
Connecticut Yankee are secrets hidden from the children of King
Arthur's time—a curious ability to use the forces of nature, some
glimmerings of social justice. But to what purpose have Hartford
and the nineteenth century used their knowledge? It is a world of
slaves still as it was in King Arthur's day. The human animal
cannot lift himself to heaven by his own bootstraps, and heaven
will not stoop to lift him. For a "clammy atmosphere of reverence,
respect, deference," it has substituted smartness, vulgarity, irrev-
erence.

As one slips back and forth between the two worlds the satire
takes on vaster perspectives; it cuts deep into all civilizations, for
all alike are sham, all have issued from the conquest of man's native
intelligence by his superstitions that are too useful to his masters
to be dissipated. Clearly in Mark Twain's philosophy of history
the hopes of the Enlightenment are fading. Passionately dedicated
to the program of the Enlightenment—freedom, individuality,
humanitarianism, democracy—his faith in reason, free will,
progress, was burning low, in presence of the historical record.
The determinism that lurked at the bottom of John Locke's
psychology, unperceived by the French idealists, was revealing
itself to Mark Twain and he was already trimming his sails to the
chill winds blowing from the outer spaces of a mechanistic cosmos.

More immediately of course *A Connecticut Yankee* is an attack on the aristocratic romanticism of Sir Walter. There is little
loitering in the great hall—except to comment on the coarseness
of the knights and ladies—and much poking about in unlovely
secret places where one comes upon a rare collection of human
animals thrust away in the *oubliettes* or pigging together in mean
huts. Few chapters in American literature are so noble in their
saeva indignatio, so beautiful in their stern simplicity, as certain
sketches of the king's progress through his realm—not a royal
progress but a peasant's. There are no tears in them, they go far
beyond that. The scene in the smallpox hut where the wife is glad
her husband and daughters are dead—they are either in heaven or
hell, it makes little difference, for they are no longer in Britain
and so are happy; and the scene of the young mother hanged for
stealing a piece of cloth of an ell's length or so, hanged that property in Britain might be safe—such pictures reveal how far he had
traveled from the days of *Roughing It*. He was no longer a good

Federalist-Whig concerned about exploitation and the safeguards of property. Although he voted the Republican ticket he made merry over the tariff [56] and he frankly hated the dominant Republican property-consciousness. Like Lincoln he was for the man rather than the dollar when the rights of the two clashed. In these later years he was steadily drifting to the left, on the side of the social underling, sympathetic with those who do the work of the world. "He never went so far in socialism, as I have gone," said Howells, "if he went that way at all . . . but from the first he had a luminous vision of organized labor as the only present help for workingmen. . . . There was a time when I was afraid that his eyes were a little holden from the truth; but in the very last talk I heard from him I found that I was wrong, and that this great humorist was as great a humanist as ever." [57]

It is good for an American to read *A Connecticut Yankee*—and *Joan of Arc* as well; for in them is a flame that sears and shrivels the mean property-consciousness which lays a blight on every civilization. In the peasant girl of Domrémy, the rapt mystic led by her Voices, Mark Twain found his ideal, the lily that bloomed out of the muck of medieval times; and as he contemplated her life and work he was lifted to the plane of worship. She had waged heroic warfare against the embattled lies and shams and treacheries of a sordid age, and that she should have died at the stake was inevitable. What other reward was to be expected from bishops and kings and suchlike spawn of the devil? Not till the people grow to manhood can any savior help them, and in that day they will need no savior but themselves. The Sieur Louis de Conte struggles with the idea confusedly.

I believe that some day it will be found out that peasants are people. Yes, beings in a great many respects like ourselves. And I believe that some day *they* will find this out, too—and then! Well, then I think they will rise up and demand to be regarded as a part of the race, and that by consequence there will be trouble. Whenever one sees in a book or in a king's proclamation those words 'the nation,' they bring before us the upper classes; only those; we know no other 'nation;' for us and the kings no other 'nation' exists. But from the day I saw old D'Arc the peasant acting and feeling just as I should have acted and felt myself, I have carried the conviction in my heart that our peasants are not merely animals, beasts of burden put here by the good God to produce food and comfort for the 'nation,' but something more and better. You look incredulous.

[56] See Chapter 33.   [57] W. D. Howells, *My Mark Twain*, p. 43.

Well, that is your training; it is the training of everybody; but as for me, I thank that incident for giving me a better light, and I have never forgotten it.[58]

No Bayard ever did his devoir more knightly to his lady than Mark Twain to Joan, finding in the noble drama of her life the romance he had not found at Arthur's court. The knights of the Round Table were "but ghosts fighting in the fog," but Jeanne D'Arc was human and lovable and divine. And then the outlet through which his idealism had found release slowly closed in, and he was left alone with his comfortless speculations. What profits it to rail at the damned human race when man has about as much chance for happiness as a blind puppy in a sack? The bitter lot of humanity is due not to institutions alone or chiefly, it is a part of the mad plan of a bleak mechanical universe. For Mark Twain the solid earth was dissolving, leaving only a rack behind. It is futile to lament. A sympathetic heart, indeed, is the last and bitterest irony—for why weep over an evil exhalation! "*Life itself is only a vision, a dream . . . Nothing exists save empty space—and you.*"

In a little while you will be alone in shoreless space, to wander its limitless solitudes without friend or comrade forever—for you will remain a *thought*, the only existent thought, and by your nature inextinguishable, indestructible. But I, your poor servant, have revealed you to yourself and set you free. Dream other dreams, and better. Strange, indeed, that you should not have suspected that your universe and its contents were only dreams, visions, fiction! Strange, because they are so frankly and hysterically insane—like all dreams . . . the silly creations of an imagination that is not conscious of its freaks—in a word that they are a dream, and you the maker of it. . . .[59]

So, like Cabell, Mark Twain asserts that man must build within and by letting his dreams flow out create for himself such shelter as he can against the chill of the eternal void. A flea on the epidermis of earth, nevertheless he is thought and thought is deathless. To such a conclusion did the buoyant youth of *Roughing It* arrive in the dun twilight years. *The Mysterious Stranger* is only *Tom Sawyer* retold in the midnight of his disillusion.

What an ending for a child of the Gilded Age! In his youth a complete frontiersman, with vast potential wealth within him, he hewed and hacked at his genius, working the easiest veins,

<hr/>

[58] *Joan of Arc*, Chapter 37, p. 290.
[59] *The Mysterious Stranger*, p. 151.

exploiting the most accessible resources, wasting much to cash in on a little. And when in the end the fool's gold turned to ashes in his mouth, as a frontiersman still he pursued his way alone, a solitary pioneer exploring the universe, seeking a homestead in an ironical cosmos, until overwhelmed by the intolerable solitude he made mock at all the gods. What a commentary on the Gilded Age!

CHAPTER III

CHANGING THEORY

UNLIKE as were Thomas Bailey Aldrich, Walt Whitman, and Mark Twain, they belonged equally to an America that was passing. In consequence of the silent drift towards consolidation new philosophies were preparing that were to rephrase the familiar American ideals and adapt current political and economic theory to the needs of the new order. For a decade or more the significance of that drift was obscured by the last great wave of decentralization that swept across the prairie commonwealths; but when the frontier had been pushed to the Pacific Northwest and the free lands had passed into private ownership, the movement of consolidation gathered momentum swiftly. Primarily economic in its origins, it went forward on even foot with the industrial revolution. The vast increase in population, the unprofitable expansion of agriculture, the augmenting resources of liquid capital, the new potentialities revealed by industrialism, were all engaged in the work of transforming a scattered agricultural people into an urbanized industrial people.

And then came the railways to hasten a movement that was implicit in the nature of things. Effective nationality in America issued more immediately from fluid communication than perhaps any other cause.. A depressing spirit of isolation—of provincial aloofness—had lain like a heavy weight on the colonial mind. The barriers of distance were made formidable by a rugged untamed country, and to open up free communication was an arduous undertaking. Yet easy communication must be provided if economic development were to go forward. In the early years of the nineteenth century vast plans and great outlays of money went into the work of linking the sundered portions of the country by a system of waterways. The Erie canal, the great lakes, the Ohio and the Mississippi, were creating their own America, picturesque and individual, when the process of differentiation was rudely broken across by the iron rails that ran East and West, disregarding natural barriers and breaking down traditional frontiers. It was the railways that tied the continent effectively together, providing the needed transportation to make possible a national economic system. With the laying of the Union Pacific rails in the late sixties the destiny of America as a self-sufficient economic unity was fixed. Henceforth for an indeterminate period the drift of tendency would be from the outlying frontiers to industrial centers, and with that drift would come far-reaching changes in the daily routine of life. The machine would reach into the remotest villages to disrupt the traditional domestic economy, and the division of labor would substitute for the versatile frontiersman the specialized factory-hand. A new urban psychology would displace the older agrarian, and with the new psychology would come other philosophies in response to the changing realities.

I

WINDS OF ECONOMIC THEORY

So profound a revolution could not fail to dislocate the foundations of all traditional schools of thought. Economic and political theory were both thrown out of their earlier beds to flow in new channels. By force of gravitation the main stream of economic theory—like the main stream of political theory—poured into the broadening channels of capitalism, and only the lesser vagrant currents followed the old channels of agrarianism or the new channels of proletarianism. There was much speculation on the disturbing phenomena of the great change, and current economic theory was slow to settle into the conformities of a school. It divided sharply, not only between the advocates of capitalism and agrarianism, but between those who accepted the classical English theory and those who believed that economic conditions in America warranted an independent American school. The first group of professional economists—Henry C. Carey, Francis A. Walker, David A. Wells—made its appearance, and a very considerable group of amateurs—free-lance economists and fireside theorists—contributed to the speculation of the times in the measure of their intelligence. These latter have received scant attention, since the battle went against them; nevertheless they do not deserve to be forgotten, for most often they were an expression of the social conscience of the times—a homely protest against the exploitation of farmer and workingman by the rising capitalism.

But because they essayed to turn the course of "manifest destiny" they were ignored or roughly ridden down, and only one of them— Henry George—is still widely influential.

In the primitive early days of America economic theory had been a simple homespun product, woven on fireside looms, and following simple domestic patterns. With the rise of industrialism it passed into the keeping of stockbrokers and textile manufacturers and retail merchants who were looked upon as authoritative expounders of the new science of wealth. In his *Elements of Political Economy*, first published in 1837 and for forty years a standard textbook in American colleges, Francis Wayland accepted this view and offered an apology for treating of the subject at all. "It may possibly be urged," he said, "that the Author, having had no experience in mercantile business, should have left this subject to be treated of by practical men." In the days of Henry Clay this view established itself in the halls of Congress, where politicians who had never heard of Ricardo were on profitably intimate terms with Nick Biddle, and respected the interests of influential constituents far more than the principles of Manchesterism. With the appearance of professional economists the breach between economic theory and legislative votes widened to a chasm. Ignored by the politicians except in so far as their views fell in with the current paternalism, the economists retreated to the quiet of the schools and there spun their webs quite harmlessly. Youthful undergraduates were fed on a modified English classical theory in which the pessimism of Ricardo and Malthus, bred of the bitter dislocations of English industrial life, was diluted with an optimism more suited to the temper of the new world.

The academic economists, it must be confessed, were in an unhappy position, not unlike that of the earlier Calvinists. They lived as remote from the realities of life as did those old ministers. Trained in the orthodox English school they felt bound to defend *laissez faire;* yet as members of universities dependent on wealthy patrons they could not well offend powerful interests that wanted none of their free-trade theory. On the whole they stuck pretty manfully to their guns, and from Wayland to Sumner they upheld the abstract principle of free competition; but what they could do in other ways to appease the wrath of the protectionists they did heartily, and the steady rapprochement of academic economic theory and capitalism was foreordained in the nature of things academic. Agrarian and proletarian economics were granted no hearing in the colleges. Other schools than the English classical were not countenanced, Henry George was ridiculed and the left-wing European economists—great thinkers like Sismondi, Saint-Simon, Louis Blanc, Bastiat, Proudhon, Engels, and Karl Marx—were pretty much ignored by professors of economics in the America of the Gilded Age. Something of the intellectual sterility of the genteel tradition descended upon our academic economists; yet amongst them were vigorous and capable minds that must not be overlooked.

I

HENRY C. CAREY

Henry C. Carey, son of the vigorous Irish Republican, Matthew Carey, who made *The American Museum* one of the ablest of the eighteenth-century American magazines, may perhaps be justly called our first professional economist. The eighty-six years of his life were filled with enormous labors in the twin fields of economics and sociology. He did his own thinking from a basis of facts that he was at great pains to gather and tabulate, and his intellectual unfolding followed naturally the current material development of the mid-century. His statistics, of which he was excessively fond, no doubt were as unreliable as most statistics that economists love to dabble in, and like other purveyors of columned figures and impressive charts he certainly leaned too heavily on his knotty staff; but unlike academic economists such as Francis Wayland he tried to keep his thinking in contact with reality and in consequence his studies possess a solidity that is still impressive.

Although his father had early been interested in Hamilton's national system and for a time was president of a Philadelphia society concerned in furthering a protective tariff—for which the great German protectionist List published a number of letters in 1827—Carey began as a follower of the classical school, and in the thirties he published a treatise on political economy that expounded the Manchester doctrine of free-trade. But under the stirring leadership of Henry Clay the American System was making headway fast, and the facts of American expansion impressed him as earlier they had impressed the young List on his visit here. Turning statistician, he soon discovered, as he believed, certain fallacies in the English classical school, and he proceeded to examine afresh the Ricardian theory of rent. (The change came in 1848.) According to this most celebrated of all economic doctrines rent is measured by the difference in productivity between the best land, which is settled first, and the poorest, which social need later brings under cultivation; and hence in every growing community the increment of rent constantly increases at the expense of both labor and capital. But in the America which Carey was acquainted with, and where the story of social development was being swiftly recapitulated, the facts seemed to him to prove quite otherwise. Here the poorer lands were settled first, because their physical condition made them more easily available, and only later, when social pressure increased and larger means were available, were the rich bottom-lands cleared and the marshes drained.

As a result of his narrow interpretation of Ricardo's doctrine of social fertility, Carey lost faith in the Ricardian theory and turned frankly to the American scene to discover, if possible, a more adequate explanation. Soon the seeds of his intense nationalism were bearing their fruit. An inherited dislike of England led him to fear its industrial preëminence, and he abandoned the ideal of an international division of labor for the ideal of independent nationality, with America developing its individuality through the exploitation of its own resources. Free-trade, he came to believe, is international, it results in establishing a "single factory for the whole world, whither all the raw produce has to be sent whatever be the cost of transport"; whereas any society waxes individual and strong in the measure that it develops variety of employment with its demand for mutual help and service. Only through such associations can man develop his capacities and further his mastery of nature. His patriotism thus became involved in his economics and for years he waged a relentless warfare against Manchesterism. Not only were the English doctrines false to American fact, he pointed out, but they were vicious Tory doctrines which if followed here would keep America poor for the benefit of England. The great idea which came finally to dominate his thinking is suggested by the title of a pamphlet, written in 1852, *The Harmony of Interests: Agricultural, Manufacturing, and Commercial*—a work that suggests Frédéric Bastiat's *Les harmonies économiques*, published in 1850, and influenced by Carey's earlier speculations.[1] It was an age much given to discovering harmonies and Carey was

---

[1] See Gide and Rist, *A History of Economic Doctrines*, pp. 282–284, 327–331.

not behindhand in the business. In the introduction he traced the ills of contemporary economic life to the Manchester theories of rent and population—theories which had thrown their black shadows over English Parliamentary programs of relief and perverted the normal unfolding of western civilization. In conse- · quence the "tendency of the whole British system of political economy is the production of discord among nations."[2]

In the background of Carey's mind was a Physiocratic dislike of the sterile middleman which sharpened his antagonism to an international division of labor, and a sensitive social conscience that was concerned at the ruthless exploitation of English mill-hands. An ardent believer in natural liberty and convinced of its beneficence, he restricted economic freedom within national boundaries. The harmony of interests is local and not international—the tying together of the several parts of the whole. Beyond the national boundaries it ceases. The pessimism of the English school with its iron law of wages and its Malthusian law of population was harshly repugnant to his buoyant optimism. From these vicious roots, he was convinced, sprang the principle of isolation and differentiation—that producer and consumer must live apart, with the corollary that the poor must seek new lands in far countries to supply the places of those from which they have been thrust, there to produce agricultural staples to exchange for the manufactured goods produced in thickly settled countries—a principle that taxes both producer and consumer in the exact measure of transportation tolls, and benefits exclusively the sterile middleman. Applied to America the policy of free-trade must keep this country dependent upon England—keep it agricultural for the benefit of British merchants; and the program that Carey outlined, the complete sufficiency of which he never doubted, was a return to the policy of Adam Smith, to that "general harmony of interests" that must result from bringing the farmer and artisan into neighborhood communities, fashioning the raw materials where they are produced and consuming the farmer's produce where it is grown. Adam Smith "saw well," says Carey, "that when men came thus together, there arose a general harmony of interests, each profiting his neighbor, and profiting by that neighbor's success, whereas the tendency of commercial centralization was toward poverty and discord, abroad and at home."[3]

[2] *Miscellaneous Works*, Preface to *Harmony of Interests*.   [3] *Ibid.*

To his death in 1879 Carey was the most distinguished as he had been the most tireless advocate of a system of protection for American manufactures. He was one of the most pugnacious pamphleteers of a pugnacious generation.[4] He was a co-worker with Horace Greeley in the labor of convincing a suspicious people of the common benefits to be got from a subsidy to a class; and their joint influence gave respectability and popularity to the appeals of business men and politicians. Between 1849 and 1857 he "was the virtual editor of the *New York Tribune*" in all matters regarding protection. His chief antagonist in the long struggle was William Cullen Bryant and the *Evening Post;* and he made frequent appeal to Bryant to meet him in a pamphlet debate that should bring before the public both sides of the great question of protectionism. Bryant's refusal did not lessen his ardor, and in successive pamphlets he laid before the American people a well-rounded argument for tariff subsidies that ranks him in the history of economic thought with Friedrich List, the great German apostle of a nationalist economic system. American manufacturers owe a heavy debt to Henry Carey.

In these early years of industrialism the manufacturer was still dependent on the banker, and industrial development was held back, Carey came to believe, by a false financial policy imposed on the county by the bankers. From his boundless enthusiasm for the ideal of a national economy sprang likewise his unorthodox views on money that so greatly annoyed his fellow economists. Individual in his thinking on this as on other subjects, he espoused theories that to dogmatic bullionists like David A. Wells seemed incendiary at a time (during the post-war years) when so many Americans were bitten with "money heresies." On this theme his patriotism and his democratic sympathies ran together. He was opposed to the bullion system because it struck at nationalism. An English system, devised by Lombard Street, did not answer the needs of America. The price of gold is established in a world market and the flow of bullion is always toward the great centers already glutted with money. To throw the money of the world into a common pool was to subject the money of poorer and remoter countries to the control of the great financial capitals. Free-trade and the gold standard were the twin weapons forged by England for world-

---

[4] All told he published at his own print-shop some 3000 pages of pamphlet material of his own writing.

wide economic conquest, and for America to adopt a financial policy that held her subject to Lombard Street, seemed to Carey the height of folly. Gold follows the balance of trade, and until America had built up an adequate domestic economy her specie would continue to drain off, leaving too scanty a supply to do the necessary work of society.

The solution, he believed, lay in the creation of an independent national currency; and an efficient national currency, he held with Bishop Berkeley, was one that was non-exportable, that remained at home to do the day's work instead of gadding about. To provide such a medium of exchange he proposed a currency founded on the national credit—a "national system," he argued, "based entirely on the credit of the government with the people, and not liable to interference from abroad." [5] It was on such grounds that Carey supported the greenback issues and favored the remonetization of silver. The ideal of "societary circulation," he pointed out, was credit—"that great step towards civilization which consists in substituting *letters of credit* for material money"; and because "the steady and regular use of the *letter of credit* known to the world as the 'greenback,' or that other known as the 'national bank note,'" [6] tended to wean the minds of men from dependence on specie, he was warm in their favor.

With a sound national system, let foreigners take our gold for whatever balance of trade they can impose upon us, having no use among ourselves for any coin money except what we can retain under a wholesome foreign commerce.

What we most need today is the establishment of that monetary independence which results from maintaining absolute command over the machinery of exchange used within our borders, leaving to the gold dollar the performance of its duty of arranging for the settlement of balances throughout the world.[7]

Carey's insistence on a plentiful supply of money laid him under the charge of being an advocate of "cheap money," and therefore one of those wicked persons known as "inflationists." The charge in the main was true. He was pungent in his contrast between the prosperity of war times when an abundant currency released all the energies of the American people, and the stagnation that

[5] *Contraction or Expansion? Repudiation or Resumption? Letters to the Hon. Hugh M'Culloch, Secretary of the Treasury*, Philadelphia, 1866, p. 20.
[6] *Ibid.*, p. 22.
[7] Quoted in W. Elder, *Memoir of Henry C. Carey*, p. 13 (Philadelphia, 1880. With bibliography).

followed upon contraction. "Cheap money—low interest—enabled our working men to prosper," whereas dear money—high interest—was bringing distress and hardship. Every reduction in the amount of currency decreases the purchasing power of the people, and slows down the circulatory system. The attempt to retire the greenbacks he regarded as a class attack on the common welfare of the country. "To that end the greenback, everywhere claimed as the people's money, has by those in high places been denounced, small as is the quantity, when compared with the real need for it." [8] Paper money is "democratic in its tendencies," passing from hand to hand and never seeking a bank vault to hide in.

A war upon what is called "paper money" is . . . a war upon the poor in favor of the rich; and that the war being made upon it has precisely that effect is proved by the fact, that the western farmer is now being so impoverished by reason of such a reduction in the price of corn and oats that the former is being used as fuel, while the latter sold at 8 cents a bushel, [while] houses and lots in the neighborhood of Wall Street [are] commanding . . . prices such as had never before been heard of.[9]

Considering Carey's reputation as an economist and his wide influence, such doctrine, in the eyes of all "sound-money men," was distinctly pernicious. He was giving aid and comfort to the apostles of inflation and repudiation, and he suffered many a sharp attack. But that would not deter a warrior grown gray in battle, and in the very last year of his life he fell upon the bullion theory with the ardor of a young man. He would not suffer the bankers to go unrebuked in their mad attack on the prosperity of the country; he would not be silent while a policy of contraction, that so early as 1866 had reduced the per capita circulation to $12.50— according to his statistics—was still in full swing after the disastrous lesson of 1873. He had much in common with Peter Cooper, who in 1876 took up the battle against Wall Street for a "democratic" monetary system. The blood of the two old men, both born in the last decade of the eighteenth century, had not grown cold or sluggish with long years, but responded ardently to the great cause of democracy that had inspired their youth. That Carey's national system was a house divided against itself—that industry and finance were engaged in a mortal combat for supremacy—he

[8] *Shall We have Peace? Letters to President-elect Grant*, p. 39.
[9] *Contraction or Expansion? etc.*, p. 20.

probably never quite realized. He was concerned that America should be free to create and enjoy the wealth that lay in the potentialities of the continent, and to that end he would have money serve industry, and not industry money.

2

FRANCIS A. WALKER

The social conscience of Carey was colored with an optimism that was the spontaneous expression of a generation that set no limits to the beneficent development of American industrialism. No storm-clouds had yet gathered on the horizon; no hostile systems challenged the sufficiency of capitalism. But a change was at hand. By the end of the seventies the complacency of the Gilded Age was disturbed by the rise of pestilent heresies in the shape of new economic dogmas. The surplus-value theory of Marx and the unearned-increment theory of Henry George were spreading widely through America, to the unsettlement of susceptible minds; and the Knights of Labor were preparing to launch a general attack against the whole system of capitalistic exploitation. Carey had sufficed the wants of his simpler day, but there was need of a new champion to wield the sword of pure Ricardian doctrine against these later heresies.

Francis A. Walker, son of the economist Amasa Walker, Brigadier General in the Civil War, Professor at Sheffield Scientific School and later President of the Massachusetts Institute of Technology, was to be the self-appointed champion of industrialism, the official economist of the Gilded Age, and forerunner of a long line of academic purveyors of economic dogma. As the author of a college textbook that superseded Francis Wayland's naïve *Elements of Political Economy*—a work that had served innumerable college generations as a quarry of economic doctrine— he elaborated a complete system of economics with a geniality that went far to popularize the "dismal science" with vast numbers of undergraduates; and as an authoritative apologist for entrepreneur profits he rendered a service to capitalism that quite erased his little Ricardian peccadillo of free-trade prejudice. There runs through his solid pages the confident optimism of his generation— an optimism that discovers in the heresies of socialism and single-tax the only storm-clouds on the fair American horizons. He saw no reason to question the ultimate good of industrialism, or to fear any deep-seated clash between labor and capital. He carried water easily on both shoulders, for he was so fortunate as to have worked out to his complete satisfaction, a magic economic formula that should return both to master and workman their just shares of the total production. In the light of his exegesis there could be no Marxian struggle of the classes. The captain of industry must no longer be regarded with sour aspect as a parasite upon labor, but as a fellow worker, the creator of those profits which are not subtracted for his benefit from the portion of labor. From Ricardo to Marx the economists had been barking up the wrong tree in their analysis of the rewards of the entrepreneur.

The classical school of the Gilded Age was in like position with the eighteenth-century Calvinists; they must either abandon their dogmas or reinterpret them to meet current needs. Walker was too good a Ricardian to abandon them, so he proposed to reinterpret them. The urgent problems to which he addressed himself were the sources of profits and of wages; and the examination of those problems led him to his theory of the function of the entrepreneur and to a rejection of the classical wage-fund theory. He refused to discard his suit of Ricardian clothes as Carey had done. They could never go out of style, he believed, so long as honest thinking was respected. He accepted most of the Ricardian dogmas without question. "Capital," he asserted soberly, "arises solely from saving. It stands always for self-denial and abstinence," and interest is the "reward of abstinence." But one important dogma, the classical wage-fund theory, he insisted on stripping away. He was too genial an optimist to rest content with the bleak conception that the margin of subsistence circumscribes the rewards of labor, and too enlightened an apologist of industrialism to assert that "profits are the leavings of wages." He could not hope to erect a theory suitable to the Gilded Age on such skimpy hypotheses, and he scourged them from the temple of economic law. Wages, to be sure, are the leavings after rent, interest, and profits have been deducted from the total production; but vast and dangerous misconceptions have arisen in regard to the portions that accrue to these several partners, and in particular mischievous perversions touching the share of profits. This was the crux of the problem of distribution and until the nature of profits should be determined the question of wages would remain to befuddle weak heads.

The heart of Walker's doctrine, therefore, is his theory of profits. He proposed to show that according to the true law of profits this flexible increment is never a moiety wrested from labor, but an additional earning of management that justly accrues to him who creates it. The doctrine from which he deduced his theory of the entrepreneur was the Ricardian theory of rent. On this point Walker was the most loyal of Ricardians, and he violently attacked Carey for repudiating the classical dogma. In a word "Ricardo's doctrine can no more be impugned than the sun in the heaven," he asserted, "and those who mouth at it simply show that they do not know what it was Ricardo taught." [10] What was needed was to understand its wide implications rather than to seek to destroy it— to trace in all its reaches the doctrine of fertility and discover how in other spheres than land the difference between fertile and unfertile measures the return upon economic endeavor. For the great doctrine of fertility, Walker pointed out, following Mill, is capable of expansion to cover wider fields than rent; it applies equally to management and labor; it broadens out into a comprehensive principle that exactly measures the most bitterly disputed of the several increments, the increment of profits.

This theory of fertility, introduced into the law of distribution, is Walker's most interesting contribution to economic speculation. By it he supplemented the trinity of land, capital, and labor—or in terms of distribution, of rent, interest, and wages—with a new entity—management and the earnings of management. The argument is highly ingenious. Assuming a no-profits employer at the lowest scale of the entrepreneur system, by analogy from the Ricardian no-rent grade of land, he asserted that similarly "profits are measured upwards from the level of the no-profits class of employers," and hence "it appears that the gains of the employer are not taken from the earnings of the laboring class, but measure the difference in production between the commonplace or bad, and the able, and shrewd, and strong management of business." [11] Profits, then, are an added increment of management, secured by foresight and business skill, the fruit of managerial fertility; and since they flow solely from the entrepreneur they belong to him alone and no portion may be justly claimed for rent, interest, or wages. The complete theory he states thus:

[10] *Land and its Rent*, p. 108.
[11] *Political Economy*, pp. 242, 348.

Under free and full competition, the successful employers of labour would earn a remuneration which would be exactly measured, in the case of each man, by the amount of wealth which he could produce, with a given application of labour and capital, over and above what would be produced by employers of the lowest industrial, or no-profits, grade, making use of the same amounts of labour and capital, just as rent measures the surplus of the produce of the better lands over and above what would be produced by the same application of labour and capital to the least productive lands which contribute to the supply of the market, lands which themselves bear no rent.[12]

It is a persuasive argument of which Walker was vastly proud. The germ of it later historians of economic thought have traced to Senior and John Stuart Mill, who had suggested the idea of "differential rent," or "rent of ability," which is the reward of "all peculiar advantages of extraordinary qualities of body and mind." [13] From whatever source it issued, the usefulness of such doctrine in the days of an expanding industrialism, and the ends it might serve in counteracting proletarian philosophies, are too evident to need comment. The Marxian dogma of surplus value—that profits are stealings from wages—was certainly calculated to breed dissatisfaction in weak proletarian heads. Marx was a good Ricardian in his major postulates and the Ricardians had failed to analyze adequately the true sources of profits; because of such failure the classical school had underestimated the social beneficence of the capitalistic system. Chained to the iron law of wages the school had been forced to envisage a bleak future with labor kept always at the margin of subsistence. From this pessimism Walker proposed to rid economic theory, by showing that entrepreneur profits augment the wage fund and hence that the entrepreneur is the benefactor rather than the exploiter of labor. With his business skill the captain of industry, like the inventor of a new machine, lays open new sources of wealth for all, and if he gains much for himself he gives more to society; for every improvement in business methods accrues in the end to society as a whole, for the new technique soon becomes a common possession.

The validity of Walker's theory of profits does not concern us here; it is a matter for economists to determine. To one who is under the spell of no doctrinaire system the theory seems some-

[12] *Quarterly Journal of Economics*, April, 1887. Quoted in Gide and Rist, *A History of Economic Doctrine*, p. 551.
[13] *Ibid.*, p. 549.

what too neat with its assumption of "free and full competition";[14] and in its conscious purpose to glorify the captain of industry it is freighted rather too heavily with the spirit of the Gilded Age. It not only throws the door wide to exploitation but it invites everybody to the feast. Yet the work of the apologist was only half done. Having established to his satisfaction the law of profits, Walker was prepared to take equally high ground in determining the increment that falls to labor. To glorify profits and at the same time defend the pessimism of the wage-fund theory, would have been foolish tactics in presence of the Marxian surplus-value theory; proletarian discontent must be dealt with and Walker was prepared to deal with it. Having ascertained exactly the several increments due to rent, interest, and profits—which in his system are rigidly determined by economic law—he confidently assigned all the residual increment to wages. Labor not only gets all it earns, he argued, but far more, since what does not fall to the just shares of the other partners falls to it—that is the "whole remaining body of wealth." If it be recalled that the total social fund of inventions, machinery, trade processes, systems of transportation, business methods, are alike in the service of all employers—the no-profit entrepreneur equally with the high-profit—it follows that the individual employer can derive from such social wealth no modicum of profit above and beyond what his individual fertility has produced. Where then can the income from such social fund flow except to wages? "Every invention in mechanics, every discovery in the chemical art, no matter by whom made, inures directly and immediately" to the benefit of labor.[15] This, to be sure, on the hypothesis of "full and free competition," which may be interfered with by various means but which in the long run prevails. How else shall one explain the constant rise in the wage-scale that has marked the Industrial Revolution and that has gone hand in hand with vast profits to the entrepreneur class?

It was a robust optimism that could lay down the theory that labor is "the residual claimant to the product of industry." Although Walker prided himself on his discovery, it seems to have made slight impression on later economic thought. Like too many members of the classical school the apologist of the Gilded Age

---

[14] For a critical examination see Gide and Rist, *A History of Economic Doctrine,* pp. 551–558.
[15] *Political Economy,* pp. 251–258.

failed to keep his feet on the plebeian earth; and his conclusions suggest how great mischief *a priori* reasoning may work in the speculations of academic gentlemen. A moderate dash of realism might have lessened his buoyant optimism; but Walker was too warm an admirer of capitalism, too eager to assert the beneficence of industrialism, to inquire curiously into the everyday facts of current exploitation. As a realistic statistician he was far inferior to Carey. But why demand a plodding realism of the economist when all America was romantic? If the economic theory of General Walker was a pleasant blend of Ricardo and Colonel Sellers, would it not hit the taste of the age to a nicety? Its sturdy optimism was a soothing antidote to the Jeremiads of the Marxians and the shrill demands of the single-taxers. The Gold Coast of America looked to its official economists for a confutation of all economic heresies, and who was so well equipped for that business as a doughty Colonel Sellers armed with a sharp Ricardian sword?

In this brisk work Walker engaged with gusto. In his onslaught upon Marx and Henry George he was untroubled by doubt. He first demolished the structure of their theory and then impugned their honesty. His condemnation of single-tax is bold and sweeping. There is a bitter asperity in his denunciation of the economic heresies of *Progress and Poverty*, and he dismisses the proposal to tax unearned increment with the comment, "Every honest man will resent such a proposition as an insult."[16] His discussion of the economics of the question is only casual and he hastens back to the safe haven of Ricardian doctrine.[17] In his commentary on the Knights of Labor he is somewhat vindictive for a well-bred gentleman. He charges the syndicalistic attack on the profits system to immigrant foreigners, asserts that the law of profit fertility is an insuperable obstacle to any proletarian control of industry, and finally damns it as un-American. The honest, native American "knows that for himself and his children the way is open clear to the top"; his "spirit is that of civility, reciprocity and fair play"; and he concludes:

Had it been left to our native population alone, not one of those violent and reckless attacks upon production and transportation, which have, within the past two or three years, shocked the whole industrial system and have come near to produce a general crisis of trade, would ever have taken place.[18]

[16] *Land and its Rent*, Preface, p. vi.   [17] *Ibid.*, pp. 181–182.
[18] *Political Economy*, p. 394.

Yet in spite of his genial optimism he discovered specks on the fair picture of society. To the Ricardian logic the stupidity of men is a constant irritant; if only men were rational the path of progress would be so much easier! After economic law has been demonstrated with the finality of a Euclidian theorem, it is disconcerting to see how the multitude will not be reasoned with, but persist in following after the last false prophet who cries in the market-place. The clamor raised by single-tax was especially annoying. "That such an argument," he remarked a bit testily, "should for a moment have imposed upon anybody, is enough to give one a new conception of the intellectual capabilities of mankind." [19] Fortunate it is for society, he concludes, that while man proposes, economic law disposes. False prophets will have their little day, but from their secure watch-tower the Ricardians calmly look out upon a world of which they alone hold the key.*

II

THE CONSCRIPTION OF POLITICAL THEORY

When the social fabric is being torn rudely across by a changing economics, political theory and practice will suffer from the attendant confusions. The America of the Gilded Age accounted itself a democracy and was outwardly content to make use of the familiar democratic machinery; but until it was determined whether majority or minority rule should prevail, whether the well-being of the many or the property of the few should be the chief object of government, there would be no serious effort to create a political state for adequate social control. In the meantime the old individualisms would range the land seeking what they might devour, and the common attitude toward the political state would remain one of good-natured contempt. A shambling government, corrupt and incompetent, awakened no man's hope or pride, and amidst the slovenly anarchisms of the times, with a crude exploitation in the saddle, the state would be pretty much ignored except when its services might prove useful to such exploitation. The plutocracy would oppose the erection of a vigorous state until such time as it felt strong enough to control its activities. The principle of the majority-will held grave potentialities that

[19] *Ibid.*, p. 433.
* In his original plan Professor Parrington included a third subsection on W. G. Sumner, but evidently decided against its inclusion.—*Publisher*.

might threaten the eventual mastership of wealth, and until the
plutocracy had created its strongholds within the framework of
the democracy it would bitterly oppose any extension of democratic
control.

Broadly two great movements were going forward side by side
in the unconscious drift of political tendency—the democratic and
the plutocratic. The former, drawn chiefly from agrarian and
labor elements with a considerable following of the middle and
professional classes, was determined to carry forward and supplement the Jacksonian movement. It was honestly concerned for
the development of the democratic principle. It would purify
government by the application of civil service reform, it would
steadily enlarge the bounds of social control of economic forces,
and it would strengthen the political state to enable it to cope with
corporate wealth and constrain the ambitions of the plutocracy
into conformity with democratic ends. To such a democratic
program the plutocracy was necessarily opposed. It professed the
warmest loyalty to the abstract principle of democracy while
bending every energy to emasculate effective democratic control.
The problem confronting it was the familiar Federalistic problem—
how to protect the minority from the majority and set property
interests above human interests; but the problem had been immensely complicated by the strategic advances made by democracy. The democratic principle could not be easily thrust aside,
it must be undermined. And so while awaiting the time when it
should be strong enough to set up boldly its mastery of society,
plutocracy took refuge in two principles, the superman theory
and the *laissez-faire* theory, both of which it asserted to be democratic, the very essence of democracy. The former was "The public
be damned" theory, which held that the economic leaders of society must be left free to manage their properties as they saw fit;
and the latter was the familiar doctrine of individual initiative,
that looked with suspicion on any interference by the political
state with economic activity. If a bureaucracy may stick its nose
into the citizen's private affairs what becomes of individual liberty?

But the plutocracy was building its real defenses elsewhere.
Shrewdly aware of the potentialities of a Constitution that had
been designed for the protection of property interests, it followed
two main lines of development: it furthered the popular develop-

ment of a cult of the Constitution by praising the excellence of a system of checks and balances, and spreading the view that to tamper with any provisions of the instrument was little short of sacrilege; and at the same time it bent every energy to extend the range of judicial prerogative and bring the legislative branch under control of the judiciary. It sought extra-constitutional indulgences that were dispensed by the courts in the name of the police power. The way had been prepared by Marbury vs. Madison and Dred Scott vs. Sanford, and during the Gilded Age a broad path to judicial control was opened by the elaboration of the "due process of law" principle discovered in the fourteenth amendment. With the development of the plutocracy the extension of the doctrine of judicial review went forward rapidly, providing an impregnable defense for property interests that promised ill for the principle of democratic control in the interests of the common well-being. The democracy was being driven from the inner keep of the castle.

While the real struggle was thus going on in the court-room, with the outcome in the hands of the judges, political speculation was playing havoc with certain of our oldest and most cherished doctrines. Pursuing the path suggested by Webster and Francis Lieber, it turned away from the particularism of Calhoun to explore the reaches of a consolidating nationalism. The inevitable drift towards unity—whether democratic or plutocratic—was daily gathering momentum. The destruction of the states-rights program and party had cleared the ground for a new conception of the dignity and powers of the political state. With the social shift from dispersion to centralization the federal government was destined to grow in authority; and political theory was destined to follow the same course, seeking to justify in principle what was being accomplished in fact. The end of the philosophy of dispersion was in sight. The tide was running toward an exaltation of the doctrine of sovereignty, with the consequent exaltation of the abstract political state. As the individual coalesced in the mass, the rights and dignity of the individual would lessen in the presence of an engulfing sovereignty. The traditional doctrine of natural rights was in for a slashing attack. Centralization must destroy the shambling Jacksonian structure and erect in its place a grandiose organic theory.

During the Gilded Age a number of systematic studies of political theory appeared, amongst which the most significant were, Woolsey's *Political Science, or the State* (1877), Bryce's *The American Commonwealth* (1888), Woodrow Wilson's *The State* (1889), and Burgess's *Political Science and Constitutional Law* (1891). Of these the formal studies of Woolsey and Burgess may serve to illustrate the changing thought of the times. Both are academic reflections of the current drift of tendency, and both reveal the academic sympathy with the master movement of centralization. The work of Woolsey was a revision of classroom notes used between 1846 and 1871 and strongly colored by pre-war views; the work of Burgess was the first-fruits of the influence of German speculation on the nature of the leviathan state.

I

THEODORE WOOLSEY

Theodore Dwight Woolsey, professor of Greek and president of Yale, was an heir in direct succession of Connecticut Federalism. Nephew of Timothy Dwight, a minister, and distinguished member of the social oligarchy that in its decadence still held Connecticut opinion in a strong grip, he could scarcely escape a predilection for the moralistic authoritative dogmatisms that marked the old Connecticut *régime*. The principle of coercive authority had lain at the heart of the political theory of Timothy Dwight, and Theodore Woolsey was true to his Puritan antecedents in asserting the supremacy of authority over liberty. The only important element in his thinking that sets him apart from his uncle was the influence of Francis Lieber, whose conception of organic growth in social custom he made his own, and whose disciple he professed to be. Naturally he retained the old Puritan dislike of leveling—the traditional Connecticut distrust of democracy. He would have no weakening of authority, no Jacobean license; and for anarchism, socialism, communism, which he reckoned the nastiest spawn of Jacobinism, his abhorrence was what one would expect of a Connecticut Federalist. The two ponderous volumes that he issued in 1877 are learned studies that bear on their dun pages many a tell-tale mark of earlier times. In them Theodore Woolsey was renewing the fight against an infidel philosophy that with its doctrine of natural rights denied the authority of the godly to police society.

In harmony with Lieber and Calhoun he rejected the romantic

doctrine of natural rights, and substituted a composite social-moralistic conception, that from John Winthrop and Roger Williams to Channing and Emerson had colored the Puritan thought of New England. Natural rights, he asserted, are those which belong to man by reason of the nature God has endowed him with; and the state is a moral agent, arising out of custom, to secure and guarantee such rights. It is "as truly natural as rights are, and as society is"; for established in the social nature of man it is the natural repository and guardian of his rights in a social order. It is an expression of the teleological purpose that underlies all things. The manner in which Woolsey elaborated his moralistic theory will be evident from the following passages:

The considerations that men exist together in society, that they have an irresistible impulse towards society, that their perfection of soul and of outward condition can be secured only in a social life, and, on the other hand, that recognition of rights and obligation alone make a social life a tolerable or even a possible thing, and that wherever men reflect on their own nature they admit the existence of certain classes of rights and shield them by public power, show a divine purpose which none who believe in a Creator of the world can deny. The Creator of man, having made him such that his temporal, moral, and spiritual perfection can be found only in society, prepared his moral feelings for the life for which he was destined. The destination for society; the means within human nature by which it is fulfilled; the means by which the individual and the community, when brought into society, are able to secure the good and avoid the evils possible in a state of coexistence—these form a complete, harmonious whole, which manifest comprehension of view and forethought. It is provided in our nature, when it is not perverted—that is, when it does not swerve from the true idea of human nature—that we shall form societies under law. A state of society is a state of nature, and the only true one.

When therefore *natural* rights are spoken of, we can accept the term, if it be used to denote such rights as grow out of our nature, and may be inferred from the destination to which it points us. Another and a heathenish kind of sense was attached to the words, when they were taken to mean the rights, or rather uncontrolled liberties, which men possessed in a state of human nature in which there was no organized society or government. . . . [Such a theory] contemplates men as enjoying certain powers of free action in this state of nature, and these powers must serve for a foundation of their state as members of society, or so many of them as it cannot be shown that they gave up, in order to make a state of law and order possible. In other words, the theory of the derivation of these rights from a state of nature may take a hypothetical shape, and deduce rights from what a man could do in a state of things which exists only in a jural fiction. . . .

We find no fault with the objects which the theories had in view, but with the want of conformity to truth. It must be pronounced, in *the first place*, contrary to fact, that such a state of nature ever existed. Man has always been under law; he is a ζῷον πολιτκον. . . .

Secondly, if it could be shown that he had such an origin, it would prove nothing.[20]

Having thus established both society and the state in the nature of man, and dismissed the romantic interpretation of natural rights as heathenish, Woolsey turned to examine the true sphere and function of the political state. He rejected in the main the *laissez-faire* view of Mill and Spencer, but he refused to go so far as Burgess. He will have no omnicompetent state. A just mean must be laid down between authority and liberty, and that mean he discovered in the dictum, "The sphere of the state . . . may reach as far as the nature of man and needs of man and of men reach"; [21] that is to say, its control runs far beyond mere police powers, and concerns itself not only with material ends but with the "intellectual and aesthetic wants of the individual, and the religious and moral nature of its citizens." A state swollen to great powers he regarded as likely to swallow up liberty in paternalism, and a state immediately responsive to the popular will is certain to run into "extreme democracy." His ideal government he discovered in the rule of the Connecticut oligarchy, under which a homogeneous people, with simple agrarian habits, disciplined by religion and responsive to moral leadership, enjoyed a stable government administered by proved executives. Unfortunately with the nineteenth century began a decline in American government, resulting from economic changes, the growth of cities, lower-class immigration, and the "gradual reception of doctrines of political rights, which belong to extreme democracy." Such pernicious doctrines, in his judgment, were: the short term of office, popular election of judges to hold for a fixed period instead of for life, the debasement of the representative system by subjecting the representative to his constituents, and the spoils system.[22] In a later study he added two other evils: direct legislation through the initiative, and a popular referendum on war and peace.[23]

In spite of an imposing display of classical learning these two stout volumes reveal a childlike ignorance of *Realpolitik*, a naïve

---

[20] *Political Science*, Vol. I, pp. 23–25.   [22] *Ibid.*, Vol. II, p. 141.
[21] *Ibid.*, p. 216.   [23] *Communism and Socialism*, p. 232.

inability to grasp the significance of economic groupings that under-lie all political alignments. Neither as minister nor as college pres-ident did Theodore Woolsey learn anything about the robust materialisms which any realistic political theory must take into great account. His knowledge of ancient Greek institutions no doubt was adequate, but his knowledge of American constitutional development was singularly inadequate. He accepted without question the argument of Story and Webster that the phrase, "We the people," proves the original, consolidating intention of the document; he discussed the history of party government in the United States without touching on the economic alignment of agrarianism and capitalism; and he could discover only one thor-oughly admirable political party—"the upright federal party." He extols the Supreme Court as the triumph of the American Constitution, without considering the desirability of a judicial veto on legislative enactments, or suggesting a potential alignment of the judiciary with the master forces of a generation. The moralistic bias of his thought is perhaps sufficiently revealed in a comment on the functions of the judges. "In a higher sense, they are not representatives of the community nor of its chief magistrates, but of justice and of God. . . . They are in fact more immediately servants of God than any other men who manage the affairs of a country, because expediency, departure from law or from the con-stitution, is for them in no circumstance a thing to be conceived of."[24] Mark Twain, it would seem, was not the only humorist of the Gilded Age.

In his later years Woolsey was much disturbed by the spread of collectivist doctrine, and in the thick of the economic unrest of the times he felt it to be his duty to assist in stemming the advance of such doctrine. In his great work on political theory, he demolished the communist-anarchist-socialist arguments in a few pages, and then remarked with excellent candor, "There is an extensive literature, relating to the subject . . . with much of which I am not familiar." Fearful that he might not have delivered a death-blow, after further reading he returned to the attack three years later, and in 1880 published a volume entitled *Com-munism and Socialism*. For so difficult a business he was even then inadequately equipped. He did not realize the magnitude of his task. Marx's *Capital* could not be undermined in ten pages,

[24] *Political Science*, Vol. II, pp. 330–331.

even with the help of Cairnes, Mill, and Ricardo, and a political scientist with a theological background was scarcely competent to untie the close-knit threads of the Marxian economics. His exposition in consequence is incomplete and faulty; it largely over-looks the Marxian philosophy of history and ignores the doctrine of economic determinism. What troubles him most is the lack of religious faith amongst socialists. The validity of a theory he is satisfied to test by the morality of the theorist. One can easily guess that President Woolsey's opinions had turned into dogmatic conviction before a page of the literature to be examined had come under his eyes. Yet that so shallow a book should have issued from an academic pen will surprise no one who is aware of the incredible number of shallow books that actually have issued from academic pens. Provocative social thinking and the American university seem never to have got on well together.

In the fact that Woolsey's speculations on the nature of the state were accounted significant contributions to political science by his generation of Americans, the historian may find added confirmation of the shallowness of the Gilded Age. A stale Connecticut Calvinism, molding in the corner of the cupboard, is poor food to nourish thinking, and a man who knows nothing about the deeper springs of political struggle is singularly un-qualified to elaborate a science of the state. Theodore Woolsey's weighty volumes were a dignified attempt to rehabilitate the old Connecticut Federalism and suit it to the taste of a new age. But what measure of political intelligence can one expect of a people fed on pious fictions by their most authoritative expounder of the noble art of government?

2

JOHN W. BURGESS

Woolsey has little to say about sovereignty. The speculations of Austin had not reached his quiet study, and the need for a coercive state in harmony with a centralizing industrialism was not likely to be realized by a man whose eyes were turned back fondly to a simple village life. It was left for a younger generation to examine the problem of sovereignty, and to that business John W. Burgess turned with zest. A thoroughgoing Austinian, a disciple of the German state-cult, a Hegelian, he would seem to have been ill fitted to interpret the functions of the state to America. And yet by virtue of his European detachment he saw clearly the direction in which America *

IV

BUTTRESSING THE DEMOCRATIC THEORY

I

A DEMOCRATIC ECONOMICS—HENRY GEORGE

While the academic economists were thus providing a new body of capitalistic theory, from the ranks of the people came a group that was bent on bringing economic principles into greater conformity to what they considered democratic needs. The economics of bankers and manufacturers they regarded as a selfish class economics and they proposed to democratize the body of economic thought as Tom Paine and Jefferson had democratized the body of political thought. Since the days of John Taylor such amateur economists had been plentiful in America, and in the post-war days when the country was in the throes of the Industrial Revolution, they sprang up at every cross-roads. George Henry Evans, Horace Greeley, Peter Cooper, Parke Godwin, Wendell Phillips, Albert Brisbane, Hinton R. Helper, "Coin" Harvey, were only a few out of the many who in their own way were seeking in economics a road to freedom. They were not formal economists; they were little read in the history of economic thought; in so far as they may be accounted a school they were mostly the unclaimed progeny of French Physiocratic theory who did not recognize their own father. Yet they were vastly concerned to bring economic theory into some sort of realistic contact with the facts of American experience and the ideals of democracy; and their immediate objective was the overthrow of current Manchester principles and the erection in their stead of a body of theory based on the needs of the producer and the consumer rather than the middleman.

Of this characteristic native group, largely ignored by our formal historians, by far the ablest and most influential was Henry George, a thinker created by the impact of frontier economics upon a mind singularly sensitive to the appeal of social justice, singularly self-

* The discussion of Burgess was not completed by Professor Parrington. At this point he planned a third section, "The New Ally: the courts: the police power and the fourteenth amendment; the injunction." None of this section was written, but he has dealt with these subjects *passim.—Publisher.*

sufficient in its logic. He remains still our most original economist. Beyond the Ricardian theory of rent, with its corollary of unearned increment, he owed little to Europe and nothing to academic American economists. From the first he was a free-lance, returning to the origins of things—as Tom Paine had advised long before— and thinking "as if he were the first man who ever thought." His major doctrines he arrived at largely independently, ignorant of the fact that his *impôt unique* had been earlier elaborated by the Physiocratic school, till long after he had come to identical conclusions. His matured philosophy was the outcome of the meditations of a Jeffersonian idealist contemplating the divergence between the crude facts of exploitation all about him and the eighteenth-century ideal of natural justice; and he became, in consequence, the voice of idealistic America seeking to adjust the economics of a rapidly changing society to the ends of democratic well-being. The passion of the reformer was in him, but wedded to the critical mind of the analyst; and this accounts for the wide appeal of *Progress and Poverty* that for thousands of Americans removed economic theory from the academic closet and set it in the thick of political conflict. Henry George humanized the dismal science and brought it home to the common interest. With his extreme simplification no doubt he fell into the same error the classical school had fallen into before him; he left too many elements out of his equation; but he succeeded in the same way they had succeeded—he made of economic theory a weapon to use in the struggle between the exploiters and the exploited. After *Progress and Poverty* the social economist could cross swords with the Ricardians.

Henry George is readily enough explained in the light of his environment. He was intellectually native to the West, but it was the West of the Gilded Age with its recollections of an earlier agrarian order. Upon the gigantic exploitation of post-war times, carried forward in the name of progress, he threw the experience of two hundred and fifty years of continental expansion. That experience had undergone a subtle change as the settlements moved through the Inland Empire, a change marked by the spirit of capitalistic expansion with its crop of unearned increment. On the frontier, land speculation was often the readiest means to wealth. To the west of the Allegheny Mountains land had long been the staple commodity, with the buying and selling of which every community was deeply concerned; and from the dramatic repetition of that experience in California, Henry George clarified the principle upon which he erected his social philosophy, namely, that a fluid economics begets an equalitarian democracy and homespun plenty, and that with the monopolization of natural resources a static economy succeeds, with its attendant caste regimentation and augmenting exploitation. In the days when he was meditating his social philosophy, California was still in the frontier stage of development, but amidst the hurrying changes a fluid economics was visibly hardening to the static, with a swiftness dramatic enough to impress upon him the significance of a story that had been obscured in earlier telling by the slowness of the dénouement. The vast cupidity of business in preëmpting the virgin resources of California, and in particular the technique of Leland Stanford and the Central Pacific Railway group, provided an eloquent object-lesson that set him to examining the long history of land-jobbing in America in its remoter social bearings. From such inquiry emerged the cardinal principles of an economic theory that must be reckoned the ultimate expression of a school of thought that beginning with Quesnay a hundred years before, and first interpreted for America by John Taylor and the Jeffersonians, was finally buried in a common grave with the kindred doctrine of natural rights.

It was no accident that his mind fastened upon land monopoly as the deeper source of social injustice. As a child of the frontier he thought in terms of land as naturally as the money-broker thinks in terms of discounts. His psychology was that of the producer rather than the middleman. Land, with all its potential wealth of field and orchard and forest and stream, with its unmeasured resources of coal and iron and oil and timber, was the fruitful gift of nature to man; and the true measure of social well-being, he believed, is the measure in which labor is free to use such natural resources for productive purposes. Land monopoly was an ancient evil that had laid its blight on every civilization. The expropriation of natural resources was the origin of rent, and rent was a social tax parasitic in nature. Unearned increment was a moiety wrested from the producer, that waxed ever greater with the increase of production. Henry George was well aware how deeply rooted in American psychology was the love of unearned increment. Since the far-off days when the agent of the Transylvania Land Company wrote in 1775 that the Ohio Valley abounded in land-mongers, the rage for expropriative speculation had mounted steadily; and the railway land-grants of his day were a fitting climax to a policy that in every generation had brought forth such fruits as the Yazoo frauds. The land question was a perennial western problem. For years Horace Greeley in the *Tribune*, had spread amongst the farmers the "Vote Yourself a Farm" propaganda. The protest of the small western settler against the middleman policy of the government in alienating great blocks of the public domain to speculative companies, had added thousands of votes to the Republican party, and the result was the Homestead Act of 1862. But the fruits of the Act were partly destroyed by huge grants to railway promoters, and the time had come, George believed, when the problem must be envisaged in all its complexities and the American people brought to understand how great were the stakes being gambled for.

The disease had so long been endemic in America that the remedy must be drastic. No patent nostrums would serve. The vividness of his experience in the West had thrown into sharp relief his earlier experiences in the East, and made him distrustful of all social panaceas that hopeful idealists were seeking in Europe. With any form of collectivistic theory he would have nothing to do. Marxian socialism he looked upon as an alien philosophy, inadequate in its diagnosis and at fault in its prescription. The ills of America—perhaps of Europe as well—must be cured by another regimen. *Progress and Poverty* grew out of his experience as he watched the heedless alienation of the public domain. It was his reply to the policy of preëmption, exploitation, and progress of the Gilded Age. Philadelphia-born, he early suffered in his personal fortune from the periodic hard times that ran so disastrous a cycle in the days when America was in thoughtless transition from an agrarian order to an industrial. His scanty schooling came to an end before he had reached his fourteenth year, and at sixteen he saw no better opening in life than to ship before the mast to Australia. On his return he learned to set type, but times were bad and opportunity declining to knock at his door, he worked his way through the Straits of Magellan, landing in San Francisco in 1858, on his way to Salem, Oregon, where he worked for a time in a shop. With the exhaustion of the diggings he made his way back to San Francisco, and began a long series of restless ventures in the newspaper field, with only his hands for capital—none very successful, none quite a failure, but returning him useful dividends in the form of a serviceable prose style. At twenty-two he plunged into an improvident marriage with a girl of eighteen, and the next dozen years brought many privations to the little family.

Fate had not yet taken Henry George in hand to lead him into his life work. All the economics he then knew had been learned in the rough and tumble ways of a western print-shop. In 1869, at the age of thirty, while on a business trip to New York City, he was confronted by the contrast between wealth and poverty there nakedly exposed—so unlike what he had known at San Francisco. It was a prod to his social conscience, and as he contemplated the wretchedness of the East Side he registered a vow to explore the hidden causes of social disease. He had given no serious thought to economic questions, and now almost casually he went to the Philadelphia public library to look into John Stuart Mill's *Political Economy*. He accepted Mill's views on wages without critical examination, and wrote his first important article—on the Chinese question in California. In the meantime a group of California railway promoters had been buying and selling legislators in their work of building up private fortunes out of a public monopoly; and it was the contemplation of wealth acquired by such methods, together with the gamble of land speculation in Oakland in consequence of the proposal to establish there the western terminal of the continental railway, that clarified for Henry George the great principle he was to expound in *Progress and Poverty* ten years later.

The first drift in his intellectual development had been a drift back to the old Jeffersonianism from which the country was swiftly moving. As an editor he was an outspoken Democrat of the primitive school, opposed to protectionism, subsidies, a centralizing political state, and the corruption that follows in the train of paternalism as sickness follows infection. In a pamphlet written in 1870, he expounded his political faith thus:

> Railroad subsidies, like protective duties, are condemned by the economic principle that the development of industry should be left free to take its natural direction. They are condemned by the political principle that government should be reduced to its minimum—that it becomes more corrupt and more tyrannical, and less under the control of the people, with every extension of its powers and duties. . . . They are condemned by the experience of the whole country, which shows that they have invariably led to waste, extravagance and rascality; that they inevitably become a source of corruption and a means of plundering the people.[25]

[25] George, *Life of Henry George*, pp. 216–217.

Having thus indoctrinated himself in the Jeffersonian liberalism with its foundations laid in natural rights and its conception of a decentralized society, the following year, at the age of thirty-two, he sat down to the serious elaboration of his views. *Our Land and Land Policy, National and State*, was an explorative pamphlet that went to the heart of the problem as he had come to understand it. The kernel of the work is the question of the relation of land to labor, of rent to wages; and the conclusion to which it led was the doctrine of the social ownership of socially created values, which justice requires shall return to society in the form of an equalized tax that shall absorb the unearned increment. Around this fundamental doctrine was grouped a considerable body of ideas that had been expounded by earlier liberals. How much he borrowed and how much he arrived at independently, cannot easily be determined; such diverse thinkers as James Harrington, Locke, the Physiocrats, Tom Paine, Karl Marx, John Stuart Mill, William Ellery Channing, might well have contributed to this provocative document, if George had been acquainted with them. Like Harrington was the assumption of economic determinism—that ownership of the land implies the rulership of society. From the school of Locke came the conception of natural rights, but interpreted rather in terms of Tom Paine and of William Ellery Channing. From Mill came the conception of unearned increment; from Marx the law of concentration; and from the Physiocrats the conception of a natural order and the doctrine of an *impôt unique*. And all this set in a framework of American economic history, which reveals with shrewd insight the disastrous tendency of the traditional policy of land alienation in great blocks to middle-men, with the attendant rise of rent.

How intimately he was related in his thinking to the French liberals of the eighteenth century, may perhaps be sufficiently suggested in his interpretation of the doctrine of natural rights—a doctrine the new realistic school from Calhoun to Woolsey and Burgess was subjecting to critical analysis. By uniting the individualism of Locke's doctrine of property with the Physiocratic doctrine of social well-being, he gave a sharp turn to the conception that, like Jefferson's, set it widely apart from the exploitative interpretation preferred by the Hamiltonian followers of Locke. The gist of his conception is thus set down:

Now the right of every human being to himself is the foundation of the right of property. That which a man produces is rightfully his own, to keep, to sell, to give or to bequeath, and upon this sure title alone can ownership of anything rightfully rest. But man has also another right, declared by the fact of his existence—the right to the use of so much of the free gifts of nature as may be necessary to supply all the wants of that existence, and which he may use without interfering with the equal rights of anyone else; and to this he has a title as against all the world.[26]

Much of Henry George is compressed within these few lines, that suggest as well the diverse liaisons of his thought. In his conception of the right of every man to himself he is in agreement with William Ellery Channing, who used the argument in his attack on slavery, and with Emerson, Parker, and the Transcendental radicals generally. It is an interpretation of natural rights that sprang easily from the Unitarian-Transcendental conception of the sacredness of the individual, and that was given wide currency by the anti-slavery propaganda. From his deduction that the right to property flows from the right to self, came his theory of tax-equity that was to play a major rôle in the formulation of his principle of taxation. If society may not justly take from the individual what the individual has created, it must seek its revenues elsewhere than in a personal-property tax; and where should it look if not to those values which society has created? The inalienable right of the individual to what he has produced does not extend to the appropriation of wealth he has not produced, and a sharp line is drawn between the rights of the individual and the rights of society, between production and exploitation. Herein lies the justification of the single-tax—a principle derived by crossing Locke with the New England school.

From the classical economists Henry George got little. He had a quiet contempt for them he was never at pains to conceal. He was convinced that they had distorted the whole science of economics. As the earlier Tories with their sacred *arcana imperii* had done with political government, they had involved economics in abstract theory, removing it from the comprehension of the common man. At the best they had dehumanized it to the status of a dismal science, with their postulate of an economic man and their pessimistic outlook. At the worst they had shaped it into a potent weapon for the exploiting class, who gravely invoked economic law—which none understood—to justify class policies of

[26] *Ibid.*, p. 223.

state. In an address delivered at the University of California, Henry George paid his respects to the classical school in these words:

> The name of political economy has been constantly invoked against every effort of the working classes to increase their wages or decrease their hours of labour. . . . Take the best and most extensively circulated textbooks. While they insist upon freedom for capital, while they justify on the ground of utility the selfish greed that seeks to pile fortune on fortune, and the niggard spirit that steels the heart to the wail of distress, what sign of substantial promise do they hold out to the working man save that he should refrain from rearing children? . . .[27]

For political economy thus degraded from its high place and become the slut of private interest, Henry George proposed to do what Tom Paine had done for political theory a hundred years before—he would transfer it from the closet to the market-place by exposing the shabby *arcana imperii* and bringing it within the comprehension of common men. He would bring home to the popular intelligence a realization of the dynamics of economic law and its bearing upon social well-being, that men might plot a fairer course for society. This was the deeper purpose of *Progress and Poverty*—to humanize and democratize political economy, that it might serve social ends rather than class exploitation. *The Rights of Man* and *Progress and Poverty* may be reckoned complementary works, applying to related fields the spirit released to the modern world by the great thinkers of Revolutionary France. The foundations on which they both rest is the eighteenth-century conception of natural law, all-comprehensive, beneficent, free, enshrined in the common heart of humanity, and conducting to the ultimate of social justice.

As a necessary preliminary to his purpose, Henry George was forced to clear the ground of old growths. Before he could declare the truth he must uproot certain of the Malthusian and Ricardian heresies. He must substitute a sociological interpretation, based on historical reality in western civilization, for a set of economic abstractions, based on the political and economic accidents of England in post-Napoleonic days. The Manchester school, it must be remembered, was an embodiment of the aspirations of the rising middle class; it was a philosophical attack upon the vexatious restrictions laid upon capitalism by government in the hands of the landed aristocracy. It conceived of economic principles as of con-

[27] *Ibid.*, p. 277.

cern only to the owning classes, and its theory took a special and narrow form from the current struggle between the landed and capitalistic interests. In a Parliamentary debate over the corn laws in 1814, Alexander Baring, the banker, assumed that the working classes had no interest at stake. To argue that they were affected, he said, was "altogether ridiculous; whether wheat was 130s. or 80s., the laborer could only expect dry bread in the one case and dry bread in the other." [28] In Francis Wayland's *Elements of Political Economy*, published in 1837, a similar narrow view of the field of economics was expressed. That an adequate political economy must be social, that it must be something very much more than a merchant's *vade mecum*, or handbook of profit rules, Henry George grasped as clearly as Ruskin; and he attacked certain of the Manchester principles with the ardor of a social prophet. Of these the classical wage-fund theory seemed to him the most vicious, and he was at vast pains to prove that wages are drawn from the produce of labor and not from a preëxistent capital-fund. Having established this to his satisfaction, he turned to consider the economic effects of monopolistic expropriation of natural resources, and discovered the explanation of the augmenting poverty of civilization in the shutting out of labor from the sources of subsistence, that is in land monopoly.

The argument is based on the Ricardian theory of rent. Though George rejected the classical wage-fund theory, he accepted without qualification the classical rent-theory, and discovered the kernel of his philosophy in the doctrine of social fertility. If rent is the difference between the income-value of a given piece of land and that of the least valuable in the neighborhood, it measures the difference between the yields per acre on the richest and the leanest soil with a like outlay of labor and capital. So in an urban community rent arises from what may be called social fertility— that is, from a monopoly-value in a given neighborhood. Such monopoly-value arises from strategic location; the desirability of a given tract for dwelling, factory, or shop. The number of persons daily passing will determine the rental value for shop purposes; the the accessibility to docks, railways, raw material, power, markets, labor-surplus, will determine its rental value for factory purposes. In every such case, however, it is society and not the individual

[28] Quoted by Wesley Clair Mitchell in *The Trend of Economics*, edited by R. G. Tugwell, p. 5.

that augments rent, and this unearned increment increases with the growth of the community. From every advance of civilization it is the landlord who profits. He is a social parasite, the nether millstone between which and material progress the landless laborer is ground.

In every direction, the direct tendency of advancing civilization is to increase the power of human labour to satisfy human desires—to extirpate poverty and to banish want and the fear of want. . . . But Labour cannot reap the benefits which advancing civilization thus brings, because they are intercepted. Land being necessary to labour, and being reduced to private ownership, every increase in the productive power of labour but increases rent—the price that labour must pay for the opportunity to utilise its power; and thus all the advantages gained by the march of progress go to the owners of land, and wages do not increase. . . [29]

Labour and capital are but different forms of the same thing—human exertion. Capital is produced by labour; it is, in fact, but labour impressed upon matter. . . . The use of capital in production is, therefore, but a mode of labour. . . . Hence the principle that, under circumstances which permit free competition, operates to bring wages to a common standard and profits to a substantial equality—the principle that men will seek to gratify their desires with the least exertion—operates to establish and maintain this equilibrium between wages and interest. . . . And this relation fixed, it is evident that interest and wages must rise and fall together, and that interest cannot be increased without increasing wages, nor wages be lowered without depressing interest.[30]

There is no inherent antagonism between labor and capital, Henry George was early convinced. The Marxians with their theory of a class war were mistaken in their analysis. It is rent that is the true source of social injustice, and the clash of interests in society lies between the producer and the parasitic rent-collector. In every society the appropriation of measured increment has enslaved the ownerless. In all civilizations, from ancient Peru to modern Russia, it has subjected the worker to exploitation. Helot, villein, serf, are only different names for a common slavery, the profits of which go to the landlord. In modern times the Industrial Revolution has changed the form of serfdom, only to intensify and embitter it. The Manchester factory-hand was in worse plight than the medieval villein after the Black Plague. Dispossessed of his acres by the enclosure movement, he had been thrown into the hoppers of industrialism and ground to pieces. He was helpless in

[29] *Progress and Poverty*, Book IV, Chapter 4.
[30] *Ibid.*, Book III, Chapter 5.

the hands of the masters, who with their monopoly of land and the machine, in control of the common heritage of trade processes, raw materials, transportation, credit, and the law-making and law-enforcing machinery, were taking from labor an augmenting toll of its production. Hence the close correlation between material progress and proletarian poverty. Hence the logical outcome of the Industral Revolution, when it should have run its course, was the reduction of the worker to the level of a slave, compared with whose material condition the status of the southern bond-slave was enviable. The southern apologists of slavery had been right; the negro on the plantation enjoyed advantages denied to wage-labor under industrialism.[31]

Having thus analyzed the forces at work in modern society, and wedded a flamboyant material progress to a slattern poverty, Henry George proposed his sovereign remedy—the return to society of social values, hitherto expropriated by means of the private ownership of land, and the removal of the burden of indirect taxation from the back of productive labor. The Ricardian theory of rent, interpreted in the light of eighteenth-century *laissez faire*—of free competition, of a beneficent natural law, of social justice—conducted to unforeseen social issues. If labor and capital are individual, the fruits of both should return to their producers. Society has no just claim on what society has not produced, and the individual has no just claim to that which his labor or capital has not produced. Render unto Cæsar the things that are Cæsar's, and to the individual citizen the things that are his—such to Henry George was the sum of the law of distribution. Land monopoly was a refined denial of natural rights. "The equal right of all men to the use of the land is as clear as their equal right to breathe the air—it is a right proclaimed by the fact of their existence."[32] Unearned increment was the shackles wherewith labor was bound. In the name of social justice strike those shackles from the limbs of men and progress would never again have its ears filled with the wailings of poverty. The workman would once again sing at his work, and the sunshine of well-being fall pleasantly on the land.

A brilliant thinker, with a passionate sympathy for the exploited of earth, this knight-errant from out the newest West ardently believed in the sufficiency of his social philosophy to all

[31] See *Ibid.*, Book VII, Chapter 2.   [32] *Ibid.*, Book VII, Chapter I.

needs. In him the French Revolutionary doctrine came to its most original expression in America. No doubt, like his progenitors, he oversimplified the problem. Society is more complex than he esteemed it; individual motives are more complex. It is perilous to subordinate psychology to abstract theory; the ideal of justice is always running afoul of immediate and narrow interest. Later academic economists have dealt sharply with Henry George, but what have they done to justify their magisterial tone? The science of economics is still cousin-german to philosophy in its fondness for spinning tenuous subtleties; it is still system-ridden, still too much the apologist for things as they are. From its servitude to a class Henry George essayed to deliver it. In fastening upon monopoly as the prime source of social injustice, he directed attention to the origins of exploitative capitalism. He did more than any other man to spread through America a knowledge of the law of economic determinism. He opened a rich vein and one that needs further exploring. The suggestive principle of unearned increment calls for further expansion to embrace other forms than rent, to fit it to the needs of a complex society. What he seems not to have seen was the wider range of economic determinism—that changes come only when the existing order has become intolerable to great classes, and the grip of use and wont is loosened by the rebellions born of exigent need. "For ever the fat of the whole foundation hangeth to the priest's beard," asserted a quaint Beggars' Petition in appeal to Henry VIII against the monasteries, and in that comment were the seeds of the Reformation. When the beards are few to which the fat hangs, the time is ripe for an upheaval. An arch-idealist, Henry George would hasten the change by appeal to reason. Like Godwin and Tom Paine he believed that reason will make its own way, forgetting that reason waits upon interest, and the day of its freedom is long delayed. Yet if he was oversanguine, why account that to his discredit? *

* The discussion of Henry D. Lloyd, planned as the second subsection, was not written.—*Publisher*.

CHAPTER IV

THE BEGINNINGS OF CRITICISM

FOR many thoughtful Americans the welter of frontier individualism was a severe trial to their faith in American institutions. An ambitious industrialism colliding with a shambling Jacksonian democracy was forecasting consequences to government and to society that intelligent men could not shut their eyes to. The America of Fisk and Gould, of Boss Tweed and the *Crédit Mobilier* scandal, was far from satisfying the requirements of any rational civilization. After a hundred years to have come to such heroes, to have bogged down in such filth, was an outcome to the great experiment that one could not contemplate with pride. It was no time to be silent. No people was ever saved by dumb preachers. The present generation was answerable for the new evils that were springing from the graves of the old, and intelligent Americans must not lose their heads in the thick of the common hurly-burly. So amidst the ruck and clamor of the times a tiny note of criticism was lifted up, timid and uncertain at first, but growing more confident and more strident as the decade grew older. It was not searching criticism. Sooner or later it was pretty certain to run into a blind alley of moral indignation, overlooking the major issues and leaving the vital factors of the problem unconsidered. Yet such as it was—shallow and feeble enough often to excite wonder in a later generation—it marks the rise of a spirit of skepticism towards the blowsy doctrine of manifest destiny that since the fifties had been blowing about the land.

The determining factors in the situation confronting criticism were political and economic, and the immediate problem that pressed for solution was the problem whether an undisciplined people, wedded to an old-fashioned agrarian democracy, could cope with an ambitious industrialism that was quite cynically buying and selling the political state. To deal with that problem most of the critics were singularly ill equipped. Two generations of constitutional debate, seasoned with a dash of equalitarian dogma, had left them intellectually lean and impoverished. They had forgotten the sober realism of the eighteenth century that never overlooked the intimate ties between economics and politics, and with no anchors down in the plebeian mud they were likely to drift helplessly in the moral squalls they were always blowing up. The more distinguished critics—those who commanded the most serious attention—were in a particularly unfortunate situation, for not only were they uninstructed idealists with no understanding of *Realpolitik*, but they had been reared in the classical tradition and their minds were saturated with a decadent aristocratic culture. To many of them the present evils of America served only to quicken an inherited skepticism of democracy. How can society expect to function adequately, they asked, without capable and honest leadership; and how can such leadership be hoped for in a rough and tumble democracy that loves the noisiest demagogue? Of this very considerable group of belated Federalists James Russell Lowell was the most distinguished representative. In the middle seventies he had come to believe that America was suffering from too much democracy, and that competent government could be had only by working back to the responsible Federalism of earlier times, with leadership reclaimed by the better elements of society. To the economics of the problem—the antagonistic interests of capitalist, proletarian, and farmer, with their struggles to control the political state—he gave no serious thought, but he viewed with instinctive suspicion the mounting ambitions of labor and he foresaw only evil from the bitter unrest of the farmers.

A second very considerable group, of which George William Curtis may be taken as spokesman, rejected all such antiquated Federalistic hopes as the foolish dreams of defeatists. They held fast to their faith in democracy, but they were convinced that more adequate democratic machinery must be provided. The root of the evil, they had come to believe, was political and must be sought in the vicious Jacksonian spoils system. With every change of administration to turn over the country to hungry partisans to devour, was not democracy but the negation of democracy? Government would not function satisfactorily until a trained civil service was provided, and the need of the hour, they pointed out, was an honest civil service reform. A third group, very much smaller than the others, of which Edwin Lawrence Godkin was the spokesman, was inclined to trace the plentiful evils of the times to an unwise paternalism, asserting that the real

source of the common political scoundrelism was the lauded Amei ·
ican System devised by Henry Clay, as a result of which govern ·
ment was seduced from its proper business of keeping the peace
and was turned into a fairy godmother to shower gifts on favored
interests. The only cure for the evil was to divorce business
and politics and reëstablish in practice the police theory of government.

In the thinking of all three groups little consideration was given
to the social consequences of the venture on which America had
entered with the vigor of thoughtless youth. Concerning the ultimate consequences of the collision between a shambling democracy and an ambitious industrialism, few troubled themselves
greatly. To find those who confronted the problem frankly and
realistically, one must search out obscure men, labor leaders for
the most part, or *déclassé* radicals like Wendell Phillips. The
middle-class mind refused to see what its feet were stumbling over.
In consequence the Gilded Age produced no critics of industrialism
comparable to the great English critics—Carlyle, Kingsley, Ruskin,
Morris, Tawney; no social philosophers like the great continental
expounders of proletarian ideals—Marx, Engels, Bakunin, Sorel;
no left-wing economists like the great French school—Louis Blanc,
Bastiat, Proudhon. The genteel culture of America was no better
than bankrupt in presence of brutal reality, quite unequipped to
interpret the sprawling America that was transforming itself before its eyes into something it hated but did not understand. The
time for searching criticism had not come, and would not come
until the Industrial Revolution had created in America a proletariat such as swarmed in the English black country and amongst
the hovels of continental cities. Nevertheless such criticism as
there was must be taken into consideration, and for our present
purpose it will suffice to single out three spokesmen—a grizzled
warrior of the earlier renaissance who had the courage to face unpleasant fact, and two critics who brought to bear on political
themes the best culture of the time. With these may be conveniently grouped certain novelists who more or less casually suffered
their pens to deal with social problems.

I

THE NEW ENGLAND CONSCIENCE AND CAPITALISM— WENDELL PHILLIPS

Social criticism was by no means a new thing in America. For half a century it had filled all ears with its strident clamors, and from it had issued the motley group of reform movements that had been cheered or mocked at by thousands. From Channing and Cooper down to Parke Godwin and Horace Greeley it had been mustering its forces, vivid and picturesque figures for the most part—men and women like Fanny Wright, George Henry Evans, and Hinton R. Helper; ardent souls who beyond the dun horizon discovered a golden morrow that only awaited the rising of a new sun, and who lectured and wrote and argued till pretty much all America had caught something of their contagious enthusiasm. In this work New England came eventually to take the lead, and the golden forties were a time when in many an obscure Yankee head programs of reform were fermenting like a vat of malt. But unfortunately an excess of eagerness wore out the first enthusiasm, and when the shackles had been loosened from the negro bondmen the militancy of the New England leadership subsided and the tired New England conscience went on vacation.

But in these slothful times the conscience of one great New Englander was not tired, though he gave it no rest while life lasted. Wendell Phillips was a soldier of Puritan soul who did not lay down his arms in '65, but for nearly a score of years warred upon the injustices of the Gilded Age as he had warred before upon the obscenities of negro slavery. No sooner was the cause of abolitionism won—a cause to which he had sacrificed much in ease and the good opinion of Beacon Street, but from which he had gained more in self-respect and the decent opinion of mankind—than he turned to whatever new work offered. The lovers of justice, he knew very well, can indulge themselves in no vacations, for the devil is on the job day and night, and while the assailants sleep he is at work repairing any breaches in the walls of his citadel. When conscience is tired he counts on gaining his greatest victories.

The love of freedom has always been a dangerous possession in Massachusetts, given to exploding in unforeseen moments and unexpected places. No one could have foretold—certainly not he himself—that Wendell Phillips would put away all his Brahmin loyalties and devote forty-seven years to an unresting attack on the diverse Toryisms from which he and his class had hitherto prospered. Son of the first mayor of the city and a distinguished member of the Boston gentry, he was a patrician in the fullest Boston sense. All the loyalties of his caste summoned him to uphold the Brahmin authorities, but something deep within him, a loyalty to other and higher ideals, held him back. When a frock-coated mob laid its hands on Garrison to lynch him for abolition propaganda, he drew back; he refused to follow the Mayor and the Colonel of his regiment and other gentlemen if they betrayed the Boston for which their grandfathers had fought. An instinctive love of justice held him back. A fierce indignation flamed up within him at the wrong done a citizen of Massachusetts for exercising his natural right of free speech, and in that wild hour he discovered that he was a child of '76 with the mentality of a revolutionist. His conscience was aroused and he proceeded to put it in the safe keeping of Ann Terry Greene, a brilliant young woman of radical mind, who quickened his sense of social justice as Maria White was to quicken Lowell's. There was to be no backsliding in his case. From the December day in 1837 when he replied to Attorney-General Austin's slanders of the Revolutionary fathers in Faneuil Hall, to the end of a life filled with enormous labors—a life daily stabbed by Tory hornets, and that at the last is said to have inspired the remark of Judge Hoar that he did not attend the funeral of Wendell Phillips but he approved of it [1]—he followed his conscience into many an unpopular cause and spoke for those for whom few were willing to speak.

The story of his anti-slavery labors belongs to an earlier time and need not be recounted here. His devotion to abolitionism equaled Garrison's and his services were as great. It is rather the nineteen years that remained to him after Appomattox that are of present concern—what later battles he fought and how he bore himself in those battles. It was a difficult time for Puritan liberalism, face to face with a new age that had forgotten the old liberalisms. The Grand Army of Abolitionism had disbanded and new armies of other causes had not yet been recruited. Garrison and Edmund Quincy and Whittier had laid aside their arms, and Lowell had long since settled back into a comfortable Brahminism; the long struggle had left them drained of their energy. But for Wendell Phillips the

[1] See Charles Edward Russell, *The Story of Wendell Phillips*, p. 53.

battle was not over; it was unending and he was enlisted for life. At a vast meeting that marked the formal close of the abolition movement he took leave of his old associates with these words: "We will not say 'Farewell,' but 'all hail.' Welcome, new duties! We sheathe no sword. We only turn the front of the army upon a new foe." [2] He had long spoken for prohibition, woman's rights, the abolition of capital punishment, and he now joined heartily with the courageous women engaged in such reform work. But more provocative business was at hand, and more dangerous—causes that touched the northern pocketbook as abolitionism had touched the southern. The banker's exploitation of the national currency, and the manufacturer's exploitation of factory labor—these were issues that a cautious man who was careful of his good name would not meddle with. But Wendell Phillips was never cautious and his good name had long since been flung to the wolves. And so in the evening of his days, with a courage that took little counsel of expediency, he embarked on a campaign that had for its ultimate objective the impregnable citadel of State Street. He would destroy capitalistic exploitation in all its works. It was as hopeless a battle as King Arthur's "last, dim, weird battle of the west," and entered upon as courageously.

How he came to hold the heretical views on money and labor that he expounded from the lecture platform cannot easily be traced. Perhaps they came from the radical fringe that envelops every great social movement; perhaps they were the inevitable expression of his left-wing temper. A man who had fought all Tory programs for thirty years must eventually come to hate the ways of capitalism, and so confirmed a democrat as Wendell Phillips would be certain to espouse the doctrine of thorough. One who had passed through the fires of abolition nullification, who had spoken of the Union as "built i' the eclipse and rigged with curses dark," who had repudiated his citizenship and equaled Garrison in contempt for a slave-protecting Constitution, would have pretty well cleared his mind of conventional respect for capitalistic law and order. He was not impressed by political cant. He had taken the measure of existing law and order and was casting about for a juster law and a more generous order.

In these later years, as a program of social reconstruction took shape in his mind, he was coming to essential agreement with the

[2] Quoted in Martyn, *Wendell Phillips: The Agitator*, p. 372.

program of socialism. With the Marxians he based his thinking upon economics, and his final objective came to be the substitution of coöperation for the profit-motive. As ardently as Horace Greeley he asserted the rights of labor. As early as 1860–1861 he had come to recognize a similarity in the economic status of the wage-slave and the bond-slave, and in 1865, in a speech on the eight-hour movement, he accepted as true the southern thesis that in western civilization all labor, whether bond or wage, was unfree, held in the grip of a master, bought and sold in the market; [3] and now that the shackles had been struck from the negro, it remained to strike them from the wage-earner. To turn the negro from a bond-slave to a wage-slave would be a sorry ending of abolitionism; but such must be the inevitable outcome, he believed, unless all labor should win freedom. The question of the hour for Wendell Phillips had become the question of the relation of labor and capital.

In his thinking on the currency question—a question that became acute in the seventies—he was soon caught up by the Greenback movement. It may have been that his contact with Thaddeus Stevens helped to mold his views on the money question; yet that he should have become a Greenbacker was foreordained. He had no amiable illusions in regard to State Street. As a tribune of the people he had long been intimately acquainted with its ambitions, and he would not turn over the country to its custodianship. He would have no bankers' control of the national currency, to augment or deflate as banking profits dictated. His democratic sympathies recoiled from a class control of the common medium of exchange, and in 1875 he offered a drastic solution of the vexing question that brought down on his head all the wrath of State Street. His plan provided for three things: the rejection of the national banknote system; the issue of honest greenbacks, secured by the wealth of the country, and receivable in payment for all debts public and private—not dishonest greenbacks like the old, which the government had repudiated at issue by refusing to accept them in payment of custom dues; and finally the retirement of interest-bearing bonds and the return to a cash basis for government business. How deeply he felt in the notorious matter of credit manipulation is suggested in the following passage with its echoes of an older America that looked with suspicion on a consolidating capitalism.

[3] See *Speeches*, Second Series, p. 139.

Three times within a dozen years, [he said] capitalists with their knives on the throat of the Government, have compelled it to cheat its largest creditor, the people; whose claim, Burke said, was the most sacred. First, the pledge that greenbacks should be exchangeable with bonds was broken. Secondly, debts originally payable in paper . . . were made payable in gold. Thirdly, silver was demonetized, and gold made the only tender. A thousand millions were thus stolen from the people.[4]

At other times he went further. Speaking on the labor question in 1872, he said:

I say, let the debts of the country be paid, abolish the banks, and let the government lend every Illinois farmer (if he wants it), who is now borrowing money at ten per cent., money on the half-value of his land at three per cent. The same policy that gave a million acres to the Pacific Railroad, because it was a great national effort, will allow of our lending Chicago twenty millions of money, at three per cent., to rebuild it.[5]

When we get into power, there is one thing we mean to do. If a man owns a single house, we will tax him one hundred dollars. If he owns ten houses of like value, we won't tax him one thousand dollars, but two thousand dollars. . . . We'll double and treble and quintuple and sextuple and increase tenfold the taxes. . . . We'll crumple up wealth by making it unprofitable to be rich. . . . You will say, "Is that just?" My friends, it is safe. Man is more valuable than money. You say, "Then capital will go to Europe." Good heavens, let it go! If other States wish to make themselves vassals of wealth, so will not we. We will save a country equal from end to end. Land, private property, all sorts of property, shall be so dearly taxed that it shall be impossible to be rich; for it is in wealth, in incorporated, combining, perpetuated wealth, that the danger of labor lies.[6]

The mad wicked ravings of a demagogue, such talk was accounted by sober financiers of Boston. But it was rather the talk of an honest equalitarian who understood how incompatible was property rule and the ideal of equality. The arch-enemy of a worthy civilization, Wendell Phillips had become convinced, was private capitalism with its dehumanizing profit-motive. There could be no adequate civilization, no Christianity, until coöperation had displaced competition, and men were become equal in economic rights as they were in franchise rights. At a Labor-Reform Convention held at Worcester on September 4, 1871, resolutions drafted by him were adopted—resolutions that reveal "just where Mr. Phillips stood for the last thirteen years of his life."

[4] Quoted in Martyn, op. cit., pp. 412–413.
[5] Speeches, Second Series, p. 176.
[6] Ibid., p. 167.

In this "full body of faith," and in two later speeches—*The Founda-tion of the Labor Movement*, and *The Labor Question*—the man who called himself "a Jeffersonian democrat in the darkest hour," wrote down as the great objective of the labor party the principle that has long been accepted as the cardinal plank of the Socialist platform.

We affirm, as a fundamental principle, that labor, the creator of wealth, is entitled to all it creates.

Affirming this, we avow ourselves willing to accept the final results of the operation of a principle so radical,—such as the overthrow of the whole profit-making system, the extinction of all monopolies, the abolition of privileged classes, universal education and fraternity, perfect freedom of exchange, and . . . the final obliteration of that foul stigma upon our so-called Christian civilization—the poverty of the masses. . . . *Resolved*, —That we declare war with the wages system, which demoralizes alike the hirer and the hired, cheats both, and enslaves the workingman; war with the present system of finance, which robs labor, and gorges capital, . . . war with these lavish grants of the public lands to speculating com-panies, and whenever in power, we pledge ourselves to use every just and legal means to resume all such grants heretofore made; war with the sys-tem of enriching capitalists by the creation and increase of public interest-bearing debts. We demand that every facility, and all encouragement, shall be given by law to co-operation in all branches of industry and trade, and that the same aid be given to co-operative efforts that has heretofore been given to railroads and other enterprises. . . .[7]

When he was about to take the platform on another occasion his wife is reported to have said to him, "Wendell, don't shilly-shally!" Certainly in this pronouncement, and in the speeches supporting it, there is no shilly-shallying. He will have no halfway measures, but goes straight to the economic core of the problem. Pretty much all of Marxianism is there, even to the class war. The capitalists had whetted their swords and he would have labor put its sword likewise to the grindstone. If the war were cruel, where did labor learn it—"learned it of capital, learned it of our enemies." In a world of economic concentration where caste follows property accumulation he had come to rest his hopes on the international solidarity of labor. The cause of democratic justice was committed to the keeping of the workingman, and if he were defeated in his hopes the future was black indeed. The American Revolution and the French Revolution had prepared the way gloriously for a greater event, the revolution of labor.

[7] *Ibid.*, pp. 152–153.

He was not afraid of revolution. In America he hoped the battle would be fought with ballots, but if it must come to bullets, so be it. The Paris Commune met with his heartiest approval: "I have not a word to utter—far be it from me!—against the grandest declaration of popular indignation which Paris wrote on the pages of history in fire and blood. I honor Paris as the vanguard of the Internationals of the world." [8] And in the Phi Beta Kappa address, delivered in 1881 before all the assembled conservatisms of Boston, the old warrior with seventy years upon his head, went so far as to defend Russian Nihilism.

Nihilism is the righteous and honorable resistance of a people crushed under an iron rule. Nihilism is evidence of life . . . the last weapon of victims choked and manacled beyond all other resistance. . . . I honor Nihilism, since it redeems human nature from the suspicion of being utterly vile, made up only of heartless oppressors and contented slaves. . . . This is the only view an American, the child of 1620 and 1776, can take of Nihilism. Any other unsettles and perplexes the ethics of our civilization. Born within sight of Bunker Hill, in a commonwealth which adopts the motto of Algernon Sydney, *sub libertate quietem* ("accept no peace without liberty"); son of Harvard, whose first pledge was "Truth"; citizen of a republic based on the claim that no government is rightful unless resting on the consent of the people, and which assumes to lead in asserting the rights of humanity,—I at least can say nothing else and nothing less; no, not if every tile on Cambridge roofs were a devil hooting my words! [9]

"It was a delightful discourse," said one gentleman, "but preposterous from beginning to end." The doctrine was strange to Harvard ears—wicked and perverse. And strange and disconcerting also was his roll-call of great and noble deeds done in America in which Harvard scholarship had had no part. To an audience of Brahmin scholars it was not kind to say, "The greatest things have not been done for the world by its bookmen"; nor this, "It is not the masses who have most disgraced our political annals. I have seen many mobs . . . I never saw or heard of any but well-dressed mobs, assembled and countenanced, if not always led in person, by respectability and what called itself education." [10] It was a curious scene—that gathering in a Harvard hall listening to a son of Harvard who had gone to school to other teachers than those brought up on Brahmin culture. The liberalism of the forties was speaking to a generation that was concerned about other

---

[8] *Ibid.*, p. 154.   [9] See *Ibid.*, pp. 356–359.   [10] See *Ibid.*, p. 347.

things than a just and humane civilization. Wendell Phillips was hopelessly old-fashioned in America of the Gilded Age—a lone Puritan in a land of Yankees. He used to speak of himself grimly as "that Ishmael"; his home, he said, was the sleeping-car and his only friends the brakeman and the porter. He spent his strength and his earnings with generous prodigality, and when he died the only treasures he had laid up were in heaven. He was the last survivor of the great age of Puritan conscience, and the words he spoke of Theodore Parker may well stand for his epitaph: "The child of Puritanism is not mere Calvinism—it is the loyalty to justice which tramples under foot the wicked laws of its own epoch."

II

MORALITY AND POLITICS—GEORGE WILLIAM CURTIS

A child of Puritan conscience also was George William Curtis, like Wendell Phillips sprung from the Puritan gentry, but unlike him wanting in a passionate Hebraism that sought justice in all the byways and would not turn aside from pursuing it. A reformer but never a radical, he was a gentleman who was a lifelong friend of civilization. An idealist, he refused to serve the gross materialisms that swept so many of his fellows from the old moorings, but throughout a long and honorable career he preserved unshaken his early faith in republican ideals and the way of liberty. As an abolitionist he faced hostile audiences with admirable poise, and as a civil service reformer he fought off the attacks of greasy politicians with quiet contempt. A cultivated gentleman, high-bred if not heroic, was George William Curtis.

Born in Providence, Rhode Island, of excellent stock, living most of his life in New York City whither his father had removed to engage in the banking business, he was brought up in affluence and spent his days amidst dignified surroundings. Broad-minded and generous, with wide sympathies and urbane manners, he followed his conscience and weighed life in the scales of Puritan morality. He was no friend to compromise or expediency, yet he was content to serve God in the station whereunto he had been called, declining to turn rebel and become an outcast and pariah. Endowed with excellent parts, his training was unusually fortunate. At eighteen with his brother Burrill he went to Brook Farm, where he spent two profitable years in an atmosphere he found stimulating. After

quitting Brook Farm he passed the better part of two years at
Concord with his brother, living at farmhouses, helping with the
crops, and for a time indulging in an experiment not unlike Thoreau's at Walden Pond. Then followed four years overseas—from
1846 to 1850—rambling about the continent, sloughing off the
provincial asceticism of New England, and practicing his pen by
means of letters and diaries. On his return he drifted into journalism, wrote several volumes of travel essays and social satire,
caught the Lyceum infection, then at its malignant stage, lectured
voluminously to pay off an unfortunate debt, wrote for *Putnam's
Magazine*, became connected with *Harper's Weekly*, finally settling
into the Easy Chair of *Harper's Magazine*, from which comfortable
seat for years he sent forth gracefully pointed comments on manners, society, politics, life, yet more and more turning to politics as
his particular field and serving as volunteer political mentor and
critic to the Gilded Age.

Of his several early ventures into the field of polite letters little
need be said. The work of a high-spirited young man, they were
a cross between Nathaniel Parker Willis and Thackeray with a
suggestion of Disraeli. He took his place naturally as a member of
the New York group of littérateurs who were gaily exploiting the
conventional sentimentalism of the fifties. With its pose of clever
sophistication the New York school could do no good to a serious
young writer, and the pretensions of the new-rich society of the
town were a cordial invitation to go wrong. *Nile Notes of a Howadji*
(1851), written before the young traveler had caught the current
note of social satire, was a conscious correction of the ascetic
Puritanism imbibed at Concord, and with its frank delight in the
sensuousness of the East it gave offense to the professional blue-
stockings of the time. But in *The Potiphar Papers* (1853) he turned
to satirize New York society, then hastening to transform itself
from a staid Knickerbocker world into a Gold Coast of social
climbers. That his treatment of the theme should have been a
slighter edition of Thackeray's *Vanity Fair*—less searching and
more sentimental—might be guessed even if we did not know how
greatly Curtis loved and admired the English satirist. "He seems
to be the one of all authors who takes life precisely as he finds it,"
he wrote of him. "If he finds it sad, he makes it sad: if gay,
gay. You discover in him the flexible adaptability of Horace,
but with a deep and consuming sadness which the Roman never

knew, and which in the Englishman seems to be almost sentimentality.[11]

But in spite of their excellent model these sketches do not now
seem so sprightly as they seemed to his fellows on the staff of
Putnam's Magazine. Moralism scented with patchouli is no longer
the vogue, and they have long since been laid away with the hoops
and crinoline of the fifties. His most important venture in polite
literature—if indeed even that deserves the name important—was
Prue and I (1856), written in a golden summer when his pen was
dipped into the inkwell of love and he foresaw the years of his life
lengthening out in the most intimate of companionships. They are
charming essays in contentment that teach the familiar lesson that
the only abiding riches are the riches of mind and character. The
old bookkeeper in black coat and white tie who voyages to the
realms of romance while watching from the Battery outgoing ships,
has discovered the vicarious pleasure of the imagination, and the
Aurelia of his dreams is Prue as she was in her youth, and both are
Anna Shaw to whom soon after he was married. The first three
sketches—"Dinner Time," "My Chateaux," and "Sea from the
Shore"—are humorous and tender fancies in the graceful Victorian
manner; but "Titbottom's Spectacles" is Hawthorne-like in the
tenuous play of a grotesquely moralistic fancy, and the succeeding
sketches reveal the exhaustion of the vein. Later he tried his hand
at a novel—*Trumps*—but it refused to turn into anything but a
tract and in the early sixties he settled down in the Easy Chair
which he had first occupied as early as 1853.

Thereafter to his death in 1892 his work followed three diverse
lines. For thirty years he was essayist, orator, and political critic,
to a generation sorely in need of wise and urbane counsel. His
audience was wide and his influence great, and to his work he
brought the weight of his sane and just character. Not a great
scholar and not an acute critic, he was an enlightened and sensitive
conscience, and to the bar of his conscience he summoned the
parties and policies of a heedless and selfish generation. From the
Easy Chair he sent forth his genial comment on matters of current
interest, satisfying his love of creative writing by the grace of his
talk, and recognizing his kinship with the age of Queen Ann by
adopting the words of *The Tatler*, "I shall from time to time Report
and Consider all Matters of what Kind soever that shall occur to

---

[11] Edward Cary, *George William Curtis*, p. 78.

me." But such work at the best is ephemeral, and ephemeral likewise were the polished pronouncements of the occasional orator on
which far too much time and labor were expended. But New York
City must have its spokesman for formal occasions, and after
Bryant's death George William Curtis was summoned with increasing frequency. The rich context of his speeches, elaborated
with formal dignity and embellished with literary allusions, hit to
a nicety the taste of a generation that still delighted in oratory and
preferred dignity to informality. His addresses on Charles Sumner,
Wendell Phillips, Bryant, and Lowell, are excellent examples of a
style that is no longer the fashion. In their polished sentences
eulogy is tempered with criticism, but the criticism is sympathetic
and refuses to render judgments that may strike his hearers as
severe. It would be ungracious to intrude unpleasant facts on dignified occasions.

But his most significant work during these busy years lay in the
field of political criticism, and it was as editor of *Harper's Weekly*,
from 1863 to his death, and as a leader in the movement of civil
service reform, that he made the deepest impress on the age. The
Weekly, with Nast as cartoonist, was then at the height of its
popularity and influence, and by means of its editorial page Curtis
was able to marshal a very considerable following for whatever
cause or party he espoused. He had long taken part in practical
politics, was active in caucuses and conventions, was much on the
stump and kept his fingers on party wires. Yet influential as he
was—the scholar in politics, as his own generation loved to say—he
was never a serious student of politics in the broader meaning. He
was essentially an English gentleman politician, with a fine scorn
of mean and sordid policies, a warm love of country but an equally
warm love of civilization, devoted to the cause of liberty, a friend of
justice, yet with all his excellent traits an inadequate political philosopher. Like Lowell's his horizon was curiously limited. Abstract
political theory did not interest him and he never critically examined
diverse systems of government. Of economics he was as ignorant
as his generation. Again like Lowell the single standard by which he
judged politics was the moral standard, and in his anxious concern for
"good government" he failed to probe deeply the sources of "bad
government." In presence of the vast corruptions of the Gilded
Age he was as helpless in diagnosing the evil as Lowell or Norton.

Such helplessness is the more surprising considering what rare opportunities he had enjoyed for intelligent understanding. During the impressionable years of youth he daily associated with the most militant group of intellectual radicals in America and heard the ideas of Saint-Simon and Fourier and Owen eagerly canvassed. Associationism as a cure for the evils of competition was the cardinal doctrine of the Brook Farmists; yet his individualism passed unaffected through all such discussions. He seems to have sympathized with the skepticism of Hawthorne rather than the faith of Ripley and Dana. Writing to his father from Brook Farm he fell into the genial transcendental vein and gaily poked fun at those who would make the world over.

No wise man is long a reformer, [he wrote] for Wisdom sees plainly that growth is steady, sure, and neither condemns nor rejects what is, or has been. Reform is organized distrust. It says to the universe fresh from God's hand, "You are a miserable business; lo! I will make you fairer!" and so deputes some Fourier or Robert Owen to improve the bungling work of the Creator.[12]

It was as a transcendental optimist that he set out on his travels in 1846. The Europe he visited at the age of twenty was seething with discontent that was to flame up in the revolutionary year of '48, yet though he wandered leisurely through Italy, Hungary, Germany, France, and was at Paris during the great overturn, the evidence that his biographer has gathered indicates that he was not deeply affected by the experience. Unlike his friend Margaret Fuller, who was a passionate volunteer in the struggle of Mazzini at Rome, or like Dana, who followed the movement closely as foreign correspondent, he felt none of the promptings of a revolutionist. A romantic sympathy for Kossuth is clearly indicated, but his feelings carried him little further than that. Even in England, seething as it was with the proletarian unrest that culminated in the great Chartist movement, he came upon little to quicken his transcendental pulse. It was not till he got back home and found himself in presence of negro slavery that his reforming ardor took fire and he proposed to engage in the business of "organized distrust." He threw himself into the cause with enthusiasm and spoke from many an abolition platform. Then came the war and during those passionate years he was swept unconsciously along the path of consolidation, emerging from the fire a confirmed Hamiltonian with transcendental democratic leanings.

[12] See *Ibid.*, pp. 25–26.

Have you thought [he wrote Charles Eliot Norton in 1864] what a vindication this war is of Alexander Hamilton? I wish somebody would write his life as it ought to be written, for surely he was one of the greatest of our great men, as Jefferson was the least of the truly great; or am I wrong? Hamilton was generous and sincere. Was Jefferson either? [13]

Such Hamiltonian sympathies suffice to explain some of his votes in the New York Constitutional Convention of 1867, of which he was a member. He advocated the appointment of the attorney-general and certain other state officers, opposed the principle of municipal home rule, and approved the extension of the authority of the state over local police systems. With Tammany Hall and Boss Tweed before his eyes it was perhaps natural that he should have sought in the power of the up-state voter some external control over the city machine. But in spite of such obvious leanings towards the Whig branch of the Republican party Curtis was never a Whig. The transcendentalism he had imbibed at Brook Farm remained with him to color much of his thinking and restrain him from an uncritical advocacy of capitalism. He never went over body and soul to the new gospel of exploitation. He never lent a willing ear to the seductive appeals of the American System. He early became a free-trader and throughout his life was opposed to all tariffs and grants and subsidies. Discovering in the principle of liberty the cardinal principles of American democracy, he was disposed to accept a wide application of *laissez faire;* yet when it opened the door to extortion he was willing to curb an anti-social individualism. When in the seventies it was proposed by the western farmers that a national railroad should be built from Chicago to the Atlantic seaboard, Curtis looked upon the proposal with sympathy as likely to rescue the farmer from extortionate tolls.[14] Unlike Dana and Godkin, he declined to grow bitter and lose his head over the economic proposals of the western agrarians. In the sharp alignment between agrarianism and capitalism he stood in the main outside both parties, and although opposed to greenbackism he discussed the question with moderation and good sense—a rare thing in those blatant times.

But it was political decency rather than capitalistic or agrarian programs that he was chiefly concerned about. He looked to his conscience as guide and as editor of *Harper's Weekly* he used his influence to cleanse America of the corruption he abhorred. Week

---

[13] See *Ibid.*, pp. 180–181.   [14] See *Harper's Weekly*, Sept. 20, 1873.

after week he appealed to the American voter to turn rascals out of office and put honest men in. The corrupt political machine was the source of the evil, and the machine had grown powerful through its control of patronage. There would be vicious government so long as politicians could create a machine by means of the spoils system. Two remedies, he believed, were necessary to cure the evil—independent voting and civil service reform; and to the spread of these two ideas he devoted the last twenty years of his life, thereby bringing on his head much abuse and incurring eventually a break with the Republican party.

His troubles began with his proposal of independent voting. To that party-ridden generation on whom the passions of war had fastened a tyrannical machine, the scratching of the party ticket seemed no better than treason. It was a Copperhead device to undo the results of the war and reëstablish the rebel leaders at Washington, and it needed courage to advocate it publicly. Curtis put the matter fairly in a speech to Independent Republicans at New York in 1880:

The first powerful and conclusive remedy for the tyranny of the machine . . . is scratching. The word has become a sneer, a taunt, a bitter reproach, but the test of the power and effectiveness of the remedy is the fury with which it is assailed. . . . The machine denounces scratchers as lustily as Laud denounced the Puritans, or George III the rebellious Yankees, or slave-driving Democrats Republican woolly heads. . . . The scratcher is the minute-man of politics. He is always in light marching order. He has only to consult his own knowledge and conscience, and with one stroke his work is done. Fortunately, also, his stroke may be as secret as his ballot. Those who do not choose to publish the fact need not be known, and may smile serenely at the blind fury of those whose plots are quietly foiled. This is the reason of the impotent anger with which scratching is assailed. It cannot be reached. . . . Scratching is denounced as dishonorable. Oh, no! the secret ballot is not dishonorable. The shot of the Middlesex farmer from behind a tree was no more dishonorable than the immortal volley from behind the breastworks of Bunker Hill.[15]

He then proceeded to lay open what seemed to him the core of the problem:

But useful as scratching is as a corrective, it does not strike at the heart of the machine, and it is therefore *only* a corrective and not a radical remedy. That remedy can be found only by finding the source of the power of the machine, and that source is official patronage. It is the command of millions of the public money spent in public administration; the control

[15] *Orations and Addresses,* "Machine Politics and the Remedy," Vol. II, pp. 157–159.

of the vast labyrinth of place, with its enormous emoluments; the system which makes the whole Civil Service, to the least detail and most significant position, the spoils of party victory; which perverts necessary party organization into intolerable party despotism. It is upon this that the hierarchy of the machine is erected. Strike at this system strongly, steadily, persistently, and you shiver the machine to pieces.[16]

Seeing his duty clearly, Curtis did not spare himself, but while most of his fellows were seeking fame or wealth for themselves he gave his time and strength without stint to the cause, and it was due to his efforts more than to those of any other man that a reform in the civil service was eventually brought about. He had to fight his way against bitter opposition. It was charged that he was seeking to create in America an undemocratic bureaucracy. His old friend Charles A. Dana—from whom he had become estranged—was quite frank. "Above all I do not believe," he said, "in the establishment in this country of the German bureaucratic system, with its permanent staff of office-holders who are not responsible to the people, and whose tenure of place knows no variation and no end except the end of life." [17] But it was the politicians who fought most bitterly, and when to civil service reform he added the sin of bolting the party, throwing over Blaine and supporting Cleveland, he was subjected to plentiful insults. Nevertheless as the leader of the Mugwumps, preaching to a party-ridden generation the gospel of independency, he did his country a real service. He could not foresee, of course, how easily the menace of the independent voter was to be met; how through the control of both party machines and both nominees by the political bosses the independent would have only the choice betwixt tweedledum and tweedledee, and in disgust would largely refrain from voting. But the open and crying political evils of the Gilded Age he saw clearly, and in seeking to lessen them he proved himself a useful citizen as well as a cultivated American.

III

ENGLISH LIBERALISM AND POLITICS—GODKIN AND "THE NATION"

The severest critic of the Gilded Age was Edwin Lawrence Godkin, founder of the *Nation*. More caustic than George William Curtis, equipped with a complete social philosophy, and armed with

[16] See *Ibid.*, p. 160.   [17] J. H. Wilson, *The Life of Charles A. Dana*, p. 466.

perfect self-assurance, he devoted thirty-five years to the task of instructing America in the principles of government as those principles were understood by John Stuart Mill. He was at once an idealist and a realist, and the intellectual history of the critic is revealed in the shift from the one to the other. To Godkin the English liberal—who had studied the American experiment from overseas—as to Karl Schurz the German liberal, America was the torchbearer of the democratic faith; and any defection from the cause, any betrayal of that faith, was a desecration of the temple of liberalism by its own priesthood. Liberalism, he was persuaded, was the handmaid of civilization; the hope of any rational progress, rested on the principle of free inquiry and free endeavor. To God-kin, therefore, and to Schurz and the hundreds of European liberals who sought refuge here following the *débâcle* of the revolutionary hopes of 1848, it was a matter of deep import that America should remain true to its liberal tradition, trusting freedom, refusing to repeat the unhappy experience of a Tory Europe. He would say to America what John Wise had said nearly two centuries before: "Ye have been called unto liberty, therefore hold your hold, brethren! Pull up well upon the oars, you have a rich cargo, and I hope . . . day-light and good piloting will secure all." But he would do more than that; he would pull an oar himself; and with high hopes, at the age of twenty-five, he cast in his lot with America to serve the cause in whatever ways might offer.

Godkin came of an English Protestant strain that for seven centuries had lived in County Wexford, at the extreme southeastern point of Ireland. He was neither Scotch like the men of Ulster, nor Irish like his neighbors of Kilkenny and Wicklow, but as English in blood and temperament as Jonathan Swift. Educated at Queen's College, Belfast, he studied law for a time at Lincoln's Inn, went through the revolutionary years of 1848–1851 with their great hopes, and entered the field of journalism as correspondent for the London *Daily News* during the Crimean War. In 1856 he came to America with the intention of entering the law, but returned to journalism. During the Civil War he was correspondent for the *Daily News* of London, laboring to counteract British Tory opinion that ran strongly pro-South, and marshal the forces of English liberalism on the side of the North. Three months after Appomattox he founded the *Nation* as an organ of criticism, through the columns of which he proposed to appeal to the intelligence and the conscience of America in support of the principles of Victorian liberalism.

For this excellent work of criticism Godkin was provided with a sound equipment. Endowed with a vigorous intellect, he kept his mind free from shifting fogs and rarely mistook immediate for ultimate ends. His training had been in a distinguished tradition. His father was a Presbyterian minister and journalist, and the strain of robust dissent that contributed so richly to Victorian liberalism came to him as a birthright. He was "brought up," he said, "in the Mill-Grote school of radicals." "When I was in college," he wrote in later years, "I and the young men of my acquaintance were Liberals, in the English sense. John Stuart Mill was our prophet, and Grote and Bentham were our daily food." [18] Already his heart was overseas; America as it had been described by de Tocqueville was his "promised land," the home of a free democracy on which his hopes for civilization were fixed. His first book, written at the early age of twenty-two, was a history of the land Kossuth was striving to set free, and he there defined the word democrat as he had come to interpret it—the democrats, he said, are "all those whose hopes and sympathies are not bound up in a party or class, but look for the welfare and progress of humanity as the goal of their striving." [19]

Thus he wrote in the aftermath of the revolutionary years of 1848–1851. But the glowing idealism of the young radical was to suffer discouragements and setbacks from the experience of later years. One suspects that his liberalism never possessed the whole of him, never grew from within out, but was overlaid on a nature fundamentally aristocratic that at heart preferred Tory to liberal ends. Though as a young man he spred his canvas to the winds of liberalism, he was always a little distrustful of the bellying sails and he never quite liked the crew. There is a curious suggestiveness in his changing attitude towards England and English society. He had quitted the old world out of dislike for it, and a dozen years later he declined to go back except as a "last extremity." "It would be going back," he said, "into an atmosphere that I detest and a social system that I have hated since I was fourteen years old." [20] At the bottom of this repugnance was an obstinate pride. He was ambitious, capable, and sensitive, and a caste society that refused

[18] Ogden, *Life and Letters of Edwin Lawrence Godkin*, Vol. I, p. 11.
[19] *Ibid.*, Vol. I, p. 17.   [20] *Ibid.*, Vol. II, p. 140.

to open its doors to him he looked upon as pernicious. To assert that his espousal of democracy was due to his brusque rejection by a more distinguished mistress, is a severe judgment, yet it is a judgment that his friend Henry Holt quite frankly implied.[21]

He had come to America in the hope of getting on in the world. He had a strong regard for social position. His standards were severe and his sympathies so narrow as to lay him open to the frequent charge of snobbery. He would mingle in none but good society, and it was easier in America than in England to gain entrance to good society. Until he had made his mark he would not go back; but when as a distinguished editor he ventured to return, and found himself accepted by the best people, his hatred for the English social system oozed away, and the eager delight he experienced in upper-class society was an unconscious testimony to the value he had set upon a system from which as a young man he had been excluded. Godkin was too English to make himself over into an American, too natively aristocratic to be a democrat. A disciple of John Stuart Mill, he lacked the complete intellectual integrity of Mill that brushed aside all caste prejudices and personal ambitions, as he lacked his vast intellectual accumulation. Godkin's liberalism was founded on Mill, but it was never quite Mill.

The philosophy to which, as a disciple of the Bentham-Mill-Grote school, the young Godkin gave his allegiance, was a Utilitarian adaptation of *laissez faire*—the doctrine that the greatest happiness of the greatest number is the ultimate social objective, and that such objective can be attained only through the completest liberty under the sway of reason and justice. As presented by John Stuart Mill it was a singularly persuasive philosophy that awakened a response in every generous mind. Liberty, he insisted, is the thing chiefly to be desired, for where men are free they will shape social organisms to their needs. Man is both an economic and a political animal, and the difficult problem of the political philosopher is to keep the one from trespassing upon the rights of the other. The economic man, under the drive of the acquisitive instinct, regards the political state as an ally in the present business of acquisition; and the political man looks upon business as subject to strict regulation and control in the interests of the state. To prevent this meddlesome interference of each with the other, Mill laid down the principle of liberty in terms as uncompromising as

[21] *Nation*, July 8, 1915, p. 47.

those of the Physiocrats. The "sole end," he asserted, "for which mankind are warranted, individually or collectively, in interfering with the liberty of action of any of their number, is self-protection," and "the only purpose for which power can be rightfully exercised over any member of a civilized community, against his will, is to prevent harm to others. His own good, either physical or moral, is not a sufficient warrant." [22]

From this excellent school the young Godkin emerged a political theorist of no mean ability; somewhat too dogmatic, perhaps, a bit overconfident of the finality of his logic, but with a shrewd dialectic, quick to separate reality from pretense, severe upon all flummery and buncombe. That his philosophy was sharply opposed to the current tendencies of American political life he saw clearly: to Whiggery with its ambitious paternalisms; to centralization with its glorification of a Bismarckian state. His thought was erected on a foundation of *laissez faire*, and he sharply differentiated economics and politics. As a realist he recognized differences in individual capacity, but he was keenly suspicious of any attempt on the part of government to compensate for such differences. Any interference with natural law, he was convinced, entailed greater evils than benefits. Economic competition is a struggle between individuals, and government must content itself with its proper rôle of policeman to keep the peace. With Mill he refused to recognize the state as a separate entity. He never confused the personnel of government with "what is called 'the state'"; and as he contemplated the honesty and capacity of the several members who administered government in a given commonwealth, he was disinclined to entrust them with regulative powers. Disinterested honesty and capacity, it seemed, too rarely got into office, governments were too little acquainted with common morality, to justify hopes of equalizing the inequality of nature by political means.

To the sound philosophical equipment brought from England Godkin added a very considerable understanding of American political history. The ten years spent here before the founding of the *Nation*, had been employed in getting at home upon the new scene. He had carefully checked the findings of de Tocqueville and was convinced that the French critic had gone far astray in his interpretation of the great American experiment. In his analysis of democratic tendencies he had fallen into the fallacy of *post hoc*

[22] *On Liberty*, Chapter I.

ergo propter hoc, with the result that he had got the cart before the horse; and in an article published in the *North American Review* of January, 1865, Godkin entered the lists in defense of America against the criticisms of English Tories founded on such fallacies. In its emphasis on historical realism "Aristocratic Opinions of Democracy" is a surprisingly modern study that might almost have been written by one of our younger historians. It is an interpretation of our political development in terms of environment, and it traces the rise of democracy to the leveling influence of decentralization. For a hundred and fifty years, he pointed out, old-world habits and customs, the spirit of aristocracy, prevailed in the closely grouped settlements along the Atlantic seaboard, where physical conditions restrained the tendency to social disruption; but with the breaking through of the Appalachian barrier, and the influx of new waves of immigration, the conditions were prepared for a vast movement of decentralization. It was the Inland Empire that made possible the democratic revolution in America. "How was it," he asks, "that that democratic tide, which within the last fifty years, has overwhelmed everything, during the previous hundred and fifty years gave so few signs of rising?" And his reply to the question antedates Professor Turner's theory of the frontier by thirty years:

> If we inquire what are those phenomena of American society which it is generally agreed distinguish it from that of older countries, we shall find . . . that by far the larger number of them may be attributed in a great measure to what, for want of a better name, we shall call "the frontier life" led by a large proportion of the inhabitants, and to the influence of this portion on manners and legislation, rather than to political institutions, or even to the equality of conditions. In fact, we think that these phenomena, and particularly those of them which excite most odium in Europe, instead of being the effect of democracy, are partly its cause, and that it has been to their agency more than aught else, that the democratic tide in America has owed most of its force and violence.
>
> The agency which, in our opinion, gave democracy its first great impulse in the United States, which has promoted its spread ever since, and has contributed most powerfully to the production of those phenomena in American society which hostile critics set down as peculiarly democratic, was neither the origin of the Colonists, nor the circumstances under which they came to the country, nor their religious belief; but the great change in the distribution of the population, which began soon after the Revolution, and which continues its operation up to the present time.[23]

[23] "Aristocratic Opinions of Democracy," in *Problems of Modern Democracy*, pp. 25–26, 30–31.

Godkin was thirty-four when he entered upon his life work of pouring a stream of fresh and free thought upon the ways of the Gilded Age. It was somewhat in the spirit of Matthew Arnold that he interpreted the function of criticism. "The highest allegiance of every man," he wrote Norton in 1865, "is due to liberty and civilization, or rather civilization and liberty"; [24] and the creed of the *Nation*, which Godkin unconsciously modified as culture dispossessed liberty in his affections, may be summed up in the words democracy, individualism, morality, culture, to the end of a free life in a humane and well-ordered society. Throughout the Gilded Age this transplanted English liberal was the high priest of criticism in America. His caustic intelligence played ironically about the current shibboleths and fetishes, reducing them to shreds and patches. He could discover little that was good in the Gilded Age, in its tariffs and land grants, its *Crédit Mobilier* and other scandals, its buccaneer plutocracy, its undisciplined proletarianism, its bitter agrarianism; and he was prompted to a severity of judgment that easier-going natures thought harsh. Enemies sprang up in his every footprint; but too much was at stake, he believed, to temper his criticism to flabby minds, and he laid about him with what he considered a fine impartiality.

It was a cold plunge into a dirty pool, and a nature less robust would have scrambled out quickly. His realism was a profound discouragement to his idealism, and his native aristocracy of temperament closed his mind to the virtues of certain homely American liberalisms. As an intellectual he distrusted all Jacksonian frontier freedoms. The doctrine of liberty did not appear to advantage in the garb of agrarians and proletarians; Thaddeus Stevens and Terence V. Powderly were an ungainlier breed of libertarians than Gladstone and Mill; with such leadership it seemed to Godkin that liberty was running away with civilization and a smash-up was likely. It was the duty of the *Nation*, therefore, to arouse the culture of America to its political obligations, to the end that the custodianship of liberty should be taken over by the intelligence of America. It proved a discouraging job, and slowly on the horizon of his mind rose the shadow of the doubt that had troubled de Tocqueville and Cooper and Fisher Ames— must a democracy prove a leveling influence that destroys a fine individuality and a generous social culture? Careless of his trus-

[24] Ogden, *op. cit.*, Vol. II, p. 48.

teeship, was not the American democrat throwing his heritage to the demagogue and the spoilsman?

As he watched the scrambling heedlessness of the times his liberalism oozed away, his democratic faith lost its sanctions, and he slowly drifted to the right and the dead-sea of pessimism. The mass was too powerful in America, and the mass was shot through with the spirit of selfish leveling. The democracy had been distorted by the frontier, and the sense of responsibility, of individual duty, was well-nigh atrophied. The vulgar West threw its crudity upon all America. "I do not like the western type of man," Godkin confessed to Norton; and to another friend who praised California, he wrote, "No scenery or climate I had to share with western people would charm me." He never spared his mordant adjectives in commenting privately on all America west of the Hudson River. In his gloomy later years he found consolation in Brahmin culture. For years he lived in Cambridge, and in the company of Lowell and Norton he felt at home. Here were democratic gentlemen worthy of his ideal. If all America were only like Cambridge his faith in a cultivated liberalism would be justified. In those years he called himself "an American of the *vieille roche*," which being interpreted, meant a liberal of the Brahmin school.

The immediate problems on which Godkin was called to pass judgment brought him into the thick of the struggles of the Gilded Age. As an editor he confronted the bitter antagonisms that sprang from the rivalries of the farmer, the wage-earner, and the industrial capitalist. Each group was seeking to enlist government on its side and use the political state for special and narrow ends. To a disciple of Mill all such attempts were no better than treason to democracy, and when such treason was justified by what he considered specious economic theory Godkin's hostility was edged with acerbity. All the trenchant dogmas of his philosophy—his police theory of the state, his Ricardian *laissez faire*, his individualism—rushed to the attack of such impudent impostors. With no organized forces at his back he made war on every major group in America. He essayed to rally the scattered minority of the intellectuals and overthrow the citadel of economic power by appeal to reason. It was magnificent but it was scarcely war. The culture of the Gilded Age was undisciplined, lacking faith and unnurtured in philosophy, fastidious rather than vigorous—the poorest of material for shock troops. It applauded every clever thrust of its captain, but preferred to keep its own hands unsoiled. In consequence, to the end of his life Godkin was a leader without a following, little more than a voice crying in the wilderness.

For the rising plutocracy Godkin felt the scorn of a gentleman for the vulgar new-rich. Its hands were dirty, and it was soiling all American life. Its gospel of Whiggery, that under pretense of furthering prosperity had turned Congress into an auction room, was an insult to his Manchester liberalism. Just as surely as government meddles with subsidies and tariffs and grants, he pointed out, will it be defiled. Men are but indifferent honest, and if statesmen are not to become mere political hucksters they must stand apart from the temptations of business. The plea for a national economy had brought Congress to the *Crédit Mobilier* scandals, and it would breed other scandals so long as it was heeded. The only cure for Whiggery was to destroy it. In a scathing leader he early paid his respects to the Whiggish system of governmental subsidies:

> The remedy is simple. The Government must get out of the "protective" business and the "subsidy" business and the "improvement" and the "development" business. It must let trade, and commerce, and manufactures, and steamboats, and railroads, and telegraphs alone. It cannot touch them without breeding corruption. We care nothing about the wonderful stories we hear about what can be achieved in the way of "promoting industry" by all these canal and steamboat and railroad schemes. Were the material prospect twice as tempting, the state could not profitably meddle with them, because neither it nor any other government in the world *can command the virtue necessary to carry them on.* This is not a matter of speculation; we know it as a matter of experience. It is almost as much as this Government can do to maintain order and administer justice. It may one day be able to do a great deal more, but not until a great change has occurred in the social condition of the country. We have gone far enough, heaven knows, on the road of "protection" and "promotion," and have found at every step that it leads straight to the bottomless pit; that for every hundred dollars voted by these poor men to whom we pay scanty wages for passing bills at Washington, we lessen, and perceptibly lessen, the stock of individual honor, of self-respect, and of public spirit, of a loyalty to ideals, to which far more than to any triumphs of material industry, we must look for continued national greatness. We are making money fast enough in all conscience; what needs fostering just now is honesty.[25]

Godkin found it exceedingly difficult to foster the austere honesty that he desired in the body politic, and in his fury at the

[25] *Nation*, January 30, 1873, p. 68.

common political scoundrelism he came to ascribe much of the virus that was poisoning America to the party of western agrarians. He was rapidly drifting to the right and the defense of capitalism, and as the agrarian platform was slowly built up of successive planks—greenbacks, free silver, subtreasuries, railway regulation, the income tax—he turned upon it all the batteries of his wrath. Godkin never understood the American farmer, but he professed to understand economics and political science, and the agrarian platform aroused his implacable hostility. In his frequent discussions of the currency question, a question that for thirty years was a subject of passionate debate, he was at some disadvantage. Intellectually he was ill equipped to deal with it. Although a Ricardian he failed to grasp Ricardo's quantitative principle of money or the function of paper currency. As a gold-standard advocate he accepted the English monetary system as it was given form by the Parliamentary Bank Act of 1844, and he would have no tampering with it. To Godkin money was a measure of value, and a fluctuating standard, implied in the quantitative theory, was as immoral as a fluctuating yardstick. The use of greenbacks—"rag money"—he reckoned a scheme by which dishonest debtors might cheat their creditors.[26] He was forced to regard gold and silver as commodities, fluctuating in price with supply and demand; but he looked upon them as possessing a stable natural value that placed them beyond political manipulation. Any attempt to disturb this natural value by artificial means he called dishonest.[27] He was almost indecent in the vehemence of his adjectives applied to the "dishonest money men." He called the Greenbackers "communists," [28] and speaking of the Grangers, he said, "There is nothing unnatural or deplorable in a Granger turning from one form of swindle to another." [29]

By the middle nineties it was hard to distinguish Godkin's views on the agrarian program from those of a Wall Street banker. In discussing free silver he abandoned economic principles and fell to mouthing like any newspaper writer. The currency question he regarded as a simple question of public morality. There was only one issue, the issue between honest and dishonest money.

[26] See "Public Opinion and the Currency," *Ibid.*, February 27, 1873; "The Political Situation in 1896," in *Problems of Modern Democracy.*
[27] See "On Gold and Silver," *Ibid.*, July 6, 1876.
[28] *Ibid.*, May 25, 1876.
[29] *Ibid.*, June 1, 1876.

"The demand for free-silver coinage is a demand for a division of property," [30] he said in the early days of the campaign of 1896, and a fortnight later he took extreme ground:

. . . the bold and wicked scheme of repudiation . . . is presented without a blush in the platform. Upon this question the campaign must be fought. If the party of repudiators cannot be put down, the republic cannot be preserved and is not worth preserving.[31]

Such pronouncements bear none of the earmarks of dispassionate criticism. It may seem severe to suggest that they are the comments of a very ignorant or shallow critic, blinded by his prejudices; yet it is true. The equipment of Manchester economics with which he had outfitted himself in the late forties, was no longer adequate in the nineties; yet he seems not to have been aware of the fact. The mid-Victorian still regarded himself as an authority on all economic questions, although he seems to have done no serious reading in economic theory for half a century, and was scarcely conscious how far he had drifted towards the right. The old liberal was fighting the battles of capitalism with weapons as antiquated as the old cap-and-ball musket. "The great trouble with all silverites and currency lunatics, North and South," he said, "is that, when monetary crises arise, they cannot be got to go to the right quarter for information"—a comment that one might retort upon Godkin himself. The intellectual knew far less about money than "Coin" Harvey, whom he would have laughed at.

The same drift to the right is evident in the pronouncements on the Populist movement of the times. Writing on "The Kansas Situation," when the farmers' unrest was becoming militant, he remarked:

Such an unexpected outbreak as this of the last two or three years shows at least that it is not only in the cities, where the foreign-born swarm, that demagogues may thrive and the doctrine of revolution be preached.[32]

The "ravings of the Farmers' movement" he regarded as no more than a "vague and visionary discontent," that was seeking political cures for its economic ills. The hard times from which the West was suffering were the result of economic law. It was not the currency or excessive railway rates that were the cause. The vast

[30] "The Issue of the Campaign," *Ibid.*, July 2, 1896.
[31] "The Platform of Revolution," *Ibid.*, July 16, 1896.
[32] *Ibid.*, January 19, 1893.

extension of railway systems had brought under cultivation too many acres, and the reduction of transportation costs would serve only to bring additional acres under cultivation, thereby increasing competition and forcing prices still lower. High railway rates were the surest safeguard against further extension of an industry much overdeveloped; and for state legislatures to attempt to fix railway tariffs by law—to attempt to control economic forces by statutes—was sheer folly. In discussing the celebrated Illinois railway legislation Godkin spoke in defense of the roads:

> The locomotive is coming in contact with the framework of our institutions. In this country of simple government, the most powerful centralizing force which civilization has yet produced has within the next score years, yet to assume its relation to that political machinery which is to control and regulate it. . . . The corporations of course contested the validity of the law. If the legislature could establish one rate at which they should do the work of transportation, it could establish another. They were fighting for their lives and property; it was against taxation without representation. . . . An arbitrary power is claimed in the supreme legislative body to decide on the reasonable rates of the cost of private services. Just as three hundred years ago the price of bread and labor was regulated by act of Parliament, so now the cost of transportation is to be fixed by a jury of twelve men. . . . Thus far, therefore, the results of the Illinois railroad war must be regarded as rather portentous than satisfactory.[33]

The "watered-stock hallucination," that had taken possession of the agrarian mind and aroused such bitterness, he dismissed with a curious comment that did no great credit to his intelligence.

> There is . . . one difficulty in the way, which is the difficulty common to many of the proposed reforms in railroad management—the practice alleged has absolutely no existence except in the heated brain of the agitators who have imagined it. There are no roads in the United States on which any attempt has been made to increase the freight earnings in proportion to the watered stock or debt.[34]

The passions aroused by the campaign of '96 swept Godkin from his moorings and left him adrift. He quickly convinced himself that the real issue at stake was the moral integrity of the nation. As he studied the platforms and leaders he found little comfort in either. For McKinley he had the contempt of the intellectual for a purveyor of heavy platitudes, and he flayed him in a two-

[33] *Ibid.*, April 10, 1873.
[34] "The Watered Stock Hallucination," *Ibid.*, October 9, 1873.

column leader with his old skill.[35] But for Bryan, the "boy orator of the Platte," his dislike passed the bounds of decency; and for the Chicago convention that put him in nomination—"the roaring mob" with its "Populistic, anarchistic platform"—his contempt outran his command of invective.

No such collection of inflammatory and reckless men ever put themselves on exhibition in a national convention. Beside them the Populists are lamb-like, and the socialists sucking doves. The country has watched their mad proceedings with disgust and shuddering, only impatient for the coming of November to stamp out them and their incendiary doctrines.[37]

To what lengths his overheated brain carried him in those political dogdays, how starkly reactionary he had become, is suggested by his comment on the plank in the Democratic platform attacking the scandal of injunctions:

This blow at the courts shows how true are the instincts of the revolutionaries. They know their most formidable enemies. Judicial decisions have again and again drawn the fangs of confiscatory and revolutionary legislation, and the courts have come more and more to stand as the great bulwarks of property and personal rights.[37]

Godkin's last years were not happy. The wave of imperialism that swept over England and America, with its Boer War and Spanish War, brought him acute concern. The world that he knew was slipping from its moorings, and he was fearful of the seas into which it was plunging. The conquest of the Philippines seemed to him a badge of national degradation. Writing in November, 1899, he said:

We are dragging wearily in the old way, killing half a dozen Filipinos every week, and continually "near the end." The folly of ignorance and rascality we are displaying in the attempt to conquer and have "subjects" would disgrace a trades union.[38]

As he watched the tedious process of subjugation he inclined to attribute to Kipling a large share of the current imperialism. "I think most of the current jingoism on both sides of the water is due to him," he wrote a few weeks later. "He is the poet of the barrack-room cads," a "most pernicious, vulgar person"; and his

---

[35] "Prosperity's Advance Orator," *Ibid.*, June 18, 1896.
[36] "The Chicago Platform," *Ibid.*, July 16, 1896.
[37] "The Platform of Revolution," *Ibid.*, July 23, 1896.
[38] Ogden, *op. cit.*, Vol. II, pp. 238–239.

"White Man's Burden," cabled to America and printed on the front pages of the newspapers as a message to imperialist America, must have rubbed across Godkin's raw nerves. The pious cant of Kipling's imperialism was a bitter cup for a disillusioned liberal. The Jubilee with its fulsome laudation of "fat, useless royalty," was fittingly commemorated by this noisy poet of imperialism, and Godkin turned away from it all in disgust.

But turn where he might he found no comfort. His old dreams of a free and enlightened democracy rising in America, were dead. Victorian liberalism had been laid away in the grave of John Stuart Mill, and only its ghost was walking in these latter times. Godkin's last days were bitter, and the gloom that was settling upon him crept into his letters. It is a malady common amongst liberals, and how deeply it had struck in is revealed in such passages as these:

I am not sanguine about the future of democracy. I think we shall have a long period of decline . . . and then a recrudescence under some other form of society.[39]

I do not know what the future of our modern civilization is to be. But I stumble where I firmly trod.[40]

Things look very black. I think that while money-making will long continue on a great scale, the government will shortly undergo great changes which will be presided over not by men of light and learning, but by capitalists and adroit politicians.[41]

I came here fifty years ago with high and fond ideals about America. . . . They are now all shattered, and I have apparently to look elsewhere to keep even moderate hopes about the human race alive.[42]

The idealist is prone to be exigent in his demands upon civilization. He marks out a straight path to the goal of his hopes, and takes it greatly to heart when society chooses to follow other ways to other ends. Godkin's mind was keenly critical, but his sympathies were narrow and his prejudices great. It is well to be a friend to civilization, but it is foolish to set up as a custodian; for civilization, like Topsy, will shift for itself. A just and liberal government is an excellent ideal, but it is one for which few amongst the mass of men greatly care; and because America chose to follow its own nose, because it would not become like the America of his dreams, Godkin allowed his heart to fill with bitterness. It is true that his recompense for long years of labor was scanty; the Gilded Age

[39] *Ibid.*, Vol. II, p. 199.
[40] *Ibid.*, Vol. II, p. 217.
[41] *Ibid.*, Vol. II, p. 243.
[42] *Ibid.*, Vol. II, p. 237.

was not to be frightened from its fleshpots by his warnings. But long ago it was said, "Wisdom crieth in the streets and no man regardeth her," and why should Godkin have become discouraged with civilization because certain blackguard years clove to their blackguardry, instead of mounting to the somewhat arid heights he pointed out? One must choose at the last between tolerance and pessimism, and Godkin chose pessimism.

It is difficult today to understand his great influence with cultivated readers of his generation. In part perhaps it was due to his crisp assurance. He put things so plumply, he wrote so brilliantly, that his readers were persuaded he must think as neatly. Yet his trenchant prose style cannot hide a certain slightness of matter. His later comments tended to become ever thinner and shriller—not criticism at all, but the sharp expression of aging prejudice. When he talked about the tariff he had Mill at his elbow; but when he talked about the agrarian or the proletarian movements he was little more than a blue-jay scolding at a world he disliked. Unlike his great master he did not go forward to meet new times; he did not reinterpret Victorian liberalism in the light of the lessons taught by the Industrial Revolution; but by standing still he did liberalism a real disservice.

IV

FICTION CONSIDERS THE STATE OF THE COUNTRY

It was only a question of time before the novel would throw off the inhibitions of the genteel and turn to consider the state of the country. A changing social order would not fail of reflection in the pages of fiction, and as the novelists fell to scrutinizing the familiar scene, comparing the reality with the patriotic professions, it was certain that the workings of democracy would come in for sharp criticism. In the last decades of the century the problem novel spread swiftly, expanding the field of its inquiry, and seeking to understand the new ways. Making its first essays in the familiar field of the political, it soon turned to consider the economic problems arising out of the new industrialism, espousing either capitalism or labor as the social sympathies of the author might determine. The class passions of the times found a reflection in its pages, and in consequence the sociological novel became increasingly a repository of the social ideas of a perplexed and troubled generation.

I

THE POLITICAL NOVEL

Of the early political novels three are of sufficient interest to reward attention: *The Gilded Age* (1873), *Democracy* (1881), and *An American Politician* (1884). The first, written by Mark Twain in collaboration with Charles Dudley Warner, is a satire of Gilded Age ways with particular attention to the political corruption of General Grant's administration. The fictional disguise is slight. The actual Washington is presented vividly and familiar figures —Ben Butler, Oakes. Ames, President Grant, Secretary Boutwell —move through the scene. The central figure, Senator Dillworthy, was modeled upon Senator Pomeroy of Kansas, who had recently lost a reëlection through an unlucky exposure of an attempt to bribe the Kansas legislature. The heroine, Laura Hawkins, is a western lobbyist who in order to put through a congressional steal under pretense of providing an industrial school for the freedmen, twists Congressmen about her fingers, turns adventuress and ends in tragedy. Out of the West comes the spirit of corruption that the respectable East is unable to withstand, until the itch of speculation infects the whole country. It is Colonel Sellers who embodies the slackness of frontier political morals, that in turn vitiates his political principles. The genial Colonel is quite frankly a Greenbacker.

> The country is getting along very well, [he said] but our public men are too timid. What we want is more money. I've told Boutwell so. Talk of basing the currency on gold; you might as well base it on pork. Gold is only one product. Base it on everything! You've got to do something for the West. How am I to move my crops? We must have improvements. Grant's got the idea. We want a canal from the James River to the Mississippi. Government ought to build it.[43]

The analysis is not penetrating. The real sources of political corruption—the rapacious railway lobbyists that camped in brigades about the capitol building—are passed over, and attention is fastened on small steals—the Knobs University bill and the Columbus River Navigation scheme—that do not touch the real rascals of the day. The implication is unmistakable that the source of corruption is the Jacksonian West with its heritage of the spoils spirit. The Federalistic East is victimized by the rapacities

[43] Vol. II, Chapter 13, p. 128.

of mid-western politicians with their religious cant, their talk of the rights of the people and the greatness of the plain democracy. Senator Dillworthy is fairly unctuous in his oily Christian spirit, and Brother Balaam is his fellow. The portraits, one suspects, need not be taken seriously as pictures of the chief apostles of preëmption and exploitation. To have sketched the real leaders of the great barbecue might have involved too many unpleasantries.

Democracy, written seven years later, is an inferior book in every way, less penetrating, less amusing, less creative. To essay to penetrate the dark places of political jobbery through the eyes of a society woman, too high-bred to turn lobbyist and inveigle secrets out of ambitious politicians, is sufficiently absurd, yet not uncharacteristic of the Henry Adams whose home was a distinguished salon and who in pottering about the political world of Washington deceived himself in thinking he had his finger on the web of intrigue. It is an amazing book for such a man to write. The attitude is that of the kid-gloved reformer who goes in for civil service reform, and who views the uncultivated West as the source of all political corruption. The hero, Senator Silas Ratcliffe of Peoria, Illinois, like Senator Dillworthy, is a past master in political organization who covers his dishonesty with religious cant. The economic sources of political corruption are ignored, and the evil is traced to the principle of democracy. Whatever political convictions are in the book are expressed by Representative Gore, a civil service reformer from Massachusetts, and quite evidently Henry Adams himself; and the conclusion is thus set forth:

"Do you yourself think democracy the best government, and universal suffrage a success?"

Mr. Gore saw himself pinned to the wall, and he turned at bay with almost the energy of despair:

"These are matters about which I rarely talk in society. . . . But since you ask for my political creed, you shall have it. I only condition that it shall be for you alone, never to be repeated or quoted as mine. I believe in democracy. I accept it. I will faithfully serve and defend it. I believe in it because it appears to me the inevitable consequence of what has gone before it. Democracy asserts the fact that the masses are now raised to a higher intelligence than formerly. All our civilization aims at this mark. We want to do what we can to help it. I myself want to see the result. I grant it is an experiment, but it is the only direction society can take that is worth its taking; the only conception of its duty large enough to satisfy its instincts; the only result that is worth an effort or a risk. Every other step is backward, and I do not want to repeat the past.

I am glad to see society grapple with issues in which no one can afford to
be neutral."

"And supposing your experiment fails," said Mrs. Lee; "suppose society destroys itself with universal suffrage, corruption, and communism."

". . . I have faith; not perhaps in the old dogmas, but in the new ones.
. . . faith in science; faith in the survival of the fittest. Let us be true to
our time, Mrs. Lee! If our age is to be beaten, let us die in the ranks. If it
is to be victorious, let us be first to lead the column. Anyway, let us not be
skulkers or grumblers. There! have I repeated my catechism correctly?
You would have it! Now oblige me by forgetting it. I should lose my
character at home if it got out."[44]

And the conclusion of the matter is thus summed up:

"I want to go to Egypt," said Madelaine, still smiling faintly; "democracy has shaken my nerves to pieces. Oh, what rest it would be to live in
the Great Pyramid and look out forever at the polar star!"

Not a hint of the Industrial Revolution; not a hint of the sordid
Whiggery that was fouling American politics; not a suggestion of
any creative social philosophy on which to establish an adequate
theory of democracy. A dreary place at best, with no faith in human nature and no trust in democratic machinery, but only a
gentlemanly belief that an antiquated Federalism may somehow
pull this venture in republicanism out of the bog in which Jacksonianism had mired it. No wonder Henry Adams would not set his
name on the title-page, but left it an orphan to make its own way
in the world. In his life of John Hay, William Roscoe Thayer has
explained the situation thus:

The Adamses, the Hays, and Clarence King formed an inner circle,
which somebody named "The Five of Hearts," and out of this came, in
1882, a novel entitled *Democracy*, a strikingly clever satire on Washington
society. Its authorship was at once attributed to them, but one after another denied it. If it was a joint product no individual could monopolize
the credit; and as it seems to have been read chapter by chapter to the
group, and discussed by them all, it might be said, technically, to be a
composite. Clarence King is still commonly regarded as its author; and
there are many supporters of Hay; but I believe that only Mr. Adams
possessed the substance, and style, and the gift of Voltairean raillery which
distinguish it.[45]

Mr. Thayer is generous in his praise.

An American Politician is even less consequential as a political
study than *Democracy*. Marion Crawford was a professional ro-

[44] Chapter 4, p. 78.   [45] Vol. II, pp. 58–59.

mancer and in this naïve venture into a field little known to him he carried his complete romantic kit. The political theme is tied about with so many love strands as almost to strangle it. The hero, John Harrington, we are assured is a very remarkable man, a Bostonian with a Mayflower teapot in his family treasures, an idealist of primitive Puritan intensity. But we must take him upon hearsay. Nothing that he does or says suggests his greatness. Politically the book is reduced to a little glimpse of the methods of selecting a United States senator—an Irish ward boss with twenty votes in his belt, a gentlemanly railway attorney who handles offal skillfully with a handkerchief at his nose—set in between two set speeches by the hero. The rest is Newport and the Back Bay, not quite stupid yet with no distinction. The romancer does not move easily in an unfamiliar field, and he sends his hero forth to battle for righteousness with small intellectual equipment. His speeches are heavily oratorical and his political philosophy is naïve; it is pretty much George William Curtis, the sufficiency of civil service reform and the virtues of non-partisanship.

The unreality of the book is furthered by a conception worthy of Poe—a mysterious council of three that meets in London and directs political movements in America. We are dimly aware that the council is both ancient and honorable; that it goes back historically to post-Revolutionary days and is self-perpetuating; and its uncanny power has resulted from supreme intelligence supplemented by exact information gathered during many years. In its secret archives every public man in America is tagged and docketed; his political and financial affiliations are set down in detail; and on the basis of this knowledge the cryptic three send forth instructions that are faithfully carried out. The danger to America lies in sectionalism—North, South, and West struggling for supremacy in the national councils; and upon the three rests the self-imposed responsibility of saving America from itself. The idea is sufficiently absurd, as the book is absurd. Crawford was a cosmopolitan who knew little about American political conditions, and the crisis of the novel is the Hayes-Tilden *impasse* of 1876. The influence of the novel, one may safely assume, was negligible.*

* In his original scheme Professor Parrington included Tourgée's *A Fool's Errand*, but the text shows that he decided against its inclusion.—*Publisher.*

2

THE ECONOMIC NOVEL

The theme of these earlier novels was politics as revealed by the Gilded Age; on the other hand *The Bread-winners* was one of the early economic novels. Like *Democracy* it was an outcome of the discussions of the vivacious trio, John Hay, Clarence King, and Henry Adams. Written in 1882 by Hay, it was published anonymously in the *Century Magazine* from August, 1883, to January, 1884. Hay never publicly acknowledged the authorship, and it was not until the edition of 1915 appeared with an introductory note by his son, that his name appeared on the title-page. It achieved a notable success—far beyond that of *Democracy;* was warmly praised and sharply criticized; was replied to in other novels; all of which goes to show that it fanned the coals that were smoldering in the industrial life of the day, threatening a general conflagration. It was the first recognition on the part of literature that a class struggle impended in America—a first girding of the loins of polite letters to put down the menace that looked out from the underworld of the proletariat; and as such it assumes importance as an historical document quite beyond its significance as a work of art.

The motive of *The Bread-winners* is the defense of property against the "dangerous classes"; its immediate theme is a satire of labor unions. In an introductory note to the later edition, Clarence Leonard Hay explicitly denies this. "*The Bread-winners,*" he says, "is not directed against organized labor. It is rather a protest against the disorganization and demoralization of labor by unscrupulous leaders and politicians who, in the guise of helping the workingman, use his earnings to enrich themselves." He then states the theme thus:

It is a defense of the right of an individual to hold property, and a plea for the better protection of that property by law and order. Civilization rests upon law, order, and obedience. The agitator who preaches that obedience to lawful authority is a sin, and patriotism an illusion, is more dangerous to society than the thief who breaks in at night and robs the householder.

The editor thinks well of the American workingmen. At heart they are sound; their motives are honest; but their ignorance of fundamental economic principles too easily suffers them to fall victim to unscrupulous demagogues whose only object is their exploitation. To prevent such "disorganization and demoralization of labor," which can bring only suffering and failure upon men ill prepared to endure them, is therefore the patriotic duty of the educated classes. The proletariat is groping blindly for leadership; it is stirring uneasily; if the educated classes do not offer an enlightened leadership, the laborer will follow low cunning to immoral ends and blind leaders of the blind will bring irretrievable disaster upon civilization. Selfish appeal will kindle envy and hate; the rich and prosperous will go down before brute force; the rights of property will be destroyed; law, order, and obedience will give place to anarchy.

Such, briefly developed, is Clarence Hay's exposition of *The Bread-winners;* and the exposition seems to suggest the social views of John Hay. He probably had no antipathy to labor unions which are guided in their policy by "sound economic principles" and right "morality"—as the capitalist understands such things. But labor unions which follow their own leaders, which persist in thinking out a proletarian economy, which are bent on substituting a social morality for a property morality, which refuse to be led by the "educated classes," he was bitterly hostile to. It is the unrest furthered by rebellious labor unions that he fears, and it is this that gives point and animus to his satire. That *The Bread-winners* was conceived in a spirit of beneficent paternalism towards the proletariat, the present-day reader will have difficulty in discovering. It is too frank in defense of vested interests, it looks with too stern a disfavor upon all labor leaders who refuse to accept the finality of the present industrial order, it exudes too strong an odor of property-morality, to deceive an intelligent reader. Read today it is clearly a partisan defense of economic individualism, an attack upon the rising labor movement, a grotesque satire smeared with an unctuous morality—and because of this, a perfect expression of the spirit of upper-class America in those uneasy eighties with their strikes and lockouts and Haymarket riots.

The plot of the book is slight—it is the story of the oily machinations of Ananias Offitt, a professional agitator who lives off simple honest workmen whom he seduces, organizes a secret Brotherhood of the Breadwinners, urges on riot and robbery at the time of a great strike, is checkmated by the hero—a cultivated and elegant clubman by the name of Captain Arthur Farnham—betrays his tool, and in the end is murdered by him. Fortunately for the welfare of property interests there are "honest" workmen, men like Leopold Grosshammer, who rally to the support of law and order and eventually break the strike. The love-story is provided with two heroines, and the contrast between them emphasizes the class line which property draws. The upper-class heroine is as correct and colorless as Cooper's Eve Effingham: the lower-class heroine is as vulgarly handsome and as brazen as "such people" are supposed to be. A high-school education has spoilt her for the factory or domestic service, filling her empty head with foolish ambitions, but it could not make a lady of her.

Hay was in Cleveland at the time of the great strike in 1877, and he was profoundly disturbed by the experience. Writing to his father-in-law, he said:

The prospects of labor and capital both seem gloomy enough. The very devil seems to have entered into the lower classes of workingmen, and there are plenty of scoundrels to encourage them to all lengths. . . . I am thankful you did not *see* and *hear* what took place during the strikes. You were saved a very painful experience of human folly and weakness, as well as crime.[46]

The crying evils of a buccaneer industrialism which lay behind the strikes, Hay ignored completely. To provide his idyllic background of contented labor before it is seduced by demagogues, he goes back to a decadent domestic economy. His "honest and contented workman" is a carpenter who works for another carpenter—not a factory-hand tending a machine; and when the demagogue comes with his specious appeal he is triumphantly refuted.

"What are we, anyhow?" continued the greasy apostle of labor. "We are slaves; we are Roossian scurfs. We work as many hours as our owners like; we take what pay they choose to give us; we ask their permission to live and breathe."

"Oh, that's a lie," Sleeny interrupted, with unbroken calmness. "Old Saul Matchin and me come to an agreement about time and pay, and both of us was suited. Ef he's got his heel onto me, I don't feel it."[47]

John Hay was convinced that an "educated leadership" alone could save American democracy. But unfortunately—despite his great reputation in diplomacy and statesmanship—his own education seems to have been faulty. He had lately risen into the exploiting class, and he accepted the ready-made opinions of that

[46] William Roscoe Thayer, *Life and Letters of John Hay*, Vol. II, pp. 5–6.
[47] Chapter V

class. His biographer has admirably stated his position during the days of the strike riots when he was clarifying his views:

> Those riots of 1877 burnt deep into Colonel Hay's heart. Like the rest of the world, he had theorized on the likelihood of war between Capital and Labor; but he had reassured himself by the comfortable assumption that under American conditions—equal opportunity for all, high wages, equal laws, and the ballot-box—no angry laboring class could grow up. The riots blew such vaporing away: for they proved that the angry class already existed, that the ballot-box instead of weakening strengthened it, and that not only the politicians of both parties but also the constituted authorities would avoid, as long as possible, grappling with it.
> The event was too large to be dismissed as an outburst of temper: it must be accepted as a symptom, a portent. Did it mean that a cancer had attacked the body politic and would spread to the vital organs? Was Democracy a failure,—Democracy—for more than a century the dream of the down-trodden, the ideal of those who loved mankind and believed in its perfectibility, the Utopia which good men predicted should somehow turn out to be a reality? Hay had sung his paean to liberty; Hay had throbbed at the efforts of patriots in Spain and in France to overthrow their despots; he had even exulted over the signs of democratization in England. Had he been the victim of mirage? Was Democracy not the final goal of human society, but only a half-way stage between the despotism of Autocracy and the despotism of Socialism?
> These questions he could not evade. . . . But he held, as did many of his contemporaries, that the assaults on Property were inspired by demagogues who used as their tools the loafers, the criminals, the vicious,—Society's dregs who have been ready at all times to rise against laws and government. That you have property is proof of industry and foresight on your part or your father's; that you have nothing, is a judgment on your laziness and vices, or on your improvidence. The world is a moral world; which it would not be if virtue and vice received the same rewards.[48]

John Hay, it must be recalled, had enjoyed a college education through the aid of relatives, he had been taken under the wing of Lincoln and become his private secretary, he had been thrust forward by influential politicians, and finally he had married wealth— were these things proofs of virtue in a moral world that rewards foresight and punishes improvidence? Or were they rather the marks of a skillful climber? John Hay was a charming and cultivated gentleman, but he was also a child of the Gilded Age, with the materialisms of his generation in his blood. The young man had been an Abolitionist and a political radical; the old man was a McKinley conservative whose chief claim to reputation lay in

---

[48] Thayer, *op. cit.*, Vol. I. pp. 6-7.

the "open-door" policy in China. The beginnings of this shift to conservatism seem to have coincided with his marriage to Miss Stone, daughter of a Cleveland capitalist whose interests were threatened by the great strike. He was temperamentally one of John Adams's "natural aristocrats," and having gained entrée into aristocratic circles he took the coloring of his new environment. A son of the frontier, he became a man of the world. Prosperity was necessary to him.

Professing a deep attachment to democratic institutions and hatred of all monarchical principles—in Spain and France—John Hay ceased to be a Lincoln democrat, and took his place amongst the ruling class, accepting the principles of the rising plutocracy. *The Bread-winners* is a dramatization of the Federalistic principle that government exists for the protection of property. "Remembering the date when *The Bread-winners* was written," says his biographer, "we must regard it as the first important polemic in American fiction in defense of Property." [49] John Hay had become a thoroughgoing Hamiltonian. In his younger days his sympathies had gone out to radical republicans everywhere, and he watched the rising tide of liberalism with great satisfaction. In his first visits to Europe he followed closely the liberal movements. He was a warm admirer of Castelar, eulogizing him as one of the heroic figures of modern times. In a lecture in 1869 on "The Progress of Democracy in Europe" he spoke with the zeal of an advanced liberal. But soon thereafter the ardor of his zeal lessened. On later trips to Europe he did not display a like sympathy with the program of the Social Democrats. As economic unrest crept into politics, as strikes and boycotts began to disturb his father-in-law's business, he discovered less sympathy for revolutionary movements. Political revolutions sponsored by respectable middle-class leaders, were one thing; economic revolutions sponsored by the proletariat were quite another thing. A democracy that breeds more democracy is clearly dangerous. So much as has already been accomplished is excellent, of course; but nothing further must be attempted.

There is sound strategy in offensive epithets. And so, taking counsel of fear, he applied to the current economic unrest the words most offensive to polite American ears, and called it socialism, anarchism. Without pausing to weigh the demands of the farmer

[49] *Ibid.*, Vol. II, p. 15.

and the workingman, with no understanding of the meaning of the great proletarian movement then going forward in Europe, he appealed in defense of property to the specter of economic leveling before which every good American of the eighties recoiled in horror. As early as 1869, speaking of Castelar, he said: "He has too much sense and integrity to follow the lead of the Socialist fanatics."[50] Commenting on the unsettled state of things in Paris in 1883, he wrote: "The laborers have had the mischief put into their heads by trade-unions."[51] As he contemplated the agrarian unrest of the seventies and later, he discovered in Greenbackism and Populism only another form of this hateful socialism. It was the work of agitators who were plain rascals.

He was greatly disturbed in 1875 at the state of politics, "with half the Republicans and all the Democrats inflationists at heart, and carrying on a campaign on the bald issue whether the nation shall be a liar and a thief or not."[52] And so late as 1900 he exclaimed petulantly: "This last month of Bryan, roaring out his desperate appeals to hate and envy, is having its effect on the dangerous classes. Nothing so monstrous has as yet been seen in our history."[53] Unhappily even in free America with its equal opportunity, and equal laws, there had come to be "dangerous classes"—rather a good many of them, taking the populistic farmers and discontented wage-earners into the account—so many, indeed, that John Hay grew gloomy over the outlook. And the outlook was all the gloomier because of our form of government; for is not the ultimate test of our democratic institutions the test of whether they are adequate to protect the property and "civilization" of the few against the "hate and envy" of the discontented many?

That *The Bread-winners* was a dishonest book Hay certainly could not have been brought to believe; nevertheless a Tory who covers his Tory purpose with a mantle of democracy can scarcely be reckoned intellectually sincere. The men of the seventies and eighties—cultivated and intelligent gentlemen like Godkin and Aldrich and Hay—were little more than demagogues in their fustian attacks on agrarian Greenbackers and militant labor unions; they feared and hated them too much to understand them, and they took advantage of their social position to cry them down. The "educated leadership" of the Gilded Age was a somewhat

[50] *Ibid.*, Vol. I, p. 321.   [52] *Ibid.*, p. 426.
[51] *Ibid.*, p. 414.   [53] *Ibid.*, Vol. II, p. 256.

sorry thing; it was ethically bankrupt while appealing to high moral standards. The best of such leaders were second-rate men—mediocre minds cramped by a selfish environment, imbued with no more than a property-consciousness. Of such a world John Hay in his *Bread-winners* was a distinguished spokesman and representative.*

3

THE BEGINNINGS OF THE SOCIOLOGICAL NOVEL

It was in the nineties that the sociological novel expanded into a great movement that in the next decade and a half was to engulf pretty much all American fiction and bring it into service to the social conscience. Such a development was in the nature of things. The artist would not sit forever in his ivory tower, content to carve his statuettes while the country without was turmoiled with revolution. Sooner or later he would venture forth and once he had been caught up in the swirl his art would take new forms and serve other purposes than the traditional genteel. Realism was in the air, the realism of Zola and the Russians, and from such a realism would come in America a more critical attitude towards the social revolution at work in the land.

It was the city that played havoc with our older fictional methods, as it played havoc with our traditional social philosophy. America was late in discovering the import of the huge Babbitt warrens it had been building with such fierce energy; but slowly the realities of the economic city rose to challenge the respectability of the romantic city. It was the discovery of this new lair of business that created the school of sociological fiction. The older city of literature had been a polite world wherein ladies and gentlemen drank tea and made love and talked proper scandal—a pleasant background of clubs and drawing-rooms, against which moved well-dressed figures. It was an echo of Thackeray—the world of the West End and Beacon Street and Fifth Avenue, too well-bred and prosperous to recognize slums or stockyards or stock-gambling. But with the nineties the old complacency was disturbed. A note of unrest crept into the current fiction. As the *protégés* of Mr. Howells looked out upon their world in search of reality, they discovered that polite society was being undermined. Too many

* In his plan Professor Parrington included here H. F. Keenan's *The Money-Makers*, but apparently he decided against its inclusion.—*Publisher*.

social climbers were thrusting themselves forward; too much vulgarity was displayed by the new-rich. The social primacy of the
old families was being challenged by western pork-packers. Here
was a rich field to harvest. *Le document humain* was the latest cry
of realism, and so under the inspiration of M. Paul Bourget a new
crop of realism came to fruit—clever studies in feminine psychology—the last word in contemporary reality. The social climber
was analyzed mercilessly, her shallow and silly ambitions revealed
to the least petty maneuver; her blighting influence upon an
idealistic husband or her stimulus to a money-grabbing mate, is
traced shrewdly. Such are Boyesen's *Mammon of Unrighteousness*,
Robert Grant's *Unleavened Bread*, and Edith Wharton's *House of
Mirth*—studies that were symptomatic of a generation disturbed by
the consciousness of a vulgar plutocracy rising in its midst, and yet
ignorant of the nature of the disease.

Nevertheless their vogue was brief. As economic unrest rose
more menacingly upon the horizon of the new century, realism
quickly tired of its Kate Van Schaaks and Selma Whites and Lily
Barts, and turned away to prospect for a richer vein. Psychology
was losing its fascination and social analysis was supplying a new
inspiration; M. Bourget was yielding authority to Emile Zola. Even
so whole-hearted a romantic as Mary Johnston was to turn from
tales like *To Have and to Hold* to write *Hagar*, a novel of suffrage
propaganda. There was to be not less realism but more. The
change may be summarized in the word *background*. The old
individualism had unconsciously insulated its hero from economic
contacts; he moved in a polite environment detached from the
larger play of social forces. An individualism so wanting in sociological verity could make scant appeal to the new spirit of sociology.
That old world is dead. With the rise of the philosophy of determinism came another mood. To the realism of environment that
conceived of the individual as a pawn on the chessboard of society,
M. Zola had given the name *naturalism*. It was realism wedded to
a deterministic sociology—the first reaction of a generation awakening to the subjugating power of the mass, and bent on studying the
resultant phenomena in the clear light of science. The change was
no less than revolutionary. The new school thought in terms of
group and class and movement, rather than in terms of individuals
each nursing his petty hopes and fears. The individual counts for so
little in the enveloping stream of social tendency. Let us have no

more shoddy heroes, foolish little egoisms in an unreal world; but figures of men and women, encompassed by the great stream, carried along on a resistless current. If they prove to be little better than puppets the novelist is not to blame, but society that reduces them to impotency. So the emerging school abandoned Howells and James and followed Frank Norris into the camp of the naturalists. Their work might be bad art—as the critics love to reiterate —but it was the honest voice of a generation bewildered and adrift.

The discovery of environment led imperceptibly to another discovery—the economic basis of society; and this in turn led to the rejection of the polite city of older literature. Once the eyes of the novelist opened to the significance of the economic, the world of the spenders became less significant than the world of the makers, the drones became less interesting than the workers. If a novel were to be true to American life, it must adjust its perspectives to the facts of the great American game of money-chasing; it must shift its habitat from Fifth Avenue to Wall Street, from the club to the factory. So the business man entered the portals of fiction, no longer the stock figure in broadcloth and top-hat who discarded business with his dirty collar in order to shift into respectability; but bringing with him his talk of deals and squeeze-outs, playing the great game of exploitation at his mahogany desk—the central, dominating figure in a capitalistic world. He was subjected to acute analysis—his philosophy, his ethics, the machine of industrialism he was creating, the intricate system of exploitation that he had elaborated, the jungle city that was his lair where he fought his battles. The more acutely he was analyzed the clearer it became that here was a figure greater than kings or presidents—a figure that had taken our traditional American life in his hands and was reshaping it to his ends; and that if realism were to be true to its ideal it must paint him as he was without detraction and without glorification. So of necessity the younger novelists turned from polite society to economics, and fell to dramatizing the life of the city jungle where business men fought their fierce battles.

The forerunner of the new school was a Norwegian-American, Hjalmar Hjorth Boyesen. An essayist and philologist, for a number of years professor of German at Columbia University, Boyesen began publishing as early as 1874, and thereafter contributed freely to the several fields of the essay, poetry, and fiction; but it was not until 1891 that he opened the new vein of realism which he worked industriously the remaining four years of his life, the life brought to a premature close in 1895. Three novels belong to this last phase of his work: *The Mammon of Unrighteousness* (1891), *The Golden Calf* (1892), and *The Social Strugglers* (1893). The books made considerable stir upon their publication, for they were the nearest approach to the Tolstoian type of realism which till then had appeared in America. They contain in germ many of the ideas which the later city realists were to amplify and develop; but these ideas were still entangled in the mesh of the current psychological realism and their sociological bearings obscured. In consequence they largely failed of their purpose, and within a decade they had fallen into oblivion. They are of interest today chiefly as historical documents of the early nineties.

In the preface to *The Mammon of Unrighteousness* Boyesen sets forth his purpose thus:

My one endeavor in this book has been to depict persons and conditions which are profoundly and typically American. I have disregarded all romantic traditions, and simply asked myself in every instance, not whether it was amusing but whether it was true to the logic of reality—true in color and tone to the American sky, the American soil, the American character.

This, very evidently, is the realism of *milieu*—an endeavor to catch the reality of atmosphere; and as such it is of no great significance. In his choice of "types," moreover, he reflected the current taste. The crude self-made millionaire who dimly conscious of failure founds a university; the young idealist who fails because he is conscientious and the young realist who succeeds because he has no scruples against playing the game; and the aristocratic climber who marries to further her social ambitions—these are the stock figures of the realism that was to culminate in Robert Grant's *Unleavened Bread*, nine years later. But in the delineation of the character of Horace Larkin—the hero of a book that does not realize its promise—the note of the new realism is heard distinctly for the first time. The business man frankly breaks with the old ethics and erects a new ethics in conformity with his ambition; and it is the elaboration of the ethics of the Will to Power that justifies one in regarding *The Mammon of Unrighteousness* as a first study in the new city realism.

Horace Larkin, like Herrick's Van Harrington, is a Nietzschean who learned his ethics not from the German philosopher, but from the world of cut-throat business. It is the flower of the competitive system. The old pretense that business is an uplifting and civilizing agency—that trade breaks down barriers and carries in its shipments the gospel of fraternity and good will—is flung out on the scrap heap. Horace Larkin is no smug hypocrite. He faces the facts frankly; he will not deceive others any more than himself.

He was a beast of prey, asserting his right of survival; nothing more. If he succumbed to sentiment (and it is far easier to succumb to it than to resist it) he would merely be eliminating himself from the battle of existence as a potent and considerable force, and consigning himself to the rear ranks. And he felt in every fibre of his being that he was born for leadership.[54]

. . . nobody has a right to sacrifice himself to anybody else. If he does he simply eliminates himself from the struggle for existence, proves his unfitness to survive. It is natural for every strong man to try to make every other life tributary to his own; but the man who consents to make his life tributary to somebody else's is from Nature's point of view a weak man. . . . She may allow him to exist in a small way; but what is existence without predominance? . . . The man who is in advance of the morality of his age is, for practical purposes, a fool. It is no use quarreling with Fate; and in the United States the average man is the Fate that rules us and determines our place in the world.[55]

"The majority of our politicians are a low-lived lot, and many of them corrupt. But they have the courage to be American—crudely and uncompromisingly American—and that is, in my eyes, a virtue which is not to be lightly rated."

"And may I ask, Mr. Larkin, what do you mean by being American?"

"Being frankly, ably, enterprisingly plebeian. It is the plebeian after all, who shall inherit the earth—"

"I beg your pardon. According to the Bible it is the meek."

"I must differ with the Bible, then; for the meek, in my experience, if they inherit anything, never manage to keep it. It passes, sooner or later, into the hands of the strong, the self-assertive, the grasping. But these, as you will admit, are plebeian characteristics. A universally prosperous, comfortable, impudent, and enterprising mob—that is the goal toward which we are steering; and in my opinion it is a good and desirable one."[56]

This is a note that is to be heard more insistently as the new realism went further in its probing. Armed with this conviction Horace Larkin set forth as a conqueror, and it only adds to the dramatic fitness of things that in his rise he came across a will to power stronger, cleverer, than his own. Kate Van Schaak climbs upon his back to rise with him; she buys him with her money and social position, and having made the deal she realizes on the invest-

[54] Chapter XXXI. [55] Chapter XXXVI. [56] Chapter XXXIII.

ment. She is mistress henceforth, and the Nietzschean smiles at the irony of the situation.

In the third work Boyesen fails to maintain the level of *The Mammon of Unrighteousness*. *Social Strugglers* is simpler, more dramatic, better told. It carries the reader forward more easily. But it belongs with such novels of social analysis as Charles Dud-ley Warner's *The Golden House*—mildly critical of the vulgarizing influence of the new-rich, mildly sympathetic with the slum workers —rather than to the new realism. The heroine—daughter of a new-rich family that has come to New York to climb socially—awakens to the realization of parting ways: one the path of luxury which the four hundred travel, the other the path of service which leads to the slums and settlement work. It is a sentimental awakening, not an intellectual, induced by the hero, who on the fringe of the four hundred is mildly discontented with the ways of luxury. The vague idealism of the latter has been stirred by the Toynbee Hall experiment in London, and the persuasiveness of the lover rather than the conclusions of the thinker carries Maud Bulkley away from her conventional moorings.

The movement of the book is little clogged with sociological discussions; there is too little, indeed, to justify the conclusion. Only once does Philip Warburton lift the curtain upon the idealism which ostensibly is the determining factor in his life.

"I frankly confess that I am something of a red. I think the world is out of gear, and I can perfectly well conceive of a civilization far better than ours, without yet proposing any radical amendment to human na-ture. . . ."

There was to Maud something so wholly unexpected in this ebullition that she scarcely knew what to say. She had never philosophized concern-ing life and its problems; nay, she had never suspected that to a person who had money enough, and the access to good society, it could present any problems whatever. She knew that some terribly disreputable, shaggy, and wild-faced foreigners came here from Europe and proposed to turn our admirable civilization upside down; but that a gentleman of Warbur-ton's culture and social standing could sympathize with such criminals had never occurred to her as a remote possibility. . . .

After this disturbing introduction Warburton proceeds to dis-close what being "a red" means to him in the way of social revolu-tions:

"Have you ever heard of a London experiment known as Toynbee Hall?" he asked. . . .

"Yes: it's a place in the slums, where young men of good family go to live; isn't that it?"

"Yes; and, do you know, that is to me the most beautiful modern instance of a real desire to help the poor and helpless—to lift the world to a higher level. It is what I should like to do myself—and what I shall hope some day to do. . . ."

"Then you really think it a misfortune to be rich?" she ejaculated. . . .

"Yes, if wealth entails the loss of human sympathies, as in nine cases out of ten it seems to do, I regard it as a misfortune. If it means, as in this country it seems to mean, the loss of vital contact with humanity, the contraction of one's mental and spiritual horizon, a callous insensibility to social wrongs and individual sorrows, a brutal induration in creature comforts and mere animal well-being, the loss of that divine discontent and noble aspiration which alone makes us human—if it means this or any part of it, it is the greatest calamity which can befall a man. And it is because Christ foresaw that these were the natural effects of great wealth, and the security and ease which it engenders, that he declared that it was easier for a camel to pass through the eye of a needle than for a rich man to enter the kingdom of heaven." [57]

That is all. There is no dramatic justification of Warburton's views; they are without motive and foundation. *Social Strugglers* does not advance far along the path of the new realism.

As the years drew nearer the new century, the business man usurped an ever larger place in American fiction; the romance which had been sought in the deeds of 1776 was now discovered in the achievements of enterprise. It was the unconscious testimony of literature to the hold which business had got on the imagination of Americans. In the golden days of the "full dinner-pail," following the great victory of '96, the Captain of Industry reached the apogee of his fame. The voice of detraction had not yet been lifted against him; the muckraker had not yet set forth on his devastating career. To young reporters on city papers looking ambitiously towards fiction as the goal of success, what could offer greater appeal than the unwritten romance of Wall Street and the Stock Exchange? They had described it for the daily news columns, they had seen it extolled on the editorial page, why not dramatize it in fiction? Here was the real interest of America—the only reality that signified; yet the novelists had stupidly overlooked it, because they lacked the journalist's sense of news values, his *flair*.

Of the abundant crop of fiction which resulted from this discovery, no more characteristic examples need be sought than *The*

[57] Chapter VII.

Short Line War (1899) and *Calumet "K"* (1901), written in collaboration by Samuel Merwin and H. K. Webster. Their popular
success was immediate and maintained surprisingly. The former
ran to six editions, the last in 1909; the latter, to twelve editions,
the last so late as 1915. They are brisk stories, all action stripped
of descriptive superfluities, with plenty of newspaper punch:
dramatizations of hustle and bluff and the tricks of a cut-throat
game. Charlie Bannon, hero of *Calumet "K,"* is the boss who does
things, who is on the job, who takes long shots and "makes good"
—a "movie" hero of efficiency. He has no time nor inclination to
think, possesses no philosophy, asks no questions and is troubled by
no doubts or scruples; his fertile brain and cool nerve make him a
first-class fighting man, and he fights as the good soldier should on
orders from above. The hero of *The Short Line War*, Jim Weeks, is
another Bannon with the same fertile brain, cool nerve, calm
tenacity of purpose, quick decisiveness, and the same lack of
intellectual interests. In war it is sound strategy to strike quick
and hard; and the Captain of Industry, let it be clearly known, is a
war captain. To play the game hard, to beat the other fellow by
whatever means serve, that is the ideal of a competitive *bourgeoisie:*
not to be too nice about the law, for everybody knows that the law
is the chief weapon of the strong; not to cherish foolish idealisms,
for everybody knows that success alone pays. No more heartless,
brutal, anarchistic books could be conceived—a mad philosophy for
a mad world.

The broad movement towards a realistic portrayal of the economic city produced its eddies and minor currents, which at times
brought such a commotion of the waters as to appear like the main
current. Such was the flood of political novels which came with the
new century and lasted well upwards of a decade. These were a by-
product of the muckraking movement—a part of the propaganda
of the group of young insurgents within the Republican party who
were bent on rescuing the party from control of the old bosses, and
who prepared the way for the more significant movement of Progressivism which followed. Such studies as Francis Churchill
Williams's *J. Devlin—Boss* (1901), and Elliott Flower's *The Spoils-
men* (1903), were early examples; and Winston Churchill's *Coniston*
and *Mr. Crewe's Career* were probably the most notable. They were
journalistic for the most part, *exposés* of the "Boss" and the evils
of the political machine. The "Boss" is painted in various guises, as

brutal, cunning, thoroughly vicious, or as a man who plays the game with the same unsocial conscience that marks the capitalist. Most frequently Lincoln Steffens is followed and the human side of the "Boss" is "played up" equally with his political cunning. It is the characteristic journalistic touch—a bit cheap but immensely effective. As the movement of naturalism gained headway it became increasingly apparent that the "Boss" was only a part of the "System," and the political novel merged in the economic. These brisk studies constitute, however, a suggestive episode in our history—the literary echo of our political history between the years 1900 and 1910.

Little in the way of social analysis was to be expected from a group of clever journalists. They were reporters of fact, transcribers of externals. They note the social unrest, but it is little more than an undertone of the chorus of prosperity—a snarl of inconsequential criticism. It is the sting of a troublesome mosquito that is brushed off by the Captain of Industry who is too busy with big projects to bother about insects. Such is Will Payne's *Mr. Salt* (1903)—a sympathetic study of a coal-baron who is caught in the panic of '93 but pulls out and rises higher. To provide dramatic contrast there is the ineffective idealist who is growly and surly— "The whole thing is rotten—the whole business scheme. It's just a gold brick game operated by Salt and his kind. I'd like to stick a fuse to it and touch it off." [58] It is feeble enough—this protest. The rebel joins wildly in the great strike, is struck down by the hand of the law, rebels and strikes again and gets nowhere. Only a bitter, ineffective hate rankles in his heart, while Salt goes on triumphantly to greater power and a sort of moral regeneration through love—a regeneration that does not interfere with his keeping the title-deeds to his loot. An earlier study—*The Money Captain* (1898)—seemed to give promise of honester work than this. It is the story of a struggle between a corrupt gas-magnate and an enterprising editor whose *exposé* puts the magnate afoul of the law as interpreted by the magnate's judges, and who is saved from disaster by the timely death of the "duke." At the end is a touch of prophecy, quite startling in its forecast. These money-kings with their strong prehensile fingers are the spawn of a common plebeian America; the world of the makers is vulgarly democratic; but there follows the age of the spenders, and that shall be finely, altruistically

[58] Chapter IX.

aristocratic. The death of the hero "expunged from his fortune that color of greedy vulgarity and left its gold untarnished."

Dexter, for all his success, was a figure in the common democratic foreground of business; he was intimately and solely of the great everyday warp and woof of toil. He bore all his fruit at once—when he died. An heirship was required to give the fortune value. . . .

In a way it was fine and beautiful—all that huge accumulation of pillage coming to the white, firm hands of this pretty, amiable capable, good-hearted woman. The sudden substitution of her graceful and gracious figure for the swart and iron figure of the duke was like an apt transformation scene, prophetic of the future.[59]

These earlier books are mere preliminary sketches—first studies in economic backgrounds, hesitating between admiration and censure—satisfied to exploit the "human interest" in the dour figure of the money-grabber. The clever newspaper men did not know enough to do better, more realistic work; they saw the daily activities of business but they understood little of economics, less of sociology. And the new realism was soon to yield itself captive to sociology—to inscribe the name of Zola boldly on its pennant and go forth to conquer. It was Frank Norris who wrote the pronunciamiento of the new school, boldly, magnificently, with immense faith in the finality of his own conclusions. *The Responsibilities of the Novelist* was to become the textbook of the young naturalists.

[59] *The Money Captain*, Chapter 22.

PART TWO: NEW PATTERNS OF THOUGHT

CHAPTER I

DISINTEGRATION AND REINTEGRATION

THE figures of the Gilded Age, colossal yet grotesque, belonged to an America that was passing. Another world of thought and experience was rising above the horizon—a world in which the divinities were science and the machine—that was to disintegrate the traditional society of the dispersion and reshape the plastic materials in new forms. The long tide that for two centuries and a half had been running out had come at last to the turn. For six generations the pattern of life had been woven by the impulse of dispersion that in scattering men along a wide frontier had disintegrated the philosophies and rejected the social order brought from the old world, transforming America into such a society of free men as the Enlightenment had dreamed of—decentralized, individualistic, democratic. Dispersion, disintegration, individualism, anarchism—such was the inevitable drift under the compulsions of a fluid economics and frontier ways, of which the ultimate philosophical expression had been Thoreau at Walden Pond, discovering in his bean patch the same anarchistic principles that Godwin had learned of the French naturists—of which the prophet had been Walt Whitman, dreaming amidst the formless crowds of Manhattan his generous dreams of the democratic brotherhood—and of which Jay Gould the sordid wrecker in Wall Street was the prosaic reality.

Then had come the Industrial Revolution that in creating great cities and in drawing men from the plow to the machine was to undo in a few brief years the long work of the dispersion, repudiate the ideals of the Enlightenment, and provide a new pattern for a consolidating urban society. Thenceforward the drift was increasingly toward concentration, with its compulsions to reintegration and conformity—the imperious subjection of the individual to a standardizing order, the stripping away of the slack frontier freedoms in the routine of the factory, the substitution of the ideal of plutocracy for the ideal of Jacksonian democracy. And this revolutionary work of the machine was hastened by the new spirit of science that spread silently through the land, effecting a revolution in men's thinking as great as the machine was effecting in men's lives. Provincial America had been theological- and political-minded; but with the staying of the dispersion and the creation of an urban psychology, the ground was prepared for the reception of new philosophies that came from the contemplation of the laws of the material universe. The incoming of science had two immediate results: the application of technology to industry that was to further the Industrial Revolution; and the impact on speculative thought of the newly discovered laws of science that was to create a new philosophy. In the second of these twin influences lay an intellectual revolution that was to disintegrate the old theological cosmos, push far back the boundaries of space and time, reorient the mind towards all ultimate problems, and bring into question all the traditional faiths—political and social as well as theological and philosophical. Out of science was to come a new spirit of criticism and realism that was to set the pattern for later thought.

The story of disintegration and reintegration is a striking chapter in American life, a story that runs through two generations—the generation that came to maturity in the seventies, and the generation that came to maturity in the nineties. Between 1870 and 1900 the broad movement of thought passed through two sharply differentiating and contradictory phases: the extension of the philosophy of the Enlightenment, and the final rejection of the Enlightenment in consequence of a more rigid application of the law of causality in the light of a mechanistic universe. During the seventies biological evolution was interpreted in the light of earlier philosophies that had come out of the eighteenth century. It was reckoned a fulfillment and justification of the ideals of the Enlightenment, sanctioning the doctrine of progress that had risen from the conception of human perfectibility by a teleological conception of cosmic progress, glorifying the ideal of democratic individualism, and putting the seal of scientific approval on the philosophy of anarchism that had been the flower of two and a half centuries of the dispersion. And then in the nineties the clouds drew over the brilliant Victorian skies. With the substitution of physics for biology came a more somber mood that was to put away the genial romanticism of Victorian evolution, substitute a mechanistic conception for the earlier teleological progress, and reshape its philosophy in harmony with a deterministic pessimism that denied purpose or plan in the changing universe of matter. It was an unconscious return to the dark spirit long before brought hither by Puritanism from the complexities of English society—the spirit that dominated Calvinistic dogma before it disintegrated in the freedoms made possible by the great dispersion.

The great changes came swiftly because the machine had made ready the soil. Farmers and bankers do not think alike; country and town create different psychologies. A simple, decentralized America had been content with theology and metaphysics, and the intellectual history of New England for two hundred and forty years is not greatly skimped by being compressed into three words, Calvinism, Unitarianism, Transcendentalism. What was true of New England was true of America generally, except for the lesser influence of metaphysics. So long as society was mainly agricultural—and in those portions where the frontier spirit lingered on into later days—the church would retain its dominant influence and theology would still bound men's thought. But with the revolutions in economics and industry, with the rise of an urban society, the mind of America was making ready for the reception of science and the realism that was eventually to spring from science.

Venturesome pioneers had been at work long before, digging about under the thick crust of theology. Even in theocratic Massachusetts Increase and Cotton Mather had professed a zeal for scientific investigation, and the latter was vastly proud of his membership in the Royal Society. In the eighteenth century Franklin and Rittenhouse and William Bartram were evidences of a new spirit, and at Yale College President Ezra Stiles made a small beginning of scientific study that was swept away by his successor Timothy Dwight. In the early decades of the nineteenth century an interest in science was spreading widely, as *Silliman's Journal* witnesses. Asa Gray, Le Conte, and Agassiz encouraged the general interest in geology, and in the sixties and seventies Lewis H. Morgan turned to anthropology and R. L. Dugdale stimulated sociology by his significant study of the Jukes family.

Our present concern, however, is not with the contributions of America to abstract science, but rather with the changing mental attitude that resulted from familiarity with scientific methods— the shift from deductive reasoning to inductive investigation,

with the consequent breakdown of theology and the slow drift
from metaphysical idealism to scientific materialism; and such a
changing attitude concerns us because of its enormous influence
on the fabric of our later thinking, the total body of our intellectual
and cultural life. Considered in this light the intellectual revolution that resulted when the mind of America, long shaped by
theological dogmas, turned away from those dogmas to consider
the new universe presented by science, cannot be made too much
of. With the pushing out of the frontiers of space and time, the
discovery of a vast impersonal cosmos that annihilated the petty
egocentric world of good and evil postulated by the theologians,
the substitution of universal energy for a beneficent providence,
the conception of a ceaseless flux and flow that took no account
of teleological ends, the assumption of universal law and universal
causality, the mind of America quitted its quiet theological re-
treats and set forth on a great adventure that was to carry far and
the results of which were to unsettle what before had been sure.

In this great work we have been engaged since European science
first rose on our horizon a half-century and more ago. To speak
exactly, it is not so much science that has taken possession of the
mind, as certain postulates of science, certain philosophies presumably derived from science and justified by science, which we
have felt bound to incorporate in our thinking as a hundred years
before the conclusions of the Enlightenment had been incorporated.
In that earlier philosophy of the Enlightenment the whole drift
had been towards a dissolvent individualism, a disintegration of
the earlier integration. In the new interpretation after 1870 the
emphasis came to rest on the whole rather than the parts: in
sociology, upon the historical growth of human societies; in biology,
upon the evolution of the higher from lower forms. The individual,
thus conceived of socially and politically, is no longer an isolated,
self-determining entity, but a vehicle through which is carried the
stream of life, with a past behind and a future before. He is a portion of the total scheme of things, tied by a thousand invisible
threads to the encompassing whole. From the parts to the totality,
from freedom to determinism—such has been the drift of thought
that science has laid upon us and from which there is no easy escape.

With the advent of such a conception the long movement towards
philosophical anarchism was brought to a stop. The integrating

principle of unity must eventually shoulder aside the disintegrating principle of individualism; order must supersede willfulness. In the outcome a conception so coercive was to deny all the aspirations of our traditional social philosophy, surrendering society to a new regimentation and reducing the individual to an impotent victim of things as they are. Out of it was to spring the passionate protests of later rebels like Theodore Dreiser and Thorstein Veblen. Yet for the moment the rigid determinism of the premise was overlooked and man was accepted as the first-born and heir of God's benevolent universe. In the seventies the new postulates of science were looked upon as no other than fresh sanctions for the Comtean principle of continuity—of evolution from lower to higher in biology, of growth and progress in sociology. It was this middle ground that Herbert Spencer came to occupy in the minds of his American disciples—holding to the older individualism with its implications of anarchism, yet creating a cosmic philosophy that foreshadowed the eventual dwarfing of the individual.

I

THE VICTORIAN MOOD

The sturdy optimism that was a genial hallmark of the Victorian, was erected on more substantial foundations than a middle-class prosperity arising out of the Industrial Revolution; it was founded on a systematic philosophy, built of excellent materials and laid up with nice mortar-work, to which many hands contributed and in the finality of which many minds believed. Its master idea was the conception of growth, a conception that by contrast with the ideal of the static of earlier times, was profoundly revolutionary. Perhaps the most stimulating suggestion that came out of the Enlightenment, it was evolved by Turgot in France and by Price and Priestley in England, from the psychology of John Locke. If the human mind at birth is an empty vessel, wanting in innate ideas and waiting to be filled by sense perceptions, or if—to accept the familiar figure—it is a clean slate on which the finger of experience writes what it will, then it follows from the philosophy of Locke that the shaping of the individual is determined by the environment that cradles him. It is not an unfolding from within but a molding from without. Hence the idea of growth, and hence the vast preoccupation of the Enlightenment with sociology—or the science of environment—the hand of the sculptor that models the plastic clay. From such a conception the principle of progress was an inevitable deduction.

I

SOCIOLOGY AND THE ENLIGHTENMENT

It is convenient, if not quite exact, to trace the rise of the new gospel to Condorcet, who in the midst of the Terror and whilst in hiding from the Jacobins, wrote his stimulating *History of the Progress of the Human Mind* [1]—a work that was early reprinted in America and profoundly influenced Jefferson, who professed to find its principles exemplified in the history of his native Virginia. Condorcet was a humane and liberal spirit, a mathematician, a physicist, a sociologist, one of those eager Revolutionary minds passionately devoted to the creation of a more generous social order; and his celebrated work deserves a distinguished place in the history of social thought. He begins as a good Lockean with the psychology of sense perception, on which he erects his entire superstructure. Here is his opening paragraph:

Man is born with the faculty of receiving sensations; of perceiving and distinguishing the simple sensations of which they are composed; of retaining them, reproducing them, combining them; of comparing these combinations; of grasping what they have in common and what sets them apart; of fixing signs on all such objects in order to reproduce them more clearly and to facilitate new combinations.[2]

He then proceeds to trace the growth of the scientific attitude from the time of Bacon, till it culminated in the rise of social science, with the new politics of natural rights and the new conception of man as perfectible. It is commonly believed that the philosophers of the Enlightenment were speculative dreamers who created a fantastic natural man that flouted the sober realism of experience. Such a notion is grossly absurd. Condorcet was immersed in the scientific spirit of his age; it was to science that he looked for guidance and he had acquired a remarkable understanding of the data already gathered in western Europe. When he set down the following passages, therefore, he was writing not as a speculative dreamer, but as a sociologist who relied solely on

[1] The French title is, *Esquisse d'un tableau historique des progrès de l'esprit humain.* See *Œuvres*, Vol. VI, Paris, 1847.
[2] *Œuvres*, Vol. VI, p. 11, Paris, 1847.

scientific inquiry to find a way out of the social mess into which western civilization was plunged by the selfish stupidity of rulers who were hostile to scientific truth.

After long errors, after having lost their way in incomplete or vague theories, the publicists have finally come to recognize the true rights of man, to deduce them from this single truth, that he is a being endowed with sense perceptions (*un être sensible*), capable of shaping a train of reasoning (*capable de former des raisonnements*), and of acquiring moral ideas.[3]

Finally, we have seen a new doctrine appear. . . . It is that of the indefinite perfectibility of the human species, a doctrine of which Turgot, Price and Priestly, were the first and most distinguished apostles; it belongs to the tenth epoch, in which we shall develop it broadly.[4]

In such passages is contained the kernel of Condorcet's philosophy, the grounds of that hope for human betterment which awakened his generous sympathies. The *Esquisse* is a noble contribution to the work which the heirs of the Enlightenment, from Turgot to Comte, so eagerly and hopefully engaged in—the work of tracing scientifically the changes of the past in order to forecast the path of the future. After dividing the history of social evolution into nine periods, Condorcet projects the outlines of the tenth which is still to come.

If man can predict, with almost complete assurance, the phenomena of which he knows the laws; if, while they are still unknown in him, from the experience of the past he can forecast, with much probability, the events of the future; why should one regard as a chimerical undertaking the attempt to trace with some likeness the picture of the future destiny of the human species, in accordance with the facts of its history (*d'après les résultats de son histoire*)? The sole ground of faith in the natural sciences is this idea, that the general laws, known or unknown, that rule the phenomena of the universe, are necessary and constant; and on what grounds would this principle be less true for the development of the intellectual and moral faculties of man, than for the other operations of nature? Finally, since opinions formed from the experience of the past, in matters of the same kind, are the sole rule of conduct for the wisest men, why should one deny the philosopher the right to rest his conjectures on the same base, provided he does not attribute to them a certainty beyond that which springs from the number, the constancy and the exactness of his observations?

Our hopes for the future state of the human species may be reduced to these three important points: the destruction of inequality between nations; the progress of equality amongst a common people; finally, the

[3] *Ibid.*, p. 176.   [4] *Ibid.*, Vol. VI, pp. 194–195.

growth of man towards perfection (*le perfectionnement réel de l'homme*). May not all nations one day approach the state of civilization to which have arrived the most enlightened peoples, the freest, the most emancipated from prejudice, such as the French and the Anglo-Americans? The vast distance that divides these peoples from the servitude of nations subject to kings, from the barbarism of African tribes, from the ignorance of savages, must it not gradually disappear? [5]

Condorcet was an idealist, and the grand object towards which he was working was an adequate social philosophy that should interpret justly the evolution of civilization. True to the genius of the Enlightenment he believed that in reason and in the moral sense man possessed the keys to his own progress—that the general reason under the guidance of humane feeling must assure a progressive amelioration of life that will eventuate in the common well-being of men in a rational society. The age of the Enlightenment, he believed, had "opened new paths to the political and moral sciences," and laid bare what to him were "the true principles of social happiness." The American Federalists, who were prodigal of vituperative rhetoric in assailing all French theorists, might have read the pages of Condorcet with profit.

The idea of progress with its corollary of a philosophy of history, thus elaborated by Condorcet, was taken over by Saint-Simon, but came to its most elaborate expression in the work of Auguste Comte. The grandiose philosophy of history to which Comte gave the name of Positivism, was an attempt to formulate the law of progress in civilization; and his dynamic sociology, which emerged naturally from his conception of history, was an attempt to apply that law to society. That the principle of progress is the law of nature Comte professed to discover in the unity of all natural processes and the historical unfolding of all systems; there are no breaks and no fresh beginnings, but everywhere and always, continuity. From this principle emerged the Comtean law of historical evolution with its three phases: the theological, the metaphysical, and the scientific-industrial. If continuity is the law of nature, such continuity presupposes an objective—presumably benevolent; and in view of such continuity towards a benevolent objective, it is only logical to endeavor to dispose the forces of society in harmony with the teleological purpose, and through the application of positive knowledge hasten the advent

[5] *Ibid., Dixième Époque*, pp. 236–237.

of the Golden Age. Hence the grand science, hitherto neglected, is sociology. Earlier generations had placed the Golden Age in a dim past; Comtean philosophy, in harmony with the Enlightenment, placed it in the future as the ultimate goal of an evolving society. To forecast the lines along which such progress will move, to read the future as a child of the past, became therefore a prime objective of the new school of history. The tracing of social laws was the great business at hand, and as the founder of a new social science Comte carried further and systematized the work begun by the Physiocrats. Before Comte history had been little more than chronicles, without pattern or meaning, unconcerned with the sources of change and providing no basis for forecast; after Comte history became an interpretation and a philosophy.

One would have supposed that Positivism would have appealed to American intellectuals, as it appealed to liberal English thinkers like Mill and Spencer. Not only has the American mind taken kindly to sociology, but the history of America, as Woodbridge Riley has pointed out, offers too pat an illustration of the Comtean law of progress to be overlooked.[6] The three centuries of American existence—the seventeenth with its theocracy, the eighteenth with its abstract theories of political rights and its faith in constitutions, and the nineteenth with its industrialism based on science—would seem to be pages out of the Positivist philosophy of history. That Comte made so slight an impression on the mind of New England was due, no doubt, to the current influence of transcendentalism with its metaphysical backgrounds. Although eager young intellectuals like John Fiske might accept it while awaiting a more adequate evolutionary philosophy, the country was not yet ripe for Positivism. When that time came it was Spencer rather than Comte who became the master of American intellectuals—Spencer and in a lesser degree John Stuart Mill. Both Spencer and Mill had come under the influence of the French sociological school, and it was through their writings that the new social philosophy penetrated America.[7]

2

BIOLOGY AND THE ENLIGHTENMENT

The appeal of Spencer to the generation born after the Civil War was extraordinary. Ardent young minds, for whom the candles

[6] *American Thought*, p. 172, New York, 1915.
[7] Woodbridge Riley, *American Thought*, Chapter XI.

of theology were burnt out and who were seeking new light to their feet, were drawn to him irresistibly. Young rebels who had thrown off the guidance of their elders and were bent on discovering fresh paths through the tangle of dead faiths—independent souls like Hamlin Garland and Jack London and Theodore Dreiser who were to become leaders of the realistic revolt against the genteel tradition in life and letters and faith—went to school to him to prepare themselves for the great work of freeing the American mind from the old theological inhibitions. Young men in colleges no longer read *Butler's Analogy*, as their fathers had done before the war, but turned with zest to Spencer's *Data of Ethics* to discover a more scientific theory of conduct. Everywhere the influence of the great Victorian penetrated, and wherever that influence spread the old theological prepossessions disintegrated. It is probably no exaggeration to say that Spencer laid out the broad highway over which American thought traveled in the later years of the century.

If the supreme excellence of Comte, as has been suggested by Lester F. Ward, was his insistence on the ultimate unity of all processes of nature,[8] if before him the continuity of forces had been inadequately understood, his intellectual kinship with Spencer cannot fail to be remarked. The latter's master conception, which he arrived at independently of Darwin and which life-long he applied systematically to the several fields of thought, was the master creative conception of the nineteenth century—the conception of pervasive unity and organic growth. In his well-known phrase it was the law of continuous development from the homogeneous to the heterogeneous, from the simple to the complex; and this principle he found exemplified in the total history of nature and man. Here then is the Comtean law of continuity, but vastly strengthened and given a cosmic significance by deductions from the new science. Lamarck and Darwin laid the foundations for Spencer's philosophy, as Condorcet and Saint-Simon had provided the backgrounds for Comte. Trained thus in the new school of biology, Spencer erected his synthetic philosophy upon the broadest foundations; the principle of organic evolution sufficed to explain for him not only the history of civilization, but the total history of life in a physical universe; and biology, psychology, sociology, politics, ethics—all the congeries of ideals and institutions and bodies of knowledge that shape civilization—were but

[8] *Ibid.*, p. 401.

variant expressions of the development from the homogeneous to the heterogeneous.

The final effect of the synthetic philosophy was not to overset but to confirm the major postulates of the Enlightenment. In his social theory are unforeseen confirmations of the glowing hopes of Turgot and Condorcet. From his studies in biology Spencer had come to think primarily in terms of the individual, and only secondarily in terms of the species and the genus. Now variation is the mark of the individual, for strictly considered, nature knows no duplication of life forms, but always and everywhere individual differentiation; yet since likenesses are far greater and more cohesive than unlikenesses, the instinct of gregariousness impels individuals to associate in ever larger groups, interacting through association and coöperation, whence arises a human society that tends continuously to pass from the simple to the complex. On these two major premises then—individual variation and the instinct of association—Spencer established his social and political theory; and when the elaborate data drawn from biology and ethnology and psychology are stripped away, the underlying conceptions reveal a curious likeness to the master principles of French romantic philosophy. This likeness becomes more striking as he explores the fields of sociology and politics; and his final deductions tally so closely with earlier theory as to warrant a disciple of Jefferson in becoming a disciple of Spencer.

There is no break between Condorcet and the synthetic philosophy. The great Victorian completed the work of the Enlightenment. In establishing his individualism on the principle of biological variation, Spencer was only restating in scientific terms the earlier metaphysical individualism; in establishing his psychology upon an unbroken sequence "from the simple reflex action by which an infant sucks, up to the elaborate reasoning of the adult man," with its corollary of continuously expanding powers, he was rebuilding on the foundation of Locke, a fresh argument for the doctrine of indefinite development, or perfectibility; in establishing his sociology on the organic principle of "natural development," which shapes the individual to social ends, with an accruing wealth of individuation that is the final objective of true social life, he justified the French enthusiasm for liberty as the great desideratum, but liberty enriched and augmented by association in a free society; and finally, in establishing his ethics on the principle that "increas-

ing fullness of life is the 'end' of evolution," and the "highest conduct is that which conduces to the greatest length, breadth, and
completeness of life"—that the ultimate criterion of social ethics is
justice and that "every man is free to do that which he wills, provided he infringes not the equal freedom of any other man"—he
rephrased the earlier Godwinian principle that rational liberty
under the reign of justice is the ultimate end of society.[9]

That Spencer's social theory should have been shot through with
older ideals is not surprising when one considers his origins and
training. Sprung from radical nonconformist stock, a congenital
rebel, extraordinarily self-sufficient and coming to intellectual maturity in the tempestuous forties with their Benthamism, their
Chartism, their exigent democracy, he was molded by forces that in
large part were a reëmbodiment of the aspirations nullified by the
Napoleonic wars and the Tory reaction, and now come again to
birth. As a consequence his political theory, like Mill's, was deeply
affected by the revolutionary heritage. He accepted the social
contract as a "theoretical, though not a historical, basis of political
authority and institutions";[10] the doctrine of natural rights, which,
with Jefferson, he interpreted in terms of the rights to life, liberty,
and the pursuit of happiness; and the theory of a constantly
diminishing political state, on the hypothesis that the ultimate
form of society—as in Godwin's *Political Justice*—will, be anarchistic.

At least, such he conceives to be the forecast suggested by the
law of social evolution. As the coercive authority of the political
state diminishes, its place will be supplied by the cohesive force of
association, until voluntary coöperation extends to all the necessary
functions of society; and since the state tends to disappear with the
growth of a rational society, the great desideratum is an adequate
sociology rather than a political theory. The net result, therefore,
of Spencer's wide studies was a fresh justification, based on the
findings of Victorian science, of the master principles of eighteenth-
century speculation; its individualism, its liberalism, its passion for
justice, its love of liberty and distrust of every form of coercion.
The power of the majority must be curbed equally with that of the
minority and he concluded his *The Man versus the State* with the

[9] For a brief exposition of Spencer's major ideas see, William Henry Hudson,
"Herbert Spencer," in *Philosophies Ancient and Modern*, London, 1908.
[10] William Archibald Dunning, *A History of Political Theories from Rousseau to
Spencer*, New York, 1920, p. 400.

well-known words, "The function of Liberalism in the past was that of putting a limit to the powers of kings. The function of true Liberalism in the future will be that of putting a limit to the powers of Parliament." In the scientific speculations of the great Victorian the aspirations of romantic thought came to fresh vitality; embodied in a comprehensive evolutionary system they were given a fresh currency. Herbert Spencer completed the work begun by Locke a hundred and fifty years before, and his *Synthetic Philosophy* brought to conclusion the greatest intellectual movement of modern times.

As the young intellectuals, trained in the school of Spencer, looked out on the universe in the last quarter of the nineteenth century, they discovered, amid all its complexities an encompassing unity, a continuous growth, a creative purpose; and from such assumptions they justified the theory of progress, cosmic in scope and plan, that opened wide the doors to a vaster future. If in the backgrounds of their minds lurked the conception of determinism, it gave them no concern, for a benevolent determinism that shapes all things to a divine end, is no monster to be feared. In the evolutionary science were the grounds of a genial optimism that nothing could shake. If they had lost something of the jauntiness of the transcendental faith that beheld God plowing furrows at Brook Farm, they were armed with a scientific faith that by tapping stones and comparing fishes they should find His plan in an evolving series of life forms. Browning's Fra Lippo was a good Spencerian in his vigorous pronouncement:

> This world's no blot for us,
> Nor blank; it means intensely, and means good:
> To find its meaning is my meat and drink.

That progress was the law of the universe was held to be axiomatic by the new evolutionary school, and the American read in the new philosophy an added confirmation of a prepossession common to all Americans since Franklin and Jefferson, and become the common faith after the War of 1812. In sober minds it led to a complete reshaping of the outlook upon life, and in unbalanced minds it ran riot in all sorts of blowsy enthusiasms. Freedom, love, benevolence, progress towards a millennial perfection—these were the clarion notes in a huge symphony in praise of human perfectibility that assaulted American ears in the Gilded Age. Not Henry

Ward Beecher alone was the prophet of the new day. In the early seventies Mrs. Victoria Woodhull, one of the minor prophetesses, established a paper dedicated to the high end of "the Universal Religion of the Future . . . the Universal Home . . . the Universal Science, called Universology, based on the discovery and demonstration of Universal Laws . . . and an accompanying Philosophy of Integralism"—the "organ of the most advanced thought and Purpose in the World . . . the Organ of Cardinary News . . . News of the Aspiration and Progression of Mankind toward Millennial Perfection." [11] By contrast with such rhythmic enthusiasms the familiar lines of Tennyson are sober prose.

> Yet I doubt not thro' the ages one increasing purpose runs,
> And the thoughts of men are widen'd with the process of the suns.

How logically to young intellectuals of the seventies it all followed from the premises! If man is a rational being, potentially excellent and capable of indefinite development, the idea of a humane and rational progress in civilization is an inevitable deduction; and the evolutionist above all men was certain to build into his philosophy the cardinal idea of a unified progress, but given a cosmic sweep, accepted as the master principle in all fields of the material and the spiritual. It was the law of life, as the static was the law of death. No thinker who had grasped the idea of organic growth, could escape its larger implications; and no student in the seventies could think seriously without coming upon it.

3

THE END OF THE HOPES OF THE ENLIGHTENMENT

Then a film of haze slowly gathered upon the face of the brilliant sun and the light of men's hopes grew dimmer. As physics encroached upon the interest in biology, and leadership in speculation based on scientific findings passed from Spencer to Ernst Haeckel, young Americans of the next generation found the membership of the current philosophical trinity changed for them, and instead of unity, growth, purpose, they discovered unity, flux, chance. Purpose had disappeared from the grim face of the material universe, and they found themselves in the coils of a determinism that was more likely to prove malignant than benevolent. The idea of

[11] Quoted in Constance Mayfield Rourke, *Trumpets of Jubilee*, p. 201.

progress slipped quietly from their minds, and in its stead was only a meaningless and purposeless flux of things. But unity remained to bind the individual upon the whole and dwarf him to a pin-point in a vast macrocosm. The intellectual history of the last quarter of the nineteenth century—in America as well as elsewhere —in its teleological aspects is the history of the shift from the benevolent evolutionism of Spencer to the mechanistic materialism of Haeckel, with all the dislocations and readjustments involved in the cataclysmic change; and *The Education of Henry Adams*, that curiously suggestive study in disillusion, is saturated with the pessimism that followed upon the transition—a pessimism exuding from the contemplation of the bleak unity of a mechanistic universe. Of the earlier period before hope was gone, he wrote thus:

For the young men whose lives were cast in the generation between 1867 and 1900, Law should be Evolution from lower to higher, aggregation of the atom in the mass, concentration of multiplicity in unity, compulsion of anarchy in order; and he would force himself to follow wherever it led, though he should sacrifice five thousand millions more in money, and a million more lives.[12]

Was there purpose in it all? To this Adams and the younger men more and more declined to make answer. Yet this much is clear, for them the end of the theological age had come, and the end also of the great hopes of the Enlightenment. The idea of progress was given over henceforth to the middle class to become the plaything of material expansion.

II

THE SCHOOL OF SPENCER—JOHN FISKE

Of the distinguished group that labored to naturalize in America the philosophy of evolution John Fiske was the most authoritative spokesman. As a brilliant popularizer of the Synthetic Philosophy, and an historian who applied the Comtean law of continuity to the American past, he brought to the Gilded Age the revolutionary influence of English and French thought. Deeply immersed in Victorian speculation, he threw over his acquisitions the genial mood of his generation and infused the doctrines of evolutionary science with the spirit of religion. He reveled in the cosmic philosophy of Herbert Spencer, but within the material cosmos the scientists were revealing, controlling its eternal flux, he perceived a

12 *The Education of Henry Adams*, p. 232.

directing will that was shaping man's destiny to noble ends. New England scholarship had served God for too many generations to put aside its teleological prepossessions, and John Fiske was too completely New England to deny his spiritual obligations. The duty laid upon his conscience was plain. It was not enough to lay open to the New England mind the wealth of evolutionary science; he must justify its conclusions by binding them back upon the old faith and discover God revealed in biology as before he had been revealed in the Bible. And so in the heyday of Spencerian influence, before the bleak conception of a mechanistic universe had risen upon the horizon of men's thought to disperse the genial glow of optimism, this learned son of Connecticut was the prophet in America of the new order of thought.

John Fiske was a brilliant Yankee with a voracious appetite for ideas and a passion for cosmic syntheses. In certain respects he was the most richly endowed of the young students of his generation of Americans. Intellectually curious and acquisitive, he refused to be confined by orthodox fences but ranged far in pursuit of knowledge. The pale negations of the current New England theology, on which he had fed in his youth, soon lost their savor, and following his natural impulses he sought out the strongest food available. While still in his teens he had absorbed Emerson, Theodore Parker, and other New England radicals, and was reaching out for an ampler diet. That was in the late fifties, when a new cosmos was taking shape in men's minds and old faiths were disintegrating. The several rivulets of science—geology, zoölogy, chemistry, physics— that hitherto had followed diverse and vagrant courses, were slowly converging and making ready to mingle their waters in a vast common stream. Some further dredging needed to be done first, and on that great job Darwin had long been patiently engaged. It was a time of high hopes and young John Fiske, about to enter Harvard College, was not one to miss the significance of so great an awakening.

Amidst his quiet Connecticut lanes he had already been making his own discoveries. Although he had early gone through a form of conversion to dogmatic Calvinism he had not long been content with its arid provender, but turned to the English disciples of Positivism—George Henry Lewes, Buckle, Mill—and was absorbing Comte with the help of Voltaire and Goethe. In June, 1860, two months before taking his examinations for advanced standing at Harvard, he came upon a prospectus of Herbert Spencer's proposed system of philosophy, and this boy of eighteen was one of the first dozen Americans to subscribe to the undertaking. It was a golden day in his life, that was to determine his whole intellectual development. He became a devoted disciple of Spencer, dedicating his labors to the great cause of evolution. To that end he felt called to study prodigiously. As a Harvard undergraduate he found it difficult to treat his conventional instructors with due respect, for while his classmates were struggling with Greek roots he was exploring the whole field of philology and rioting in Comtean sociology. Instead of exhausting his energies with the usual undergraduate themes, he wrote in his junior year, at the age of nineteen, a critical examination of *Buckle's History of Civilization* for the *National Quarterly Review;* and while preparing for his final examinations he wrote a learned article on "The Evolution of Language" that was accepted by *The North American Review.*

Such intellectual precocity, suggesting to timid souls a lack of respect for orthodox opinions, was not without its dangers. From his first entrance to Harvard he was marked by certain tutors as a dangerous influence. Positivism and evolution were in ill repute in the college circles, and he was eventually summoned before the faculty and admonished for undermining the faith of Harvard undergradutes. Outside the college he was becoming known as the "young atheist of Cambridge." The reasons for such a reputation were quite sufficient to Unitarian dogmatists who had forgotten the cardinal principle of Unitarianism—the principle of devout free thought—for young John Fiske had already gathered a huge pile of combustible materials that threatened the established orthodoxy. Before entering Harvard he had planned to write a history of early Christianity, but his interest in science drew him into other fields—the new sociological interpretation of history that he discovered in Grote's *History of Greece*, and the broad field of scientific speculation that opened to him in Humboldt's *Cosmos*. To this latter field he turned greedily, reading amongst other works Cuvier's *Règne Animal distribué d'après son Organisation,* Herschel's *Outlines of Astronomy*, Laplace 's *Système du Monde*, Agassiz's *Zoölogy* and his *Essay on the Classification of the Animal Kingdom* (1857), and with the joy of a great discovery Darwin's *Origin of Species* (1859). From Agassiz's defense of special creation he dissented vigorously, and this dissent prepared him for an enthusiastic reception of Darwin's careful exposition. Certainly no other young student in America followed so closely or so intelligently the unfolding of the English school of evolutionary thought. In solid acquisition and in intellectual curiosity he was far in advance of Henry Adams, then a young diplomat in London.

Upon his graduation in 1863 he determined upon the law, read through the two-year course of the Harvard Law School in nine months, was admitted to the bar, waited two years for clients who never came, threw it over, and turned to his first love, the life of the scholar. He had his eye on a chair at Harvard, but so long as the old orthodox *régime* lasted no opening offered there. In the first year of President Eliot's administration (1869) an opportunity was provided and he was invited to give a course of lectures in Holden Chapel on the Positive Philosophy. The opposition was still too strong to permit the offer he sought—a chair in history—but he was eventually given a place as Assistant Librarian, where he spent five years amongst the books of Gore Hall. Driven to other means of support he turned to lecturing, was received with immense applause in London, and thereafter to the end of his life he suffered much of his vast energy to drain off into that most fruitless of jobs for a creative mind. A certain genial egoism was to blame for his playing willingly the rôle of lackey to women's clubs. He liked to talk to sympathetic audiences, and he was greatly effective on the platform. The inevitable result was that he fell short in accomplishment of the fine promise of his early years. His style became diffuse, his materials picturesque rather than solid, his thinking flabby. Pretty much all his significant work was done before he was forty.

The greater part of Fiske's intellectual life, despite his later incursions into certain waste places of history, was dedicated to the indoctrination of the American people in the principle of evolution as that principle was outlined in Spencer's *Synthetic Philosophy*. He was a man of one idea, but that idea was so vast and germinal, so comprehensive in its implications and so constructive in its suggestions, as to set afoot the greatest intellectual revolution in western civilization. He called himself a philosopher, but he meant by the term not a metaphysician, but a cosmic historian whose business was to interpret the universe in the light of the great laws that science was revealing. By 1860 science had revealed three such general laws: the law of gravitation, the law of biological variation and the survival of the fittest, and the law of the conservation of energy; and from them Spencer had deduced the principle of a unitary cosmos, with a common force sustaining both the organic and the inorganic, working to a single "far-off divine event, to which the whole creation moves." An intimate friend of Fiske's, and an ardent Spencerian, puts the intellectual situation in these terms:

> The conceptions of the Universe generally held at the time when Fiske was in college were fragmentary and chaotic, each phenomenon or each group of phenomena being, like language, a special creation of an anthropomorphic God, turning out different jobs piecemeal like a man. The conception of one power behind all had been a dream of not a few philosophers and poets, but as a fact comprehensible by the average mind, it was not known until the discovery about 1860 of the Conservation of Force. About the same time was discovered the unity of all organic life, in its descent from protoplasm, and the identity of its forces with those of the inorganic universe. The nebular cosmogony, the persistence of force and the biologic genesis, united together, showed the power evolving, sustaining and carrying on the entire universe known to us, to be *one*, and constantly acting in one unified process; and that every detail—from the most minute known to the chemist, physicist and biologist, up to the greatest known to the geologist and astronomer, and including all known to the psychologist, economist, and historian—was caused by a previous detail. It having been established that the same causes always produced the same results, these uniformities were recognized as Laws, and it was also recognized that conduct in conformity with these laws produced good, and conduct counter to them produced evil. . . .
> These great discoveries were at once grasped by Fiske's great intelligence, and welcomed with enthusiasm. To their dissemination he mainly devoted his next twenty years, and to their illustration in the origins and foundation of our national commonwealth, the rest of his career.[13]

While still at Harvard, as a result of the publication of his two undergraduate essays already referred to, he was sought out by Edward L. Youmans and urged to join with him in spreading the new evolutionary philosophy.[14] Youmans was an ardent proselytizer who had volunteered for the job of instructing the American people in the meaning of science. He attached himself to Spencer as spokesman and publicity agent, and was on the lookout for helpers. Encouraged thus by Youmans, Fiske threw himself impetuously into the work of furthering the new philosophy of

[13] Henry Holt, *Garrulities of an Octogenarian Editor, with Other Essays somewhat Biographical and Autobiographical*, Boston, 1923, pp. 327–328.
[14] See John Spencer Clark, *Life and Letters of John Fiske*, Vol. I, pp. 273–278.

evolution. As the task unfolded before his maturing mind it came to involve three major problems: to dissociate in the popular mind the potential theism of Spencer's *First Principles* from the materialism of Comte's Positivism, with which it was widely confused; to elaborate the teleological implications of evolution and demonstrate that the grand objective of all natural processes was "the production of happiness, and that, despite occasional lapses, all records of them prove that, on the whole, they tend not only to produce happiness, but to increase it";[15] and finally to apply the principles of the cosmic philosophy to historical writing and reveal how the law of evolution determines the forms of social institutions —to do more adequately in the field of American history what Buckle had tried to do in a larger field without the aid of evolution.

In all his intellectual interests and attitudes Fiske was a complete New England Victorian, but scarcely a British Victorian. In his erection of the doctrine of progress into a cosmic law, and in his resultant optimism, he was at one with Spencer and the English group. But he was a son of New England before he was an evolutionist, and although he had broken with the grotesque, anthropomorphic dogmas of Calvinism, he remained profoundly religious, and like Henry Drummond he sought to transfuse science with spiritual qualities. He was effectively a Unitarian, the leader of the Cambridge intellectuals who were carrying on the work that Theodore Parker would have done had he lived twenty years longer—the work of bridging the chasm between science and religion. To that end his vast concern with teleology—that God is the great wellspring out of which flows the unfolding cosmos, and that the unfolding is guided and controlled to beneficent ends. Natural law, working in a realm of causation, and shaping matter to forms more and more complex, to John Fiske was no other than the beneficent purpose known to theology as Divine Providence.

Pretty much all that he had to say on the question is contained in the four volumes of *Outlines of Cosmic Philosophy*, published when he was only thirty-two. Written with great enthusiasm and complete confidence, it was an attempt to summarize and restate the conception of cosmic evolution as Spencer had defined it in *First Principles*, and partly elaborated it in his *Biology* and *Psychology*. It was a timely presentation, and with its lucid exposition of the evidence drawn from the several fields of science it furthered

[15] Henry Holt, *op. cit.*, p. 328.

the spread of the evolutionary philosophy. But it sought to do more. Not content with arraying in due order the scientific proofs of a vast unitary cosmos—as Spencer had done—Fiske essayed the rôle of apologist and supplemented the facts of science with ontological and teleological speculations. Whereas Spencer had remained agnostic, refusing to speculate on the unknowable, and clearly implying a deterministic cosmos, Fiske took high theistic ground, asserting that evolution implies the existence of a creative mind, vaster than the anthropomorphic conceptions of theology and far nobler, whose cosmic plan unfolding in the material universe compels a belief in a benevolent God, and a belief also in the "eternal source of a moral law which is implicated with each action of our lives, and in obedience to which lies our only guarantee of the happiness which is incorruptible." And this "eternal Power, not ourselves, that makes for righteousness"—to use Arnold's phrase which Fiske was fond of quoting—is making also for altruism and the spirit of love that lies at the heart of Christianity; for is not the prolongation of infancy with its demands on altruism—a principle that was Fiske's contribution to evolution, of which he was justly proud—a master biological device for individual variation? In consequence the evolutionist becomes not only a theist, but a Christian in the truest meaning of the term. The fatherhood of God and the brotherhood of man—to which New England Unitarianism had come to restrict its dogmas—are in reality "two great interrelated cosmic truths—the existence of righteousness as an active principle in the Infinite Power or Reality back of the cosmos, and its correlative manifestation in the altruistic consciousness of man."[16]

Such speculation concerning the unknowable exercised an increasing fascination for Fiske as his deeply religious nature slowly colored the acquisitions of the scientist, and in a succession of tracts—*The Destiny of Man* (1884), *The Idea of God* (1885), *Through Nature to God* (1899), and *Life Everlasting* (1900)—he definitely rejected the negative attitude of agnosticism that was a common mark of the English evolutionary school, and turned to outline the religious faith of an evolutionist. George Eliot's dictum that God is unknowable and immortality is unthinkable, was too thin a diet for his robust nature; instead he elaborated the argument that faith in God and immortality is reasonable in the light of

[16] John Spencer Clark, *op. cit.*, Vol. II, p. 50.

the evolving cosmos that science was revealing. To John Fiske that cosmos was not bleak and impersonal, a vast congeries of physical forces that reduced man to the status of a flea on the epidermis of earth, but the expression rather of a benevolent will unfolding in accordance with a divine purpose. "The process of evolution is itself the working out of a mighty Teleology, of which our finite understandings can fathom but the scantiest rudiments." To Henry Holt this recovery of teleology was Fiske's great contribution to evolutionary thought.

He did more just there than any modern philosopher, perhaps than any philosopher, to show that this teleology is beneficent, and to restore in this way the attitude of mind which it may not yet be too late to call Faith in God and Immortality.[17]

No doubt it was due to such emphasis on the theistic implications of evolution that the doctrine was so quickly accepted in New England amongst the Unitarians and liberals; but for Fiske it marked the end of his intellectual leadership. After the battle had been won he turned away to engage in less fruitful activities, no longer followed keenly the new discoveries of science, and finally set himself to write the history of America. The venture on the whole was not fortunate. In his attempt to reinterpret the American past he suffered from grave handicaps, an inadequate knowledge and an inadequate philosophy. He was led into the field of history by his interest in the English school of Grote and Maine and Stubbs and Freeman, and his ultimate purpose was to present "the drama of American civilization, of which the political organization of the United States was the crowning feature, as an evolutionary development from antecedent causes and of great significance to the future civilization of the world." [18] But for this undertaking he was inadequately equipped and his conscious search for a Comtean continuity in social growth did him a real disservice. The economics of historical change he seems never to have considered, and his analyses of social forces are never acute or penetrating. Although he attempted to apply sociological evolution to history he was really little more than a political and military historian with a special fondness for wars and the details of battle strategy. In his first venture, *American Political Ideas*—written for his London lectures of 1880—he simplified American political develop-

---

[17] Henry Holt, *op. cit.*, p. 339.
[18] John Spencer Clark, *op. cit.*, Vol. II, p. 456.

ment to two germinal ideas—the town meeting and the principle of federation, and these two conceptions he traces back to the Teutonic folkmote and the Teutonic principle of shire representation. The theme with which he deals is thus stated in the preface:

The government of the United States is not the result of special creation, but of evolution. As the town-meetings of New England are lineally descended from the village assemblies of the early Aryans; as our huge federal union was long ago foreshadowed in the little leagues of Greek cities and Swiss cantons; so the great political problem which we are (thus far successfully) solving is the very same problem upon which all civilized peoples have been working ever since civilization began. How to insure peaceful concerted action throughout the Whole, without infringing upon local and individual freedom in the Parts,—this has ever been the chief aim of civilization, viewed on its political side; and we rate the failure or success of nations politically according to their failure or success in attaining this supreme end. When thus considered in the light of the comparative method our American history acquires added dignity and interest, and a broad and rational basis is secured for the detailed treatment of political questions.[19]

Only a New England historian could write so naïvely as that, for only to a New Englander does the town meeting become a germinal source of American democracy. Not a great historian, Fiske ceased to be in his wandering later years a great intellectual influence. The rare promise of his young manhood he never fulfilled, but like his generation he suffered his energies to be dissipated and he ended in a somewhat blowsy optimism. To Henry Holt he was a very great and learned man, but to a later generation it is difficult to make out his vast stature. Nevertheless as a purveyor of Victorian science to the American people he did a useful and important work.

[19] John Fiske, *American Political Ideas*, Preface, pp. 4–5.

CHAPTER II

THE SKEPTICISM OF THE HOUSE OF ADAMS

In the welter of change that resulted from the revolutionary transitions of the Gilded Age, one man at least stood apart, skeptical about the worth of the current revolutions, unconvinced that all the hurly-burly meant a rational progress. To Henry Adams skepticism early became a habit. Doubt persistently dogged his footsteps and the more critically he examined the ways of his generation of Americans, the more certain it seemed to him that any were unworthy the name of civilization. He was not at home in the new world of the Gilded Age; and as he watched the disintegrations of the older New England in which he had been brought up, an incurable nostalgia seized upon him and he set about seeking another home where he might live the good life he had not lived heretofore. The America of the Gilded Age was alien to him; its gods were not his gods, nor its ends his ends. And so began for him a long pilgrimage of the spirit that was to carry him far and return him at last with no solider gains than a handful of curious relics in his pilgrim's scrip.

The sturdy New England character, with its self-sufficing individualism and granite integrity, never came to finer flower than in the Braintree-Quincy house of Adams. Intellectually curious, given to rationalism, retaining much of the eighteenth-century solidity of intellect and honest realism, refusing to barter principle for the good will of men, the Adams line produced no more characteristic offshoots than came in the fourth generation. In Charles Francis Adams, Jr., Henry Adams, and Brooks Adams, the family virtues of independence, intellectual integrity, and disinterested criticism, found abundant expression. All three were children of an earlier century, endowed with the solidest Yankee-Puritan qualities of mind and heart, unyielding as the rock ledges of their native fields; and they found the experience of living in the late nineteenth century, of adjusting their eighteenth-century minds to the demands of a sordid capitalistic order, a difficult business. Though they tried to bridge the chasm between the two worlds, though they

212

honestly sought some working compromise that would suffer them to share in the work of their generation, they met with failure. It was not possible for the House of Adams, with its old-fashioned rectitude, to accept the ways of the Gilded Age, and in the end they turned aside from the main-traveled road to follow their own paths.

I

CHARLES FRANCIS ADAMS—THE BUSINESS FAILURE

Of the three Charles Francis Adams most nearly succeeded in his experiment of a *rapprochement* with capitalism, with the result that his life came nearest to shipwreck. Perhaps there was less of the Adams granite in his character. He refused to turn rebel but consciously sought to win the prizes offered by his generation, training himself to serve financial interests, making overtures to business, and achieving a very considerable financial success. Yet nothing was more incongruous than an Adams serving as lackey to State Street, and when after abundant experience he came finally to realize it he turned away to pick up the scattered threads of a life largely wasted. For years he had suffered from a long maladjustment. When he quitted the army at the close of the war with the brevet rank of brigadier-general, he found himself adrift. The world of his youth was gone and the future seemed drab and unpromising. Intellectually he was caught between tides. The traditional idealisms had burnt out in the bitter struggle, and in the sterile post-war years his Puritan nature found no adequate nourishment. The crusading ardor was gone, and the new world of science had not yet risen on the horizon of young men who had given their youth to the army. In 1865 he came upon John Stuart Mill's essay on Auguste Comte, which he said revolutionized his whole mental attitude—"I emerged from the theological stage, in which I had been nurtured, and passed into the scientific. . . . From reading that compact little volume of Mill's . . . I date a changed intellectual and moral life." Yet from this accidental foray into Victorian rationalism he got little more than a sense of release from a dead Puritanism. Creative intellectual enthusiasms were not to be his portion.

Disillusioned with the law, over which he had been pottering, and wanting to ally himself with the dominant forces of his generation, he "fixed on the railroad system as the most developing force and largest field of the day." He delved into the history of certain railways and established a reputation as a student of transportation. For upwards of a quarter century—from 1866 to 1890—as a member of different public commissions and finally as president of the Union Pacific system—Jay Gould's road—he devoted his best energy to the work, only to be disillusioned in the end. In 1912 he wrote this confession:

Indeed, as I approach the end, I am more than a little puzzled to account for the instances I have seen of business success—money-getting. It comes from a rather low instinct. Certainly, as far as my observation goes, it is rarely met with in combination with the finer or more interesting traits of character. I have known, and known tolerably well, a good many "successful" men—"big" financially—men famous during the last half-century; and a less interesting crowd I do not care to encounter. Not one that I have ever known would I care to meet again, either in this world or the next; nor is one of them associated in my mind with the idea of humor, thought, or refinement. A set of mere money-getters and traders, they were essentially unattractive and uninteresting. . . . In the course of my railroad experiences I made no friends, apart from those in the Boston direction; nor among those I met was there any man whose acquaintance I valued. They were a coarse, realistic, bargaining crowd.[1]

Yet not till he had reached his late fifties did he finally cut the ties that held him to the "bargaining crowd," and turn to the business of salvaging the remnant of his days. He gave himself over with zest to the writing of Massachusetts history, but it was then too late to do notable work. He had laid too many offerings on an altar he had come to loathe. Not a lifelong student like Henry, he had been unable to gather great stores of knowledge. Not a militant rebel like Brooks, he had never been given to searching inquiries into the laws of civilization. And so when he found himself free at last, he set himself to the business of local chronicles. That was better than nothing; it was the one thing in his life he took solid pride in; the work was honestly and capably done; but it was small savings from a lifetime of conscientious work. His venture into the realm of business had been a disaster.

II

HENRY ADAMS—INTELLECTUAL

From a similar disaster Henry Adams was saved by an early disillusionment. His efforts at *rapprochement* were little more than a gesture. While casting about after the war for a promising opening

[1] *Autobiography*, pp., 190–195.

for a career he hit upon finance as a likely field and published a number of essays that drew attention to him. But it was quite impossible for him to go forward along such lines. He was too completely the intellectual, too aloof from his generation in spirit and will, to ally himself with the economic masters of the Gilded Age. Sooner or later he would go his own way, and luckily good fortune took the matter in hand promptly. No suitable opportunity offering, he was dragooned by family and friends into an assistant-professorship at Harvard, where he spent seven years trying to explain to himself and his students the meaning of the Middle Ages. Those years were his introduction to history. The passion of the student was in his blood, and he turned with zest to brood over the scanty records of past generations, seeking a clue to the meaning of man's pilgrimage on earth, trying to arrange the meaningless fragments in some sort of rational pattern, in the hope of discovering an underlying unity in what seemed on the face only a meaningless welter of complexity and irrationality. A rationalist, he followed his intellect in an eager quest for the law of historical evolution, and he ended fifty years later in mysticism. It was a natural outcome for a lifetime of rationalizing—a compensation for the mordant dissatisfactions that issued from the restless play of mind.

Dissatisfied with his labors he quitted the Harvard post in 1879 and thereafter made his home at Washington in the atmosphere of politics. From the Middle Ages he turned to the American past and set out to explore the period during which the first Adams had played his part. He could not deal with narrow parochial themes; he would not fall into the "sink of history—antiquarianism," that satisfied Charles Francis Adams. From the beginnings of his intellectual life he had been concerned with the ideas and ideals that presumably lie behind periods and civilizations; so he went back to what he regarded as the great age of American political history, to inquire into the meaning of the struggle between Federalism and Jeffersonianism for control of the venture in republicanism. But finding little satisfaction there, as he had earlier found none in Victorian England, where he had studied closely contemporary English statesmen—Palmerston and Lord Russell and Gladstone— only to convince himself that they were bankrupt of ideas and morality, and had nothing to teach concerning the good life, he abandoned the field, threw over his familiar studies, and set about the great business of reëducating himself.

From his long studies in the American past one significant thing had emerged—he had come to understand the source of certain of his dissatisfactions with current American ideals that set him apart from his fellows. He had gone back to his own origins and had traced the rise of the defiant Adams prejudices that were as strong in the fourth generation as they had been in the first. The Adams family was eighteenth-century—Henry Adams had come to understand—and he himself in mind and education and prejudices, was of that earlier time. He was a child of Quincy rather than Boston—a simple world with simple virtues that capitalism and industrialism were destroying in the name of progress. From such village loyalties he could not rid himself. Perhaps in reason he should not have preferred that earlier homespun world; but affection does not heed logic, and as Henry Adams traced the decline of Quincy to Hamilton's financial policy that started the new capitalism on its triumphant career, he was filled with bitterness. It was a vulgar order that was rising and an evil day. Since 1865 the bankers had ruled America, and they were coming finally to cajole the American people into accepting their vulgar ideals and putting their trust in a bankers' paradise. As he watched the temples of the new society rising everywhere in the land, his gorge rose at the prospect. He had no wish to dwell in a bankers' paradise. Dislike of a capitalistic society was in his blood. From father to son all the Adamses had distrusted capitalism and hated State Street. The "only distinctive mark of all the Adamses," he said late in life, "since old Sam Adams's father a hundred and fifty years before, had been their inherited quarrel with State Street, which had again and again broken out into riot, bloodshed, personal feuds, foreign and civil war, wholesale banishments and confiscations, until the history of Florence was hardly more turbulent than that of Boston."[2]

And so when at the climax of the capitalistic revolution he watched the change going on noisily all about him, when the transition to the bankers' paradise was called progress and capitalistic feudalism was hailed as the advent of Utopia, he seemed to himself a somewhat pathetic anachronism. Shades of the prison house were falling about him. "He had hugged his antiquated dislike of bankers and capitalistic society," he said bitterly, "until he had become little better than a crank."

[2] *The Education of Henry Adams*, p. 21.

He had known for years that he must accept the régime, but he had known a great many other disagreeable certainties—like age, senility, and death—against which one made what little resistance one could. . . . For a hundred years, between 1793 and 1893, the American people had hesitated, vacillated, swayed forward and back, between two forces, one simply industrial, the other capitalistic, centralizing, and mechanical. In 1893, the issue came on the single gold standard, and the majority at last declared itself, once for all, in favor of the capitalistic system with all its necessary machinery. All one's friends, all one's best citizens, reformers, churches, colleges, educated classes, had joined the banks to force submission to capitalism; a submission long foreseen by the mere law of mass. Of all forms of society or government, this was the one he liked least, but his likes and dislikes were as antiquated as the rebel doctrine of State rights. A capitalistic system had been adopted, and if it were to be run at all, it must be run by capital and by capitalistic methods.[3]

But while he clung tenaciously to his obsolete prejudices in favor of an earlier century, the pugnacious realism of that century was oozing out of him. The middle years of his life, between the acceptance of the Harvard post in 1870 and the final break with Victorianism in 1892, were intellectually an unhappy period. He was losing his grasp on realities and becoming narrowly and exclusively political-minded. It was not good for him to live daily in the presence of politics. In so "far as he had a function in life," he said of the Henry Adams of 1877, "it was as stable-companion to statesmen, whether they liked it or not."[4] The term "statesmen" was of course only a polite euphemism for the breed of politicians who played their sordid game under his critical eyes. He was rarely under any illusions in regard to them except when blinded by friendship. Certainly his etchings of Grant and Blaine and Sherman and Conkling and other servants of democracy were done with acid.

Yet in all his penetrating comment on men and measures there is a curious failure to take into account the economic springs of action. He had let slip the clue old John Adams had followed so tenaciously. An acute historian, not thus wanting, would never have traced the triumph of the gold standard to the "mere law of mass," would never have substituted a physical determinism for an economic, would never have confused the principle of mass with a minority. How far an intelligent man and a competent historiar. could go astray in his criticism of current ways is suggested by the curious novel *Democracy*, that he wrote in 1880 while living in the

[3] *Ibid.*, pp. 343–344.   [4] *Ibid.*, p. 317.

daily companionship of John Hay and Clarence King. In dealing with the phenomena of political corruption he had none of the acuteness of old John Taylor of Carolina, who would have put his finger unerringly on the cause, or of the first Adams. If he had written *Democracy* after he had studied the funding operations of the Federalists under Hamilton's leadership, very likely he would have dealt with the problem more searchingly; but in 1880 Henry Adams revealed no more critical intelligence than did Godkin or Lowell or other critics of the Gilded Age.

The historical work done during those middle years at Washington was abundant and excellent, marked by rigorous use of sources, a dispassionate attitude towards partisan issues, and excellent form. It was easy for an Adams to take middle ground between Jefferson and Hamilton, however much his sympathies inclined to the former. In all this work, however, in the *Life of Albert Gallatin* (1879), in *John Randolph* (1882), as well as in the nine-volume *History of the United States during the Administrations of Jefferson and Madison* (1889–1891), the point of view remains too narrowly political, with the result that it fails to thrust into adequate relief the economics of the great struggle between agrarianism and capitalism; and without that clue the interpretation is wanting in substantial realism.

By 1891 he was convinced that he had got all he could from the curdled milk of politics, and he became dissatisfied with his work. There can be little doubt that it was a growing realization of the inadequacy of his analysis of social forces that determined him to abandon the field he had tilled so long and set about the business of reëducating himself. If *Mont-Saint-Michel and Chartres* and *The Education* tell anything about Henry Adams they reveal that his dissatisfactions welled up from deep springs within himself—from the consciousness of his failure to penetrate beneath the surface, to probe the hidden forces that move the puppets on the historical stage. He had long been seeking an adequate philosophy of history—for a unity behind the multiplicity—and in these early years of the nineties he was stimulated by Brooks Adams, who was then deep in his theory of the law of civilization and decay and had come to lean heavily on the principle of economic determinism.[5] "Brooks Adams had taught him," he said later, "that the relation between civilizations was that of trade," and stimulated by this

⁵ *Ibid.*, pp. 338–339.

rediscovery of the philosophy of the first Adams he set about the business of orienting himself to the realm of science, of substituting for a meaningless political interpretation a broader philosophical interpretation.

Very likely it was his reading in the sociology of the Enlightenment that first turned his thought to the philosophy of history—chiefly Turgot and Comte. Speaking of the years 1867–1868 he said he "became a Comteist, within the limits of evolution."[6] He had long been interested in such clues as science offered—in the geological theories of Sir Charles Lyell and the biological deductions of Darwin. But the theory of biological evolution with its implications of a benevolent progress from the simple to the complex, failed to satisfy him; and he turned to the physical sciences for a guide, discovering as the ultimate reality behind all appearances—force. This physical principle he transferred to the field of sociology. Coal-power, electrical power, he concluded, were to civilization what the gaseous theory was to physics. It was a creative suggestion and it revolutionized his conception of history. It runs through all his later speculations and provided the basis of his thinking. "Adams never knew why," he said, "knowing nothing of Faraday, he began to mimic Faraday's trick of seeing lines of force all about him, where he had always seen lines of will."[7] "To evolutionists may be left the processes of evolution; to historians the single interest is the law of reaction between force and force—between mind and nature—the law of progress."[8] "The great division of history into phases by Turgot and Comte first affirmed this law in its outlines by asserting the unity of progress."[9]

Thus by the aid of the physical sciences Henry Adams came back to the philosophy of determinism—a conception that may lead either to pantheism or to mechanism as one's temperament determines. In such a choice there would be no doubt which way Henry Adams would go; he must somehow reconcile determinism and progress, he must discover unity in multiplicity—and that unity and progress he found in a mystical pantheism. "Continuous movement, universal cause, and interchangeable force. This was pantheism, but the Schools were pantheist . . . and their deity was the ultimate energy, whose thought and action were one."[10]

[6] Ibid., p. 225.
[7] Ibid., p. 426.
[8] Ibid., p. 493.
[9] Ibid., p. 493.
[10] Ibid., pp. 428–429.

How creatively this pantheistic mysticism was to determine his later thinking is sufficiently revealed in the pages of *Mont-Saint-Michel and Chartres*. With incredible labor Henry Adams had at last made his way out of the Sahara of politics in which he had long wandered.

Phrased in less transcendental terms his philosophy of history, as he came finally to understand it, was expressed thus:

> The work of domestic progress is done by masses of mechanical power— steam, electric, furnace, or other—which have to be controlled by a score or two of individuals who have shown capacity to manage it. The work of internal government has become the task of controlling these men, who are socially as remote as heathen gods, alone worth knowing, but never known, and who could tell nothing of political value if one skinned them alive. Most of them have nothing to tell, but are forces as dumb as their dynamos, absorbed in the development or economy of power. They are trustees for the public, and whenever society assumes the property, it must confer on them that title; but the power will remain as before, who- ever manages it, and will then control society without appeal, as it con- trols its stokers and pit-men. Modern politics is, at bottom, a struggle not of men but of forces. The men become every year more and more creatures of force, massed about central power-houses. The conflict is no longer between the men, but between the motors that drive the men, and the men tend to succumb to their own motive forces. This is a moral that man strongly objects to admit, especially in mediaeval pursuits like poli- tics and poetry, nor is it worth while for a teacher to insist upon it.[11]

From a civilization thus tyrannized over by coal-power and elec- trical power, he turned away to discover if possible a civilization in which men had lived the good life that he longed for; and in his second incursion into medieval times he found what he had long been seeking. Two centuries, from 1050 to 1250, came to represent for him in the evening of his days the crown and glory of all human endeavor; the first century with its Norman Mont-Saint-Michel and its *Chanson de Roland*, with its forthright strength and sim- plicity, its uncritical acceptance of life and God, its hope encom- passed by a sufficing unity—a strong, naïve, credulous world, yet with men's minds buttressed like their cathedrals by a faith that held in equilibrium the soaring arches of their aspirations, with every cranny and nook flooded with radiant color: and the second century, that expressed itself in the cathedral of Chartres, with its adoration of the Virgin, its courtly love of Guillaume de Lorris and Marie de Champagne, its passionate mysticism of Saint Louis and

[11] *Ibid.*, pp. 421–422.

Saint Bernard and Saint Francis, and its soaring scholasticism of Thomas Aquinas—a tender, feminine age, that worshiped woman and erected its altars to Our Lady of Love rather than to Our Lady of Sorrows, that found in Isolde the ideal woman and expressed itself in Eleanor of Guienne and Blanche of Castile, in Héloïse and Marie de Champagne, more adequately than in Richard Cœur-de-Lion, till it finally went the way of mortality "with the death of Queen Blanche and of all good things about the year 1250":—to such idealization of medievalism did this child of Puritanism come in the wistful twilight of his days. He had never evaded life, nor professed himself satisfied with mean or cheap substitutes, but had sought persistently till he had come to believe that the good life had been lived once, though it might not ever be lived again. So much at least was clear gain, even though it should end in wistfulness.

Mont-Saint-Michel and Chartres is a beautiful book, the more beautiful because of its wistfulness; and the theme that runs through its pages is a denial of the values that embodied for his countrymen the sum of all excellence. It is an account of certain happy generations—so few amongst the countless many—who worshiped in love, before fear had come to the western world and crept into the message of the church; a love that elevated Mother Mary above the Christ of the Cross, and that in her shrine at Chartres would allow no hint of sorrow or suffering to appear, but represented her as looking out upon the world with a gracious and regal kindliness and mercy, quick to succor and to forgive—the spirit of love that suffices life in all its needs. *Mont-Saint-Michel and Chartres* is rich and tender and wise, perhaps beyond anything else that his generation of Americans wrote, with a mellow scholarship that walks modestly because it has learned how little it knows. Yet in its every implication it is a sharp and searching criticism of Boston and America of the nineteenth century. It repudiates every ideal of a generation that had gambled away the savor of life—that does not comprehend "and never shall," the greatness of that earlier time, "the appetite" for living, the "greed for novelty," "the fun of life." [12] It was precisely these things, unimportant though they might seem to the acquisitive mind, that Henry Adams had missed in his own life and passionately resented having missed. To come to know great men and great deeds and great ages is perhaps of doubtful expediency for one who must live amongst small men; and Henry

[12] *Ibid.*, p. 139.

Adams was forced to pay a heavy penalty for his catholic under-standing and sympathy.

The profound suggestiveness of *Mont-Saint-Michel and Chartres* lies in the skill with which the brilliant threads of medieval art and thought and aspiration are woven into a single pattern, and the splendor of its unity traced to a mystical *élan* that found its highest expression in faith. It was the ideal of love that he discovered in the golden twelfth century—love above law, above logic, above the church and the schools: a love that explains for him the passionate worship of Mother Mary, together with the new *"courtoisie"* that sought to shape manners and morals to humane ends. The human-ity of the Virgin set her above the Trinity, as the humanity of Saint Francis set him above Thomas Aquinas, for all the latter's soaring scholasticism. To one who entered those bygone times through the portals of Chartres cathedral, it was natural to interpret the total age in the light of the gentle smile of the Mother of God, and to feel her presence as a transforming spirit amongst men. Has any other Yankee interpreted so lovingly the mission of the Virgin, as Henry Adams analyzed it in such a passage as this?

True it was, although one should not say it jestingly, that the Virgin embarrassed the Trinity; and perhaps this was the reason, behind all the other excellent reasons, why men loved and adored her with a passion such as no other deity has ever inspired: and why we, although utter strangers to her, are not far from getting down on our knees and praying to her still. Mary concentrated in herself the whole rebellion of man against fate; the whole protest against divine law; the whole contempt for human law as its outcome; the whole unutterable fury of human nature beating itself against the walls of its prison-house, and suddenly seized by a hope that in the Virgin man had found a door of escape. She was above law; she took feminine pleasure in turning hell into an ornament; she delighted in trampling on every social distinction in this world and the next. She knew that the universe was as unintelligible to her, on any theory of morals, as it was to her worshippers, and she felt, like them, no sure con-viction that it was any more intelligible to the Creator of it. To her, every suppliant was a universe in himself, to be judged apart, on his own merits, by his love for her,—by no means on his orthodoxy, or his conventional standing in the Church, or according to his correctness in defining the nature of the Trinity. The convulsive hold which Mary to this day main-tains over human imagination—as you can see at Lourdes—was due much less to her power of saving soul or body than to her sympathy with people who suffered under law,—divine or human,—justly or unjustly, by acci-dent or design, by decree of God or by guile of Devil. She cared not a straw for conventional morality, and she had no notion of letting her friends be punished, to the tenth or any other generation, for the sins of their ancestors or the peccadilloes of Eve.

So Mary filled heaven with a sort of persons little to the taste of any respectable middle-class society, which has trouble enough in making this world decent and pay its bills, without having to continue the effort in another. Mary stood in a Church of her own, so independent that the Trinity might have perished without much affecting her position; but, on the other hand, the Trinity could look on and see her dethroned with almost a breath of relief. . . . Mary's treatment of respectable and law-abiding people who had no favours to ask, and were reasonably confident of getting to heaven by the regular judgment, without expense, rankled so deeply that three hundred years later the Puritan reformers were not satisfied with abolishing her, but sought to abolish the woman altogether as the cause of all evil in heaven and on earth. The Puritans abandoned the New Testament and the Virgin in order to go back to the beginning, and renew the quarrel with Eve.[13]

Thus at last, in another land and a remote age, Henry Adams found the clue that explained for him his own failure and the source of the dissatisfactions that had tracked him doggedly through his far wanderings. He had come to understand the reasons for the sterility of his Massachusetts past, and the last shreds of his Puritan-Federalist heritage were cast off. In comparison with the vision that came to him in the choir of Chartres, how unspeakably poor and mean were the activities he had portrayed in *Democracy*, or even those he had dealt with in his history of the early days of the republic. He had discovered the highest existence in emotional response to noble appeal; the good life was the unified life, possible only on a grand scale in those rare and great periods of social *élan* when the individual is fused in an encompassing unity. Of that golden age of the Transition—so he finally cast up the account— "the sum is an emotion—clear and strong as love and much clearer than logic whose charm lies in its unstable balance."

The Transition is the equilibrium between the love of God—which is faith—and the logic of God—which is reason; between the round arch and the pointed. One may not be sure which pleases most, but one need not be harsh toward people who think that the moment of balance is exquisite. The last and highest moment is seen at Chartres, where, in 1200, the charm depends on the constant doubt whether emotion or science is uppermost. At Amiens, doubt ceases; emotion is trained in school, Thomas Aquinas reigns.[14]

. Of all the elaborate symbolism which has been suggested for the Gothic cathedral, the most vital and most perfect may be that the slender

[13] *Mont-Saint-Michel*, pp. 276–277.   [14] *Ibid.*, pp. 321–322.

nervure, the springing motion of the broken arch, the leap downwards of the flying buttress,—the visible effort to throw off a visible strain,—never let us forget that Faith alone supports it, and that, if Faith fails, Heaven is lost. The equilibrium is visibly delicate beyond the line of safety; danger lurks in every stone. The peril of the heavy tower, of the restless vault, of the vagrant buttress; the uncertainty of logic, the in-equalities of the syllogism, the irregularities of the mental mirror,—all these haunting nightmares of the Church are expressed as strongly by the Gothic cathedral as though it had been the cry of human suffering, and as no emotion had ever been expressed before or is likely to find expression again. The delight of its aspiration is flung up to the sky. The pathos of its self-distrust and anguish of doubt is buried in the earth as its last secret. You can read out of it whatever else pleases your youth and con-fidence; to me, this is all.[15]

One may enter the past, of course, through such portals as one chooses; but one is likely to choose the portals that promise to open upon the world of one's desires. It was a fortunate accident, no doubt, that led Henry Adams to Chartres to study the cathedral glass under the guidance of John La Farge; nevertheless it finally determined for him his total interpretation of the Middle Ages and of all history, and that interpretation followed naturally a subtle ancestral bias. Even in his rebellion against his past he could not get away from it, but like Ruskin and John Henry Newman he came to affirm—whether rightly or wrongly, who shall say?—that the singular glory of the Middle Ages was the mystical *élan* that came to expression in the adoration of the Virgin. As a child of generations of Puritans he came back finally, in the twilight of his studies, to the great ideal of faith. And yet it is not without sugges-tion that William Morris, who more nearly than any other modern expressed in his daily life the spirit of the Middle Ages, never con-cerned himself much with the medieval church—neither its cathe-drals nor its scholasticism nor its miracles—never talked about an age of faith, would scarcely have understood, indeed, what was meant by the drive of a mystical *élan;* but discovered the secret of that earlier civilization in the gild rather than the church, and traced the source of the haunting beauty that clings to all its works to the psychology of craftsmanship that found delight in shaping the raw material to the craftsman's dreams.

The difference between Morris and Adams is great enough, and at bottom it is the difference between the artist and the intellectual; yet it is a pity that Henry Adams, with his wide acquaintance in

[15] *Ibid.*, p. 383.

England, should never have known the one Victorian he should most have delighted in—the nineteenth-century craftsman who found in his workshop the good life the historian dreamed of, and was unhappy because it had been lost. Perhaps it would not have greatly changed the latter's interpretation. He was not a pagan in temperament to enter sympathetically into the medieval world that Morris had discovered and of which the Church was only a drapery—a drapery that never quite covered a frank *joie de vivre* that was an emotion far more realistic and human than any mystical *élan*, and that persisted long after the apogee of faith in the early twelfth century, filling all the later Middle Ages with its abundant beauty till it was finally destroyed by the economic revolution that came out of the Reformation. But at any rate he might have been led by such knowledge to set the craftsman beside the poet and the schoolman and the mystic—the nameless artist who wrought such marvels beside the patron who took care to have his name and his arms emblazoned on window and wall to remind posterity of his generosity; and certainly, his interpretation of the Middle Ages would not have suffered by such addition. Instead, an excessive intellectualism drove him back upon the naïve.

The disillusion of Henry Adams is abundantly instructive to the student of our flamboyant transition, so different from the golden Transition. Here was an honest man and an able—none honester and none abler in his generation—who devoted his life to finding a path out of the maze of middle-class America, that should lead to a rational and humane existence. He was never overconfident of his conclusions. All arrogant dogmatisms he had long since left behind; they had become for him pathetically futile and foolish. Creeds and faiths, whether in religion or politics or economics, he no longer subscribed to; but a certain residuum remained, from his long meditations—a sense of interfusing unity, mystical, pantheistic, that his lurking skepticism dealt tenderly with. "*Inter vania nihil vanius est homine*," he asserted as a skeptic, and as a mystic he replied, "Man is an imperceptible atom always trying to become one with God. If ever modern science achieves a definition of energy, possibly it may borrow the figure: Energy is the inherent effort of every multiplicity to become unity." [16] In these later years he called himself half whimsically a "conservative Christian Anarchist" [17] and the explanation probably is to be found in his

[16] *Mont-Saint-Michel*, p. 332.   [17] *The Education*, p. 405.

shift from intellectualism to emotion as the crown of a satisfying life. "The two poles of social and political philosophy seem necessarily to be organization or anarchy; man's intellect or the forces of nature." [18] In rare and happy periods—as in the glorious Transition—freedom finds its fullest life in a spontaneous drawing together of the whole; but as the social *élan* dies away, institutions, organization, remain. Thomas Aquinas follows Saint Francis, form remains after emotion has subsided. Nevertheless the free man must cling to his freedom, in spite of society, in spite of the political state.

Absolute liberty is absence of restraint; responsibility is restraint; therefore, the ideally free individual is responsible only to himself. This principle is the philosophical foundation of anarchism, and, for anything that science has yet proved, may be the philosophical foundation of the universe; but it is fatal to all society and is especially hostile to the State. [19]

Though he lived in the midst of a centralizing politics and found his friends in such servants of centralization as John Hay and Henry Cabot Lodge, Henry Adams had no faith in the dominant ideals. He was never a friend to an acquisitive society with its engrossing political state. In the light of his favorite dictum that "Power is poison," he may perhaps be regarded as an old-fashioned Jeffersonian; it is another evidence of the persistence of his eighteenth-century mind. He was an arch-individualist who would go his own way and reach his own conclusions, quite unconcerned that his views were wholly at variance with those of his generation. How could it be otherwise? How should men who lived in the counting-house understand even the language of this pilgrim returned from other and greater worlds? It was foolish to talk of what he had seen. And so when he wrote *Mont-Saint-Michel and Chartres* he published it privately, and was incredulous when it was proposed to republish it and give it to the world. What had he, or the twelfth century, to say to the land of Theodore Roosevelt and Pierpont Morgan? Was not this America of theirs peopled by the descendants of the *bourgeoisie* who, six hundred years before, resentful at having been cheated—as they supposed—in their heavy investments in shrines and churches of Our Lady, had turned away from all such unprofitable business, and put their savings in lands and houses and ships and railways and banks—of which

[18] *Mont-Saint-Michel*, p. 344.   [19] *Ibid*, p. 372.

things politics was the sluttish servant? How should one who had known Saint Francis and Eleanor of Guienne take such men or such a world seriously?

III

BROOKS ADAMS—REBEL

The difference between Henry Adams and Brooks Adams is, perhaps, sufficiently revealed in the distinction between the intellectual and the rebel. The youngest of the brothers was a militant nonconformist, a searching and outspoken critic of all the faiths of his generation. In Brooks Adams the family skepticisms were pointed and barbed, and the family distrust of capitalism issued in a broadside attack upon the hateful system. Few Americans of his day were so little pleased with the bankers' Utopia dreamed of by the middle class, or subjected the capitalistic mind to such critical analysis. Not content with rejecting that Utopia, he pursued his studies in the history of western civilization with a view to determining whether the economic mind, instead of being the friend and ally of a human society—as it professed to be—were not rather the foul wellspring of a disintegrating egoism that must destroy every civilization that yields to its siren appeal. In the theory he eventually elaborated, the capitalistic mind proves to be a greedy spider spinning his web to catch the simple imaginative minds—warrior and priest and artist and craftsman—and suck them dry. The sterile middleman becomes master of society and with the inevitable enslavement of the producer, and the drying-up of production at its source, civilization withers and decays, to be followed by another cycle in the long struggle between the creative and acquisitive instincts.

None but a congenital rebel could have arrived at such conclusions from the studies in which his youth was passed. As a son of the house of Adams the profession of the law was the predestined path to politics and diplomacy, and like Charles and Henry he devoted his younger years to the ancestral study, receiving such training as the Harvard Law School could give. He made greater progress than his brothers, eventually getting so far as to write legal treatises; but finding such work a bit arid he supplemented his legal studies with the writing of Massachusetts chronicles. His dissatisfactions seem to have culminated in the late eighties, during the lean years that preceded the crash of 1893; and he turned away from local chronicles to speculate on the deeper causes of social vigor and decline. The result was the publication in 1895 of *The Law of Civilization and Decay*, a study in social dynamics that took its point of departure from psychology, and based its conclusions on physics and economics. Before Henry Adams he elaborated the theory that civilization is the product of social energy, and social energy obeys the physical law of mass, accelerating or retarding in ratio to the density of population reduced to order. As society draws together in great centers its activity increases until exhaustion finally slows it down; whereupon follows a period of disintegration that breaks up the integrated mass and disperses its energy. The social ebb and flow, therefore, is always from decentralization to centralization and back again to decentralization, and as it flows it thrusts into the foreground different types of mind that express themselves in diverse ideals.

The master types that appear and disappear in this ceaseless flux are determined by two psychological drives that always and everywhere shape human activity—fear and greed: the one culminating in the social rule of the priest, the other in the social rule of the usurer. Decentralization with its isolation breeds the imaginative mind which, seeing more devils than vast hell can hold, turns to the priest for succor—to one who deals in miracles and professes to be able to fend off malignant powers, and who in consequence grows rich by his traffic in relics and rises to economic power. But imagination produces as well the creative mind that finds in isolation the promptings to revery, expresses its dreams in terms of beauty, and fashions a realm of art in which to dwell. Priest, artist, and warrior,—shrine, cathedral, and castle—were the creation of medieval times, the naïve products of the golden age of decentralization. Whereas centralization, with the rubbing away of singularity by daily contact and the greater rewards that lie open to activity, breeds automatically the economic mind—a mind that is necessarily unimaginative, practical, competitive, acquisitive, skeptical, preferring administration to creation, and setting exploitation as the single object of activity. And since centralization offers increasing rewards to greed, the economic mind subdues the imaginative, and the money-lender with his control of wealth rises to mastery. As he expropriates the resources of society he inevitably dominates the political state. His wealth enables him to maintain a hired police to safeguard his gains, until expropriation having run its course, the police fail to hold in check the mass of the exploited, and an unmartial class discovers that money can no longer buy security against the strength of numbers. The usurer is overthrown, his wealth is expropriated, and the social cycle must be run again.

This suggestive theory, which he works out with conspicuous skill in his interpretation of the Middle Ages and the rise of capitalism, implies a perennial conflict between fear and greed, that turns finally upon the relative development of the arts of attack and of defense. Centralization, it is clear, results from the superiority of the former; when attack is superior to defense the lesser strongholds of exploitation must fall and the defeated must become subject to the coalescing masters. After the disruption of the Roman Empire western Europe created its feudal system, by means of which the baron in his stout castle flouted the centralizing ambitions of the impotent monarchy; and it was not till the wealth of the church and of the *bourgeoisie* was thrown on the side of the king, and the development of the art of attack through the use of gunpowder, that the rise of the monarchical state was possible. But having aided the king to reduce the power of the barons, thereby rendering trade secure on a large scale, the *bourgeoisie* turned against the medieval church with its vast wealth that invited expropriation. In the primitive age of faith, under the dominion of fear, the burgesses had spent their money prodigally to build shrines and churches and cathedrals—in France alone between the years 1170 and 1270, eighty cathedrals and nearly five hundred large churches had been built, that by a calculation made in 1840, would cost a billion dollars to replace [20]—but with the development of the economic mind such amazing expenditures seemed wasteful, and the *bourgeoisie* looked about for a cheaper way of salvation. The money cost to the worshipers of saints and relics was a sharp prod to their skepticism as to the efficacy of such worship. This explains for Brooks Adams the origins of the Reformation; it was due to the economic dissatisfaction of the burgess class; the church had grown rich and grasping from its monopoly power. Speaking of the rise of English Lollardry, he argued:

The Lollards were of the modern economic type, and discarded the miracle because the miracle was costly and yielded an uncertain return . . . gifts as an atonement for sin were a drain on savings, and the econo-

[20] See Henry Adams, *Mont-Saint-Michel*, pp. 94–95.

mist instinctively sought cheaper methods of propitiation. The monied class, therefore, proceeded step by step, and its first experiment was to suppress all fees to middle-men, whether priests or saints, by becoming their own intercessors with the deity . . . [and] as the tradesman replaced the enthusiast, a dogma was evolved by which mental anguish, which cost nothing, was substituted for the offering which was effective in proportion to its money value. This dogma was "Justification by Faith," the cornerstone of Protestantism. . . .

But the substitution of a mental condition for a money payment led to consequences more far-reaching than the suppression of certain clerical revenues, for it involved the rejection of the sacred tradition which had not only sustained relic worship, but which had made the Church the channel of communication between Christians and the invisible world. That ancient channel once closed, Protestants had to open another, and this led to the deification of the Bible. . . . Thus for the innumerable costly fetishes of the imaginative age were substituted certain writings which could be consulted without a fee. The expedient was evidently the device of a mercantile community, . . . and made an organized priesthood impossible. When each individual might pry into the sacred mysteries at his pleasure, the authority of the clergy was annihilated.[21]

With warrior and priest superseded by the tradesman as the dominant type—the imaginative mind by the economic—came the inevitable triumph of greed over fear. The ancient defenses of the church were razed and it stood naked to its enemies. In presence of the skepticism of the burgesses it could no longer sell its miracles in the open market, could no longer persuade men that it was God's vicegerent with powers of binding and loosing; and with its divine sanctions gone, its wealth-hoards lay unprotected before the cupidity of king, noble, and commoner. The spoliation of the monasteries was the prelude to the long movement of the Reformation in England, and made possible its success. So long as the church retained its lands and treasure it could not easily be overturned; so a greedy King and greedy nobles took effective measures to disarm it, and having got their hands on the substantial plunder they left to Genevan ministers the lesser business of disputing over the form and doctrine of the new church. The revolution had already been accomplished; and this revolution—the transfer from priest to layman of a third of the wealth of England—was but prelude to still greater revolutions that were preparing, and which began with the pouring into England of the gold and silver from the Spanish treasure-ships. The spoiling of Rome and the spoiling of the Spaniard were both buccaneering adventures undertaken by zealous Protes-

[21] *The Law of Civilization and Decay*, pp. 150–151.

tants. Drake and Hawkins—pirate and slaver—were "hot gospel-
lers," ready to fight, plunder, or rape for the glory of God and the
profit of England; and it was such men who diverted to London the
flood of Spanish-American silver that issued from the rich mines of
Potosi.

Potosi was discovered in 1545, and from that event Adams dates
the rise of the commercial activity that was to prepare the way for
the Industrial Revolution, which came to flower two centuries later.
This vast upheaval that destroyed the older feudal England, was
the immediate outcome of the plundering of India that brought to
London the vast treasure-hoards of the East. The eviction of the
peasants from their lands had already provided a plentiful supply
of cheap labor, the machinery of credit and exchange had been
created, and with this immense influx of capital the Industrial
Revolution was a matter of course. The manufacturers seized
control of England and ruled till approximately 1810, when their
authority was disputed by the financiers who gradually displaced
them. The Bank Act of 1844, which yielded the control of the
currency to the bankers, marked the definite transfer of sovereignty
to Lombard Street; Samuel Lloyd, the banker, completed the
work begun in 1523 by Thomas Cromwell, burgess-adventurer—the
work of bringing England under the authoritative sway of the
principle of greed. Since 1844 western civilization has lain helpless
under the heel of the usurer, who levies his tax upon production by
expanding and contracting the currency at will, and rules society
through his control of the political state. The triumph of the
economic mind is complete.

The aristocracy which wields this autocratic power is beyond attack,
for it is defended by a wage-earning police, by the side of which the legions
were a toy—a police so formidable that, for the first time in history, revolt is hopeless and is not attempted. The only question which preoccu-
pies the ruling class is whether it is cheaper to coerce or bribe.[22]

The Law of Civilization and Decay is an extraordinarily provocative study, the main principles of which he elaborated and applied
in later historical studies, the result of which was to emphasize for
him the determining influence of economics and geography in the
rise and fall of empires.[23] Equipped thus with a comprehensive

---

[22] *Ibid.*, p. 292.
[23] See *America's Economic Supremacy*, New York, 1900; *The New Empire*, New
York, 1902.

philosophy of history, he turned in a later work to examine certain aspects of the play of social forces in America, in the light of universal social experience. The particular object of his inquiry in *The Theory of Social Revolutions* is the machinery of social control developed in America during the movement of capitalistic centralization, and its probable adequacy to meet the future stresses of acceleration. The problem of security for the capitalistic order resolves itself, he decides, into the problem of a sufficient protective police; and since every non-military master class must depend upon some form of mercenary Swiss guard, the solution in America has assumed a form not uncommon in earlier European experience, but which every European country has learned at bitter cost to reject. In the face of a strong anti-militaristic public sentiment that forbids a coercive army and navy, the financial masters have had recourse to the courts; and it is the eventual effect of such perversion of the courts to non-judicial ends that he considers in this frank inquiry.

Historically, he points out, the courts have at times exercised two diverse functions, the judicial and the political; and the problem of justice and equity before the law, it has been found by long and bitter experience, resolves itself into the total separation of the one from the other. The judicial function is that of impartial arbitrament in accordance with an established *corpus juris;* it is judgment and not will. The enactment of the law, on the other hand, is a political function, residing in the legislature. When therefore, the courts exercise the political function, they not only assert that the judicial will is sovereign, but they engage in a perilous struggle for mastership and involve themselves in all the passions of partisan objectives. Every "dominant class, as it has arisen, has done its best to use the machinery of justice for its own benefit." The temptation to such perversion is perennial; it is the particular and besetting temptation of an unmartial monied class; and in times of social stress it becomes acute. In revolutionary crises—as in England under Lord Chief-Justice Jeffreys and in France under the Revolutionary Tribunal—the political function overrides the judicial, the last protection of the individual is swept away, and society lies helpless before the ruling power. Thus to pervert the legitimate functions of the courts is a dangerous game to play—most dangerous for a non-military group for whom the courts are protectors; and yet it is precisely this game that capitalism in America, heedless of the teachings of experience, has long been playing. Using the courts as a police power it has brought contempt upon them and thereby weakened the arm upon which alone it can hope to rely in periods of acute stress. In short, capitalism has assumed the functions of sovereignty in America, but it has refused to assume the responsibilities of sovereignty. To gain immediate ends it has shut its eyes to future consequences; and what those future consequences are likely to be Brooks Adams is at pains to point out.

The kernel of his argument, obviously, lies in the thesis that the federal courts have assumed political functions; and into this question he delves with the equipment of the lawyer added to that of the philosophical historian. "Politics," he asserts realistically, "is the struggle for ascendancy of a class or a majority." Under the "American system, the Constitution . . . is expounded by judges, and this function, which, in essence, is political, has brought precisely that quality of pressure on the bench which it has been the labor of a hundred generations of our ancestors to remove."[24] Hence, "from the outset, the American bench, because it deals with the most fiercely contested of political issues, has been an instrument necessary to political success. Consequently, political parties have striven to control it, and, therefore, the bench has always had an avowed partisan bias."[25] From so anomalous a situation two curious developments have resulted: in the rôle of guardians of the Constitution the courts have assumed sovereign powers over the legislature, and at the same time, by a clever non-judicial hocus-pocus they have declared themselves superior to the Constitution, possessed of the prerogative of dispensation. How the first came into being Adams traces in detail from the time of Marbury vs. Madison in 1803, when Marshall asserted a supervisory jurisdiction over Congress, to Standard Oil Company vs. United States in 1911, when the Court amended an act of Congress that Congress had declined to amend. How the second came into being is a curious story. It arose, according to Adams, from the rigidity of a written constitution, that having been interpreted narrowly must somehow be stretched to meet public needs. In such an emergency the "Supreme Court of New York imagined the theory of the Police Power," saying in effect, "in our discretion, we suspend the operation of the Constitution, in this instance, by calling your act an exercise of a power unknown to the framers of the Constitution."[26]

[24] *The Theory of Social Revolution*, p. 45.   [25] *Ibid.*, pp. 47–48.   [26] *Ibid.*, p. 128.

In other words, having, by the assumption of sovereignty, nullified the legislative power from which relief would naturally come,
and having awakened a hostile public opinion by its narrow interpretation of contractual rights, the court was embarrassed and
looked about for a loophole of escape; and the most convenient
loophole was the novel doctrine of judicial prerogative:

> No legislature could intervene, and a pressure was brought to bear which
> the judges could not withstand; therefore, the Court yielded, declaring
> that if impairing a contract were, on the whole, for the public welfare,
> the Constitution, as Marshall interpreted it, should be suspended in favor
> of the legislation which impaired it. They called this suspension the opera-
> tion of the "Police Power." It followed, as the "Police Power" could
> only come into operation at the discretion of the Court, that, therefore,
> within the limits of judicial discretion, confiscation, however arbitrary
> and to whatever extent, might go on.[27]
> The effect of the adoption by the Supreme Court of the United States
> of the New York theory of the Police Power was to vest in the judiciary,
> by the use of this catch-word, an almost unparallelled prerogative. They
> assumed a supreme function which can only be compared to the Dispensing
> Power claimed by the Stuarts, or to the authority which, according to the
> Council of Constance, inheres in the Church, to "grant indulgences for
> reasonable causes." I suppose nothing in modern judicial history has ever
> resembled this assumption. . . .[28]

It is this amazing principle of the judicial prerogative which
sets the Courts above the Constitution and grants them the privilege of dispensing Indulgences, that has perverted their functions
from the judicial to the political. If Indulgences are for sale, naturally the wealthy will buy them. And since corporate wealth is regarded by the judiciary with a more than friendly eye, it rarely
finds difficulty in securing such Indulgences as it seeks. The
Courts have become, in consequence, not so much the Swiss Guards
of capitalism, as a pliant sovereign lord who dispenses rewards to
his favorites. The capitalist is "the most lawless" of citizens. In
his attitude towards the state he is essentially anarchistic; he
evades or nullifies a law that he does not like, while clamorous for
the enforcement of a law that works in his favor.

> If the capitalist has bought some sovereign function, and wishes to
> abuse it for his own behoof, he regards the law which restrains him as a
> despotic invasion of his constitutional rights, because, with his specialized
> mind, he cannot grasp the relation of a sovereign function to the nation

[27] *Ibid.*, p. 93.   [28] *Ibid.*, pp. 91–92.

as a whole. He, therefore, looks upon the evasion of a law devised for public protection, but inimical to him, as innocent or even meritorious.

This attitude of capital has had a profound effect upon shaping the American legal mind. The capitalist, as I infer, regards the constitutional form of government which exists in the United States, as a convenient method of obtaining his own way against a majority, but the lawyer has learned to worship it as a fetish. Nor is this astonishing, for, were written constitutions suppressed, he would lose most of his importance and much of his income. Quite honestly, therefore, the American lawyer has come to believe that a sheet of paper soiled with printers' ink and interpreted by half-a-dozen elderly gentlemen snugly dozing in armchairs, has some inherent and marvellous virtue by which it can arrest the march of omnipotent Nature. And capital gladly accepts this view of American civilization, since hitherto capitalists have usually been able to select the magistrates who decide their causes.[29]

The skepticisms of the House of Adams came to their frankest expression in the writings of Brooks Adams. The passion for social justice had brought him at last to a philosophy of history that made him a trenchant critic of the American of his generation. He rejected alike the humanitarian optimism that, from Condorcet to Herbert Spencer, had inspired generous souls with hope for future progress—and that even Henry Adams clung to—and the economic optimism that from the beginnings of the westward movement had inspired acquisitive souls with the hope of continuous gain. Nothing perhaps marked him more clearly as a rebel than his denial of the god worshiped by his fellows. The gospel of progress was for him no more than a fetish of the economic mind. In the ebb and flow of civilizations under the attraction of fear and greed, what justification was there for faith in a benevolent progress? His lot had been cast, unfortunately, in an age of capitalism, when the acquisitive mind was triumphing over the imaginative, the banker over the priest and craftsman and mystic; but he could see no reason in heaven or earth to brag of that fact, and he would have held himself a fool to apply the term progress to the spread of greed that was crowning the usurer as master of men. A thorough skeptic, with the comfortable illusions of his generation dissipated, he was in worse plight than Henry Adams, for he had created no golden twelfth century as a refuge against the present.

But if he was under no illusions, he was under no intellectual tyrannies; he had cleared his mind of all middle-class fetishes and could look out calmly upon a mad world. After a century and a

[29] *Ibid.*, pp. 213–215.

quarter this youngest of the House of Adams was still true to the sturdy intellectual honesty of his race. He refused to cry up a fool's paradise where his fellows were crowning the banker as king—professing to serve high ends while seeking vulgar profits: he would not shut his eyes to disagreeable truth or hold his tongue. In Brooks Adams one can almost hear the voice of the first Adams elaborating his doctrine of determinism, pointing out to a romantic generation the unpleasant realities that confuted its optimism, expatiating on the abundant follies of men that lay snares in their own path, yet clinging to a faith in justice that has become old-fashioned. Possibly Brooks Adams is not to be reckoned a great figure, but he was an honest man and worthy of his name—no mean accomplishment, for all in all the Adams family is the most distinguished in our history.

CHAPTER III

VICTORIAN REALISM

IT was not till the eighties that the movement of realism in fiction began to excite wide interest, and then began a brisk and often acrimonious discussion of the merits and shortcomings of the new technique that filled the pages of the literary magazines. The prejudices against it were many and robust. To most Victorians realism meant Zola, sex, and the exploitation of the animal, and all the pruderies of the Age of Innocence rose up in protest against defiling letters with such themes. The judgment of Aldrich's on realism—"A miasmatic breath blown from the slums"—was a characteristic Yankee echo of Tennyson's condemnation, "wallowing in the slough of Zolaism." All the high priests of the genteel rallied to combat such a desecration of literature, and when it knocked at the door of a respectable magazine in the person of Stephen Crane's *Maggie* the editor could do nothing else than turn it into the street. In the late nineties, when *Jude the Obscure* appeared in one of the family magazines, even the great reputation of Hardy was reckoned a poor excuse for such an offense to morality.

American taste was still romantic, and from his villa at Florence, F. Marion Crawford regularly sent forth heavy romances that were regarded as contributions to our literature. In defense of his wares he threw into the discussion of realism a compact little volume, *The Novel; What It Is*, in which he defined the novel as a pocket drama, the chief interest of which lies in the plot—a retort courteous to Howells's contention that plot is childish and a story ends well that ends faithfully; wedding bells at the end are of no interest to grown men and women, but rather what life brings after the wedding bells. To the aid of Crawford came the brilliant Scot, Robert Louis Stevenson, the literary idol of America in the nineties, whose brave tales were on every center-table. A confirmed romantic, Stevenson could not resist breaking a lance in the cause, and his *Humble Remonstrance* was a persuasive defense of the perennial appeal of romance.

But in spite of protests the spirit of realism spread quietly through the lesser works of fiction and the high-flown romantic was laid away in the grave of John Esten Cooke. The new realism was a native growth, sprung from the soil, unconcerned with European technique. In its earlier expression it inclined to a romantic or idyllic coloring, but as it developed it came to rely more and more on the beauty of truth. This primitive realism issued chiefly from the local color school of the short story, but it was supplemented by the sociological school. The influence of Lowell and the *Atlantic Monthly* on the development of the realistic short story had been encouraging, and in the next decade that development was to go forward swiftly. With the exploitation of local materials came a sharp division on sectional lines, and as Howells pointed out, America was soon parceled out geographically into local groups. Edward Eggleston in southern Indiana, George Washington Cable in New Orleans, Charles Egbert Craddock in eastern Tennessee, James Lane Allen in Kentucky, Octave Thanet in Arkansas, Sarah Orne Jewett and Mary Wilkins Freeman in New England, were representative of the new concern for local truth in fiction that was to tell against the romantic. In fixing attention on narrow and homely fields they were turning towards realism, for the charm of their work lay in fidelity to the *milieu*, the exact portrayal of character and setting. With the spread of an interest in the local the vogue of the strange and the remote declined and a quiet sobriety of tone displaced the romantic. The way was being prepared for a more adequate realism. "Nothing could testify with more force," said H. H. Boyesen in 1894, "to the fact that we have outgrown romanticism than this almost unanimous desire, on the part of our authors, to chronicle the widely divergent phases of our American civilization." [1]

But that waited upon profound changes in the American outlook on life. In the seventies and eighties conditions were not ripe for it and the naturalism that in France, Russia, Germany, and Scandinavia, was carrying everything before it, was still alien to the American temper. It was not so much that it offended our innate Puritanism as that it seemed to us belied by the open facts of American life. The psychology of the dispersion still marked us. Although we were feverishly building great cities we were still emotionally a country people, far from urban-minded. We still thought in terms of the slack earlier freedoms, uncritical of our

[1] *Literary and Social Silhouettes*, p. 73.

ways, untroubled about the future. For the American born before the Civil War, naturalism was impossible; his mind had not been shaped by the industrial city or come under the dominion of science. The traditional outlook on life was unchanged; he still clung to the old moralities, the old verities, the old faith in the goodness of life in America. The intellectual revolution must be gone through with before naturalism should be at home in America, a native expression of native conditions; and it would then be a vehicle only for writers born and bred in the new city environment. In the meanwhile—in the genial years when the earlier optimisms still veiled the harsher realities of science and industrialism—the movement of realism got under way in the work of two distinguished craftsmen who, bred up in Victorian culture, interpreted life in terms of the middle and upper classes.*

II

HENRY JAMES AND THE NOSTALGIA OF CULTURE

There is a suggestion of irony in the fact that one of our earliest realists, who was independent enough to break with the romantic tradition, should have fled from the reality that his art presumably would gird itself up to deal with. Like his fellow spirit Whistler, Henry James was a lifelong pilgrim to other shrines than those of his native land, who dedicated his gifts to ends that his fellow Americans were indifferent to. Life, with him, was largely a matter of nerves. In this world of sprawling energy it was impossible to barricade himself securely against the intrusion of the unpleasant. His organism was too sensitive, his discriminations too fine, to subject them to the vulgarities of the Gilded Age, and he fled from it all. He early convinced himself that the American atmosphere was uncongenial to the artist.[2] The grotesqueries of the frontier irruption, the crude turmoil released by the new freedoms, were no materials to appeal to one in search of subtleties, to one who was a lover of nocturnes in gray. And so, like Whistler, he sought other

* The first subsection of this chapter in the Contents is entitled "William James and Pragmatism." None of this appears in the manuscript, and it seems likely that Professor Parrington planned to transfer the subject to a later part of the book. The numbering is, however, left as it is given in the Contents.—*Publisher.*

[2] "Civilization at its highest pitch was the master passion of his mind, and his preoccupation with the international aspects of character and custom issued from the conviction that the rawness and rudeness of a young country were not incapable of cure by contact with more developed forms." Pelham Edgar, *Henry James, Man, Author,* pp. 40–41.

lands, there to refine a meticulous technique, and draw out ever thinner the substance of his art.

The explanation of the curious career of Henry James, seeking a habitation between worlds and finding a spiritual home nowhere, is that he was never a realist. Rather he was a self-deceived romantic, the last subtle expression of the genteel, who fell in love with culture and never realized how poor a thing he worshiped. It was the first mistake of Henry James that he romanticized Europe, not for its fragments of the medieval picturesque, but for a fine and gracious culture that he professed to discover there. With the naïveté of the Age of Innocence he assumed that an aristocratic society—shall we say that of Mayfair or the Quartier Saint Germain?—is a complex of subtle imponderables that one comes to understand and embody only through heritage; and it was an assumption even more romantic that these imponderables were so subtly elusive as to escape any but the subtlest art. Like Edith Wharton he erected this suppositious culture into an abstract *tertium quid*, something apart from social convention or physical environment, something embodied in the choicer spirits of a class that for generations presumably had cherished them. Born of an unconscious inferiority complex in presence of a long-established social order to which he was alien, this romanticization of European culture worked to his undoing, for it constrained the artist to a lifelong pursuit of intangible realities that existed only in his imagination. The gracious culture that James persistently attributed to certain choice circles in Europe was only a figment of his romantic fancy—a fact that after long rambling on the Continent and nearly forty years' unbroken residence in England, he came finally to recognize. It was this failure to find the substance of his dream that imparted to his work a note of wistfulness. He had quitted the land of his birth to seek his spiritual home elsewhere, yet increasingly he came to question the wisdom of his act. He suffered the common fate of the *déraciné;* wandering between worlds, he found a home nowhere. It is not well for the artist to turn cosmopolitan, for the flavor of the fruit comes from the soil and sunshine of its native fields.

The spirit of Henry James marks the last refinement of the genteel tradition, the completest embodiment of its vague cultural aspirations. All his life he dwelt wistfully on the outside of the realm he wished to be a free citizen of. Did any other professed

realist ever remain so persistently aloof from the homely realities
of life? From the external world of action he withdrew to the inner
world of questioning and probing; yet even in his subtle psychological inquiries he remained shut up within his own skull-pan. His
characters are only projections of his brooding fancy, externaliza-
tions of hypothetical subtleties. He was concerned only with
nuances. He lived in a world of fine gradations and imperceptible
shades. Like modern scholarship he came to deal more and more
with less and less. It is this absorption in the stream of psychical
experience that justifies one in calling Henry James a forerunner of
modern expressionism. Yet how unlike he is to Sherwood Anderson, an authentic product of the American consciousness!

III

WILLIAM DEAN HOWELLS AND THE REALISM OF THE COMMONPLACE

From such nostalgia, that left a note of wistfulness in his pages,
William Dean Howells was saved by his frank and undivided
loyalties. Intellectually and emotionally he was native to the
American soil, and however widely he might range he remained
always a conscious American. He had no wish to Europeanize his
mind; he felt no secret hankerings for the ways of Mayfair or the
culture of the Quartier Saint Germain. The homely American
reality satisfied the needs of his art, and he accepted it with the
finality of Walt Whitman. If he failed to depict it in all its sprawling veracity, if much of its crude robustness never got into his
pages, the lack was due to no self-imposed alienation, but to the
temperament of the artist and the refined discretions of his environment.

The current school of realism is inclined to deal harshly with
Howells. His quiet reticences, his obtrusive morality, his genial
optimism, his dislike of looking ugly facts in the face, are too old-
fashioned today to please the professional purveyors of our current
disgusts. They find his writings as tedious as the gossip of old
ladies. To their coarser palates his respectable commonplace is
as flavorless as biscuit and tea. Yet it must not be forgotten that
for years he was reckoned new-fashioned. Whatever may be one's
final judgment on his work it is certain that for twenty years he was
a prophet of realism to his generation, the leader of a movement to

turn American literature from the path of romanticism and bring it face to face with the real and actual. It was not his fault that the ways of one generation are not those of another, and it is well to remember that if his realism seems wanting to a generation bred up on Theodore Dreiser, it seemed a debasement of the fine art of literature to a generation bred up on Thomas Bailey Aldrich. Realism like dress changes its modes.

The Howells we know best was not a simple child of the frontier, like Mark Twain, whom all could laugh with and love because the sallies of his wit awakened a native response. He did not remain completely native to the older folk-ways. He was rather a composite of the ideals reckoned excellent by the post-war generation— an American Victorian, kindly, urbane, tolerant, democratic, accepting America as a land that God's smile rests on, and convinced that here, wedded to a generous democracy, culture must eventually produce offspring finer than the world has hitherto known. Bred up in the mystical Swedenborgian faith, he shrank from all fleshliness and loved purity with the devotion of a Galahad. A child of the Ohio frontier, he retained to the last the western feeling of democratic equality. An adopted son of Brahmin Cambridge, he immersed himself in culture—Italian, English, Yankee— and served the ideal of excellence with a lifelong devotion; a reverent pilgrim to the shrine of truth, he followed such paths as his generation knew to lay his art at the high altar. In all these things—in his ample culture, his kindly democracy, his high standards of workmanship—as well as in the instinctive reverences of a clean and sweet nature, he was an embodiment of the best in American life, a child of Jacksonian democracy who made use of his freedoms to serve the excellent cause of culture.

But he was much more than that, and if the critics who are wont to damn his Victorian squeamishness would penetrate to the inner core of Howells they would discover an intellectual, alert and sensitive to changing currents of thought, seeing with his own eyes, pursuing his own ends, who wrought out for himself a culture that was individual and native. If he was not, like Henry Adams, plagued with an itch of curiosity, he traveled widely in the realm of the mind. Culture meant to him open-mindedness, familiarity with diverse schools of thought, a willingness to venture upon the unorthodox and to defend the unpopular. He was never a child of the Gilded Age. He was unsoiled by its vulgarity, unconcerned with its sordid ambitions. Neither at heart was he a child of Brahmin culture. He loved Lowell and Norton and Godkin and Aldrich, and he wanted to be approved by them; but he ranged far more widely than they, into places they thought indiscreet. The mature Howells came to stand apart from Brahminism, dissatisfied with a literary Toryism, convinced that a sterile genteel tradition could not suffice the needs of American literature. His very drift toward realism was a negation of the Brahmin influence. On the whole it was unfortunate that he lived so long in the Cambridge atmosphere. The New England influence may not have been a factor in shaping his too leisurely technique, but certainly it postponed the day of his intellectual release. If he had removed to New York a decade earlier, before his literary method hardened into rigidity, his technique might have changed with his more radical intellectual outlook and become the vehicle of a more adequate realism than he ever achieved.

But the significant thing is that the mind of Howells refused to imprison itself in Brahmin orthodoxies, but set forth on perilous expeditions while Lowell and Norton were discreetly evading the intellectual heresies raging outside their libraries. While Henry James was moving towards aristocratic Mayfair, Howells was journeying towards the proletarian East Side. The scientific revolution seems early to have washed in upon him, undermining the theological cosmos of his youth and turning him into a liberal freethinker. His scientific views very likely came to him secondhand, through the medium of literature; but with his wide reading in Continental fields—Spanish, French, German, Scandinavian— he could not fail to become saturated with the evolutionary view then permeating all current letters. In this he was only following with John Fiske and Henry Holt and Henry Adams the path of a new orthodoxy; nevertheless in applying the scientific spirit to fiction and espousing an objective realism, he quite definitely broke with Brahmin tradition. And when, under the guise of fiction, he turned to social questions, and wove into the placid texture of his work the vexing problem of social justice, he ventured on perilous ground where his Brahmin friends would not follow. To espouse the teachings of Herbert Spencer was one thing, to espouse the teachings of Karl Marx was quite another.

Howells came late to an interest in sociology, held back by the strong literary and aesthetic cast of his mind. But in the eighties, when he had reached middle life, he was no longer able to ignore or evade the economic maladjustments of the Gilded Age. The social unrest that was coming to bloody issue in strikes and lockouts gave him acute concern, and slowly under pressure of a sensitive social conscience there began a quiet intellectual revolution that was to transform the detached observer of the American scene into a Marxian socialist. A democrat, a lover of his kind, a just soul endowed with a tender conscience, an idealist who dreamed of a brotherhood of free men who should create in America a civilization adequate to human needs, what else could he do? He loved peace but war was all about him. And so in the mid-afternoon of life he turned to the work of spreading the gospel of social democracy in the America of the Gilded Age. He had no private or personal causes to serve. He had not, like Godkin and Dana, given hostages to fortune in the shape of a newspaper or magazine; he had no call to be partisan to his own interests. He was free to plead the cause of justice in his own way and at his own time. It is easy for the later radical to sneer at him as a parlor socialist who talked well but carefully refrained from disturbing the capitalistic machine from which he drew his income; but that is to ignore the courage of the artist in confronting a hostile world. He stood stoutly for the rights of workingmen that the passions of the times swept rudely away. When the Haymarket Riot in Chicago brought its shameful hysteria, and all respectable America was crying for blood, Howells was one of the few intellectuals who spoke for justice, one of the few who held aloof from the mob spirit, thereby bringing on his head a wave of criticism. It was a brave thing in 1886 to speak for the "Chicago anarchists."

But it was not till his removal to New York, where he found himself at the center of the great revolution, that he set about seriously studying the ways of plutocracy. For the student of Cambridge society it involved a mental upheaval. The urbanity of his literary manner conceals for most readers the intensity of emotion that underlies his quiet style; yet it is clear enough that having examined the ways of private capitalism and considered its works, he rejected it. Thenceforth to the end of his life he hated the thing and quietly preached against it. His affections went back fondly to the earlier agricultural order that had shaped his youth, and in the character of Dryfoos, in *A Hazard of New Fortunes*, he suggests the moral degeneration that he believed followed in the train of the substitution of a speculative capitalist economy for the wholesomer agrarian economy. But though, remembering his frontier youth, he might prefer the older ways, he was realist enough to understand that capitalism was the order of his generation, and he turned eagerly to explore the new proletarian philosophies that came out of Germany. Howells was the first distinguished American man of letters to espouse Marxian socialism. For a cultivated American in the Gilded Age to sympathize with proletarian theory and to proclaim himself a socialist, was enough to excite amazement in his fellows. In the eighties American social thought was still naïve and provincial. Old-world theories were as alien as old-world institutions, and in spite of the wide interest aroused by *Looking Backward* the intelligent American in 1890 knew as little about Marxianism as he knows today about Bolshevism.

The doubts and hesitations that troubled Howells during these years of changing outlook, are skillfully dramatized in *A Hazard of New Fortunes*. The story of the removal of the Marshes from New England to New York, told with more than usual leisureliness, is the story of the transition from the peacefulness of his earlier literary life to the anxieties of his later thought. Slowly into a story of the familiar Howells commonplace comes the note of social dissension. Antagonistic social philosophies meet and clash, and the movement draws inevitably to the great climax of the strike that brings tragedy into the scene. Of the mood that grew upon him as he wrote he afterwards said:

It became, to my thinking, the most vital of my fictions; through my quickened interest in the life about me, at a moment of great psychological import. We had passed through a period of strong emotioning in the direction of humaner economics, . . . the rich seemed not so much to despise the poor, and the poor did not so hopelessly repine. That shedding of blood which is for the remission of sins had been symbolized by the bombs and scaffolds of Chicago, and the hearts of those who felt this bound up with our rights, the slavery implicated in our liberty, were thrilling with griefs and hopes hitherto strange to the average American breast. Opportunely for me there was a great street-car strike in New York, and the story began to find its way to issues nobler and larger than those of the love-affairs common to fiction.[3]

The years of unrest marked by the great agrarian revolt were years of great intellectual activity for Howells, during which his

---

[3] Quoted in " The Social Consciousness of William Dean Howells," *New Republic*, Vol. 26, p. 193.

thought ripened and mellowed. His own liberal spirit drew to him the liberal spirits of the younger generation, and he became the counselor and friend of many of the young rebels of the day. His sympathy went out to all who were concerned at the injustice of the world. He questioned the right of none to uphold his creed, nor sought to impose his own beliefs upon others. As he watched the great struggle of the times his heart was always on the side of the weak and exploited. Very likely he knew little about the economics of money and finance, over which rival partisans were quarreling savagely, but he understood the human side of the farmers' problem and it was always the balance in the human ledger that weighed with him.

He was a friend of Hamlin Garland and rejoiced when *Main-Travelled Roads* was given to the world, writing for it an introduction warmly and tenderly sympathetic. As an artist he grew concerned lest under the stimulus of B. O. Flower the zeal of the propagandist should submerge the art of the story-teller; but he had no quarrel with the "causes" that were fermenting in the mind of the young Populist, and would not lessen one whit the ardor of his social faith. Throughout the passionate campaign of 1896, that brought most of his friends to a blind and scurrilous partisanship of the gold standard, his heart kept his mind just and his sympathy for the unrequited producers served as counterbalance to the shrill vituperation of his friend Godkin. He had thought too long and too honestly to be moved by the *claque* of the press.

It was in the black days of the panic of '93 that he seems to have brooded most thoughtfully over the ways of capitalistic America, and in the following year he published *The Traveller from Altruria*, the first of his two Utopian romances in which he subjected the system of capitalism to critical analysis. It is a clever book that quite disarms the reader. Howells delivers no broadside attack on the capitalistic system, and he suggests its mean and selfish exploitation with such genial urbanity, such sly satire, as to arouse no sleeping lions. The concern in his heart is belied by the twinkle in his eye. He hints that the Altrurian critic is only the figment of a dream, and he smilingly suggests the sources of the Altrurian commonwealth in the long line of Utopian dreamers from Plato and Sir Thomas More to Bellamy and William Morris. But the urbanity is only a mask. Protected by it Howells delivers many a shrewd thrust at the ways of capitalism. American democracy does not show to advantage under his analysis. The Altrurian comes upon the canker of social injustice in every chink and cranny of life—a canker that is slowly destroying democratic America; and Howells takes a sly pleasure in contrasting our democratic professions with our plutocratic practice. There is a delightful irony in his attack on the professional classes—the professor, the minister, the writer—for their quick defense of the exploiting classes. What may we expect of the science of economics, he suggests, when our academic economists are only apologists for the existing order?

The Traveller from Altruria is a shrewd analysis of American life set against a Marxian background, and in forecasting the future Howells follows the Marxian law of concentration. The Age of Accumulation, with its gigantic monopolies gathered in ever fewer hands, prepared the way for a new order when industrialism, grown overbig, falls into the control of the state as naturally as the harvest is gathered into the granary. There was no need of a class war. When the times were ripe political means sufficed, for the democracy retained the effective weapon of the vote. Thirteen years later Howells completed his Utopian venture with *Through the Eye of the Needle*, in which he sketches in fuller detail the order of life in Altruria. It was not till men learned that coöperation is a better social cement than competition, altruism than egoism, that the new order was possible; and in this later work he depicts the kindly, rational society that emerged when men left off fighting each other and turned to working together instead. On every page the influence of William Morris is revealed—not only in the rejection of an urban society founded on the machine and a return to a decentralized anarchistic order, but in the emphasis on the psychology of work and the satisfactions that spring from free creative labor. *Through the Eye of the Needle* is curiously reminiscent of *News from Nowhere* and suggests how sympathetically Howells followed English social thought in its reaction against industrialism.

It was while he was thus engaged that he put into compact form his speculations on the theory of realism. For more than a decade he had been the most distinguished advocate of realism in America, and for longer still his successive novels had revealed to a critical world what substance and form he believed the realistic novel should possess. The immediate sources of his theory are obscure, though it is clear enough that the work of Jane Austen was a creative influence. From the school of French and Russian naturalism, then at the height of its vigor, he drew back in repulsion, and it was not till after his technique was matured that Tolstoi became an influence in his intellectual life.   It is reasonable to assume that his realism was a native growth, the result of temperament unfolding through quiet years of reading in the English classics. A quizzical observer with the gift of humor is not likely to run into romanticism, and a youthful passion for Pope and Heine is not the best preparation for it. His intense dislike of the romantic, that led him to an inadequate and partial conception of it, seems to have sprung from certain instinctive feelings and convictions that strengthened with the years: a deep and sincere love of truth, a native sympathy with the simple homely phases of life, a quiet loyalty to American fact, and a sharp distrust of the aristocratic spirit. Endowed with such feelings he came to ascribe his own partisanships to literary methods; the romantic became for him the aristocratic, and the realistic became the democratic. As an American he was content to take the common stuff of life, as he found it in America, and depict it in unpretentious sincerity. Plain American life was not only worthy of literature, he was convinced, but the only material worthy of American literature. The path to the universal runs as directly through the commonplace American parlor as through the hall of the medieval baron or the drawing-room ·of Mayfair.

In *Criticism and Fiction* (1894), Howells ascribes the rise of modern realism to the twin sources of science and democracy. From science it derives its passion for truth, for "realism," he asserts, "is nothing more and nothing less than the truthful treatment of material." "We must ask ourselves before we ask anything else, Is it true?—true to the motives, the impulses, the principles, that shape the life of actual men and women." The question, what is essential truth, that has been the apple of discord amongst the realists, Howells answers in democratic fashion by appealing to the average. The "foolish man," he says, "wonders at the unusual, but the wise man at the usual." The realist, therefore, will deal objectively with the usual and common rather than with the unusual or strange, and in so doing he draws closer to the common heart of humanity, and learns the respect for simple human nature that is the source and wellspring of democracy. In delineating truthfully the prosaic lives of common people realism reveals the essential dignity and worth of all life. The romantic, on the other hand, is aristocratic. "It seeks to withdraw itself, to stand aloof; to be distinguished and not to be identified." "The pride of caste has become the pride of taste," and romance is the last refuge of the aristocratic spirit that, defeated elsewhere, has taken refuge in culture. Not aloofness, but comradeship, is the need of the world; not distinction, but identity. Realism is the child of democracy because the realist is one who "feels in every nerve the equality of things and the unity of men," and the great artist is one with a talent "robust enough to front the everyday world and catch the charm of its work-worn, care-worn, brave, kindly face."

' To this characteristic conception that realism is democratic Howells adds certain other dicta that to his own generation seemed as true as to ours they seem doubtful: that art must serve morality, that it must teach rather than amuse, and that truthfulness to American life requires a note of cheerfulness. Art cannot flout the "eternal amenities," Howells asserted, for "morality penetrates all things, it is the soul of all things." Nor can it stand aloof, disdaining the office of teacher, for unless it "tends to make the world better and kinder" it is empty and futile; and it can do this only "from and through the truth." But the truth that will uplift society does not dwell in the kennel and pigsty; it will not be come upon by exploring the animal in man, or in wrapping the shroud of pessimism about life. In America at least, realism must concern itself with the "large cheerful average of health and success and happy life," for after all "the more smiling aspects of life" are "the more American." From such postulates Howells developed his familiar technique, which in minimizing plot, rejecting the unusual and strange and heroic, reduced his stories to the drab level that bores so many of his readers, and evokes the criticism that in elaboration of the commonplace he evades the deeper and more tragic realities that reach to the heart of life.

The criticism is just. More than any other thing this concern for the usual weakens Howells's work and renders it trivial. He does not probe the depths of emotional experience. Neither the life of the spirit nor the passions of the flesh is the stuff from which he weaves his stories. The lack—and allowing for all his solid excellence it remains grave—sprang in part from his own timid nature that recoiled from the gross and the unpleasant, and in part from the environment in which he perfected his technique. For years he

lived in an atmosphere of complacent convention, a society dominated by women, culture, and conscience. Cambridge and Boston
in the seventies and eighties were still in the Age of Innocence
greatly concerned with erecting defenses against the intrusion of
the unpleasant, reverencing the genteel in life and letters, soberly
moral and making much of the eternal verities. In such a world of
refined manners and narrow outlook what should the realist do but
report faithfully of what he saw and heard? And so Howells,
perforce, became a specialist in women's nerves, an analyst of the
tenuous New England conscience, a master of Boston small-talk.
It was such materials that shaped his leisurely technique until it
falls about his theme with the amplitude of crinoline.   •

Through these chronicles of the Age of Innocence runs a persistent note of the neurotic. There are more scruples to a page of
Howells than in any other writer except Henry James—for the
most part filmy cobwebs invisible to the coarser vision of a later
generation. The action percolates through the sand of small-talk,
welling up from the tiniest springs and stopped by the smallest
obstruction. Like Franklin's two-headed snake his characters are
in danger of dying from thirst because of much argument over the
right path to water. It is hard to weave a substantial fabric from
such gossamer threads, and when in *The Rise of Silas Lapham* endless pages are devoted to the ethical subtleties of a woman's accepting the hand of a man who the family had believed was in love with
her sister, or when in *April Hopes* the fantastic scruples of a neurotic girl are elaborated with a refinement of art worthy of a Fra An-
gelico Madonna, the stuff is too filmy to wear well. Commonplace
men and neurotic women are poor materials from which to fashion
an adequate realism, and with the passing of the Age of Innocence the scruples of Howells went out of fashion.

The fault, in part at least, must be traced to the artist's deep
reverence for New England. From his youth he had cherished an
exalted notion of the sufficiency of New England culture, and had
accepted its parochialisms as ultimate standards. To a bookish lad,
inclined to be too consciously literary, such loyalty to a declining
school could only accentuate his native aloofness from life. His
four years at Venice had been given over to an ardent pursuit of
culture, as culture was understood by Lowell and Norton. It was
the natural impulse of a sensitive mind, conscious of its limitations,
reveling for the first time in the wealth that had been denied his

frontier boyhood. His poetic *Venetian Days* was an infallible pass-
port to Boston favor, and when after his return he was taken up
by the *Atlantic* group he carried with him to Boston an unconscious
inferiority complex that did his genius an evil turn. It was natural
for the self-taught western youth to be reverent in presence of the
great of earth; but it is not well for the artist to be humble in the
presence of his masters. Unless he is something of a rebel, given to
questioning the dogmas of the schools, he will never ripen into
creative originality.

An inferiority complex is a common mark of the frontier mind
that finds itself diffident in presence of the old and established, and
Howells suffered from it greatly. For years his keen eyes lacked
their usual shrewdness in judging Boston ways, and to the end of
his life he overestimated the greatness of the men to whom his
youthful loyalty had gone out. Not only did he accept Lowell and
Holmes and Longfellow at the Boston rating, but he regarded the
lesser group of cultivated Boston gentlemen with partial eyes. It
would have been far better for his art if like Hamlin Garland he
had never been received within the charmed circle; if he had had
to make his way alone. To justify his acceptance Howells felt that
he must prove himself as completely Bostonian as the best, and in
consequence he sloughed off his western heritage, perverted his
genius, and shaped his realism to the slender materials discovered in
Back Bay drawing-rooms. The genteel tradition was in the way of
strangling his realism.

Subjected to such refinements his realism in the end became little
more than technique—a meticulous transcription of New England
conventions, the casual action submerging itself in an endless
stream of talk. No doubt Howells was true to what he saw; certainly no one has ever fixed more exactly the thin substance of the
Age of Innocence. Nevertheless the fidelity of his observation, the
refinement of his prose style, and the subtlety of his humor that
plays lambently about the edges of his words, do not compensate
for the slightness of his materials. The record he has left is not
that of a great soul brooding over the meaning of life, puzzled,
uncertain, yet tender toward the victims that fate has seized and
crushed. He was restrained by too many inhibitions to deal frankly
with natural human passions. He felt deeply and tenderly, but he
was too diffident to let himself go. It is likely that Howells never
realized the inadequacy of his temperament and the futility of his

method to any serious realism. Even in his acutest study *A Hazard of New Fortunes*, which comes upon brutal economic reality, the story is entangled in a mass of minute detail and never quite breaks through. The indecisions, the repetitions, the whimsical descriptions, the drifting talk, are all true to life, but they are not essential or vital truth. The real issue toward which the story moves—the problem of social justice and the contrasting systems of wage-slavery, bond-slavery, and social democracy—is obscured in a welter of asides and never quite reaches the front of the stage. He is more effective in such works as *Indian Summer*, when he deals with characters on vacation who play whimsically with love, and in *April Hopes*, when he dwells fondly on the infinitely eloquent trivialities of young love-making. In such studies the minute fidelity to word and gesture, the humorous playing with invisible scruple, is a pleasant substitute for solider material.

Howells had real gifts, of which he made the most. Refinement, humor, sympathy—fidelity to external manner and rare skill in catching the changing expression of life—a passion for truth and a jealous regard for his art: he had all these qualities, yet they were not enough to make him a great realist. He belonged to the Age of Innocence and with its passing his works have been laid away. He has had no followers to keep his method alive. If one may hazard an explanation of the lot that has befallen him, it would be this. Howells the artist mistook his calling. He was not by temperament a novelist. He lacked the sense of drama, a grasp of the rough fabric of life, the power to deal imaginatively with the great and tragic realities. His genius was rather that of a whimsical essayist, a humorous observer of the illogical ways of men. He was an eighteenth-century spirit—a subtler Goldsmith—set down in another age and an uncongenial world. In his later years he must have come to realize this, for more and more he turned to the essay form. There his quiet humor and shrewd observation fitted his sinuous prose style to a nicety. In such sketchy autobiography as *My Literary Passions*, and more whimsically in such genial travel essays as *Certain Delightful English Towns*, his refined art arrived at its most perfect expression. Not an original genius like Mark Twain, far from a turbulent soul like Herman Melville, Howells was the reporter of his generation—the greatest literary figure of a drab negative age when the older literary impulse was slackening, and the new was slowly displacing it. He marks the transition between the earlier idealism and the later naturalism. A humane and lovable soul, he was the embodiment of all that was kindly and generous in an America that was not wholly given over to the ways of the Gilded Age—an America that loved beauty and served culture even amidst the turmoil of revolution.

BOOK TWO: THE OLD AND THE NEW: STORM CLOUDS

BOOK TWO

THE OLD AND THE NEW: STORM CLOUDS

THE quarter-century between the panic of 1873 that rudely disturbed the revelry of the Great Barbecue, and the campaign of 1896 that broke the agrarian opposition to capitalism, was marked by a fierce agrarian attempt to nullify in America the law of concentration. The silent drift toward plutocracy was too evident to escape comment even in the Gilded Age, and the ideal of plutocracy was too repugnant to a people drenched in Jeffersonian and Jacksonian prejudices to escape bitter hostility. The pursuit of wealth was an accepted democratic right, but it was assumed to be a fair race and no favors. The use of the political state by greater wealth to lay handicaps on lesser wealth had not been in the reckoning, and the law of progress that diminished the number of beneficiaries from the national policy of preëmption and exploitation had not been so interpreted. Something was wrong with a progress that augmented poverty as it increased wealth, and with the alarmist cry in their ears—the rich are growing richer and the poor poorer—the untutored democracy of the seventies and the eighties turned to question the drift of tendency that quite evidently was transforming a democratic people into a vast engulfing plutocracy. An older agrarian America was confronted by a younger capitalistic one, and the conflict of ideals and purposes was certain to bring on a bitter debate.

In the fierce struggle that turmoiled the politics of three decades the democracy went into battle as ill-equipped intellectually as it had been a hundred years before in the struggle over the Constitution. It was reaping the harvest of the long Jacksonian slackness that, content with the vote, had given no thought to the ultimate program of democracy but had suffered the lawyers to have their way. The Enlightenment had long since been submerged by Whiggish ambitions, and since the days of the Abolition Movement there had been no serious consideration of political theory. The success of the Jacksonian revolution had brought about its undoing. The abstract principle of democracy having won common

257

acceptance, it was assumed to be competent to shift for itself.
But unfortunately a supposedly democratic state was functioning
under a Constitution designed to thwart democracy, and, interpreted by lawyers, it buttressed the rights of property far more
securely than the rights of man. Within this fundamental law
capitalism had long been entrenching itself. Its stronghold could
not be taken by frontal attack and its flanks were protected by the
courts that had assumed the high prerogative of voiding statutory
enactments by judicial decree. As a result in no other country
was capitalism so safeguarded from hostile attack; it plowed its
fields and gathered its harvests secure from disturbance.

Unfortunately the political state did not realize that it was not
in reality the democracy it professed to be. The most intelligent
liberalism of the times, failing to take into account the economic
basis of politics, was satisfied to spend its energy in Civil Service
Reform and similar tinkering with the political machinery, convinced that it was only necessary to recover the old aristocratic
sense of responsibility in political agents to perfect a democratic
government. Not till another generation did liberalism come to
understand that the democratic program was still largely unfulfilled, and set about in all earnestness to complete it; but that did
not happen till the philosophy of democracy had been far more
adequately explored and the simple faith of Jacksonianism had
been instructed by the experience of other lands. Popular discontent with the drift toward plutocracy was intensified by the successive economic crises that marked the transition from agrarianism to capitalism. The gospel of progress, it seems, had not taken
due account of the price that must be paid in social disturbances,
and the breakdowns of 1873–1879 and 1887–1896 with their harsh
dislocations aroused a spirit of revolt that issued in broad popular
movements. Those movements spun the thread of liberalism
that runs through the years from the Gilded Age to the World
War—a thread woven of the earlier liberalism that came from
the frontier, and the new collectivistic theories that came from
Europe. In the eighties and nineties it was still largely native
agrarian, but in the early years of the new century it drew heavily
on the proletarian philosophies of Europe—seeking to apply old-
world experience to American problems. Through it all runs increasingly a note of sobering realism. After a hundred years political romanticism was slowly dying in America.

CHAPTER I

THE PLIGHT OF THE FARMER

I

DEMOCRATIC REACTIONS TO PLUTOCRACY

THE Middle Border was the first to recover from the heady romanticisms of Whiggery. The malady of preëmption and exploitation quickly ran its course there and after the first enthusiasm of settlement had subsided—the staking of claims, the scramble over townsites, the bidding for railway lines—the farmer settled down amidst his corn and wheat and cattle and hogs to learn what sort of living the prairies might provide. With his feet on the sobering earth he was no middle-class adventurer, no buccaneer lying in wait for the golden argosies of Spain, but a sober realist kept sane by wind and weather and kept honest by his daily occupation of tilling and reaping.

As the first wave of settlers spread over the prairies a mood of buoyant hopefulness colored their dreams. The earlier conquest of the Inland Empire had entailed exhausting labor in preliminary clearings, and the stumpage from great forests remained for years to obstruct clean tillage; but here in the Middle Border were treeless fields of black soil, level, uncluttered by stones, inviting the plow. For ages the prairie grass had been growing there, tall as a horseman in the bottoms and plentiful on the uplands; and as the unmarked seasons passed, the potash from the decaying vegetation added a richer fertility to the soil. In natural productiveness it was the fairest portion of America, and as the land-hungry settlers made their pitch there, filing on broad homesteads and building their cabins, a mood of buoyant expectation filled the land. It was not the flamboyant spirit of the Gilded Age, but the hopefulness of those who within a few short years were to transform a wilderness into the world's granary. In his wistful account of the glamour that lay upon the prairies in those first pioneer years—a glamour that soon passed like the morning dews—Hamlin Garland was no frontier romantic but a sober historian.

259

But as the seventies gave place to the eighties a subtle change came over the mood of the Middle Border. Disappointment and disillusion settled upon a land that before had smiled in the spring sunshine. The harvest was not fulfilling the expectations of the seedtime. The changed mood came in part from the harsh toil and meager living that were the necessary price the frontiersman must pay for his small winnings. It is no holiday job to subdue an untamed land and wrest abundance and comfort from a virgin soil. Only for the young who can project their hopes into the future is it endurable; for the middle-aged and the old it is a heart-breaking task. The history of the western frontier is a long drab story of hardship and privation and thwarted hopes, of men and women broken by the endless toil, the windows of their dreams shuttered by poverty and the doors to an abundant life closed and barred by narrow opportunity. It is true that the prairies took no such toll as the forests had taken; the mean and squalid poverty through which Lincoln passed was not so common in the Middle Border as it had been along the earlier frontier. Nevertheless a fierce climate and a depressing isolation added their discomforts to a bleak existence. The winds were restless on the flat plains, and the flimsy wooden houses, stark and mean, unprotected by trees and unrelieved by shrubbery, were an ill defense against their prying fingers. In winter the blizzards swept out of the North to overmaster the land, and in summer the hot winds came up from the Southwest to sear the countrysides that were rustling with great fields of corn. Other enemies appeared, as it were, out of a void. Endless flights of grasshoppers descended like a plague of locusts, and when they passed the earth was bare and brown where the young wheat had stood. Armies of chinch-bugs came from nobody knew where, and swarming up the tender corn-stalks left them sucked dry and yellow. It is nature's way, to destroy with one hand what it creates with the other; and for years the western farmers were fighting plagues that had possessed the prairies before the settlers came.

The disillusion of the Middle Border deepened into gloom as the widespread economic depression of the times added its discouragements. A period of falling prices was curtailing industry and forcing down the market values of all produce. From such depressions a debtor community always suffers most severely, for falling produce-prices mean rising money-values and a shifting standard of value for deferred payments. The farms of the Middle Border were heavily encumbered to provide tools and livestock and buildings, and the earnings were consumed by the interest that went East to the mortgage-holders. Debt was a luxury the farmer could ill afford, and when the debt was silently augmenting by the rising value of the dollar he was forced to consider his situation. The plight into which he had fallen was graphically summed up in the phrase "ten-cent corn and ten per cent interest"—a phrase that was to become a spark to all the tinder that was gathering from frontier hardships and disappointments. Falling market-values were at the bottom of his troubles. The prices of his staples were sinking below the cost of production. With four-cent eggs, five-cent butter, ten-cent corn, and fifty-cent wheat, with more hogs and cattle than the stockyards would take, and with debts contracted at interest-rates fixed by a higher scale of values, the economic position of the Middle Border was becoming desperate, and in the later eighties a sullen bitterness took possession of the land. As the farmer sat by the kitchen stove and stoked the fire with great ears of corn that were cheaper than coal, he had ample time to contemplate his lot. Ungathered crops for which there was no market would not pay interest. There was coming to be "too much hog in the dollar," as one commentator remarked quaintly. The Middle Border, all too clearly, was strangling from its own productiveness.

It was easy for newspaper critics, armed with the wisdom of the Board of Trade, to point out that overproduction was the trouble with the western farmer, and that so vast a development of staple crops resulting from sowing the prairie states to corn and wheat was certain to bring on disastrous market slumps. It was true. Production had outrun consumption; quantity output had brought on a glut. But it was also true—as the armchair critics were not so careful to point out—that other causes contributed equally to the deflation of the western farmer, the result of which was to despoil him of the last moiety of his earnings. He was in the grip of a complex middleman organization that gouged him at every turn. The gap between producer and consumer was widening to a chasm. The railways charged twenty cents a bushel cartage for wheat from the Mississippi to Chicago, and fifty-two and a half cents to the Atlantic seaboard. The elevator companies fixed monopoly tolls, swindled the farmer in their grain-gradings, and combined to force down the market price at harvest time and raise it after the crop came under their control. The "Livestock Ring," managed by the railways, controlled the Union Stock Yards at Chicago and squeezed the marginal profits from the farmer's cattle and hogs.[1] When on the other hand he bought implements or groceries or household goods he was at the mercy of a non-competitive market, protected by patent-rights and tariffs, to which were added extortionate transportation and middleman charges.

It was his own fault, of course. Due to his own political slackness the farmer had allowed himself to become the common drudge of society. All the exploiting classes had their hands in his pockets. His was the only considerable economic group that exerted no organized pressure to control the price he sold for or the price he paid. While capitalism had been perfecting its machinery of exploitation he had remained indifferent to the fact that he himself was the fattest goose that capitalism was to pluck. He had helped indeed to provide the rope for his own hanging. He had voted away the public domain to railways that were now fleecing him; he took pride in the county-seat towns that lived off his earnings; he sent city lawyers to represent him in legislatures and in Congress; he read middle-class newspapers and listened to bankers and politicians and cast his votes for the policy of Whiggery that could have no other outcome than his own despoiling. And now in the middle eighties he began to feel the rope about his neck, and realized the predicament he was in. It was not alone the local middlemen, or even the railways—he had come to believe—that were to blame. It was the money-power of the East, the grip of Wall Street, that was strangling him—a power that controlled the government at Washington, that manipulated the currency system, and that was engaged in a scheme to augment its holdings by forcing up the value of the dollar and automatically increasing the value of the indebtedness it had gathered in its vaults. Clearly it was high time for the deflated farmer to get into politics on his own account if he were to save himself from beggary, and so during the Gilded Age began a great agrarian revolt against capitalism that was to turmoil the next quarter of a century—a revolt that was to mark the last effective organization of the farmers to combat the new order, the last flare-up of an old-fashioned agrarian America before it was submerged by the middle class.

[1] See Nevins, *The Emergence of Modern America*, pp. 163–164.

II

THE FARMER CONSIDERS POLITICS

By the early seventies it was becoming clear to the Middle Border that the policy of Whiggery took no account of the needs of the farmer. Government was indifferent to him, whether at the capital of his state or at Washington, and governmental programs —whether in the matter of protective tariffs and land-grants, in its unconcern at monopoly extortion, or in the contraction of the currency with a view to the resumption of specie payments—ran so counter to his interests that the dullest began to question the fairness of the state. It had ceased to concern itself with the welfare of the whole. The combination of paternalism and *laissez faire* that marked the Whiggery of the times could be interpreted by the suspicious farmer, indeed, only as a surrender of government to capitalism. It had lost all pretense of fairness in the distribution of governmental favors, and withheld or granted aid with the single objective of furthering the interests of powerful groups. It sanctioned the use of the state by business interests for purposes of exploitation, and declined to exercise its power in the interests of the consumer. It granted tariffs and subsidies, yet refused to regulate the monopoly power it had created. It was no longer a government of the people but a government of business, concerned for the interests of exploitation, and if the farmer were to gain a hearing he must first make himself feared.

Of necessity, therefore, the agrarian program entailed a political struggle of great bitterness. There would be no adequate relief granted until the farmers had wrested control of government from the class that was exploiting them. The battle between agrarianism and capitalism, in consequence, from the outset was a struggle for control of the political state, that beginning in single commonwealths was eventually carried to the federal government. Hope of effective aid from state governments quickly proved illusory, for when the Illinois farmers passed a law to curb the railways the federal courts set aside their enactment and bade the farmers—to use a later phrase—go home and slop the hogs. They must not meddle with matters beyond their comprehension. In consequence of such slaps in the face the farmers fell to perfecting their organizations and arousing class consciousness until there issued from the long debates of the Grange and the Farmers' Alliance the great movement of Populism that proposed to reach as far as Washington, install there the representatives of the producing classes, and refashion the political state in accordance with the democratic needs of the plain people.

So ambitious a program needed time, not only for the farmers to organize but to clarify their policy. They were ill equipped for a serious struggle. With the rise of capitalism agriculture had been steadily falling in social prestige. As a result of the decline of the landed squirearchy in the North and the overthrow of the plantation economy in the South, agriculture had lost its traditional leaders who had furnished the brains and supplied the spokesmen in earlier political struggles. In the seventies agriculture was no longer reckoned a pursuit peculiarly suitable to gentlemen. The business man had risen in social prestige as the farmer declined, and instead of being recruited from the natural leaders of society agriculture suffered a draining-off of the more energetic and capable to the cities, leaving the farms in the hands of the less-ambitious, who were supplemented in the seventies and eighties by European peasants who settled great portions of the Middle Border. With this loss of social prestige came a new urban contempt for farm life that expressed itself in "Hayseed" cartoons, and in the heedlessness of politicians who were quick to transfer allegiance from a decaying to a rising order.

The farmers of the Middle Border, drawn from many commonwealths and with a high percentage of aliens, were far from a homogeneous class-conscious group like the southern planters. Race, language, and cultural antecedents held them apart, intensifying the aloofness that was a common characteristic of the frontier. Week-days they stuck to their plows and Sundays, unlike the New England farmer, they were little given to churchgoing. The landholdings were commonly a homestead of a hundred and sixty acres, often running to an entire section of six hundred and forty acres. Much land was held idle by speculators, with the result that the isolation of the farmer—dwelling convenient to his fields rather than to neighbors—deepened the suspicious individualism that was an obsession of the agrarian mind, and unfitted him for effective coöperative effort. No political or social philosophy answerable to his needs was at hand, no intellectual leaders like Jefferson or John Taylor to adapt old-world theory to the conditions of the Middle Border, no commanding figure like Old Hickory to marshal the scattered hosts. The Physiocratic theory with its prestige of distinguished advocates and its elaborate social economics had never taken root in the Middle Border; although certain of its prejudices—that the farmer is the sole producer and the sterile middleman must somehow be got rid of—had taken possession of the western mind and largely influenced the ultimate program. But if the western farmer inherited no ready-made philosophy he was daily prodded by harsh reality. He got up and went to bed under the prick of economic necessity, and this made of him a realist and an opportunist, eager to apply homely remedies to homely ills. With the discipline got from hard times he was not easily gulled by bright young city lawyers with their handbooks of capitalistic economics. The new agrarianism of the prairies, in consequence, was a hard-headed, homespun theory, fashioned on the farms, intended to serve the producer rather than the middleman. It had behind it none of the high authority of the schools, and naturally it was mocked and scoffed at by all the spokesmen—editors, lawyers, bankers, scholars, intellectuals—of the prosperous middle class. The farmer had to make his way against the embattled prejudices and contempt of the rest of America.

But before he could become a power in political councils he must organize and use his voting strength as a unit; and as early as the late sixties the work of organization was got under way. It began as a social movement with the Grange that spread widely through the South and Middle West and even gained foothold in the East, bringing together in social groups the farmer families of the neighborhood. It professed to stand outside politics and strove to awaken an interest in coöperative buying and selling, but the community gatherings were certain to find politics waiting for them at the schoolhouse door, and after the program of coöperation had been discussed the talk ran easily into political debate. From the Grange issued in the eighties the Farmers' Alliance, more consciously political in its objective, active in arousing the farmers to political action; and with the hard times that came with the turn of the decade the different groups merged in the broad movement of Populism—a militant political uprising with a definite party program and organization. The flare-up came swiftly and in the first years of the nineties the prairies were aflame and even the cotton-fields of the South were fired. · Populism swept from township to township, a militant agrarian movement, providing its own leaders—Tom Watson in Georgia, General Weaver in Iowa, Ignatius Donnelly in Minnesota, sockless Jerry Simpson in Kansas, with Hamlin Garland, and B. O. Flower, and other intellectuals rallying to the farmers' standard. It set up the banner of agrarian democracy, summoned its followers and drilled them for the battles that lay ahead. Huge meetings gathered of the farmers of a county and day-long they listened to speeches that came straight from the hay-fields and the corn-rows, speeches that were an echo of the daily experience of the farmer and the farmer's wife.

It was Mary Ellen Lease of Kansas who struck from the common bitterness a phrase that embodied the militant spirit of Populism. Week after week she traveled the prairie country urging the farmers to "raise less corn and more hell," and at her call the sunburned faces settled into grim purpose. The farmers had become class-conscious. They were enlisted in a class struggle. They used the vocabulary of realism, and the unctuous political platitudes and sophistries of county-seat politicians rolled off their minds like water from a duck's back. They were fighting a great battle—they believed—against Wall Street and the eastern money-power; they were bent on saving America from the plutocracy; and they swept over the county-seat towns, burying the old machine politicians under an avalanche of votes, capturing state legislatures, electing Congressmen and Senators, and looking forward to greater power. In 1896 Populism gained control of the Democratic party and entered on its great campaign to establish the principle of democracy at Washington. It was the last mortal struggle between agrarianism and capitalism, and to understand it one must turn back to the long agitation over the money question.

III

THE GREENBACK MOVEMENT

If in the early nineties the currency question had come to overshadow the questions of the tariff and railway regulation, it was because that problem lay at the heart of the struggle between the rival agrarian and capitalistic economies. The control of the national monetary system by the bankers was vital to the smooth functioning of a capitalistic order, and to assure such control it was desirable that monetary standards and emissions of currency be removed from the sphere of political action and lodged in the hands of business. The problem was difficult, for the right to "coin money and to regulate the value thereof" were functions of sovereignty specifically recognized in the Constitution; and it was a series of moves designed to transfer such functions to private groups that brought on a long political debate over systems of currency.

The intellectual background against which the struggle was set may be sketched briefly. Despite the long battle over the Bank in Jackson's time, little serious thinking on the principles of money and currency had been done in America. Financiers and economists alike followed the current English school, and since the appearance of the famous Bullion Report of 1811 that school had adhered to the intrinsic-value theory of money. While accepting banknotes as a useful medium of exchange, the English classical economists held that only coin is real money, and that the issue of notes must bear a definite ratio to the amount of coin and bullion in the vaults. Money is not a creature of the law. Government cannot create it. Rather it is a convenient token of labor done, and the stamp of the mint is only a certification of weight and fineness. There are but two ways, indeed, in which government can acquire money— through taxation and by borrowing. The "natural operation of the specie standard" was reckoned one of the fundamental "laws of trade," and for government to tamper with it—setting aside the intrinsic-value principle by the emission of irredeemable paper money—was to violate the sanctity of contracts, cheat creditors, increase prices, and disorder business. The law of supply and demand answered all the needs of money regulation.

This was no more than the application of the current theory of *laissez faire* to the problem of currency. But between the Bullion Report of 1811 and the Parliamentary Bank Act of 1844, English theory and practice had undergone two important modifications: the vast development of credit had suggested a free use of banknotes based on securities other than coin or bullion, and the bimetallic standard had been superseded by the gold standard. By the terms of the Act of 1844 all banknotes were to be issued against securities and gold and silver coin and bullion in the bank vaults. The margin of issue was fixed at fourteen million pounds sterling. The total amount of banknotes thus "issued on the Credit of such Securities, Coin and Bullion," might not be increased, but within the limits set the Bank was free to increase or decrease issues at will. The Act further provided that "whereas it is necessary to limit the Amount of Silver Bullion on which it shall be lawful . . . to issue Bank of England notes," it should "not be lawful for the Bank of England to retain in . . . said Bank at any time an Amount of Silver Bullion exceeding One Fourth Part of the Gold Coin and Bullion." . . . [2] That gold should eventually have thrust silver aside was natural. In addition to its convenience as a commodity for international shipment, it was less in quantity, not widely dispersed or popularly held, and therefore more easily controlled by the money-brokers. With the function of government restricted to coining such gold as came to the mint, the whole business of currency emissions, with the attendant power of inflation and deflation of credit, would lie in the hands of the bankers who became the custodians of the national monetary system.

During the bitter discussions of currency policies that followed the dislocations of the Civil War, the two most authoritative spokesmen in America on the subject were Senator John Sherman of Ohio, for years Chairman of the Senate Committee on Finance, and David A. Wells, statistician, special Commissioner of the Revenue Bureau, and a scholar deservedly distinguished as an economist. In their views on the currency question both were followers of the classical English school. In two speeches in the Senate, of January 27, 1869, and January 24, 1870, the former stated his position definitely. "Let us," he said, "recognize as an axiom that nothing but coin is real money before we undertake to deal with the currency"; and in another place, narrowing his definition in terms of the English Bank Act, he asserted, "We must . . . recognize the immutable law of currency; and that is, there is but one true standard, and that standard is gold." [3] The weakness of paper money, he believed, was its instability; the ratio of exchange with gold fluctuates too greatly to make it a safe or convenient medium of business. "Last year the fluctuation in paper money amounted to forty-five per cent. Gold, however, remained as stable as the eternal hills, because it was not only the product of labor, but it was labor and value itself." [4] One may make of such an assertion what one will, but it is clear that John Sherman thought ill of the greenbacks, and wanted substituted for them a system of banknotes.

[2] *The Statutes at Large: 7 & 8 Victoriae*, Vol. 84, pp. 188–189.
[3] *Speeches and Reports on Finance and Taxation*, pp. 188, 190.
[4] *Ibid.*, p. 233.

It is impossible [he argued] to give a currency issued by a Government the flexibility to meet the movement of the exchanges. . . . It must have a flexibility which will enable it to be increased in certain periods of the year, and to flow back again into the vaults of the bank at others. I am convinced . . . that in time it will be wise to retire our United States notes and all forms of Government circulation, and depend upon notes issued by private corporations.[5]

Brief as these passages are, they suffice to make clear Sherman's position. He accepted without question the English theory and practice, and he wished to shape American legislation in conformity with them. The experience of the Civil War, and—shall we add— his intimate connections with Wall Street,[6] had confirmed him in his preference for a *laissez-faire* policy in currency matters. He would establish the gold standard, encourage the issue of bank-notes, and turn over the custodianship of the national currency to private interests.

The position of David A. Wells was essentially similar. Wells wrote much and skillfully and he seems to have been the chief authority on whom such intellectuals as Godkin and Dana relied for materials for their editorials on the currency question. Indirectly, therefore, through the medium of editors and newspaper writers his opinions came to have wide influence. During the discussion of resumption of specie payments in the seventies his pen was particularly active. Amongst other things he then wrote *The Cremation Theory of Specie Resumption*, in which he advocated a policy of progressive contraction by the expedient of burning annually a fixed sum in greenbacks; *Robinson Crusoe's Money*, an exposition of the bullion theory of money for popular reading, illustrated by Nast and containing some witty thrusts at such well-known expansionists as Ben Butler, Wendell Phillips, Henry C. Carey, and Senator O. P. Morton; *Contraction*, in which he defended the thesis, "He who is not in favor of contracting the currency is not in favor of paying it, and he who is not in favor of paying it is a repudiator"; and certain other papers later gathered into his *Practical Economics* (1885).

Wells was an uncompromising bullionist and his theory of money is as simple as the doctrine of *laissez faire* on which it rests. Honest money represents labor and therefore possesses intrinsic value. The

---

[5] "Speech of January 24, 1870," *ibid.*, pp. 225–226.
[6] This laid him open to frequent and often bitter attack. See, among many, Mrs. Marion Todd, *Pizzaro and John Sherman* Chicago, 1891.

experience of the ages has demonstrated that of all commodities
gold and silver are the most convenient for the purpose and in consequence they have come to be accepted universally as real money.
Every dollar's worth of gold represents a dollar's worth of labor,
always and everywhere, measured by the test of the world's needs.
It is foolish for politicians and theorists to worry their poor heads
over the supply of money, or attempt to predetermine the quantity
best suited to the needs of business. The amount of money in circulation will always be regulated by the law of supply and demand.
There is limitless gold locked up in the treasure-house of nature, and
just so much is unlocked by human labor as the immediate needs of
the world require. Gold can neither be inflated nor deflated, for,
"There is one and the same law governing alike the supply of gold
and of wheelbarrows. They are both tools or commodities, and the
country will have and use all of either that it can use profitably." [7]
Let government keep its hands off and money will regulate itself.
"The value of the gold dollar is fixed and cannot be altered. The
value of the paper dollar is constantly fluctuating." [8] That busines
conditions would be seriously affected by the withdrawal of the
greenbacks, or that injustice would be done to debtors, Wells refused to believe. When the poison is withdrawn from the system a
state of health reëstablishes itself. "I also count as an absurdity the
idea that the business of the country is likely to be unfavorably
affected by a deficiency of currency consequent upon contraction in
the manner proposed." [9] The gold to take its place would be provided automatically by the infallible law of supply and demand.
Thus triply armed with the logic of economic theory Wells pronounced for deflation, immediate and drastic:

I desire the federal government to get out of and abandon forever and
as soon as possible this whole business of creating and issuing paper
money, be it redeemable or irredeemable, for I believe as long as the federal government continues to recognize anything as money except hard
matter-of-fact "labor representing" gold and silver, just so long the
country will not have [a] stable and unfluctuating currency. . . .[10]

Such neat logic was out of date on the day that Wells penned it.
The needs of business had outgrown the bullion theory of money

[7] *Practical Economics*, p. 54.
[8] *The Cremation Theory of Specie Resumption*, p. 10.
[9] *Ibid.*, p. 10.
[10] *Ibid.*, p. 13.

and credit was taking the place of a metallic currency. The fiction of a gold standard would be adhered to till another seismic dislocation proved its utter inadequacy to a world in confusion and it would be unofficially abandoned. Yet it was such logic that prevailed in America in post-war days, bringing acute distress upon the country as a whole and particular hardship to the Middle Border; and it prevailed because the banking interests followed a selfish and narrow policy marked out for them by the English theory and practice.

The financing of the war had been wasteful and slovenly beyond all precedent, and it had been fiercely criticized by the agrarians. It was a system, said the militant Greenbacker, Thaddeus Stevens, the like of which "no human folly had ever before witnessed." [11] When the war was over and the reorganization of the public finances was up for settlement, the bankers were shrewd enough to make the confusion serve their interests. Their great objective was to get back once more the control of the national credit that the war had taken from them. The National Bank Act of 1863—foolishly opposed by shortsighted state-bank advocates who were jealous of local rights—had been the first great step. By the provisions of the act the national banks were permitted to issue currency on the security of government bonds, in such quantities as they chose, on highly favorable terms, and the result was to drive out of circulation the wild-cat issues of state banks. But the crux of the problem was the question of the greenbacks that the necessities of the war had forced upon the government. The greenbacks were reckoned political money, the control of issues of which lay wholly with Congress. At any moment, responding to popular demand, Congress might deflate the bankers by the emission of new bills. At the time of first issue the financial interests had succeeded in vitiating the greenbacks by writing into the bill a repudiation of the issue by the government itself, and no sooner was the war over than they set about the business of retiring them. Their objective was the same end that English bankers had reached in 1844.

In the reorganization three broad policies were insisted upon by the banking interests: the speedy retirement of the greenbacks, in order to take government out of the credit market, the refunding of all debts on a gold basis, and an immediate return to specie payments. The result was a drastic policy of deflation that brought

[11] J. A. Woodburn, *The Life of Thaddeus Stevens*, p. 573.

further turmoil to the country. In ten years the money in circulation was reduced from somewhat over $2,100,000,000 to a little over a billion, or from fifty-eight dollars per capita in 1865 to seventeen dollars per capita in 1876.[12] The inevitable results followed, a swift appreciation in the value of the dollar and the automatic increase in the debt of the country, both public and private, with the fall of commodity prices. Within a decade, measured in commodity values, the liabilities of the American people were nearly doubled by the simple device of changing the standard of deferred payments. Gold might remain as stable as the eternal hills, but somehow all other commodities were shrinking daily. "Them steers," Solon Chase indeed said aptly, "while they grew well, shrank in value as fast as they grew." This remarkable result was brought about, it is well to remember, by the plea for honest money and the plighted faith of the nation. Keeping the public faith, it would seem, meant permitting the creditors to change the terms of their payments after the contract was made. "Who are these reasoners," cried Thaddeus Stevens, in disgust, "who talk so learnedly of the laws of finance and the morality of human dealings, whose consciences are so raw and stick out so far from their excited coverings that no pharmaceutist can heal their inward wound?"[13]

As a debtor community the Middle Border felt the pinch of deflation acutely, and in consequence the money question was thrust sternly upon agrarian attention. On this issue it came finally to fight its great battle, pitting its homespun experience against the authority of the bankers and the teaching of the schools. To the bankers' argument that note issues should be taken out of politics and lodged in the hands of business men, it replied that the issue of currency was a function of sovereignty, and to surrender it to private corporations, as was done by the National Bank Act, was undemocratic. The monetary system of the nation must not become the football of class interests. To the argument of the bullionists that gold was the only fixed and stable standard for deferred payments, it replied that the gold standard was too narrow a base on which to erect a monetary system for an expanding country, that it was notoriously susceptible to manipulation, and that it had been devised by Lombard Street in the interests of capitalism. Since the days of the great struggle over the Bank a remarkable

[12] *Ibid.*, p. 573.　　　　　　　　　　　[13] *Ibid.*, pp. 573–574.

change had come over the agrarian mind in its thinking on monetary affairs. In their distrust of all banks and bank-issues Jackson
and Benton had swung sharply back to the bullion theory of money.
They were militant hard-money men. But in the intervening years
a new and revolutionary conception had been slowly making its
way to recognition. In the minds of obscure economists the quantitative theory of money had risen to challenge the bullion theory.
In unorthodox pamphlets and newspaper discussion it was being
pointed out that the value of money is dependent on the amount
in circulation, that gold and silver are commodities fluctuating in
value like other commodities, and that it is the plain duty of the
state to regulate the per capita circulation in accordance with
business needs. To allow the bankers to erect a monetary system on
gold is to subject the producer to the money-broker and measure
deferred payments by a yardstick that lengthens or shortens
from year to year. The only safe and rational currency is a national currency based on the national credit, sponsored by the
state, flexible, and controlled in the interests of the people as a
whole.[14]

By far the most suggestive of these obscure pamphleteers was
Eleazar Lord, a New York banker, who for thirty-five years was a
propagandist for a new currency system and who watched the
bungling of the war finance with acute concern.[15] With the undemocratic nature of banknotes he was not concerned. As a banker
he accepted them as desirable and wished to establish them on a
sound national basis. He was in ardent sympathy with the patriotic nationalism of Henry C. Carey. The loose system of state-bank
issues seemed to him chaotic and he was earnest in espousal of a
common national system.   Lord was an acute and stimulating
thinker on monetary matters. He was one of the first Americans to
understand the significance of credit, and he was realist enough to
foresee that the system of the future would be a credit system.
This was the clue to his dissatisfaction with the bullion theory of
money, which he attacked with vigor, and to his acceptance of the

[14] See, amongst many, *Homo's Letters on a National Currency*, Washington, 1817;
Currency Explosions, their Cause and Cure, New York, 1858; *Our Currency: Some of
Its Evils, and the Remedies for them*, by a Citizen of North Corolina, Raleigh,
1861.
[15] His titles are: *Credit, Currency and Banking*, New York, 1828; *A Letter on the
National Currency*, New York, 1861; *Six Letters on the Necessity and Practicability of
a National Currency, etc.*, New York, 1862; and *National Currency: A Review of the
National Banking Law*, New York, 1863.

quantitative theory.[16] He had the scantest respect for Sherman's dogma that gold is as stable as the eternal hills because it is "labor and value itself," or for Wells's belief that the law of supply and demand automatically produces gold enough to meet the needs of business. He would treat gold and silver as commodities varying in price with supply and demand, and make no attempt to relate the money scale to their fluctuations. For years, he said, America accepted the English "standard of currency, their aristocratic definition of wealth, and their distinction between capital and credit," to its disaster.

> The so-called specie basis, whenever there is a foreign demand for coin, proves to be a mere fiction, a practical humbug; and whenever, by an excess of imports, this pretended basis is exported to pay foreign debts, the bank-notes are withdrawn from circulation or become worthless, the currency for the time is annihilated, prices fall, business is suspended, debts remain unpaid, panic and distress ensue, men in active business fail, bankruptcy, ruin, and disgrace reign.[17]

To provide a safe, flexible, and convenient currency, Lord proposed a system of national banknotes, based on the wealth of the country and responsive to the needs of a business world founded on credit.

> Necessity must teach us whether we can and must have a currency of purely representative value, wholly disconnected from the precious metals, as a basis and standard, or prolong the conflict between coin and paper, commerce and exchange. The existing theory on the subject is too firmly fixed by education, prescription, prejudice and interest, to be overthrown. . . . Such words as *safe, secured, national, uniform, economical, inalienable,* when predicated of any thing but gold as currency, are to the specie-paying theorist mere sounds devoid of significance. . . . Credit must triumph. Can any one blame the well-meaning theorist if he manifests some degree of doubt and alarm in view of the extent to which the actual use of credit, and of the confidence in the use of credit, has already attained? [18]

In the writings of these obscure economists are to be found the seeds of the later agrarian program. Some of them were clear-headed and able men, but they underestimated the power of the banking group. They failed to realize that in a capitalistic society

[16] From what source Lord, and the other amateur economists, derived their theory is not clear. It is possible, of course, to assume that it was from Ricardo and the English economists. For an analysis and rejection of the quantity theory, see J. Lawrence Laughlin, *The Principles of Money*, Chapter VIII.

[17] *A Review of the National Banking Law*, p. 8.

[18] *Ibid.*, p. 34.

no monetary system would be tolerated that was not to the bankers' liking, and that if it were to their liking they would easily convince the public that it was the only honest and just system. It was this lesson that the Greenbackers and Free Silver men were to learn. No sooner was the issue joined between paper money and the gold standard than a scurrilous hue and cry was raised by the "sound-money" men. The bitter dispute that marked American politics for more than a score of years is a classic example of the distortion of fact for partisan ends that seems to be an inevitable consequence of referring a matter of policy to a democratic electorate. Denunciation took the place of exposition, and hysteria of argument; and in this revel of demagoguery the so-called educated classes—lawyers and editors and business men—were perhaps the most shameless purveyors of humbuggery. Stripped of all hypocrisy the main issue was this: Should the control of currency issues—with the delegated power of inflation and deflation—lie in the hands of private citizens or with the elected representatives of the people? It is a question on which wide disagreement may well exist, for it involves important differences of social and political theory. But the significant thing is that throughout the years when the subject was debated in every newspaper and on every stump the real issue was rarely presented for consideration. The bankers did not dare to present it, for too much was at stake and once it was clearly understood by a suspicious electorate their case was lost. Hence the strategy of the money group was to obscure the issue, an end they achieved by dwelling on the single point of inflation and charging the agrarians with a dishonest policy of repudiation.

Certainly in the minds of many conscientious men the fear of repudiation was very real and acute, and their fears made timid souls panicky. The newspapers took their cue from this bogey and beat the drums so loudly in the cause of "honest money" that all hope of calm discussion was lost. The issue became so distorted from class feeling that later historians find it difficult to view the question dispassionately. So late as 1916 Joseph Gilpin Pyle in his *Life of James J. Hill* could still speak of the Greenback movement as a vicious scheme of "inflation, the boon of the demagogue and the dream of the great debtor class in this new country," who "increased . . . by the opening up of the West on borrowed capital, welcomed any measure that might give them a specious justification for discharging their obligations with something worth less than what they had promised to pay." Describing the genesis of the free silver movement, he·said:

Hence grew up a formidable coalition between mine owners, debtors unable or unwilling to pay, ambitious politicians, honest theorists led captive by barren and unpractical abstractions, and a host of men too ignorant to inform themselves, too impassioned by what they heard to wish to know the truth.[19]

Obviously it was not so simple—or so wicked—as that. To determine the justice of the charge of repudiation certain facts must be borne in mind. The gist of the money problem pressing so heavily on the Middle Border was the question of stabilizing the currency with a view to stabilizing prices. Under the prick of war-necessities a sharp inflation of prices had taken place. With the drastic contraction of the currency following the war, prices fell as sharply. From 1873 to 1896 a world-wide appreciation in the value of gold, aggravated by recurrent economic crises, further depressed the market values of commodities, rendering the question of the solvency of the Middle Border increasingly doubtful. Falling prices are only the obverse of rising money-values, and to stop the one it was proposed to cheapen the other, either through the issue of greenbacks as proposed by the Greenback party, or through the free coinage of silver as proposed in the plank of the Democratic platform of 1896. It was not a question of repudiation in favor of debtors, but a question of correcting an unjust deflation that favored the creditor class.

IV

GREENBACKISM AND PETER COOPER

The opposition to the program and methods of the rising plutocracy was not confined to the farmers of the Middle Border. It was nourished by a widespread distrust of banks and bank-currencies that was a heritage of the Jacksonian struggle. Amongst the leaders of the Greenback movement were many eastern men, some of wide industrial experience, whose economic views and prejudices were a hold-over from the days of John Taylor, and who discovered in the post-war finances the same class manipulations of public credit that marked the funding operations of Washington's administration. Men as dissimilar as Horace Greeley, Thaddeus Stevens, Wendell Phillips, Henry C. Carey, and Peter

[19] Vol. I, p. 485.

Cooper, made common cause with the western farmers in seeking to wrest control of government from the bankers, and establish what they conceived to be a just democratic economy. Picturesque militants grown old in warfare, they were of an earlier generation, inheritors of the ideals of simpler times before production for consumption had been superseded by consumption for profit, ardent equalitarians who would not see their hopes frustrated and America become a plutocracy without a struggle. Greeley, Carey, and Phillips have been considered elsewhere; Stevens was the last of the rugged equalitarians who followed their principles to the bitter end; and Peter Cooper was an unregenerate Jeffersonian who dedicated his last years to combating Wall Street, accepting in 1876, at the age of 85, nomination for the presidency by the National Independent Party, commonly called the Greenback Party.

Like Thaddeus Stevens an ironmaster, grown wealthy by a long life of useful and adventurous industry, builder of the first American locomotive that made possible the success of the Baltimore and Ohio railway, Peter Cooper was the most picturesque figure in New York City in the seventies. With Bryant he shared the distinction of being the patriarch of Broadway. Bred up amidst stern and harsh conditions, at a period when, he said, within his "own recollection unmarried white men could be sold for debt in the State of Connecticut," [20] he was not hardened by the struggle for subsistence. A tender social conscience mellowed an old-fashioned probity and gave character and dignity to a simple rugged nature. Transparently honest, with a certain innate austerity softened by a homely courtesy, he was not a reed to sway in every vagrant breeze, but a great oak with fibers toughened by the storms of years. Like Horace Greeley, whom he much resembled in honest kindliness, he carried the burdens of his country on his heart, and in the midst of abundant prosperity still reckoned himself his brother's keeper. By "nature and temperament a radical reformer," his strongest instinct was a quick sense of justice. He was oppressed by the poverty and misery he saw about him, and he gave so generously to all good causes that he was known to his generation as "the greatest philanthropist in the world." His chief accomplishment was the founding of Cooper Union for free instruction in "practical art and science," on which he expended a fortune.[21] But

[20] *Ideas for a Science of Good Government*, p. iii.
[21] *Political and Financial Opinions of Peter Cooper*, p. 23.

he was not one to salve his conscience with a gift of superfluous wealth. His heart was as open as his pocketbook, and he must explore to its hidden sources the infection that was breeding social injustice in the new world. His private interests never blinded him to his larger duties, but he gave his time and strength as readily as his money to whatever cause he espoused.

Such a man was morally incapable of the buccaneering exploitation that marked the Gilded Age. Between Peter Cooper and Jim Fisk was an impassable gulf; they were products of different worlds and different economies. The speculative middleman who thrust himself between the producer and the consumer, with no sense of responsibility to either, but concerned only with immediate profit, was a figure to excite the wrath of an older-fashioned industrialist who had been taught that the only just reward is the reward that comes from productive labor; and in the days of the great barbecue Peter Cooper became deeply concerned for the future of America. It was the new breed of bankers with their control of the money system that were to blame, he came to believe, and he would have reckoned himself false to the obligations of citizenship if he failed to protest against their selfish manipulation of the public credit. He had watched the callous juggling of the national finances by the money-lenders during the Civil War, and had seen a debt of some three billions nearly doubled in the decade after Appomattox by the bond-holders. The new system of National Banks that issued from the emergencies of war had come to control the financial policy of the country, and to Peter Cooper it seemed that their purpose was to perpetuate a debt that enabled them to tax the productive labor of America and to squeeze wealth from a calculating expansion and contraction of the currency. To surrender to such mercenaries the sovereign power of issuing and regulating money seemed to him the abdication of sovereignty, and in so far as he could he felt called in honor to prevent it.

It needed rare courage and complete self-sacrifice to take up the gage of battle and in his old age to renew the war that Andrew Jackson had engaged in forty years before. His good name and his honorable career could not save him from the gibes of politicians or the caustic criticism of honest men. It was a losing fight at best. The struggle had been venomous in Jackson's day when the money-power was in its infancy; and now that the banking interests had grown mighty it was as hopeless as the charge of the Light Brigade.

The cause had been lost on the day when Congress wrote into the bill establishing a legal tender for war purposes the single word "except," thereby invalidating the greenback for interest payments on bonds and duties on imports—an act that "drew tears from the eyes of Thaddeus Stevens"; and the bankers who could assert their control in war times had no intention a dozen years later of suffering that control to pass from hands that had grown enormously stronger.

Yet Peter Cooper refused to consider the outlook hopeless. With all the resources he could command he threw himself into the struggle. He scattered "more than a million of documents" broadcast—most of the matter of which he wrote; he appealed to Congress and the President, he challenged candidates, he cited the opinions of the Fathers, and when he was buried under an avalanche of votes—as Horace Greeley had been four years before—he preserved his faith in the "people's cause" and to the last day of his life kept up the great battle. "I always have been, am, and ever shall be with the poor toilers and producers; therefore I desire Congress to legislate for the poor as well as for the rich, who can take care of themselves," [22] he wrote in his ninety-second year, and the spirit that stirred in his old veins appears from such a comment as this:

I consider the persistent class legislation of Congress since the war, a worse despotism than that of Great Britain before the Revolution; because it reduces the laboring classes to periodic distress and starvation, that are worse than any despotism ever was; for monopolizing corporations, whether in the shape of banks or railroads, have no soul. [23]

Peter Cooper's political philosophy was simple and transparent. His teachers were Albert Gallatin, Henry C. Carey, and George William Curtis, and from them he drew three major ideas that had emerged from three generations of American experience: the need for a national monetary system based on legal tender; the necessity for a protective tariff; and the need for an effective civil service. The first was an adaptation of the old agrarian dislike of bank-notes; the second came out of Clay's American System as it had been elaborated by Henry C. Carey in the fifties; and the third issued from the Civil Service Reform movement of the seventies. The exigencies of the political situation, however, thrust into the

[22] *Ideas for a Science of Good Government*, p. 272.   [23] *Ibid.*, p. 271.

foreground the money question, and nine-tenths of his writings deal
with that pregnant issue. As an ardent Jacksonian he was deeply
suspicious of the rising money-power, with its corporations and
monopolies, its land-grants and railways and banks, for behind
them he saw the specter of aristocracy. "In America," he said in
1882, "we have no aristocrats except those who have sprung up in
a night—as toad-stools do in a dung-hill." [24] But class legislation
must end in creating classes, and at another time he said, "There
is fast forming in this country an aristocracy of wealth—the worst
form of aristocracy that can curse the prosperity of any country.
. . . Such an aristocracy is without soul and without patriotism.
Let us save our country from this, its most potent, and, as I hope,
its last enemy." [25]

His deep interest in political measures was quickened by an
anxious concern at the hard times that resulted from the policy of
drastic currency deflation. That matters were going ill in America
during the middle seventies every fool knew, and Peter Cooper was
only giving expression to the common knowledge in describing to
President Hayes, in a letter dated August 6, 1876, the "appalling"
economic situation. That it was equally bad in England he did not
point out.

> More than two hundred thousand men, within the last few weeks, have
> joined in "strikes" on the various railroad lines, the workshops and the
> mines of the country, on account of the further reduction in their wages,
> already reduced to the living point. That some of these strikes have been
> attended with lawless and unjustifiable violence, only shows the intensity
> of the evils complained of, and the despair of the sufferers. For four years
> past, since the "panic of 1873," millions of men and women, in this hitherto
> rich and prosperous country, have been thrown out of employment, or
> living on precarious and inadequate wages, have felt embittered with a lot,
> in which neither economy nor industry, nor a cheerful willingness to work
> hard, can bring any alleviation. Is it to be wondered at, that *enforced
> idleness* has made tramps of so many of our laboring population, or induced
> them to join the criminal and dangerous classes? [26]

After pointing out the disastrous effects of such hard times on
mining, railways, real estate, and the western farmers, he asserted
that the bankers, although they also were embarrassed, were "very
patient with their troubles. . . for they know, that *money is
appreciating in value all the time.*" He then uncovers the kernel of

---

[24] *Ibid.*, p. 261.   [25] *Ibid.*, p. 123.   [26] *Ibid.*, pp. 117-118.

his thought—that it is a sovereign duty of government to provide an adequate national currency.

> This bondage has its manifold centre and its secret force in more than two thousand banks, that are scattered through the country. All these banks, are organized expressly to loan out their own money and the money of all those, who will entrust them with deposits. These loans are made to men, whose business-lives will soon become dependent on money, borrowed from corporations, that have a special interest of their own. Such a power of wealth, under the control of the selfish instincts of mankind, will always be able to control the action of our Government, unless that Government is directed by strict principles of justice and of the public welfare. The banks will favor a course of special and partial legislation, in order to increase their power . . . they will never cease to ask for more, as long as there is more, that can be wrung from the toiling masses of the American people.
>
> Such a power should never be allowed to go out from the entire and complete control of the people's Government. The struggle with this money-power, intrenched in the special privileges of banks, has been going on from the beginning of the history of this country. It has engaged the attention of our wisest and most patriotic statesmen. Franklin, Jefferson, Webster, Calhoun, Jackson, have all spoken of the danger of such a power and the necessity of guarding against it.[27]

The solution he offered for the vexing monetary problem accorded with that of the Greenback Party,[28] namely, refusal to recharter those banks *"deceitfully styled national"* and the retirement of all bank currency; the abandonment of the policy of currency contraction; the issue of legal-tender notes to the amount last found necessary for the functions of industry and business; the rejection of a specie basis, the notes to be interconvertible with government bonds bearing interest at 3.65 per cent; issued on demand in any amount in exchange for legal-tender notes; and the establishment of a Postal Savings Bank. No man ever believed more ardently in the sufficiency of his program than Peter Cooper. It was a suggestive proposal, that only a knave would call the visionary scheme of a fool. He was tireless in explanation and argument, the quality of which may be judged from the following passage from a letter to Hayes and Tilden written during the campaign of 1877:

> The worth or exchangeable value of gold is as uncertain as other products of human labor, such as wheat or cotton. The exchangeable value of anything depends on its *convertibility into something else* that has value *at the*

[27] *Ibid.*, pp. 109–110.   [28] See *Ibid.*, pp. 59–60.

option of the individual. This rule applies to paper money as to anything else. But how shall Government give an exchangeable value to a paper currency? Can it be done by a standard which is beyond its control and which naturally fluctuates, while the sign of exchange indicated by the paper remains the same? . . .

. . . we must trust our Government with this *whole function* of providing the standards and measures of exchange, as we trust it with the weights and measures of trade. . . . We must require the Government to make this currency, at all times, and, at the option of the individual, *convertible.* But the currency must be convertible into something over which the Government has entire control, and to which it can give a definite as well as a permanent value. This is its own *interest-bearing bonds.* These are, in fact, a mortgage upon the embodied wealth of the whole country. The reality of their value is as sound and as permanent as the Government itself, and the degree of their value can be determined exactly by the rate of interest the Government may think proper to fix.[29]

The Jeffersonianism of Peter Cooper, like the Jeffersonianism of the Middle Border, had taken a bias from the confident nationalism that during the fifties so deeply colored American thought. To assure an adequate national economy, superior in its self-sufficiency to European—and especially English—policies, was a persuasive program that Henry C. Carey devoted his later life to formulating, and that men like Horace Greeley and Peter Cooper disseminated amongst their wide agrarian following. That such a program implied a paternalistic government did not trouble them. Peter Cooper accepted paternalism as a necessary governmental function. He would have the state build and own the great western railway systems; he would use the national domain for the benefit of the settler; he would not turn over the state to plunderers nor the resources of the nation to speculators. An honest man with a sensitive social conscience, he would have no hand in the great barbecue that wasted more than it consumed; but the times were heedless of the counsels of honest men, and he was loved and laughed at and ignored. Like Franklin in the Constitutional Convention, he had outlived his generation and was thrust aside by the new economy that was taking over the custodianship of America.*

[29] *The Political and Financial Opinions of Peter Cooper,* pp. 22–23.

* In his original plan Professor Parrington included here a discussion entitled "Bimetallism: A heritage of Jacksonian democracy; Ignatius Donnelly, 'Coin' Harvey," but from the references in the next chapter it seems evident that as he worked out his plan he decided to omit this.—*Publisher.*

CHAPTER II

THE DEMOCRACY OF THE AGE OF INNOCENCE

I

CAPITALISTIC ENCROACHMENTS

WITH its heritage of Jacksonianism it was natural for the agrarian movement to attempt to carry further the exploration of the democratic principle, seeking to complete the program that had been left unfulfilled by the Fathers. There were few as yet who questioned the finality of democracy as a political system or its adequacy to all social needs. The growing evils of American life were traced unhesitatingly to an imperfect democratic control of the forces of exploitation. If the plutocracy were making gains at the expense of the plain people it was due to defective governmental machinery, and the immediate problem was the readjustment of that machinery. There must be an extension of democratic control over the economics of society. The great principle of *laissez faire*, that had proved so useful in the earlier struggle against aristocratic paternalisms, was become a shield and buckler for the plutocracy that was rising from the freedoms of a let-alone policy. To curb the ambitions of that plutocracy and preserve the democratic bequest for the common benefit of all, was therefore the immediate problem of the times.

To this end two things remained to be achieved: to wrest possession of the government from the hands of the plutocracy that was befouling it, and to use it for democratic rather than plutocratic ends. The difficulties in the way were many. Entrenched behind the checks and balances of a complex constitution the plutocracy could not easily be dislodged from power; even if it were driven out of the legislative and executive branches of government it would find aid and succor in the judiciary, where a masterful corporation law was interpreted by a bench tender toward all property rights, and jealous of its sovereign prerogative of reviewing all legislative enactments. A surprising change had come over the attitude of the. governing class towards democracy. Having gained control of the machinery of government the plutocracy found no cause to quarrel with a situation wholly to its liking. It had mastered the gentle art of guiding the majority will, and secure —as it believed—in its control of the political state, it counted on an indefinite continuation of the policy of preëmption and exploitation. From such a group, whether in Wall Street or at Washington, no new theories of government were to be expected. Business men wanted to be let alone. They clung to the anarchism of the Enlightenment and were stout in defense of the principle of individual initiative. So late as 1916 a group of confirmed individualists reissued Spencer's *Man Versus the State*, with an introduction by Elihu Root, to combat the rising spirit of governmental control. They regarded the American system of government as adequate and final, and wanted no subversive changes. The Constitution had been completed by the post-war enactments that fixed the status of the negro, and for a generation thereafter—except for the silent changes wrought by the judiciary —it remained static. East of the Allegheny Mountains popular interest in political theory had come to an end. A group of academic thinkers like John W. Burgess and Woodrow Wilson, an occasional intellectual like Brooks Adams, isolated radicals like Johann Most and small Marxian groups in Chicago and New York, and leaders of the new proletarian movement like Terence V. Powderly, were still acutely concerned about political theory; but these men and their theories counted for little in the stodgy mass of capitalistic America. The political phase had passed over into the economic; politics was wholly divorced from reality.

But throughout the Middle Border and on to the Pacific Coast the spirit of political democracy was alive and vigorous. There the older frontier Jacksonianism still lingered. For upwards of a half a century creative political thinking in America was largely western agrarian, and from this source came those democratic ideas that were to provide the staple of a later liberalism. The conscious objective of this great movement was to complete the work begun by Jacksonianism, and create a political machinery that should enable the democracy to withstand the shock of the Industrial Revolution. Many thinkers contributed to the work—U'Ren of Oregon, Jerry Simpson of Kansas, Tom Watson of Georgia, "Coin" Harvey of Arkansas, General Weaver of Iowa, Ignatius Donnelly of Minnesota, Henry D. Lloyd of Chicago, to name a handful out of the mass—homespun realists who have been forgotten by a later generation, but whose labors were given to the necessary work of refashioning the political machinery of America, and whose program provided the materials for the later Progressive party. They were commoners, men of the people, unversed in the dogmas of the schools, idealists who drew their inspiration from the Declaration of Independence; they spoke for an older America that feared the rising plutocracy, and they were casting about for ways and means to cut its claws. From their labors came the Greenback Movement, the Farmers' Alliance, Populism; and from them came in turn the Progressive Movement that reaped what they had sown.

II

THIRD-PARTY MOVEMENTS

It is, perhaps, not extreme to interpret the political history of America since 1790 as largely a struggle between the spirit of the Declaration of Independence and the spirit of the Constitution, the one primarily concerned with the rights of man, the other more practically concerned with the rights of property. The humanitarian idealism of the Declaration has always echoed as a battle-cry in the hearts of those who dream of an America dedicated to democratic ends. It cannot be long ignored or repudiated, for sooner or later it returns to plague the councils of practical politics. It is constantly breaking out in fresh revolt. When the major parties have grown callous and indifferent to the wishes of the common people, it has reformulated its principles in third-party platforms. Without its freshening influence our political history would have been much more sordid and materialistic. With the exception of such sporadic outbursts as Antimasonry and Know-nothingism, the third-party movements of the nineteenth century were democratic movements, inspired by a sense of social justice, founded on the Declaration of Independence, and promulgated to recall the American people to their heritage of idealism. The Locofoco party, the Freesoil party, the early Republican party, the Greenback party, the Populist party, the Progressive party, however they differed in immediate programs, have had a common objective, namely, to set man above property as the great object of governmental concern, and preserve in America the democratic principle of equal opportunity.

Despite the fact that they failed in their immediate objectives

they served the larger purpose of reminding the major parties that
America professes to be a democratic country, and that party
platforms must be brought to square with that fact. Thus interpreted the history of party struggle since 1790 falls into three broad
phases: the Jeffersonian movement that established the ideal of
political democracy; the Jacksonian movement that established
equalitarianism crudely in practice; and the successive third-
party movements that attempted, in successive reactions, to regain
such ground as had been lost, to extend the field, and to perfect
the machinery of democratic government. Since the rise of the
slavery controversy the major parties, allied with masterful
economic groups, have persistently ignored the Declaration of
Independence, and repudiated in practice the spirit of democracy.
To prevent if possible so grave a treason to our traditional ideals,
to assert the rights of the common man against the encroachments
of a class, has been therefore the common mission of the third-
party movements. The significance of their somewhat scanty
success is something the thoughtful American may interpret as he
will.

Since Civil War days, discontent has been endemic in the Middle
Border, and it has broken out in three great political upheavals:
the Greenback movement of the seventies; the Populist movement
of the eighties and nineties; and the Non-Partisan League movement of the second decade of the present century. Issuing from a
profound resentment at the exploitation from which the farmer suffered, they mark a persistent drift away from the old Jacksonian
individualism and an advance toward a socialized conception of the
political state. Disciplined by hard times the farmers were learning a lesson from capitalistic Whiggery; if the political state had
proved serviceable to business why should it not prove serviceable
to agriculture? Why should not a democratic state consider the
producers as well as the middleman? Why should it not provide a
national currency, a national system of transportation, a democratic banking system, a standard system of grain-grading, public
elevators, crop insurance, and the like? Why should the farmer be
squeezed at every turn by private companies who did badly what
the state could do well? By 1917, in short, the Middle Border had
got far from the simple individualism of earlier days and was well
advanced toward state socialism; and it was only the ruthless
opposition of the business interests, that had no wish to see their

private preserves thus rudely invaded, that put a stop to the movement.

Back of all these agrarian programs was the greater problem of the popular control of the political state. How could the undisciplined majority hold in check the disciplined minority? How could poverty meet wealth on an equal footing? The control of politics had fallen into the hands of the machine, and the machine served property interests. Legislatures were bought and sold like corner lots; senatorships went to the highest bidder; judges were more responsive to the wishes of bankers than to those of farmers. To break the power of the machine there must be an extension of democratic control, and to that end new machinery must be provided. Hence the vast agrarian concern with political machinery. From the agrarian agitation—supplemented by proletarian and middle-class recruits—has come the Australian ballot, the Initiative and the Referendum, the Recall, the Direct Primary, and popular election of Senators. The only important agrarian principle that has not been adopted is the principle of proportional representation. If agrarianism lost its great battle over the currency, it won the battle over the income tax. Nullified by a scandalous court decision after it had been long accepted, the income tax was finally established by the tedious method of constitutional amendment—an outcome that owed much to the Middle Border. In casting up the accounts of American democracy, the largest sums must be credited to the Middle Border, as in earlier years they were credited to the Jacksonian frontier. Whether the new machinery is useful or merely cumbersome, there is much disagreement, but it is agrarian in origin and it came from an honest attempt to democratize American politics.*

* The Contents here calls for a third section on the "Populistic Program" (see p. xxxiv for details) and a fourth on "William Jennings Bryan."—*Publisher.*

CHAPTER III

LITERATURE AND THE MIDDLE BORDER*

III

HAMLIN GARLAND AND THE MIDDLE BORDER

IT was not till the end of the eighties that the bitterness of the frontier began to creep into literature. Its slackness and drab poverty had got into the pages of *The Hoosier Schoolmaster*, as its neighborliness had got into Riley; but in these earlier studies there was no brooding sense of social injustice, of the wrongs done the Middle Border by unjust laws, of the hardships that are increased by the favoritism of government. In the year 1887, however, came a significant change of temper. Three very different writers— Harold Frederic, Joseph Kirkland, and Hamlin Garland—turned to the theme of farm life, and dealt with it in a mordantly realistic vein. It was the first conscious literary reaction to the subjection of agriculture to capitalistic exploitation and it was marked by the bitterness of a decaying order.

Seth's Brother's Wife, by Harold Frederic, is a drab tale of farm life in upper York State, as bitter as any tale of the western border. It is a story of defeat, of flight from country to town. The blight of failure is upon the farming community—a blight that embitters old and young; and the sketches of country louts, of soured lives, of broken men and women, do not make pleasant reading. No gentle idyllic light rests on the landscape such as Sarah Orne Jewett discovers on the fields and villages of New England. Sabrina Fairchild, an old maid embittered by the family failure, yet clinging to the family pride and hopeful that the family prestige will be restored, is a pathetic and desolate figure, gaunt and sharp-tongued; at mortal feud with another pathetic old woman, who with her husband had emigrated from Massachusetts years before, and held herself proudly above the mean and vulgar neighborhood in which

---

* In Professor Parrington's plan the section given here was to be preceded by a first section on "Edward Eggleston and Frontier Realism," and a second on "Whitcomb Riley and Folk Romance."—*Publisher.*

288

they had settled. The slack servants, gossipy and impudent, the petty lives, the grasping ways unrelieved by any grace or beauty, and set in a world of petty machine politics, make a drab and unattractive picture. Harold Frederic quite evidently hates this countryside that bred him. He will not, like Hamlin Garland, take up the battle for it against the town. He sees no hope in political programs; he is no Populistic agrarian fighting for justice; he wants only to escape from it to the city, where life may be lived more generously. The "trail of the serpent is over it all," he remarks, "rich and poor, big and little. The nineteenth century is a century of cities; they have given their own twist to the progress of the age —and the farmer is almost as far out of it as if he lived in Alaska. Perhaps there may have been a time when a man could live in what the poet calls daily communion with Nature and not starve his mind and dwarf his soul, but this isn't the century . . . get out of it as soon as you can."[1]

Much less bitter and hopeless is *Zury: The Meanest Man in Spring County* (1887), by Joseph Kirkland, son of Matilda Kirkland, who a generation before had written sketches of the Michigan frontier. In the preface the author points out that his study is "a palpable imitation of Thomas Hardy's 'Far from the Madding Crowd,' " an "attempt to reproduce, on American soil, the unflinching realism . . . of life down in actual contact with the soil itself." It is a tale of pioneer days in Illinois, in the second quarter of the nineteenth century, and it draws a full-length portrait of the son of a Pennsylvania immigrant who struggles up from mean beginnings to prosperity. The niggardliness of frontier life is drawn unsparingly—the harsh struggle for subsistence—but there is no outcry against governmental favoritisms or the law's injustice. It is nature that must be fought and conquered, and the battle needs strong men who must subdue their finer natures and more generous impulses to the work of acquisition. Zury Prouder is a masterful fellow who bends every energy to the business of accumulation. He makes one hand wash the other, and by dint of saving and squeezing and trading and foreclosing he slowly amasses wealth and power. He is a thrifty farmer as well as a shrewd trader, but his soul is seared by the frontier meanness—squeezed into land and stock and mortgages, consumed with the passion for grabbing. It was a reaction from the skimpiness of his youth. The bitterness of

[1] Chapter IV, pp. 26–27.

poverty had entered his heart as a boy, and his life took shape from the youthful resolve—

"Dad, I'm goin' t'own a mortgage 'fore I die; mind what I say."

"Hope ye will, Zury," his father replies. "Yew'll have a holt of the right eend of the poker then; 'n' t'other feller he'll have a holt o' the hot part, same's we've got naow."

"You bet! An' it'll sizzle his hands, tew, afore I'll ever let up on him."

But Kirkland will not let Zury remain a crabbed and hard-fisted son of the frontier. As the frontier hardships grow less the soul that has been seared by poverty is awakened to more generous impulses. Late in life Zury is taken in hand by a Boston woman who had come out as a schoolteacher years before, and whom Zury had given up for a bride with a rich farm, but to whom he eventually returns. Under her care the plates of mail are stripped from his heart, his better nature expands, and the meanest man in Spring County ripens into a kindly and lovable old age. What poverty and hardship had warped and twisted, love straightens out and ennobles; the meanness of the frontier is washed away as the rich soil yields a more abundant life. It is not a great book, but it is vigorous and honest, and its earlier chapters contain some admirable bits of realism. As one of the first stories of the western farmer it is secure of a place in the history of our American fiction.

It was this same year, 1887, that Hamlin Garland, alone and brooding over his studies at the Boston Public Library, wrote his first sketches of life in the Middle Border. The romance was fading from the prairies when he took up his pen. The Golden West of Mark Twain and the bucolic West of Whitcomb Riley had both slipped into the past and the day that was rising was to bring its discouragements that seared men's hopes as the hot winds seared the fields of rustling corn. The burdens of the western farmer were heavy on his shoulders and he could foresee no time when they would be lighter. Depression had settled on the Middle Border, and Hamlin Garland returning to the familiar fields from his Boston studies felt the depression in every fiber of his being. This was his land and his people. The blight laid upon men and women and children by the drab pioneer life was a familiar fact to him. The Garlands and the McClintocks had suffered from it as their neighbors suffered, and a rebellious wrath filled his heart as he contemplated the Middle Border—the barnyards where tired men did the evening chores, the ungainly houses where tired women stood over hot stoves, the fertile acres that produced more than the markets consumed. It was a life without grace or beauty or homely charm— a treadmill existence that got nowhere. If this were the Valley of Democracy then the democracy was a mean thing and hopeless, and having himself escaped from it he would do what he could to help others escape. In the completeness of his disillusion the glamour of romance was swept away and he proposed to set down in honest plain words the manner of life lived by these Middle Border folk, and the sort of earnings won by their toil. He would speak frankly out of the common bitter experience. The way to truth was the way of realism.

To a later generation that never knew the pioneer hardships of the Middle Border, Hamlin Garland seems strangely remote and old-fashioned; yet his intellectual antecedents are both ancient and honorable. At bottom he is an idealist of the old Jeffersonian breed, an earnest soul devoid of humor, who loves beauty and is mightily concerned about justice, and who, discovering little beauty and finding scant justice in the world where fate first set him, turned rebel and threw in his lot with the poor and the exploited. As a young man, consumed with a desire to speak for his people, he espoused a somber realism, for only by and through the truth could he hope to dislodge from men's minds the misconceptions that stood in the way of justice. The Middle Border had no spokesman at the court of letters and if he could gain a hearing there he must not betray his father's household by glossing ungainly reality; he must depict the life of the western farmer as it was lived under the summer sun and the winter cold, what harvests were brought to crib and what sort of wealth was finally gathered.

And yet in the light of his total work one hesitates to call Garland a realist. Perhaps more justly he might be called a thwarted romantic, and his early rebellious realism be traced to its source in a passionate refusal to be denied the beauty that should be a portion of any rational way of living; for when later he found himself in a land of nobler horizons, unsoiled as yet by crude frontier exploitation, when he looked out upon vast mountain ranges and felt the warm sun on the gray plains, he discovered there the romance of his dreams and fell to describing the strange splendors with the gusto of a naïve romantic. *Main-Travelled Roads* and *Prairie Folks* are the protest of one oppressed with the meanness of a world that takes such heavy toll of human happiness; *Her Mountain Lover* is the expression of a frank romantic who glories in the nobility of nature's noblemen; and *The Captain of the Gray-Horse Troop* is a tale in which romance is justified by ethics and the hero discovers in the protection of a weaker race the deepest satisfactions of life. Beauty is excellent, but beauty should walk hand in hand with service—not art for art's sake, but art subdued to the higher good of humanity.

Between these extremes of a stark realism and an ethical romanticism, stand two books, separated by many years and great changes, that embody in more finished form the theme which after all was the master passion of Garland's life—the Middle Border and the rebellions it bred. *Rose of Dutcher's Coolly* is a full-length portrait of an idealist in revolt against the narrowness of farm life, and *A Son of the Middle Border* is an idyll of the past, autobiography done in mellower years when the passions of youth have been subdued to less exigent demands. These books, together with the sketches of *Main-Travelled Roads* and the militant critical theory of *Crumbling Idols*, contain pretty much the whole of Hamlin Garland that after years have cared to remember—the saga of the Middle Border in the days of its great rebellion when the earlier hopes of boundless prosperity were turning to ashes in the mouth.

The striking originality of Garland's work, that sets it apart from other studies of the local-color school, sprang from the sincerity of his reaction to environment. His intellectual development followed the needs of his ardent, inquisitive nature. After quitting the little Academy at Osage, Iowa, he went forth in quest of an education that should explain to him the meaning of life as he had known it. In this search he was singularly fortunate. He was his own mentor and he took what he needed. Boston had long been the Mecca of his dreams and when he found himself there—having made a pious pilgrimage as Howells had done a generation earlier—he threw himself upon his studies with ascetic zeal. Fortunately he enrolled in the Boston Public Library instead of at Harvard, and his formless radicalisms there found food in plenty. Though he lived in Boston some ten years and made friends, he never penetrated the inner literary sanctuary. A somewhat forlorn outsider, unknown and unvouched for, he found no welcome as Howells and Twain had found, and he never entered the pleasant circles where Holmes and Lowell and Fields and Norton and Aldrich and Howells held sway.

Perhaps that fact unconsciously determined his scornful rejection of the Boston genteel in literature; at any rate his denial of the sovereignty of the New England literary rulers left him free to follow other masters who seemed to him more significant. In his bleak little room his ear had caught the greater voices then sounding in Europe and America. His masters were men of intellectual horizons unbounded by Beacon Street and Harvard Square: Taine and Ibsen and Björnson, Turgenev and Tolstoi, Zola and Millet, Darwin and Spencer and Fiske, Walt Whitman and Henry George, and the later Howells with his deeper sociological concern and graver realism. His three great masters came finally to be Whitman, Spencer, and Henry George. To these greater names should be added that of Edward Eggleston, who had been his boyhood idol, and that of Joseph Kirkland, who did much to stimulate and guide his earliest sketches. He did not absorb all these men had to give. He could not stretch his provincial mind suddenly to compass the intellectual realm of his masters. But something he got and that something, woven into the fabric of his thinking, was to make him free. It was the best school of the times, and from his studies Hamlin Garland emerged an uncompromising radical, one of a group of eager young men who gathered about B. O. Flower, and in the sympathetic pages of the *Arena* published their divers radicalisms to a hostile world. He was ready to proclaim new social and literary creeds, ready to go forth to do battle for democratic justice and a democratic art.

The gist of Garland's new literary creed is set forth in *Crumbling Idols*, written in the earliest years of the nineties, when Chicago was preparing the setting for the World's Fair, and gathered into book form in 1894. It is realism modified by the local-color school, by French impressionism, and by Whitman—intensely individualistic, ardently social, and militantly democratic. It would sweep away every fetish of great reputations and authoritative schools, and insist that the artist confront the life that he knows and tell of it truthfully. Following the French example he calls this iconoclastic realism, Veritism. "The *theory* of the veritist," he says, "is, after all, a statement of his passion for truth and for individual expression," and he then goes on:

Art, I must insist, is an individual thing,—the question of one man facing certain facts and telling his individual relations to them. His first care must be to present his own concept. This is, I believe, the essence of veritism. "Write of those things of which you know most, and for which you care most. By so doing you will be true to yourself, true to your locality, and true to your time." [2]

But Veritism in the hands of a disciple of Taine, Whitman, Henry George, and Herbert Spencer must take on ethical values and serve the common well-being. All art, he insists, is "socio-logic," and realism is harsh because it is hopeful.

Because the fictionist of to-day sees a more beautiful and peaceful future social life, and, in consequence, a more beautiful and peaceful literary life, therefore he is encouraged to deal truthfully and at close grapple with the facts of his immediate present. His comment virtually amounts to satire or prophesy, or both. Because he is sustained by love and faith in the future, he can be mercilessly true. He strikes at thistles, because he knows the unrotted seed of loveliness and peace needs but sun and the air of freedom to rise to flower and fragrance.

The realist or veritist is really an optimist, a dreamer. He sees life in terms of what it might be, as well as in terms of what it is; but he writes of what is, and, at his best, suggests what is to be, by contrast. . . . He aims to hasten the age of beauty and peace by delineating the ugliness and warfare of the present; but ever the converse of his picture rises in the mind of the reader. He sighs for a lovelier life. He is tired of warfare and diseased sexualism, and Poverty the mother of Envy. He is haggard with sympathetic hunger, and weary with the struggle to maintain his standing place on this planet, which he conceives was given to all as the abode of peace. With his hate in his heart and this ideal in his brain the modern man writes his stories of life. They are not always pleasant, but they are generally true, and always they provoke thought. [3]

It is an excellent self-portrait of the young realist of that early time when all the rebellions of his blood cried out for expression— the troubled years between 1887 and 1893 when the Border was rising and the son of the Border found the flames of his discontent fanned by many winds. From such roots came the most acrid tales that had as yet fruited in American fiction. Few as were the stories of *Main-Travelled Roads* and *Prairie Folks*, they constitute a landmark in our literary history, for they were the first authentic expression and protest of an agrarian America then being sub-merged by the industrial revolution. No other man in our literature had known so intimately the Middle Border as Hamlin Garland— its restless swarmings from the old hive, never pausing long enough to gather the honey of the new fields, its heedless venturings for the reputed gold that lay beyond the farthest sunsets. He had re-

[2] Chapter III, p. 35.   [3] Chapter IV, pp. 51–53.

sponded to the spell that kept the pioneer moving West; the allure-
ment of the untamed prairie, the poetry of dawn and twilight. But
the poignant spell had been broken for him by the drab realities
that lay between the dawn and the twilight—the crushing round
of toil that took such heavy toll of men's development and wom-
en's happiness. He was familiar with the blight as well as the
bloom of the frontier. He had seen his uncle David McClintock
broken by the Border—the great wistful man with the soul of a
musician; he had seen his mother fail under the burden—the
cheerful, uncomplaining wife, joining with her rich voice in the
pioneer's song of "O'er the hills in legions, Boys!" And after the
disillusion of his final defeat on the bleak Dakota plains—by 1883
woodland and meadow were pretty much alienated from the public
domains and only plains and deserts and mountain valleys and
forests remained—his eyes were opened at last. "I clearly perceived," he said afterwards, "that our Song of Emigration had
been, in effect, the hymn of fugitives!" So he turned his face to the
East to seek the land of desire in Boston.

That chapter of his life was ended. He had learned that the old
romantic tales of the Border were lies to him, whatever they may
have been to earlier generations; but he had yet to naturalize himself in the realm of ideas, and analyze the experiences of his youth
in the light of current social liberalisms. He had begun that work in
1883 on his raw Dakota claim where his leisure hours were given to
Taine's theory of literary determinism, and Henry George's new
gospel of single-tax; and he carried it rapidly forward during three
years of eager reading. During those quiet months in Boston when
he was making himself at home in the world of contemporary
thought, he sketched the first of the stories of western life which
later he gathered together in *Main-Travelled Roads* and *Prairie
Folks.* "You're the first actual farmer in American fiction," said
his friend Kirkland, "now tell the truth about it." This handful of
short stories, fierce in the repressed passion of the writer's heart, was
Garland's reply to the old romantic myths of the West. In these
acrid pages life is not bucolic, it does not chew the cud of contentment "knee-deep in June," but it is stained with dust and
sweat, lacerated by raw nerves, depressed by a sense of economic
failure.

Of the lives of these labor-burdened men and women he intended
to tell the whole truth. But, as he confessed later, he could not.

"Even my youthful zeal faltered in the midst of a revelation of the lives led by the women on the farms of the middle border. Before the tragic futility of their suffering, my pen refused to shed its ink. Over the hidden chamber of their maternal agonies I drew the veil." It was hard for him to view it all with the calm detachment of the objective realist; the Border life was too deeply and intimately personal to him, it had marked him too harshly. And yet in the sense of conveying the spirit of reality he succeeded greatly, and these earliest tales remain notable work which later years have not forgotten. The subdued words of the Prologue offer the fittest of commentaries on the spirit in which they were done.

The Main-travelled road in the West (as everywhere) is hot and dusty in summer, and desolate and drear with mud in fall and spring, and in winter the winds sweep across it; but it does sometimes cross a rich meadow where the songs of the larks and bobolinks and blackbirds are tangled. Follow it far enough, it may lead past a bend in the river where the water laughs eternally over its shallows. Mainly it is long and weariful, and has a dull little town at one end and a home of toil at the other. Like the main-travelled road of life it is traversed by many classes of people, but the poor and the weary predominate.

Main-Travelled Roads, in its harsh objectivity, belonged to the earlier eighties, to the time when the spirit of unrest was still obscurely fermenting in the wester n mind, before it had clarified in definite agrarian movements and measures. It is clouded by doubt and harassed by uncertainty. No hope offers a way out of the weary tangle. Its psychology is that of the first mood of dejection that came with the failure of western agriculture with its virgin fields, its new machinery, and its specialized crops, to adjust itself to the new capitalistic order. The simple agrarian mind had not learned to play the new game. The sons of the Middle Border were children of the Gilded Age as truly as Colonel Sellers or Commodore Vanderbilt; they were plungers and speculators in land and crops; but they were no match for the Main Street plungers and speculators; and when bankruptcy instead of riches rewarded their hardships, they were embittered. Out of that very natural bitterness sprang the movement of Populism that proposed to take government out of the hands of Main Street and make it serve agriculture. It was the understanding of this fact that made Howells so sympathetic a critic of Garland. But he would encourage the artist rather than the reformer.

. . . these stories are full of the bitter and burning dust, the foul and trampled slush, of the common avenues of life, the life of the men who hopelessly and cheerlessly make the wealth that enriches the alien and the idler, and impoverishes the producer.

If any one is still at a loss to account for that uprising of the farmers of the West which is the translation of the Peasants' War into modern and republican terms, let him read *Main-Travelled Roads,* and he will begin to understand. . . . The stories are full of those gaunt, grim, sordid, pathetic, ferocious figures, whom our satirists find so easy to caricature as Hayseeds, and whose blind groping for fairer conditions is so grotesque to the newspapers and so menacing to the politicians. They feel that something is wrong, and they know that the wrong is not theirs. The type caught in Mr. Garland's book is not pretty; it is ugly and often ridiculous; but it is heart-breaking in its rude despair.[4]

Too soon, however, the will to remain objective weakened and his work took on a different note. "Obscurely forming in my mind," he says of the year 1889, "were two great literary concepts —that truth was a higher quality than beauty, and that to spread the reign of justice should everywhere be the design and intent of the artist. The merely beautiful in art seemed petty, and success at the cost of the happiness of others a monstrous egotism."[5] With this ethical conception of art he returned in 1889 to the old home, after a six years' absence, to experience a poignant reaction to the change that had come over the Border. "Another dry year was upon the land and the settlers were deeply disheartened," he wrote later. "The holiday spirit of eight years before had entirely vanished. In its place was a sullen rebellion against government and against God."[6]

Every house I visited had its individual message of sordid struggle and half-hidden despair. . . . All the gilding of farm life melted away. The hard and bitter realities came back upon me in a flood. Nature was as beautiful as ever. The soaring sky was filled with shining clouds, the tinkle of the bobolink's fairy bells rose from the meadow, a mystical sheen was on the odorous grass and waving grain, but no splendor of cloud, no grace of sunset, could conceal the poverty of these people; on the contrary, they brought out, with a more intolerable poignancy, the gracelessness of these homes, and the sordid quality of the mechanical routine of these lives. I perceived beautiful youth becoming bowed and bent. I saw lovely girlhood wasting away into thin and hopeless age. Some of the women I had known had withered into querulous and complaining spinsterhood,

---

[4] Introduction to *Main-Travelled Roads.*
[5] *A Son of the Middle Border,* Chapter XXVIII, p. 374.
[6] *Ibid.,* Chapter XXIX.

and I heard ambitious youth cursing the bondage of the farm. "Of such pain and futility are the lives of the average man and woman of both city and country composed," I acknowledged to myself with candor, "Why lie about it?" [7]

In such a mood the call of social justice was too insistent to be denied. "With William Morris and Henry George I exclaimed, 'Nature is not to blame. Man's laws are to blame'!" And so the young man of twenty-nine threw himself into the agrarian cause. He took the platform with Mary Ellen Lease and was glad of the farmers' approval of the new doctrine of less corn and more hell. Under the urging of his friend Flower he planned to put the Populist movement into fiction and wrote *A Spoil of Office*. The familiar Iowa backgrounds are in the story—the harsh lives and bent weary figures of men and women—but there is also an idealized heroine who suggests what life may become when injustice is done away with and the blighting toil is lessened—a figure who, as Grange lecturer and Farmers' Alliance speaker, may have been suggested by Mary Ellen Lease. Much inferior as it is to *Main-Travelled Roads*—a social tract rather than a work of art—we cannot well spare it from our Middle Border literature, for it has captured and preserves for later times the spirit of the passionate uprising of the farmers, and it recalls the vast hopes that fermented in that revolt —not well grounded, perhaps, but warm and human. "The heart and center of this movement," says Ida Wilbur, "is a demand for justice, not for ourselves alone, but for the toiling poor wherever found. . . . It is no longer a question of legislating for the farmer; it is a question of the abolition of industrial slavery." [8] There are echoes of an older and simpler America in these pages, of discontents that were put down but not removed—Jacksonianisms, Greenbackisms, anti-monopolistic crusades. Yet they look forward to a time when beauty and well-being shall be the common portion of those who do the work of the world. The way, alas, is "long and weary, and thousands and millions of us must die on the road, I am afraid," says the heroine; but go forward they must, along other paths than the path of capitalism.

Less significant is *Jason Edwards: An Average Man* (1891), that is an elaboration of the note, "The air is full of revolt against things as they are." It is a single-tax reply to the question of a young girl, "Are there any happy people in the world—any working people, I

[7] *Ibid.*, Chapter XXVIII, pp. 364-365.   [8] *Ibid.*, p. 245.

mean? Are they all cross and tired and worried and full of care, as we are here?" The story is two chapters in the life of a working-man—his struggle in Boston as a mechanic, and his struggle in Minnesota, whither he flees for a refuge on a homestead. Defeat awaits him in the end, and the conclusion is an illustration of Henry George's thesis that poverty is the entail of land rent. In this and in other studies done under the influence of B. O. Flower, whose appetite for reform literature was insatiable, Hamlin Garland had ceased to be an objective realist and turned propagandist, bringing down on his head the criticisms of conservative readers. One of his friends went so far as to expostulate over the folly of his course. "It is a mistake for you to be associated with cranks like Henry George and writers like Whitman," he said. "It is a mistake to be published in the *Arena*. Your book should have been brought out by one of the old established firms. If you will fling away your radical notions and consent to amuse the governing classes, you will succeed." [9]

It is the agrarian background of Garland's mind that makes him seem old-fashioned to a generation that has forgotten the agrarian roots of our past growth. He was so deeply colored by this earlier native America that he never outgrew it; and when the Populistic revolt had died down, when this last organized agrarian rebellion against the exploiting middle class had become only an episode in our history, he had outlived his day. He was too deeply stirred by Whitman's romantic faith in democracy, too narrowly a disciple of Henry George's Jeffersonian economics, to fit into an industrializing America. Despite his discipleship to European realism he refused to go with the group of young left-wing naturalists who were boldly venturing on new ways of fiction. He would not follow the path of naturalism. Of Norris's *McTeague* he said, "What avail is this study of sad lives? for it does not even lead to a notion of social betterment." [10] He could not bring himself to accept the major criteria of naturalism as they were exemplified in the work of Zola and Strindberg and Hauptmann. A native Jeffersonian, inspired by Whitman and instructed by Henry George and Herbert Spencer, would reject the somber, mechanistic background of naturalist thought. He had learned his science of the Victorian evolutionists, with their grandiose conception of a far-flung benefi-

[9] *A Son of the Middle Border*, Chapter XXXI, p. 417.
[10] *Critic*, Vol. 42, pp. 216–218.

cent progress from the homogeneous to the heterogeneous, and the backgrounds of his mind were radiant with promise. Neither a mechanistic science nor a regimented industrialism had risen in his outlook to bank the fires of his hope. No impersonal determinism had chilled his belief in man as a free-will agent in a moral universe. The vast bleak chemical cosmos that bewildered Theodore Dreiser did not rise before him to dwarf the individual nor overwhelm his aspirations. Like a French romantic of a hundred years before, he remained a confirmed optimist who believed that the future will correct the mistakes of the past, and the peace and beauty for which the human race longs lie immediately ahead. The art of the young man was becoming old-fashioned in the world of Stephen Crane; his ideals were Victorian in the days of Mark Hanna. And so after the agrarian revolt had failed and America lay fat and contented in the lap of McKinley prosperity, he found himself a man without a country, an alien in an industrializing order, and he turned away to the newer West and the romance he had always sought. While America was driving towards regimentation he traveled backward in time to recover a vanishing world of individualism, and the distance rapidly widened between them.

In those romantic wanderings through Colorado and California and into the far Northwest he found a new interest in the frontiersman's exploitation of the Indian, and in *The Captain of the Gray-Horse Troop* and *The Eagle Heart* he has wedded his social ethics to French romanticism, and endowed man in a state of nature with exalted social responsibilities. The old theme is dressed in new clothes and Captain Curtis of the Gray-Horse Troop becomes an Indian agent fighting the lawless and cruel encroachment of the frontiersmen upon the Indian rights; but the theme remains. Garland hated the frontier as fiercely as Cooper hated it, and like him he loved the clean free spaces; but when after his long and somewhat futile rambles he returned to the Middle Border, he found there a new light upon the familiar fields and in that light he wrote his saga of the Garlands and the McClintocks. This was to be his great bequest to American letters. To have sought the spirit of the Middle Border in its hopes and its defeat, to have written the history of the generation that swept across the western prairies, is to compress within covers a great movement and a great experience—one of the significant chapters in our total American history.

PART TWO: PROLETARIAN HOPES*

CHAPTER III
THE QUEST OF UTOPIA

FROM the welter of unrest of the later years of the century, with its labor struggles, its agrarian bitterness, its concern over the exhaustion of the public lands and a pinching monetary system, its acute distrust of monopolies and corporate power, sprang a very natural eagerness to forecast the future and blaze new roads that might lead to the democratic Canaan. Whither the main-traveled road would lead, discerning idealists knew only too well. To bog down in a mire of plutocracy would be a sorry ending to the great experiment; yet the mud was deepening with every mile of advance and unless another highway appeared the situation was unpromising. The crux of the problem seemed to reside in an extension of the powers of the political state, converting to social ends powers that hitherto had been serving private gain. The plutocracy was pointing the way. If the political state were fairly dedicated to democratic ends, why should not society go forward toward a true commonwealth, founded on a social economy and dedicated to common justice and the common well-being? There was need only to subordinate private interests to collective interests, and substitute coöperation for the present mad scramble of selfish individualism.

In elaboration of this pregnant thought a surprising number of social romances appeared during the last quarter of the century, that were native counterparts of the greater studies in collectivism by European thinkers. A recent study lists forty-eight titles of Utopian romances written between 1884 and 1900.[1] Of these several are communistic, and the rest are socialistic; yet in keeping with the American temper none openly makes use of the terms, and few apply the Marxian doctrine of the class war. Their appeal was directed primarily to the middle class of small business and profes-

* The first chapter of this section was to have been "Plutocracy and the Working-man," the second "The Rise of the Left." For the contents see p. xxxv.—*Publisher.*
[1] Allyn B. Forbes, *The Literary Quest for Utopia, 1880–1900.* "Social Forces," Vol. VI, No. 2, December, 1927.

sional men, and they were content to rely on political means to achieve economic ends. Troubled as was the American mind by the rise of a cutthroat exploitation, it was not yet ready to entertain ideas of direct action or trust the proletariat to enforce its will by mass strength. In one story, to be sure—Ignatius Donnelly's *Cæsar's Column* (1890)—there is a gloomy picture of the downfall of civilization caused by the class struggles; but the temper of Donnelly had lost its genial optimism through his long immersion in under-dog contests and had grown mordant and gloomy.

I

EDWARD BELLAMY AND "LOOKING BACKWARD"

When in 1888 Edward Bellamy published *Looking Backward* he gave a huge impetus to the Utopian romance. Third in the list of titles collected by Mr. Forbes, it was to have a wide influence on the thought of the times. It made instant appeal and successive editions were issued to meet the popular demand. Not since *Uncle Tom's Cabin* had an American novel reached so many readers, and Bellamy became at once a national figure, the prophet of a new industrial order. There is abundant evidence to the effect produced upon thoughtful readers. E. C. Stedman, the first critic of the times, spoke of it as a "remarkable and fascinating novel"; Frances E. Willard called it "a revelation and an evangel"; and Howells remarked on "the extraordinary effect which Mr. Bellamy's romance has had with the public." More significant still, *Looking Backward* speedily became the source and inspiration for a series of social organizations that beginning at Boston soon spread over the country. *The Nationalist* was established as the organ of the movement and thousands of eager men and women threw themselves into the work of reshaping American society to conform to the new social ideal. No doubt the enthusiasm was naïve, no doubt it sprang from a social inexperience that underestimated the complexity of the problem, yet the sources, clearly, were a sharp distrust of private capitalism and an idealistic faith in coöperation. In a pronouncement of the Boston "Nationalist Club," January 9, 1889, the cause was rested on two fundamental truths—"The principle of competition is . . . the application of the brutal law of the survival of the strongest and most cunning"; and, "The principle of the Brotherhood of Humanity is one of the eternal truths that govern the world's progress on lines which distinguish human nature from brute nature." [2]

It is not easy to trace the origins of Bellamy's interest in collectivism or the sources of his thought. A journalist and lawyer, he had studied in Germany, where presumably he had come in contact with Marxian socialism. Writing in the *Nationalist* for May, 1889, he commented thus on the origins of *Looking Backward:*

I never had, previous to the publication of the work, any affiliations with any class or sect of industrial or social reformers nor, to make my confession complete, any particular sympathy with undertakings of the sort. It is only just to myself to say, however, that this should not be taken to indicate any indifference to the miserable condition of the mass of humanity, seeing that it resulted rather from a perception all too clear of the depth and breadth of the social problem and a consequent skepticism as to the effectiveness of the proposed solutions which had come to my notice.

In undertaking to write *Looking Backward* I had, at the outset, no idea of attempting a serious contribution to the movement of social reform. The idea was of a mere literary fantasy, a fairy tale of social felicity. There was no thought of contriving a house which practical men might live in, but merely of hanging in mid-air, far out of the reach of the sordid and material world of the present, a cloud-palace for an ideal humanity.[3]

That the impulse did not come from the Marxians is sufficiently clear from his explanation of the idea of an industrial army. "The idea of committing the duty of maintaining the community to an industrial army, precisely as the duty of protecting it is entrusted to a military army," came to him, he said, from the object-lesson of European militarism. But however little he owed to the Marxians it is clear that Bellamy—the literary amateur who had dabbled in Hawthornesque fantasies—possessed a warm social conscience and a vigorous inquiring mind; and once his attention had been drawn to the evils of industrialism he would respond with the same direct competence that marked the thinking of Henry George. Nine years before *Looking Backward* he had dealt with a sociological theme. In 1879 he wrote *The Duke of Stockbridge, A Romance of Shay's Rebellion,* for the *Berkshire Courier,* which was reissued in book form in 1900. It was a hasty piece of work that falls off greatly in the latter part; yet in its sympathy for the agrarian rebels and its probing of the economic sources of the post-Revolutionary unrest, it was far removed from the temper of Federalist historians. It is an account of the tyranny of property rule—of the exploitation

[2] *Nationalist*, Vol. I, p. 18.   [3] *Ibid.,* Vol. I, p. 1.

of the debtor farmer by the creditor gentleman made possible by
the economic maladjustments resulting from the war. A bitter
discontent is in the hearts of the common people. Hatred of lawyers
and courts and process-servers, has taken the place of hatred of
Tories. Soldiers who had conquered Cornwallis were returning
home only to be conquered by writs and imprisoned by sheriffs. The
exactions of a brutal law fell upon helpless victims; taxes outran
incomes and there was no money to pay. Economic injustice was
daily whetting the edge of class bitterness. The animus of Shays's
Rebellion is compressed into a few paragraphs that suggest how
clearly Bellamy had analyzed the social struggle.

> "I use ter think ez there wuzn't no sech varmint ez a tory; but I didn't
> know nothin' 'bout lawyers and sheriffs them times. I calc'late ye could
> cut five tories aout o' one lawyer an' make a dozen skunks aout o' what
> wuz left over."
>
> "I hearn as haow Squire Woodbridge says taxes is ten times what they
> wuz afore the war, an' its sartin that there ain't one shillin' inter folks'
> pockets ter pay 'em with where there wuz ten on 'em in them days. . . .
> It seems darn curis, bein' as we fit ag'in the red coats jest ter git rid o'
> taxes." [4]

So felt the agrarian. Now for the gentleman:

> "That is the trouble nowadays, . . . these numskulls must needs have
> matters of government explained to them, and pass their own judgment
> on public affairs. And when they cannot understand them, then, forsooth,
> comes a rebellion. I think none can deny seeing in these late troubles the
> first fruits of those pestilent notions of equality, whereof we heard so much
> from certain quarters, during the late war of independence. I would that
> Mr. Jefferson and some of the other writers of disturbing democratic
> rhetoric might have been here in the State the past winter, to see the out-
> come of their preaching." [5]

Nine years after *Looking Backward* Bellamy published *Equality*,
a critical examination of economic history with a view to creating
an adequate social economics. The earlier work had drawn the
outlines of the democratic society of the future, the later supplied a
justification and a commentary. The great theme involved a two-
fold problem: an analysis of the failure of social justice under
private capitalism, and a defense of the working of social capitalism. The two threads are closely interwoven, and the effect is
heightened by the contrasts resulting from setting the two social

[4] *The Duke of Stockbridge*, Chapter II, pp. 22, 28.
[5] *Ibid.*, Chapter XXVI, p. 349.

orders over against each other. Innumerable questions, touching diverse phases, are propounded and answered. The apologist of private capitalism is pursued into every stronghold of his logic; he is assailed by a hundred vivid analogies which seek to lay bare the folly of a social system that breeds waste only to breed poverty, that puts a premium upon greed and yet takes away the security of possession, that bids the workers fight each other instead of uniting for the common welfare. But men must see a better before they will leave a worse, and so there is drawn the picture of another commonwealth that must arise when men shall put off the ass's head from their shoulders, and set intelligently to work. America is moving towards such a commonwealth, Bellamy is persuaded, and yet how slow it is to grasp the meaning of democracy! It holds back from its own good, loath to probe the depths of the revolutionary philosophy of liberty, equality, fraternity. Julian West awakes in this new world; his eyes are opened; the ass's head is gone; he knows for the first time the goodness of life in a rational society. And when in a hideous nightmare he returned to the old Boston he had lived in before he fell asleep, he tasted for the first time the full iniquity of the old pigsty arrangement. "I have been in Golgotha," he cried, "I have seen Humanity hanging on a cross!" It is knowledge of the good that must destroy the evil.

It was as a political economist that Bellamy attacked the problems of a democratic society, and his radicalism begins and ends with the interpretation he puts on the phrase. He was far from being a political economist of the schools. His contempt for the older classical dogmas was measureless. Manchesterism with its fetish of *laissez faire* he reckoned no better than a pseudo-science. " 'There were no political economists before the Revolution,' " remarks one of the scholars of the later age.[6] Such books as the *Wealth of Nations*, properly speaking, should be called "Examinations into the Economic and Social Consequences of trying to get along without any Political Economy." Before we shall get forward we must examine our terms.

Economy . . . means the wise husbanding of wealth in production and distribution. Individual economy is the science of this husbandry when conducted in the interest of the individual without regard to any others. Family economy is this husbandry carried on for the advantage of a family group without regard to other groups. Political economy, however, can

[6] *Equality*, Chapter XXII, p. 189.

only mean the husbandry of wealth for the greatest advantage of the political or social body, the whole number of the citizens constituting the political organization. This sort of husbandry necessarily implies a public or political regulation of economic affairs for the general interest. But before the Revolution there was no conception of such an economy, nor any organization to carry it out. All systems and doctrines of economy previous to that time were distinctly and exclusively private and individual in their whole theory and practice. While in other respects our forefathers did in various ways and degrees recognize a social solidarity and a political unity with proportionate rights and duties, their theory and practice as to all matters touching the getting and sharing of wealth were aggressively and brutally individualistic, antisocial, and unpolitical.[7]

A social arrangement based on an individual economy must necessarily result in such monstrosities as the system of private capitalism with its cash nexus. It is no other than an organized system of social warfare, with all the appalling waste of war. Habit has blinded our eyes or we should see the utter bankruptcy of individual competition, that prides itself on its "famous process for beggaring a nation." "Were these serious men I saw about me," cried Julian West as he watched the folly of Washington Street, with its thousand shops madly bidding against each other, its vulgar advertising and cheating and swindling, "or children, who did their business on such a plan? Could they be reasoning beings, who did not see the folly which, when the product is made and ready for use, wastes so much of it in getting it to the user? If people eat with a spoon that leaks half its contents between bowl and lip, are they not likely to go hungry?"[8] What is it but such folly which prevents society from doing the thousand things which cry aloud to be done? So long as men must fight each other for individual subsistence how shall they be able to join forces to fight the common enemies, cold, hunger, disease? Our individualism keeps us poverty-stricken; we are too poor to destroy the social squalor, too poor to save our own lives.

If competition entails irretrievable waste, he points out, the system of competitive profit involves economic suicide. It is a pistol which private industrialism points at its own head. The struggle for profit is the hidden cancer that is eating out the heart of modern society, and Bellamy examines it searchingly in the chapter, "Economic Suicide of the Profit System."[9] Under private

[7] *Ibid*, p. 189.
[8] *Looking Backward*, Chapter XXVIII, p. 314.
[9] *Equality*, Chapter XXII.

industrialism profits are the oil to the wheels of industry, which turn in response to the market. By the market is meant those who have money to buy with; and demand is brisk or slack according to the diffusion of economic means. When the buyers are satisfied and abstain from further purchases, the market becomes glutted and the wheels of production cease to turn "though starving and naked mobs might riot in the streets." Profits, however, must come out of somebody's pocket; and the greater they are the more the pocket that pays is emptied; unless replenished by other profits, taken from still other pockets, it ceases to be able to buy in like proportion. In consequence the market slacks off and the wheels of industry run slower. The manufacturer takes his profits out of his workmen, the merchant takes his out of the public—which is another term for the workman; he who takes most grows rich fastest and is most successful. Obviously, however, such riches are acquired at the expense of the public capacity to buy; and such lessening capacity is ominous of gluts and crises to ensue, with losses which must be made good by greater profits when the wheels turn again. It is only too clear that society is suffering from a chronic dyspepsia of its industrial system; it cannot digest its food. The current maxim that a fair exchange is no robbery—so confidently urged— cannot apply to the profit system, for if the exchange is fair there is no profit, and if there is no profit there will be no exchange. The further maxim that demand governs supply and supply keeps pace with demand, refers only to the profit-market, and quite overlooks the important detail of social need.

The stupidity of such a system Bellamy never tires of pointing out. His striking analogy of the stage-coach has become a classic; the less known parable of the water-tank [10] is equally vivid; a hundred other shafts are directed at the profit-theory which underlies our individual economy. Until the sway of such anarchy is broken, until society learns to regulate its industrialism on the principles of a wise political economy, there can be no hope of betterment. To create and apply this wise political economy is the urgent business of democracy if it is not to perish. It must be such an economy as shall satisfy both our ethical ideals and our material needs. It must embody the spirit of democratic solidarity and it must look beyond the demands of the profit-market to the well-being of all. It must substitute coöperation for competitive war-

[10] *Equality*, Chapter XXIII, p. 195.

fare. The criminal waste which keeps the gray wolves forever snarl-
ing at the threshold of society, must cease; the specter of poverty
which disorders the lives of men and distempers their hopes, must
be banished by the united strength of all. If democracy cannot
achieve such a democratic political economy it must flounder
through deepening bogs until finally it sinks in the morass of plutocracy.

The fatal mistake of democracy heretofore has been the insuffi-
ciency of its program. It is incredible how limited has been its
vision and how few and how minor have been its greatest revolutions. To overthrow monarchy was excellent, but it did not bring
in democracy; rather, the unchecked sway of plutocracy. "'The
people, indeed, nominally were sovereigns; but as these sovereigns
were individually and as a class the economic serfs of the rich, and
lived at their mercy, the so-called popular government became the
mere stalking-horse of the capitalists.'"[11] Political revolutions have
proved heretofore to be mere flashes in the pan; not until the economic revolution has been effected will the old tyranny be blown
to pieces:

> The second phase in the evolution of the democratic idea began with
> the awakening of the people to the perception that the deposing of kings,
> instead of being the main end and mission of democracy, was merely pre-
> liminary to its real programme, which was the use of the collective so-
> cial machinery for the indefinite promotion of the welfare of the people at
> large. . . .
> Which amounts to saying . . . that there never was a democratic gov-
> ernment properly so called before the twentieth century. . . . The so-
> called republics of the first phase we class as pseudo-republics or negative
> democracies. . . .
> Regarded as necessary steps in the evolution of society from pure mon-
> archy to pure democracy, these republics of the negative phase mark a
> stage of progress; but if regarded as finalities they were a type far less
> admirable on the whole than decent monarchies. In respect especially to
> their susceptibility to corruption and plutocratic subversion they were the
> worst kind of government possible. . . . How could intelligent men de-
> lude themselves with the notion that the most portentous and revolution-
> ary idea of all time had exhausted its influence and fulfilled its mission in
> changing the title of the executive of a nation from king to President, and
> the name of the national Legislature from Parliament to Congress? . . .
> The American people fancied that they had set up a popular government
> when they separated from England, but they were deluded. In conquering
> the political power formerly exercised by the king, the people had but

[11] *Equality*, Chapter II, p. 21.

taken the outworks of the fortress of tyranny. The economic system which was the citadel and commanded every part of the social structure remained in possession of private and irresponsible rulers, and so long as it was held, the possession of the outworks was of no use to the people, and only retained by the sufferance of the garrison of the citadel. The Revolution came when the people saw that they must either take the citadel or evacuate the outworks.[12]

The significance of the title of Bellamy's supplementary volume should now be clear. The problem of democracy always and everywhere is the problem of achieving economic equality. Without that all talk of liberty and fraternity, all equality before the law, is empty and sinister mockery. How can a man call himself citizen who must beg a fellow citizen to become his master? How shall the wage-taker treat his boss as a brother? Of what worth is equality before the law to one without a job? Democracy and servitude cannot lie down together. Wage-slavery debases the dignity of man; it puts upon him the greatest of indignities, servitude to things; it cheats him of his right to life, liberty, and happiness; it is the evil thing which degrades human society to the level of the pigsty, and puts a premium upon the hoggish instincts of men. It sows suspicion and hate between equals, changes the unsuccessful into cringing sycophants, sets its heel upon the weak and the helpless. The thing were too monstrous to be conceivable were it not the everyday fact of life—more than that, were it not the ideal of a supposedly democratic society, apologized for by our plutocratic culture, defended by all that accounts itself respectable, buttressed by the formidable turrets of the law, written down as a major premise in our treatises on political science: and all in the sacred name of individual enterprise. It is familiarity that blinds us to its evils, and makes its victims only callous or sullen. And it endures because men are deceived by its half-truths, seduced by its specious freedoms, led astray by its fatuous promises. Being taught to set the privilege of fighting above the privilege of helping, how should they not account their egoism more sacred than their altruism?

When men shall leave off bounding their democratic horizons by the old political economy and the old law, Bellamy was persuaded, they will see more clearly. The political science of private property conceived of government as a police power to safeguard the stake of

---

[12] *Ibid.*, Chapter II, pp. 19, 20, 21, 22.

the individual in society. Very well, democracy needs only to re-define the terms "stake-in-society" and "police power" to arrive at a competent philosophy. The definition of the former is ready to hand in the familiar words of the Declaration of Independence—the stake of every man in society is no less than his life, his liberty, and his happiness. To secure him in this stake is the primary function of government. The property interpretation of the stake-in-society principle was sound in its assumption of the economic as the determining basis; we need only to democratize the interpretation to arrive at our end.

"The primal principle of democracy is the worth and dignity of the individual. That dignity, consisting in the quality of human nature, is essentially the same in all individuals, and therefore equality is the vital principle of democracy. To this intrinsic and equal dignity of the individual all material conditions must be made subservient, and personal accidents and attributes subordinated. The raising up of the human being without respect of persons is the constant and only rational motive of the democratic policy. Contrast with this conception that precious notion of your contemporaries as to restricting suffrage. Recognizing the material disparities in the circumstances of individuals, they proposed to conform the rights and dignities of the individual to his material circumstances instead of conforming the material circumstances to the essential and equal dignity of man."

"In short . . . while under our system we conformed men to things, you think it more reasonable to conform things to men?"

"That is, indeed," replied the doctor, "the vital difference between the old and the new orders." [13]

As a preliminary to this necessary end of conforming things to men there must be a reinterpretation of the functions of the state. Here again Bellamy's political economy gives a surprising twist to the current police theory of government.

"In my day . . . it was considered that the proper functions of government, strictly speaking, were limited to keeping the peace and defending the people against the public enemy, that is to the military and police powers."

"And in heaven's name, who are the public enemies?" exclaimed Dr. Leete. "Are they France, England, Germany, or hunger, cold, and nakedness?" [14]

The plutocratic interpretation of the police power signifies no other than the protection of the individual in the enjoyment of the

[13] *Ibid.*, Chapter III, p. 26.
[14] *Looking Backward*, Chapter VI, p. 59.

fruits of his exploitation—that his right to keep and use what he
has got must be held more sacred than the welfare of society; that
the law, the military, the police, shall defend him in his right to do
with his winnings as he will. The democratic interpretation of the
police power, on the other hand, holds that the state must intervene
to the end that property shall serve a social and not a private interest; that the weak shall not be exploited by individual enterprise;
that all shall be protected in their right to life, liberty, and happiness. It demands an ethical basis for the social economy. The legal
maxim that a man may do as he will with his own, is open to question. The matter of ownership ceases to be a legal question of title,
and becomes a moral question of right and justice. Land, the
machinery of production, the profits of organized industry, coal,
ores, oil, lumber—are such things justly subject to private preemption? Shall the complex structure of society be bottomed on the
law of contract, or on the ethics of social justice? Substitute one for
the other and a revolution is accomplished.

Our ethics of wealth is . . . extremely simple. It consists merely in the
law of self-preservation, asserted in the name of all against the encroachments of any. It rests upon a principle which a child can understand as
well as a philosopher, and which no philosopher ever attempted to refute—
namely, the supreme right of all to live, and consequently to insist that
society shall be so organized as to secure that right.[15]

Thus in the political science of democracy the old police theory
of government merges in an all-embracing trustee theory. To a
paternal state is entrusted the protection of the interests of society.
That the welfare of all shall be faithfully served, it is essential that
the common will control and direct the machinery for the production and distribution of wealth. The anarchy of individualism must
give place to an ordered regimentation, under a centralized authority. The social meaning of property must be probed to the
bottom and the exact line between public and private rights be
marked off. This brings Bellamy to his fundamental principle—the
collectivistic organization of industry as the *sine qua non* of a democratic society. How effectively such a centralized state must wage
war upon poverty, how adequately it must protect the citizen
against the common enemies of cold, hunger, and nakedness, it was
the purpose of *Looking Backward* and *Equality* to picture. "A hor-

[15] *Equality*, Chapter XI, p. 74.

rible cockney dream," William Morris called *Looking Backward;* and by way of answer sketched his *News from Nowhere*, loveliest of Utopias with its anarchistic freedom set in country fields. Morris was an artist with an ample share of Ruskinian prejudice against the machinery that Bellamy so greatly developed; nevertheless Bellamy was far more modern and realistic in his understanding of the part the machine will play in the society of the future. To socialize the machine—to put upon it the slave-work of society, surely means much to human freedom.

Looking Backward is a brief for no particular school of socialism, although it inclines somewhat to Fabianism. Not through strikes, boycotts and lockouts, was the great change brought about, but in consequence of the spread of social intelligence and social ethics. Unionism was not the father of the Revolution, nor agrarianism its mother. Direct action and violence in any form rather hindered than helped. Class propaganda was too narrow and too selfish. The anarchists with their "red flag and talk about burning, sacking, and blowing people up," retarded the Revolution by frightening the timid and making "a thousand enemies of their professed cause to one friend." "The labor parties, as such, never could have accomplished anything on a large or permanent scale."

It was not till a rearrangement of the industrial and social system on a higher ethical basis, and for the more efficient production of wealth, was recognized as the interest, not of one class, but equally of all classes, of rich and poor, cultured and ignorant, old and young, weak and strong, men and women, that there was any prospect that it would be achieved. Then the national party arose to carry it out by political methods.[16]

To wait for the consent of all would seem to the impatient a long postponement of the millennium; yet the postponement, Bellamy argued, need not be long. The overreaching greed of private capitalism was daily hastening it. The new order must come about speedily as a necessary consequence of two forces; the compulsion of economic fact, and the stimulus of ideas. As the monopolistic tendencies of private capitalism open the eyes of the dullest to the growth of a plutocratic power beyond the control of the majority, a quick fear of the impending tyranny must lead men to question the larger scope and ultimate significance of the whole system. Under the lash of this fear their minds will open to ideas which have

[16] *Looking Backward*, Chapter XXIV.

long been knocking in vain for admission. The sources of monopolistic power will be examined, and the successive steps by which the few have gained control of the machinery of production will become clear. Already the fertile idea of the unearned increment which the land-taxers have got hold of and are spreading widely, has prepared the way for the revolutionary doctrine of the social fund. Let the common man once understand how small a portion of wealth is produced by his private effort, and how large a portion by the agency of social organization with its heritage of experience and invention, and he will understand how unjustly private capitalism appropriates what it has not earned. The conclusion that wealth should belong to him who produces it, is a deduction of the most elementary ethics; and since the production of wealth in quantity is a consequence of the social organization and social heritage, the conviction becomes irresistible that such wealth belongs to society and cannot justly be appropriated by the individual.[17] Let such an idea spread widely and the way is prepared for the taking over by the state of the machinery of production, and the assumption by it of the obligation of universal trusteeship. Then will come the Revolution. Coöperation will take the place of competition; production and distribution for the common well-being will destroy the malevolent trinity of rent, interest, and profit, which have so long held the world in poverty; the intelligent strength of all will stand between the individual and cold, hunger, and nakedness. The noble words of the Declaration of Independence will no longer be a catch-vote and a mockery to the exploited multitude, but a reality. The democratic ideal, with its social philosophy summarized in the phrase, "the only wealth is life," will destroy the last vestiges of ancient tyranny and men will be free. Rooted in economic equality the fine flower of individualism will expand as it cannot now in unfertile soil; a generous and unstinted culture will spread the spirit of kindliness through society, and a new and nobler art and religion will go hand in hand with the new fellowship.

Only too clearly Edward Bellamy was an incorrigible idealist. He looked into the future with more confident eyes than most of us; he saw in the East the quickening of a new day where we see only darkness. A child of the Enlightenment, he put his trust in the natural goodness of men. They are not inherently base and ignoble, but the victims of an evil system that breeds what is base and ig-

[17] See *Equality*, Chapter XIII—"Private Capital Stolen from the Social Fund."

noble. "The folly of men, not their hard-heartedness, was the great cause of the world's poverty. It was not the crime of man, nor of any class of men, that made the race so miserable, but a hideous, ghastly mistake, a colossal world-darkening blunder." [18] In an arid land shall we waste the little store of water, or shall we regulate it strictly, that the desert may be brought to bloom as a garden?

The labor of men, I explained, was the fertilizing stream which alone rendered earth habitable. It was but a scanty stream at best, and its use required to be regulated by a system which expended every drop to the best advantage, if the world were to be supported in abundance. But how far from any system was the actual practice! Every man wasted the precious fluid as he wished, animated only by the equal motives of saving his own crop and spoiling his neighbor's, that his might sell the better. What with greed and what with spite, some fields were flooded while others were parched, and half the water ran wholly to waste. In such a land, though a few by strength or cunning might win the means of luxury, the lot of the great mass must be poverty, and of the weak and ignorant bitter want and perennial famine.

Let but the famine-stricken nation assume the function it had neglected, and regulate for the common good the course of the life-giving stream, and the earth would bloom like one garden, and none of its children lack any good thing. I described the physical felicity, mental enlightenment, and moral elevation which would then attend the lives of all men. With fervency I spoke of that new world, blessed with plenty, purified by justice and sweetened by brotherly kindness, the world of which I had indeed but dreamed, but which might so easily be made real. But when I had expected now surely the faces around me to light up with emotions akin to mine, they grew ever more dark, angry, and scornful. Instead of enthusiasm, the ladies showed only aversion and dread, while the men interrupted me with shouts of reprobation and contempt. "Madman!" "Pestilent fellow!" "Fanatic!" "Enemy of society!" were some of their cries, and the one who had before taken his eyeglass to me exclaimed, "He says we are to have no more poor. Ha! ha!"

"Put the fellow out!" exclaimed the father of my bethrothed, and at the signal the men sprang from their chairs and advanced upon me." [19]

Like Henry George's noble study of social poverty, *Looking Backward* is a suggestive document of a generation that saw its finer spirits repelled by the vulgar individualism of the Gilded Age. In the long run, no doubt, its influence was slight and the hopes of the Bellamy Nationalists, like the hopes of the Single-taxers, were

[18] *Looking Backward,* Chapter XXVIII, p. 328.
[19] *Ibid,* pp. 328–9.

doomed to disappointment. Nevertheless it remains as a testimony to the fact that in a blatant world of preëmption, exploitation, and progress, were some who were concerned for a juster social order than the Gilded Age dreamed of—a true commonwealth that free men might build if they would.*

* At this point was to come a second section entitled "After Bellamy; 'Naturalism'; Tourgée's *Murvale Eastman*."—*Publisher.*

CHAPTER IV

THE DARKENING SKIES OF LETTERS

So late as 1893, in spite of the stark ugliness of Hamlin Garland's pictures of the Middle Border, American realism was still unlike in temper those somber etchings, burnt into dark patterns by the caustic acids of European experience, that came from the hands of Russian and German and French naturalists—sketches that in their bitter gloom seemed tragically untrue to the homelier experience of America. In appraising such difference in temper Howells ascribed it to the gulf that separated American well-being from the poverty and injustice of European societies. American realism was hopeful because American life was hopeful. The novelist in this singularly favored land must reflect the temper of a people made kindly by an abundant prosperity and democratic justice, and in the sincerity of his realism he will necessarily concern himself with the "more smiling aspects of life, which are the more American." Whoever should strike a "note so profoundly tragic in American fiction" as was struck in Dostoevsky's *Crime and Punishment*, he asserted in 1891, "would do a false and mistaken thing." [1] And in a later work he spoke casually of our "gay American horizons"— surely the most romantic phrase ever applied to a sad and joyless people by a professed realist.

But while Howells was thus summing up the achievements of American realism and somewhat overconfidently forecasting its future temper, he was in fact writing the history of a past phase. Already the clouds were gathering upon our "gay" horizons, and the current optimisms were finding less food to feed on. The economics of this happy America were coming to be regarded by vast numbers as a class economics, forecasting a less democratic future. Young men born in the early seventies, when Mr. Howells was entering upon his new realistic studies, were coming to intellectual maturity in a very different age; a new science and a consolidating economics were creating a somber temper that was eventually to produce in *An American Tragedy*, a story not greatly unlike that

[1] *Criticism and Fiction*, p. 128.

316

Russian tale which Mr. Howells, a short generation before, had pronounced impossible to American experience. Stephen Crane and Frank Norris and Theodore Dreiser were the intellectual children of the nineties, and their art was a reflection of that sober period of American disillusion.

The artist, of course, in his creative work is only mediately influenced by the current science and philosophy; yet even in his aloofness from the specific problems of the laboratory and the study he can scarcely escape the pervasive influence of the *Zeitgeist*. And so, after Hamlin Garland, the realistic novel again took a new course from the shifting winds of scientific doctrine. The generation that succeeded the rebellious son of the Middle Border came too late to maturity to share his faith in the benevolent universe of Herbert Spencer, and got little comfort from a promised Utopia that only awaited the enactment of certain statutory laws—laws that would assure economic justice to all—to lay open its hospitable realm. Far-reaching changes were coming over the temper of scientific thought. The conclusions of the physical sciences were ravaging the orderly preserves of biological evolution, with its cardinal doctrine of organic growth and historical continuity; the hurrying march of scientific investigation was leaving far behind the benevolent universe conceived of by Victorian thinkers and was coming out upon higher and bleaker tablelands of speculation. The universe that unfolded itself to chemistry and physics was vaster and colder than biological evolution with its doctrine of the conservation of energy, had imagined—a vibrating mechanism shot through with energy, that revealed itself in action and reaction, impersonal, amoral, dwarfing all the gods dreamed of hitherto; a universe in which the generations of men have shrunk to a pin-point in limitless space and all teleological hopes and fears become the emptiest of futilities. It was the conception of determinism that after long denial was at last coming to wide acceptance—a conception that underlay the thinking of such diverse men as Comte and Spencer and Marx, a conception implicit in the doctrine of continuity, in the law of causality, in the Marxian law of concentration; and now disencumbered of its teleological wrappings, disillusioned with the doctrine of progress, it was to shape the new intellectual attitude towards life.

In presence of such an extraordinary intellectual revolution the old anthropomorphisms of metaphysics and ethics were doomed, and from the revelations of physics and chemistry and psychology must come an endeavor after a fresh evaluation of man's duty and destiny in a universe of immeasurable energy. An ethics that should square with the new data of science must take its departure from the bleak fact of a depersonalized universe, wherein man is but a single form of imprisoned energy, localized for a brief instant and rising to momentary consciousness in the eternal flux, about and through whom flows the energy of an unprobed universe. As this mechanistic conception found lodgment in minds prepared by a mechanical economics, the last remaining vestiges of the old French romanticism were swept away; a benevolent, egocentric universe was become unthinkable; progress was no longer the inherent law of matter and of life; but instead, everywhere change, disintegration and reintegration, a ceaseless and purposeless flux to what final end the human mind could not forecast. Thus at a stroke the benevolent cosmos of the fathers, wherein for generations men had been providing themselves with sure refuges, was swept away; and with its passing passed the old faiths—faith in freedom of the will, in a purposive providence, in a universe that had been long in travail to bring forth man, its last and dearest offspring for whom all things work together for good. And with the decay of the traditional faiths the younger generation was left to wander as best it might upon the bleak tablelands of impersonal energy. Spencer's "ultimate of ultimates," the Permanence of Force, that follows the law of evolution and dissolution, had given way to Faraday's electro-energy that is indifferent to purpose.

The intellectual backgrounds were thus preparing for a gloomier realism than Howells's or Garland's, a realism that took its departure from two postulates: that men are physical beings who can do no other than obey the laws of a physical universe; and that in the vast indifferentism of nature they are inconsequential pawns in a game that to human reason has no meaning or rules. To assume that fate which rules human destiny is malignant, is to assume a cosmic interest in man which finds no justification in science; Man at best is only an inconsequential atom in a mechanical flux, or at worst, as Jurgen puts it picturesquely, only a bubble in fermenting swill. Such a conception, of course, made slow headway against the traditional order of thought; and if it had not been aided by a changing economics it would have found few to follow a line of reasoning that led to such unpleasant conclusions. The mind of the artist is more susceptible to concrete social fact than to abstract physical principle, and the swift centralizing of economics in the eighties and the nineties provided the stimulus for the extraordinary reversal of thought marked by the contrast between Emerson and Theodore Dreiser. Emerson was the apotheosis of two centuries of decentralization that destroyed the pessimism brought to the new world by refugees from the old, and found its inevitable expression in the exaltation of the individual, free and excellent, the child of a beneficent order; whereas Dreiser was the first spokesman of a later America once more falling within the shadow of the pessimism that springs from every centralized society shut up within the portals of a static economics; that dwarfs the individual and nullifies his will, reducing him from a child of God to a serf.

Oddly enough it was in the West that the new spirit first expressed itself most adequately; amidst a society that was taking its first steps away from the traditional philosophy of the dispersion. Frank Norris in California, Dreiser in Indiana, Sherwood Anderson in Ohio, Masters and Sandburg and Vachel Lindsay in Illinois, were the spokesmen of the resentment welling up in the American heart at the loss of the older freedom and individual dignity.*

* The manuscript ends here. The first section of this chapter was to be "Edwin Markham and 'The Man with the Hoe.'" The second was to be on "The Rise of Naturalism: Stephen Crane; Frank Norris." The first item of the addenda gives material on this subject and on the two authors. The third would have been " Fiction Discovers the City."—*Publisher.*

ADDENDA

THE material given here comes from various sources, as indicated by the notes. The syllabus referred to is that for Professor Parrington's lectures at the University of Washington, *The American Novel Since 1890* (1925). The order here follows that of the contents of this book.

ADDENDA

NATURALISM IN AMERICAN FICTION *

Naturalism originated in France. Term first used by Zola. Chief example—Flaubert's *Mme. Bovary*. Contrast between Zola and Flaubert reveals two diverse tendencies of the movement—a sociological study of background, with a multitude of characters dwarfed by the *milieu;* and psychological study of individual character.

Naturalism a child of nineteenth-century thought—offspring of Darwin, Marx, Comte, Taine. The scientific movement created a scientific attitude of mind and emphasized the law of causation. From this emerged two fruitful ideas: (1) biological determinism, (2) economic determinism. So Zola and Flaubert. Influence of Claude Bernard—"We take men from the hands of the physiologist solely . . . to solve scientifically the question of how men behave in society."

The criteria of naturalism are:

1. Objectivity. Seek the truth in the spirit of the scientist. "We naturalists, we men of science," Zola says, accepting Bernard's position, "we must admit of nothing occult; men are but phenomena and the conditions of phenomena."

2. Frankness. A rejection of Victorian reticence. The total man and woman must be studied —the deeper instincts, the endless impulses. The three strongest instincts are fear, hunger, sex. In the life of the ordinary person, the third is most critical, hence the naturalist makes much of it.

3. An amoral attitude toward material. The naturalist is not a judge, he holds no brief for any ethical standards. He records what happens. He "must possess a knowledge of the mechanisms inherent in man, show the machinery of his intellectual and sensory manifestations, under the influence of heredity and environment, such as physiology shall give them to us, and then finally, to exhibit man living in social conditions, produced by himself, which he modifies daily and in the heart of which he is undergoing constant transformation." (Zola.) This is difficult to accept. Puritanism.

* Notes for a lecture delivered at the University of California in 1922.—*Publisher.*

323

4. A philosophy of determinism. This is the vital principle of naturalism, setting it off from realism. The scientist has turned philosopher. It is the residuum of much pondering over life and its meaning, and may result from:

    a. Sociological emphasis—study of heredity and environment.

    b. A broader mechanistic philosophy—Flaubert, Dreiser.

    c. Fatalism: a world of malignant chance—Hardy.

5. A bias toward pessimism in selecting details. A reaction from the romantic conception of a purposive will.

Romance springs from the longings of a baffled and thwarted will, creating a world as we should like it wherein to find refuge. But the naturalist will tolerate no such refuge. He will envisage the truth, and the truth that he sees is that the individual is impotent in the face of things. Hence it is as the victim, the individual defeated by the world, and made a sardonic jest of, that the naturalist chooses to portray man. Always that conception creeps in. It is seen and felt throughout the texture of the story—a fate lurking in the background and visible to the reader—and at some dramatic moment the conviction comes home to the victim and is crystallized in bitter words wrenched from his baffled will. The business of the story is to lead him up to this crystallization.

There are two main forms—(1) Life is a trap. (2) Life is mean. So Strindberg's Countess Julie: "Everything is wreckage, that drifts over the water until it sinks, sinks." So Ray Pearson in Sherwood Anderson's *Winesburg, Ohio:* "Tricked, by Gad, tricked by life and made a fool of." So D. H. Lawrence: "We are prostituted, oh, prostituted by life." To Ma Westcott "Life is duty. It is a lie." This pressure may come from without—*milieu*—or from within—imperious desires—but the outcome is usually hopeless sorrow—sometimes stolid resignation, sometimes fierce protest, but with no other end than annihilation. An exception is Maugham's *Of Human Bondage.*

6. A bias in selection of characters. The naturalist commonly chooses one of three types:

    a. Characters of marked physique and small intellectual activity —persons of strong animal drives. They range all the way from morons like Norris's McTeague, Zola's Nana, and Dreiser's Jennie Gerhardt to natures like Hardy's Tess, and Sallie in *Of Human Bondage.*

    b. Characters of excited, neurotic temperament, at the mercy of moods, driven by forces that they do not stop to analyze. Such are Strindberg's Countess Julie, Sue, Emma Bovary, and the hero in *Of Human Bondage*. Sometimes this is aggravated by some physical defect, like a club-foot.

c. An occasional use of a strong character whose will is broken. Thus Hardy's Jude and the doctor in Strindberg's *By the Open Sea*. But such are comparatively infrequent.

Naturalism is pessimistic realism, with a philosophy that sets man in a mechanical world and conceives of him as victimized by that world. *Certain unconscious exaggerations of naturalism.* Since men are victimized either by outer forces—the *milieu*—or by inner drives—impulses and instincts—the naturalist from much brooding is subject to certain temptations:

1. From concern over a devastating *milieu* he may end in desiring to change that *milieu* to the end that men may achieve happiness. Hence he tends to lose his objectivity and scientific detachment, and becomes a partisan to a cause. Such was the fate of Zola. The philosopher of naturalism, in practice he abandoned his principles and became a reformer, attacking the church, the capitalistic order, etc. His *J'accuse* letter is characteristic of this. *Nana*, almost alone, preserves the naturalistic attitude. This was the failure of the first group of American naturalists—Frank Norris, Robert Herrick, Jack London.

2. From much study of inner drives of low-grade characters the naturalist is in danger of creating grotesques. Behavioristic psychology may prove to be a further temptation, in creating a "sex complex." So Masters's *Spoon River Anthology*, Sherwood Anderson, D. H. Lawrence, Frank Norris. Most common in the later American naturalists. So Brander Matthews.

3. From much emphasis on animal impulses the naturalist may turn man into an animal. Men are more than sex-driven creatures—the city is more than the slums. There are sewers, but why not accept the sewer without messing over its contents as they flow to disintegration? This is the commonest objection to naturalism. So Meredith: "The naturalist sees the hog in nature, and takes nature for the hog." It is certainly an overcorrection—a reaction against the complacent optimism of romanticism—against too much shutting of the eyes to slums and filth and sewers. To a mechanist like Dreiser, who traces life and conduct back to chemistry, or to the behaviorist, who traces it to ducts and glands, it is

rational. The charge may be true of Zola, of De Maupassant, of Anderson, of Lawrence, but it is not true of Hardy, of Maugham.

Naturalism and the Conception of Tragedy. Naturalistic books are almost inevitably tragedies, but the philosophy of naturalism that underlies them has played havoc with the Aristotelian conception of tragedy. As Ludwig Lewisohn says, it has "rendered the traditional principle of tragedy wholly archaic." According to the Aristotelian tradition, tragedy results when an essentially noble character of heroic proportions transgresses an immutable moral law by a self-originating will and suffers the punishment dealt by poetic justice. So Macbeth, Othello, Lear, Hamlet. But this assumes two thing: (1) an eternally changeless moral law; (2) the existence of a purposive will. Both of these the naturalist refuses to accept. Compare Hardy.

It became clear that the self-originating element in human action is small. The individual acts in harmony with his character, which is largely the result of complex and uncontrollable causes. It became even clearer that among the totality of moral values an absolute validity can be assigned to a few only. Hence the basic conception of tragic guilt was undermined from within and from without. The transgression of an immutable moral law by a self-originating will was seen to be an essentially meaningless conception, since neither eternally changeless moral law nor an uncaused volition is to be found in the universe that we perceive.[1]

The tragedy of naturalism lies in the disintegration and the pity or irony with which we contemplate man and his fate in the world.

Naturalism and the Traditional American Temper. The two most characteristic qualities of the American temper are Puritanism and optimism—the belief in the supremacy of the moral law, and the conviction that this is a good world that man shapes to his will. This is to be explained historically: the former is traditionally English, the latter a product of new-world economics—a decentralized society. Pessimistic determinism results inevitably from the sense of social pressure on the individual. Social complexity entails a feeling of coercive regimentation by forces too strong to contend against. These forces are both internal and external: environment or the social machine; heredity or the physical machine. The most complete dwarfing of the individual will and significance takes place in the most crowded societies, producing a corresponding philosophy and psychology. So the fatalism of the Orient and the dream of

[1] Ludwig Lewisohn, *Modern Drama*, New York, 1915, p. 3.

Nirvana. The first widespread philosophy of determinism among English people was spread by Calvinism. Predestination was an alien thought, the last expression of a world depressed by Roman regimentation and degeneration. Augustine preached that men are evil, and men are doomed. This old-world dogma was brought to America, where regimentation was impossible. A free economics created a free-will philosophy and psychology. The will to succeed. This flowered in Emerson. Philosophical optimism. The world is good, man is good: let him stand upon his instincts and there abide and the whole world will come round to him. "Trust thyself." Since Emerson's time a new world has been emerging. The old shadow is falling across the American mind. Determinism is in the air.

Complexity and American Determinism. Complexity springs from:

1. Machine industrialism. The bigness of the economic machine dwarfs the individual and creates a sense of impotency.

2. The great city reduces the individual to a unit. By machine methods of transportation and quantity output individual differences are worn away. We dress, live, think, work, play, alike. The *Saturday Evening Post* is fast regimenting the American mind. Standardization.

3. Centralization of wealth is creating a caste regimentation.

4. A mechanistic psychology. Behaviorism: stimulus and response; ducts and glands. The individual conceived as a mechanism driven by instincts and habits.

America today is the greatest, most complex machine the world has ever known. Individualism is giving way to regimentation, caste, standardization. Optimism is gone; pessimism is on the horizon. The psychology of naturalism is being prepared.

Three American writers began an experiment in naturalism in the middle nineties—Stephen Crane, Frank Norris, and Harold Frederic. The early death of all three stopped the movement, which was speedily overwhelmed by the romantic deluge and the muckraking zeal. Crane was tubercular and died at twenty-nine; Norris was cut down in the early thirties; Harold Frederic removed to England, where he died.

I

STEPHEN CRANE *

Stephen Crane was the genius of his generation. His work began
with *Maggie: A Girl of the Streets* (1893). "It was the first bit of
naturalism in American letters . . . an episodic bit of slum fiction
ending with the tragic quality of Greek drama." "The first ironical
novel ever written by an American." It was privately printed at
first, and not published until 1896. It is detached, objective,
amoral, dealing with a world without virtues but tyrannized by
taboos. It is a bit of life, beginning and ending casually. Here is
the end:

> In a room a woman sat at a table, eating like a fat monk in a picture.
> A soiled, unshaven man pushed open the door and entered.
> "Well," said he, "Mag's dead." [2]

It is a world without virtue and yet one that uses the social
taboo to condemn Mag—the only pure one of the lot. The story
was an attack on everything that was respectable in American literature—a notable achievement in a world of shoddy romanticism.
It was an affront to every instinct of the genteel tradition, and was
rejected by a public steeped in that same shoddy romanticism.

Crane's next novel was the first great American war story—
The Red Badge of Courage (1894). It was a *tour de force*, inspired
by Zola's *Le débâcle*, but more by Tolstoi—*War and Peace* and
perhaps *Sebastopol*. The individual is caught between the external
war machine and the inner instinct machine. There is a conflict of
impulses—fear, pride, the instinct of self-preservation, chiefly the
fear of fear. The hero is at the mercy of the crowd psychology and
blind chance. Crane follows Tolstoi in assuming that victories are
accidents, the outcome of a blind clash of unintelligent forces,
rather than due to strategy and generalship. The study is psychological—that of the fear of the recruit, his feeling that he alone is
marked as the target of the enemy. The impression of helplessness
is the same as in *Maggie*—both are atoms among a host of other
atoms.

Short Stories. The best are "The Blue Hotel," "The Experiment
in Misery," "The Open Boat." The first is a story of social responsibility and social guilt. The murder of the Swede is just part

* From lecture notes and the syllabus.—*Publisher.*
[2] Stephen Crane, *Works*, New York, 1926, Vol. 10, p. 216.

of the backwash of a topsy-turvy life: the victim of things. "Every sin is the result of a collaboration." The second is a story of a "hobo"—down-and-outer, who hears "the war of the city in his ear." "The protest of the wretch who feels the touch of the imperturbable granite wheels, and who then cries with an impersonal eloquence, with a strength not from him, giving voice to the wail of a whole section, a class, a people." [3]

2

FRANK NORRIS *

The most stimulating and militant of our early naturalists—the only one who wrote consciously with a definite creed. He had thought out a naturalistic philosophy under the inspiration of Zola. "He was never without a yellow paper-covered novel of Zola in his hand," wrote his brother of him. His two chief novels reveal the twin tendencies as revealed in *Nana* and *Le débâcle:* The study of the individual in his reaction to environment, and the study of social forces and their impact upon a group of related individuals.

His Work. Falls into three groups: (1) Romance—*Blix, Moran of the Lady Letty*; (2) Naturalism—*McTeague, Vandover and the Brute;* (3) *The Pit* and *A Deal in Wheat.* Between the two latter groups stands *The Octopus.* The dates of the earlier works uncertain. Commonly believed that Norris began as a romantic and worked out of it slowly. Another view that he wrote romances as a means of arriving, side by side with his serious work. Thus he seems to have begun *McTeague* about 1894—although it was not published till 1899.

Theory. His passion for truth more ardent—or more noisy—than Crane's: his objectivity less. The strong conviction of a deterministic universe was on him, but he never quite attained the scientific detachment. His nature large and eager. Like Zola he loved large canvases. This induced him rather to the sociological than to the individualistic study. *The Octopus* more representative of his genius than *McTeague.* Man in society, his theme: not mere men and women as ends in themselves. This grew on him—the second phase. The novelist must deal "with elemental forces, motives that stir whole nations. These cannot be handled as abstractions in fiction. . . . The social tendencies must be ex-

[3] *Ibid.,* Vol. II, p. 21.   * Lecture notes.—*Publisher.*

pressed by means of an analysis of the characters of the men and women who compose that society, and the two must be combined and manipulated to evolve the purpose—to find the value of x."[4] Above all, avoid propaganda.

Unskillfully treated, the story may dwindle down and degenerate into mere special pleading, and the novelist becomes a polemicist, a pamphleteer, forgetting that although his first consideration is to prove his case, his *means* must be living human beings, not statistics, and that his tools are not figures, but pictures of life as he sees it. . . .

Consider the reverse—*Fécondité*, for instance. The purpose for which Zola wrote the book ran away with him. He really did care more for the depopulation of France than he did for his work. Result—sermons on the fruitfulness of women, special pleading, a farrago of dry, dull incidents, overburdened and collapsing under the weight of a theme that should have intruded only indirectly.[5]

He never quite arrives at the amoral attitude. Ethical values persist in intruding themselves, sometimes quite incidentally, as in *McTeague*, but increasingly, as in *The Octopus* and *The Pit*.

"McTEAGUE"

Dedicated to Gates. The first considerable contribution to naturalism by an American writer. His carefully written work over which he labored five years.

Theme. A study in character disintegration that follows upon economic pressure. The unmaking of a man and woman by the caprice of events. The characters are simple. McTeague is heavy and stupid, slow in his movements but a blind bull when aroused. Trina neat and pretty but with unhappy potentialities in her thrift. In neither is there a will-to-power strong enough to give strength of character.

The Note of Determinism. A world of chance that victimizes them. The note struck by the lottery and the $5,000. By chance McTeague became a dentist, met Trina, proposed. But the chance that was making a man of him and a woman of Trina was preparing their downfall through Marcus Schouler. The wrestling-match was the turning-point. The two disintegrate together, each aggravating the weakness of the other. As Trina's neatness was pulling Mac up and making him self-respecting, so her thrift grew into miserli-

---

[4] *The Responsibilities of the Novelist*, "The Novel with a 'Purpose,' " Garden City, N. Y., 1928, Vol. 7, p. 22.
[5] *Ibid.*, p. 22.

ness under pressure of his failure to provide, and this embittered the essentially fair and generous nature of Mac.

Inner Drives. Little sex in the book after the first complication. Both Mac and Trina caught unexpectedly, yet handled differently. The latter pure naturalism. "The Woman is awakened, and, starting from her sleep, catches blindly at what first the newly awakened eyes light upon. It is a spell, a witchery, ruled by chance alone, inexplicable—a fairy queen enamored of a clown with ass's ears." [6] But in McTeague, oddly enough, the same instinct is judged and pronounced evil. Norris abandons the amoral attitude and argues that heritage from the lower life is evil. It is the weeds that spring up and stifle, as in Sherwood Anderson's "Seeds."

Below the fine fabric of all that was good in him ran the foul stream of hereditary evil, like a sewer. The vices and sins of his father and his father's father, to the third and fourth and five hundredth generation, tainted him. The evil of an entire race flowed in his veins. Why should it be? He did not desire it. Was he to blame? [7]

The entire handling of sex in Trina, from the first frightened yielding to the later docile submission to Mac's brutality, his sadism, is admirably handled from the point of view of modern psychology. Norris was not a psychologist but in this he succeeded surprisingly.

Romantic Elements. Yet even in this severe study Norris has yielded to his romantic tendencies.

1. His patent effort to give dramatic unity to the whole through the symbol of gold. An exaggeration that is almost Dickens-like, with its warping singleness. The gold tooth, the $5,000, Trina's twenty-dollar gold pieces, the imaginary gold plate of Maria Macapa, the absurd canary in the gilt cage, the discovery of the gold mine. The wonder is that he didn't give Trina gold hair instead of black.

2. The use of a minor action: Maria Macapa and old Zerkow. The same pursuit of a phantom and the same outcome in murder. McTeague and Trina are real; Maria and Zerkow are grotesques.

3. The use of foils: Old Grannis and Miss Baker. Justified in romantic literature by contrast. The self-effacing, timid drawing together contrasted with the brute directness of McTeague. They do not marry, and preserve their dream world.

[6] Frank Norris, *Complete Works*, New York, n. d., Vol. III, p. 58.
[7] *Ibid.*, p. 22.

4. The use of the revenge motive: Marcus Schouler—the dramatic pursuit into Death Valley and the end.

"VANDOVER AND THE BRUTE"

An unfinished work—but a huge and terrible torso.

Theme. Revealed in the title. The two natures of man and the sloughing-off of the higher till the wolf is left. Done with a terrible directness, till the naked man is on all fours, padding up and down in his room. A grim and sordid theme but not quite achieved. The thing got away from him. If he had chiseled it as he chiseled *McTeague*, holding it off objective and amoral, it would have been a tremendous piece. But it is insufficiently motivated.

Determinism. A study in will. Vandover set over against Charlie Geary and Dolly Haight. The latter a victim of momentary weakness; the former a victim of constitutional pliability. A sensuous egotism that grows and consumes. Geary alone survives—the egoist who drives forward ruthlessly. A study of the slow, long descent—a chain of circumstances that finally binds him hand and foot. His props knocked away one by one—partly by fate, partly by himself: his father, the girl whom he loves, his concern for respectable opinion, his art, his money. The conclusion intensely dramatic—more so than the romance of *McTeague*.

The comment of Garland on *McTeague* applies equally to *Vandover:* "What avail is this study of sad lives? for it does not even lead to a notion of social betterment." His interest is "not that of the ethical teacher."

"THE OCTOPUS"

McTeague and *Vandover* are of the city and its sordid evil ways. They are studies in psychology. *The Octopus* is of the great California valleys and the evils that have come into the farm life with the railroad. It is a study in economics—the first of a long series of such studies. One can easily see how the theme caught the imagination of Norris, how his mind felt the relief from the narrow world and sordid wretchedness of *Vandover*. A certain magnificence in Norris responded to the epic breadth of the valleys—they fired his imagination—the vast sweep and power of nature: the rich soil, the brilliant sun that lays its palpitating heat upon the land, the quick response in flowers and fruit. The land is eager to produce; its fruitfulness is overpowering. There is an epic sweep of life and reproduction here; and this epic of the soil is linked with the tragedy wrought by the Southern Pacific—the economic machinery of man's making. The facts were well known and they took hold of Norris's imagination. His sympathy is aroused and yet instead of attacking the railroad he weaves it into his deterministic philosophy.

Theme. Ostensibly the wheat. Norris planned a huge trilogy of its growing (*The Octopus*), marketing (*The Pit*), consumption (*The Wolf*—never written). In reality, the impotence of unimportant individuals in the struggle with things as they are. In *The Octopus* the individual is dwarfed by the vast spaces, he is crumpled and despoiled by the railroad. The flock of sheep destroyed by the train is only a symbol of the men and women of the valley, under the wheels of modern industrialism.

Action. A huge canvas with crowding figures and abundant action. "The canvas swarms with actualities—plowing, planting, harvesting, sheep-herding, merry-making, rabbit-killing, love, labor, birth, death"—all keyed high and swept into a palpitating background. A "strongly interwrought group of episodes," that fall into certain series of developments too:

1. The atrophy of Magnus Derrick, which might well be a story in itself.

2. The development of Annixter, "out of an absolute, yet not gross, materiality," through the love of Hilma Tree; and then their final annihilation.

3. A host of background characters—supernumeraries—that give a sense of epic sweep.

The Note of Romance. The riot of color, of life, arouse the latent romance of his nature. He cannot remain detached but projects himself into the story in the person of Vanamee. He returns to the use of the symbol as in *McTeague*—the wheat. He allows his villain to perish melodramatically. How much more convincing is the figure of Charlie Geary setting Vandover to work than S. Behrman in the hold of the vessel.

In the end he abandons the amoral attitude. After proclaiming the doctrine of determinism—that the railroads are the masters—not the puppets of men—he takes refuge in a moral order. In the large balance, the wheat remains, rectifying wrong—saving other lives to make good what it here destroys. "The larger view always and through all shams, all wickednesses, discovers the Truth that

will, in the end, prevail, and all things, surely, inevitably, resist-
lessly, work together for good." [8] Nevertheless in contemplating
the injustice done by the railroads, Norris neither demands nor
expects relief.

The Octopus exemplifies Norris' theory of broad-scale work. It
"draws conclusions from a whole congeries of forces, social development, race impulses." It "devotes itself not to the study of men
but of man."

. . . .

SIDNEY LANIER *

An original nature. Rejects both the genteel tradition and the
ideals of the rising middle class. An artist to whom life means
beauty.

He revivifies nature—is almost pagan in his adoration of the
beauty of the sun and water. A half-personification of the sun-
myth. He is essentially religious. To Longfellow and Tennyson
nature is pretty embroidery; to Emerson it is a dwelling-place of
the oversoul; to Lanier it is an object of adoration. See "The
Marshes of Glynn."

He attacks industrialism—the first of the poets to cry out against
it as a deadly blight on life and civilization. See "Corn," "The
Symphony," "The Jacquerie."

He seeks a new religion, recognizing a quantitative element.

[8] Frank Norris, *The Octopus*, New York, 1906, p. 652.
* Lecture notes.—*Publisher.*

THE INCOMPARABLE MR. CABELL *

The successive volumes of James Branch Cabell have provided the tribe of critical Jeffries with a rich vein of diversion. They have recognized no closed season in their full-lunged pursuit of the strange heirs of Mr. Cabell's invention, and such Homeric absurdities of comment have been flung at him, that he is in a fair way to become our classic example of the fatuousness of contemporary estimates. As whimsical as Bernard Shaw, as provocative as Chesterton, he is more incomprehensible than either to all readers who do not choose to like what they have not always liked. Professing to be a romancer, and defending the glory of romance with inimitable witchery of phrase, he writes no romance that lovers of convention can understand. The lovely fabrics of his tales of Poictesme are all shimmer and sheen, woven of magic and veiling mysteries, instead of the correct taffeta and grosgrain; and the brilliant stuff of his tales of gallantry is fashioned of wit and poetry, instead of the customary wigs and sword play. Those to whom romance suggests *When Knighthood Was in Flower*, will find only obscurities and coarseness in *Figures of Earth* (1921) and *Jurgen* (1919, *enl*. ed. 1921); and those who delight in the stage rufflings of *Monsieur Beaucaire*, will discover only a libertine in *The Cords of Vanity* (1909, rev. ed. 1920). And if the reader boggles at such tales what can he hope to make of that strange, ironical whimsy, *The Cream of the Jest* (1917, rev. ed. 1922)? One needs to walk warily in dealing with Mr. Cabell, or the jest of which he is such a master will turn sardonically upon the critic. In all his thinking vague hinterlands lie behind the commonplace, cryptic meanings lurk behind the obvious; and the credulous, easy-going reader finds himself puzzled, and at last floundering quite hopelessly in a land of bogs and marsh-lights. And yet was ever another writer born to us Americans so insistent upon being understood? He has elaborated his views of life and art at length, and repeated them in successive volumes over nearly a score of years; and finally in what may have been a mood of sheer disgust at the stupidity of those who buy books, he reëlaborated his philosophy and wrote it out in good

* Reprinted by permission from *The Pacific Review*, December, 1921.—*Publisher*.

set terms within the covers of a single volume. *Beyond Life* is an essay altogether remarkable for its haunting beauty of phrase, its honest agnosticism, its brooding irony. It is enough to turn one cynic to consider that so noble a book should have called forth from a reputable gentleman, presumably of good taste and sound judgment, the comment that it "contains cheap and shallow pessimistic observations on human limitations."

That *Beyond Life* (1919), with other of Mr. Cabell's books, contains "observations on the limitations of human nature," is quite obvious; for Mr. Cabell deals in comedy, and what is to become of comedy if it shall not observe those limitations and laugh at them? That it is even pessimistic may likewise be argued with some plausibility; but to assert that it is cheap and shallow is preposterous. An inquisitive mind, deeply concerned with ultimate values, cannot be cheap and shallow. And yet the fault of such widespread misinterpretation may lie in part at Mr. Cabell's own doorstep. An inveterate jester, his sallies often carry implications far beyond the obvious; his strange whimsies spring from depths of thought and emotion beyond the understanding of the careless. His attitude towards life is an odd mixture of the modern and the medieval: there is a medieval simplicity and frankness, a naïve wonder at the mystery that underlies the common, an incorrigible idealism; and this medieval attitude is drenched in modern agnosticism. He passes easily from a broad Chaucerian humor that laughs frankly at the relations of men and women, to a mystical idealization of those relations; and the problem of reconciling the humor and the ideal becomes a serious business with him. He hates the cant and dishonesty of our *bourgeois* existence, and he refuses to take seriously the host of petty concerns that most of us are very serious about. If he were less the artist he would join the disaffected and turn to rend this foolish world; but the spirit of comedy saves him and he contents himself with a jest. But the Cabellian jest uncovers depths of meditation that reveal the philosopher and the poet. In his own large meaning of the word Mr. Cabell is an economist. He is greatly dissatisfied with the "futile body-wasting," which under the "dynamic illusion known as common sense" passes for life, and is concerned to discover what abiding increment a man may get from his body during its brief existence as an entity. His mind is haunted with a sense of realities that lie beneath the surface appearances, and that insist on trickling from his pen in strange comments. It is a careless reader who is deceived or put off the scent by his whimsical vocabulary, who insists on conventional meanings for words which Mr. Cabell chooses to use otherwise than conventional persons use them. Romance and realism—words with which he plays constantly and upon which he hangs his philosophy—do not signify the spurious romance of childish minds, or the shoddy realism of practical minds. If one must insist upon translating his vocabulary into ordinary terms, let us understand that to Mr. Cabell romance and realism mean idealism and conventionalism; and to the profound distinction between these two attitudes towards life, he dedicates his work.

I have called Mr. Cabell a poet, and the justification lies in his persistent idealization of life in terms of beauty. At his birth he was endowed by an unkind fate with imagination. Now imagination may be a very pretty and amiable gift, highly useful for gilding one's egoism, putting honey in thistles, proving itself practical by arraying life in gay robes in order that it may seem an altogether lovely and desirable mistress; or it may prove a decidedly parlous faculty to play with. It can summon bogies, and terrors that are vaster and more real than bogies. A brooding imagination can work havoc with one's complacency. When Carlyle was in a mood to enjoy his nerves he would let his imagination range beyond the comfortable confines of convention, to consider the universe and the position of man therein—the black flow of time and the terrifying immensity of background against which man is set; and he would come back to dinner with Jane Welsh Carlyle with a sick stomach and an ill temper. It was not very gallant, but it was very natural to a man unnerved by what he had contemplated. Considered with open eyes reality is too overpowering for weak man, and because he could not relieve the tension with a jest, Carlyle's imagination inflicted chronic dyspepsia upon him. To conventional persons the dyspepsia and Jane Welsh Carlyle's sharp replies to her husband's ill humor, seem the important reality, and the overpowering visions of time and space that were at the root of the family discord, seem no other than romance. In this curious world of convention all things are topsy-turvy, and it needs a tremendous effort of will to set them only a little right.

To this effort Mr. Cabell's life work has been dedicated with unruffled urbanity. Like Carlyle he chooses to roam far in his philosophic quests, and like Thoreau he comes home at nightfall

with little more than a handful of stardust in his wallet. He loves
to sally forth on the greatest of adventures—the pursuit of reality
where it lies broadcast, hidden from practical eyes that refuse to
see. He is impelled by the old-wonder that has haunted men from
the beginning of their long upward climb; the wonder and the fear
of life. Now to anyone but a fool or a poet, only too plainly life is
petty and gross and inconsequential, from the moment when with
superfluous blood and pain we are brought into the world, to the
time when we return by an unlovely process to chemical elements.
It is compounded of vanity, as the old poet long ago observed.
The practical, about which we make so much pother and over which
we chatter so foolishly, is only an illusion which men hug because
it keeps them in self-conceit. Mr. Cabell refuses to accept any such
illusions at their face value. He will not be humbugged by foolish
persons who pretend to talk wisely. What is man? he insists on
asking: A parasite on the thin rind of a planet that swings silently
through interstellar space—"an ape who chatters to himself of
kinship with the archangels while filthily he digs for groundnuts."
If this is the reality to which the philosopher must come finally—
and like Hamlet Mr. Cabell does not shirk the contemplation of
graveyard facts—then must the thoughtful man accept logically
a frank pessimism, and on this foundation build such a hut as may
best shelter him for the few days of his unintelligible life. Over this
sorry conclusion Mr. Cabell broods much, and because he is a
human being with a will to enjoy life and think well of himself, he
uses every faculty to scramble out of the pit and find a pleasanter
refuge for the brief time of his existence. The idealist in him
engages the pessimist, and like so many other moderns he goes out
in quest of that which may keep him sane. It is true that man is an
ape reft of his tail and grown rusty at climbing, but is that the
whole story? It is evident that men in all times have refused to
believe that they are not something other than apes—their very
dreams seem to belie a conclusion so mean and ignoble. Is there not
some deeper *élan vital*, some hidden impulse that drives man forward and upward even while his mind is on groundnuts? "Yet
more clearly do I perceive," argues the idealist, "that this same
man is a maimed god. . . . He is under penalty condemned to
compute eternity with false weights and to estimate infinity with a
yardstick; and he very often does it. . . . There lies the choice
which every man must make—or rationally to accept his own

limitations? or stupendously to play the fool and swear that he is at will omnipotent."

This would seem to be a hard choice, but Mr. Cabell does not hesitate. He patches up his agnosticism with the will to believe, on the pragmatic grounds that it seems to work. For man "rationally to accept his own limitations," is to defeat everything worth while in life; it is to yield the battle to a black pessimism. Whereas "stupendously to play the fool and swear that he is at will omnipotent," may end in creating the will to omnipotence, and the fool in some preposterous fashion may prove that he is indeed divine. Let man but accept his logical limitations and he returns to the ape reft of more than his tail, fallen to gibbering in the mud, refusing to take hold of that rope of sand by which miraculously he has drawn himself forward hitherto. For accepting his limitations means contenting himself with material fact, and "the trouble with facts seems to be, that if one treats them out of relation to the rest of life, they become lies." In the "stupefying mist of common sense" men walk blindly. The practical, the conventional, are alien to the deeper reality which is shadowed forth by emotions and dreams; which refuses to disclose itself nakedly, but hides behind symbols, haunting the mind even while one is pottering among inconsequentials. This deeper reality itself may be but a dream, but nevertheless it possesses the power of creating a will to believe, upon which hangs man's destiny. Hence the tales which we tell ourselves are significant because through some occult process they foreshadow the thing that may be; they prod the foolish will to omnipotence to believe that we shall outgrow the ape. For grown rusty at climbing, the ape-man "however dimly, feels himself to be a symbol, and the frail representative of Omnipotence in a place that is not home; and so strives blunderingly, from mystery to mystery, with pathetic makeshifts, not understanding anything, greedy in all desires, and honeycombed with poltroonery, and yet ready to give all, and to die fighting, for the sake of that undemonstrable idea."

It is because he is terrified at the meanness of what practical men call reality, that Mr. Cabell turns away from it to find the true life in dreams. Not only are they pleasanter, they are more useful; they are all that man has to aid him in the appalling task of getting himself out of the slime, that he may walk in green fields. We need to turn Prospero's words around—our dreams are such

stuff as we are made on. They alone are real and salutary, for
amid all their ramblings they seem dimly to suggest some end;
amidst their rank egoisms they seem to foreshadow a purpose: and
may not that end and purpose be the eventual creation of a life for
man that shall be worthy of his dreams? It is illogical to assume
that man can pull himself up by his own bootstraps, but how else
shall he pull himself up? Is not man the inveterate romancer somehow blindly creating a noble romance of man? "To what does the
whole business tend?" he asks at the conclusion of *Beyond Life*,
"—why, how in heaven's name should I know? We can but be
content to note that all goes forward, toward something. . . . It
may be that we are nocturnal creatures perturbed by rumors of a
dawn which comes inevitably, as prologue to a day wherein we and
our children have no part whatever. It may be that when our
arboreal propositus descended from his palm tree and began to walk
upright about the earth, his progeny were forthwith committed
to a journey in which today is only a way-station. Yet I prefer
to take it that we are components of an unfinished world, and
that we are but as seething atoms which ferment toward its making, if merely because man as he now exists can hardly be the
finished product of any Creator whom one could very heartily
revere. We are being made into something quite unpredictable, I
imagine: and through the purging and the smelting, we are sustained by an instinctive knowledge that we are being made into
something better. For this we know, quite incommunicably, and
yet as surely as we know that we will have it thus. And it is this
will that stirs in us to have the creatures of earth and the affairs of
earth, not as they are, but 'as they ought to be,' which we call
romance. But when we note how visibly it sways all life we perceive that we are talking about God."

From this persistent will to romance—the incorrigible propensity
to follow the dynamic illusion of dreams that is so deep an instinct
of human nature—Mr. Cabell deduces a conception of art that to
careless readers seems whimsically perverse; and from it likewise
emerges the lambent irony that plays like diffused lightning about
the horizons of his thought. The function of art in society, he
insists, is to comfort and inspire man with its divine beauty.
Without the artist this is but a grim and forbidding place where
men live; and unless every man is somewhat the artist, and seeks
his compensations in the lure of romance, it must remain grim and

forbidding. It is therefore the privilege and the duty of the artist "to prevaricate tenderly about the universe"; to create for life a meaning that is not apparent, by clothing it in beauty and adducing for it a noble significance. It is his mission to lure men away from the contemplation of facts which terrify or debase, from all ignoble and depressing realism, to pursue the ideal and entice the imagination to enter and dwell in a world as it ought to be. The artist, therefore, is a Moses in the wilderness, pointing men to the Promised Land, and even enabling them to go forward and taste its fruits while they still dwell in the wilderness.

Now of all the dreams which lure men, the one universal and potent dream, Mr. Cabell asserts with Freudian understanding, is the woman dream. Its roots are deep in the ape-animal; it drives men inexorably, for upon it depends the very existence of the race. And therefore, a shrewd mother-nature has somehow transmuted its base materials into the very stuff of romance, commingling with it all high and generous impulses, making of it the loveliest dream that visits man's weak head. In consequence of which ironic transmutation this lovely dream "hoodwinks humanity through the dynamic illusion known as love, in order that humanity may endure, and the groans of a lover be perpetuated in the wails of an infant." Considered in one light this is the very "cream of the jest" that nature perpetrates upon man; but considered in another light, does it not turn out to be the supreme jest which man has perpetrated upon nature? For once he has been taught the alphabet of romance, through the crude necessity of race preservation, he has gone far in his studies, and turned romancer on a great scale. From this raw material of biological sex-love he has woven the fabrics of his religion, of his art, of his idealism; he has dipped it in gleaming dyes, twisted it to quaint patterns, fashioned from it lovely robes to cover what is ugly. It is the wellspring and source of all romance.

Through this open door of woman-worship Mr. Cabell chooses to enter his world of deeper realities. "There is in every human being that which demands communion with something more fine and potent than itself," and this something more fine and potent he seeks in the woman of his dreams. It was so when the world was young, and it will be so as long as there is youth left in the world. In early times this object of adoration was the witch-woman, the Circes and Calypsos of ancient tales; later it became the lady-mistress of chivalric ideals; today it is the dream maiden whom the young man woos but never finds in marriage, and not finding her is impelled to turn to the ever-young and ever-lovely Helens and Ettarres of old romance. A good half of Mr. Cabell's work is given over to this curious celebration of woman-worship. It is elaborated in *Domnei* (1920), in *Jurgen*, in *Figures of Earth*. In the strange tales of the land of Poictesme the drama flows from the balking and thwarting of this woman quest by the Dame Niafers and Dame Lisas of the commonplace world, to man's undoing. Nevertheless "the long, high, fruitless questing does not ever end, but, rather, is temporarily remitted for the society of Dame Niafer and of Dame Lisa. For . . . one perceives that, even in remote Poictesme, those aging nympholepts, Dom Manuel and Jurgen—they also—were heartened to endure the privileges of happily married persons by a sure faith, discreetly left unvoiced, that these hard-won, fond, wearisome, and implacable wives were, after all, just temporary makeshifts. By and by would Freydis and Helen return, at their own season."—For the dream persists in the very face of present fact, and in this lies man's hope. "In youth all men that live have been converts if but in transitory allegiance, to that religion of the world's youth—to the creed of *domnei*, or woman-worship." Now it is "the very essence of *domnei*, that the woman one loves is providentially set between the lover's apprehension and God, as the mobile and vital image and corporeal reminder of Heaven, as a quick symbol of beauty and holiness, of purity and perfection. In her the lover views all qualities which can be comprehended by merely human faculties." "If but in honor, his heart stays bound to his first and only real love, that woman of whom he never tires. Her coming is not yet. He can but wait, sustained by his sure faith . . . that some day her glory will be apparent, and he will enter gladly into her secret kingdom, and will find her kisses all that in youth he foreknew to be not impossible. . . . And meanwhile this prescience, somehow, informs all art . . . and makes it to him a vital thing. . . . And there seems to be no beauty in the world save those stray hints of her, whose ultimate revealment is not yet. . . . And it is very often through desire to express his faith in this withheld perfection, of which he has been conscious in broken glimpses from afar, that he turns artist. . . . For every art is a confession of faith in that which is not yet."

But however adroitly man has turned the jest against nature, and erected a noble palace from base materials, the jest remains, mixed with the mortar, and the structure cannot endure for long. It is insubstantial, and at any moment the cloud-capped towers may disintegrate and the dream palace disappear, leaving not a rack behind. There remains only the jest. This unhappy ending Mr. Cabell foresees, and hence emerges the profound irony that underlies all his writing. To such disillusionment must all things come. Life is no more than a comedy, played by puppets; bitter, with more tears than laughter in it; yet because tears are futile and unnerving, what remains for the gallant gentleman but to confront life with a jest? Mr. Cabell does not wholly forego his chivalric ideal even while he is contemplating the vanity of all endings in the light of their beginnings. As Horvendile the clerk, he clings to it, even though he is doomed to walk the streets of Lichfield, Virginia, in the form of Felix Kennaston, who passes—to his own incredulous amusement—as a personage of some importance, with two automobiles and money in four banks. He possesses the magic sigil of Scoteia, by the potency of which he can send forth his soul to meet Ettarre, and recover the raptures that Felix Kennaston no longer knows. But the sigil of Scoteia turns out to be the half-top of a pomade glass from his wife's dressing-table; the potency is gone; and he remains at last no more than a respectable citizen with his automobiles and money in four banks. *The Cream of the Jest* reduces the chivalric ideal to pure irony.

By a transition more natural, perhaps, to a Virginian than to another American, Mr. Cabell turns from the contemplation of chivalry to the study of gallantry; and shifts the theme of his romances from the ecstatic adoration of the Woman, whom to possess is to lose, to the gay pursuit and enjoyment of women. In "The Rivet in Grandfather's Neck" he chooses to set a decidedly shabby and roué gallantry over against a somewhat futile and antiquated southern chivalry. He loves both the gallant and the gentleman, and he spares neither; they are equally the descendants of that Cavalier ideal which flourished so rankly in the soil of the old planter society; nevertheless the quaint and lovable Rudolph Musgrave with his gentle heroics comes off distinctly better than his brilliant half-brother, the novelist John Charteris. One might, indeed, wonder at Mr. Cabell's treatment of the artist Charteris, were it not so distinctly Shavian. It is odd how similar is his conception of the artist to the definition of Shaw—one who wriggles into the confidence of women to learn their secrets only to betray them. Nevertheless Jack Charteris, the brilliant thinker and talker of *Beyond Life*, mouthpiece of the Cabellian philosophy, deserves better treatment than he gets in the story of this sorry escapade; he comes quite too near the likeness of the mountebank Sheridan. In *The Cords of Vanity* gallantry reveals itself more attractively; it is gilded with youth and wit and poetry. It is Congreve at his best, scintillating, brilliant, with a delightful affectation of pose and gesture; and it is Marlowe also, with its galloping wit steeped in pure poetry. There is the true Elizabethan rapture of fine words and lovely images and quaint conceits. "Meantime," says young Robert Townsend, "being in love, I refined upon the notions of love with the ingenuity of an Elizabethan." There you have the spirit of the book. It is more than a pretty piece of paganism; it is the brightest tale of gallantry in our literature, masterly in the restrained irony of its inimitable conclusion.

It is obvious, however, that the mood which finally will receive dramatization from Mr. Cabell cannot be summed up in the ideal of gallantry. What that mood is one finds revealed at length by John Charteris in *Beyond Life*. It is the quintessence of irony distilled from long observation of human life, but it is not Congreve, much less is it Sheridan. Those shameless and selfish roués began as artists but they ended as mountebanks; life taught them cynicism and not tenderness; it sharpened their wit and dulled their sympathy. The higher irony lay quite beyond their natures. But with Mr. Cabell tenderness, sympathy, an ardent concern for the inevitable failure that lies in wait upon aspiration, are so strong and urgent that under the governance of a mind less intellectual, they must inevitably run into sentimentality. But there is in Mr. Cabell something of the intellectual austerity of Matthew Arnold, and it conducts him to the same ends. Consider such a passage as this: "Through a merciful dispensation, we are one and all of us created very vain and very dull. . . . Vanity it is that pricks us indefatigably to play the ape to every dream romance induces; yet vanity is but the stirrup-cup: and urgent need arises that human dullness retain us (as it does) securely blinded, lest we observe the wayside horrors of our journey and go mad. One moment of clear vision as to man's plight in the universe would be quite sufficient to set the most philosophic gibbering. Meanwhile with bandaged eyes we advance: and human sanity is guided by the brave and pitiable and tireless dullness of mankind. . . . Yet how varied are the amiable activities of human dullness, which tend alike to protect and to enliven human progress! Dullness it is, of course, that brews and quaffs Dutch courage; . . . that fosters salutary optimism as to the destiny of mankind, in flat defiance of everything mankind can do, and does unblushingly. . . . And finally dullness it is that lifts up heart and voice alike, to view a parasite infesting the epidermis of a midge among the planets, and cries, *Behold, this is the child of God, All-mighty and All-worshipful, made in the likeness of his Father!* . . . These and how many other wholesome miracles are daily brought about by our dullness, by our brave and pitiable and tireless dullness, by our really majestic dullness, in firm alliance with the demiurgic spirit of romance. . . . For that to which romance conducts, in all the affairs of life . . . is plain enough—distinction and clarity, and beauty and symmetry, and tenderness and truth and urbanity."

Here then is the note that still awaits adequate dramatization in a comedy greater than he has yet written—a cosmic irony suffused with tenderness and truth and urbanity. Above all, urbanity. Mr. Cabell has played too long with the ideal of gallantry; he has devoted too much precious time to creating Millamants to fall in love with; he has listened too credulously to the voice of Congreve. "I have read," says Charteris, out of Congreve, "that the secret of gallantry is to accept the pleasures of life leisurely, and its inconveniences with a shrug; as well as that, among other requisites, the gallant person will always consider the world with a smile of toleration, and his own doings with a smile of honest amusement, and Heaven with a smile which is not distrustful—being thoroughly persuaded that God is kindlier than the genteel would regard as rational." Surely the cosmic irony that loves men's dullness because it alone can preserve them from madness, and retorts upon the cosmic terrors with a jest, is higher than gallantry and more enduring. It arrives at tolerance for all human shortcomings; it embraces high and low in its sympathies; it achieves urbanity as a final goal. It is the stuff of which great literature is made. And Mr. Cabell is creating great literature. A self-reliant intellectual, rich in the spoils of all literatures, one of the great masters of English prose, the supreme comic spirit thus far granted us, he stands apart from the throng of lesser American novelists, as Mark Twain stood apart, individual and incomparable.

THE PROBLEM NOVEL AND THE DIVERSION FROM
NATURALISM *

No sooner was naturalism fairly under way than it was well-nigh submerged under a wave of social speculation and inquiry. The years 1903–1917 were a distinctive period—a time of extraordinary ferment, when America was seeking to readjust her ideals and institutions to a revolutionary economic order that had come upon her. The popular phase was revealed in the muckracking movement, a movement which instructed the American middle class in certain elements of economics—particularly the close connection between economics and politics. But underneath, an intellectual revolution was in progress, setting steadily towards a new social philosophy. The old America had been intensely conservative, naïvely provincial and self-satisfied, compassed by a complacence founded on optimism—the gospel of the business man. The new America was eager and hopeful, impatient to square institutions to the new conditions. The total movement was profoundly democratic—a new Jacksonianism rising in protest against a menacing plutocracy.

1. *The Movement of Criticism.* The work of a vigorous social idealism. Passed through three broad phases:

a. Political. The movement of Progressivism, 1903–1912. An attempt to democratize the machinery of government to the end that the will of the majority shall prevail. Its impulse and much of its program came from Populism; and it resulted in a clarification of the issue between republicanism and democracy. An attack on the representative system and the checks and balances of the Fathers. It gave rise to a critical examination of the spirit and purpose of the Constitution.[1]

b. Economic. A growing conviction that talk of political democracy is futile except in so far as it leads to economic democracy. That power is economic in origin and that those who control the economics will control the government. The gospel of economic determinism. Certain conclusions emerged:

* Lecture notes.—*Publisher.*
[1] See J. Allen Smith, *The Spirit of American Government;* W. A. White, *The Old Order Changeth.*

1. That capitalism is no longer competitive but monopolistic.

2. That *laissez-faire*ism no longer suffices.

3. That centralization has submerged the individual citizen; that he is impotent before the leviathan corporation; and that henceforth the struggle is to be between organized groups for the control of the state.[2]

c. Literary. An examination and rejection of traditional literary and cultural ideas. An attack upon:

1. Puritan reticence and smug respectability.

2. Middle-class optimism and sentimentality.

Led by H. L. Mencken, Ludwig Lewisohn, and the younger intellectuals. The bias aristocratic.

2. *The Incoming of Old-World Thought.* The breaking-down of the older provincialism and the reception of new ideas.

a. The philosophy of collectivism. Derived chiefly from Germany and England; largely Marxian and Fabian. The conviction that the state must absorb the trust. Later the appearance of syndicalism and guild socialism, based on a distrust of the bureaucratic, omnicompetent state. Anarchism has remained alien in spirit.[3]

b. The new aristocracy. A reversion from an easy-going Jacksonianism based on the doctrine of equalitarianism. A direct denial of that doctrine and the theory of leadership. In business the doctrine of the expert and the rule of efficiency. In philosophy the doctrine of the intellectual aristocrat—a suggestion of Nietzsche and the will to power. Thus Mencken joins hands with Judge Gary in upholding the ethics of the strong. The total result an effective denial of our traditional ideal of democracy.

c. The problem novel. All this ferment entered into literature, tyrannizing in its insistence. Old forms became old-fashioned overnight. The novel was so useful that it was drafted by the new crusading enthusiasm. Romance and naturalism alike were swept away; the political novel and the economic novel took their place to arouse public opinion to action. It was the glorification of propaganda. Except for James Branch Cabell and Edith Wharton not a writer escaped. There is something pathetic in the way the

---

[2] Representative books are: C. A. Beard, *An Economic Interpretation of the Constitution* (1913) and *The Economic Basis of Politics* (1922); Walter Lippman, *Public Opinion* (1922).

[3] See Bertrand Russell, *Proposed Roads to Freedom* (1919); Richard Roberts, *The Unfinished Programme of Democracy* (1920).

harmless bleating romantics were dragged at the chariot wheels of social problems. Booth Tarkington, Mary Johnston, Winston Churchill, William Allen White, were sacrificed equally with potential naturalists like Robert Herrick, Upton Sinclair, and Ernest Poole. Their careers may be seen from Churchill, Poole, and Herrick.

1. Winston Churchill. [The most representative of the spirit of Progressivism.] A conscientious middle-class romantic. Churchill was a faithful reflector of middle-class movements. His work falls into three phases:

[a. *Romantic historical tales*. *Richard Carvel* (1899) the type of Cavalier romance. A blend of Thackeray's *Henry Esmond* and *The Virginians*, John Paul Jones added for extra historical flavor. A double background: (1) the old South of the Revolution with a Loyalist villain and a patriot hero; (2) the London of Brooks Club and a gaming aristocracy, with Charles Fox. The heroine another edition of Beatrix Esmond the hero another Henry Esmond. *The Crisis* (1910) a romance of the borderland of the Civil War: a fire-eating Southern heroine and a sober Yankee-Puritan hero. *The Crossing* (1904) a romance of the settlement of the Inland Empire. A theme not yet adequately dealt with in American fiction. The story breaks in two: the first half Churchill's best work in romance; the last half his worst.*]

b. *Political novels*. Coincided with the rise of the Progressive movement. *Coniston* (1906) a study of the legislative boss in New Hampshire. A reflection of his experience in the state legislature. How the "interests," and in particular the railroads, manage to put their bills through. Jethro Bass sells political control to the highest bidder.

Mr. Crewe's Career (1908): the same theme a generation later. Consolidation of the railroads has brought about absentee dictatorship of state politics. The boss has removed to New York and manages the legislature through his local lawyer. The philosophy of big-business prosperity rests on property rights, held in trusteeship by the corporations that fill the empty dinner pails, make and unmake business confidence. The revolt of the younger generation —Austen Vane and Victoria Flint, in whom stirs a new social conscience.

* From the syllabus.—*Publisher*.

c. *Economic novels.* Began with *The Inside of the Cup* (1913), a venture in higher criticism and social interpretation. So compare *Robert Elsmere* (1888). An attack on old dogmas and an attempt to discover the democratic springs of Christianity. The clash between the reborn Son of God and an unregenerate society, and the need to establish the Kingdom of God in this world. The church today controlled by business subscriptions. The solution to be sought in a free pulpit, supported by the common people, preaching a new social Christianity.

A Far Country (1915), a study in the emptiness of the profit motive. A background of banking—J. P. Morgan and Company. The dissatisfaction of the prodigal son who has wasted his intellectual and moral patrimony—the lawyer who sells his brain to rise and loses the things that make life worth while. His conversion brings the call to self-education.

The Dwelling Place of Light (1917), a study of the blighting effect of industrialism on the native Yankee stock that has failed to rise into the exploiting class. The restlessness of modern life due to the failure of normal instincts to find satisfaction in daily existence— an emptiness due to loss of beauty, freedom, creative craftsmanship. The search for compensation brings death and not life. A background of the Lawrence strike and syndicalism.

2. Robert Herrick. The most promising of the potential naturalists. An intellectual fascinated by the crude materialism of Chicago in the late nineties. Suffered from the inhibitions of a Puritan idealism; the problems of this raw world cried aloud for solution— the woman question, the labor question, the problem of the professions—and warped him away from naturalism, making him an easy victim of the new social enthusiasm. The key to his thought— economic determinism.

The Memoirs of an American Citizen (1905). His best work and the nearest approach to naturalism. A detailed study of the American business man—the captain of industry who rises in a competitive society by his own will. The competitive order, he perceives, requires an ethics different from the Christian ideal. The survival of the fittest means the survival of the strongest, the most cunning and unscrupulous. The realist who deals with facts discovers that he lives in a world of pigs—little pigs of the village, larger hogs of the city. To get in the trough a man must have fingers and toes and use them. The world belongs to the strong.

That which gives dignity is bigness: the larger the hog, the more imposing. Little business is dirty and petty, but big business may become poetic. To grind a mess of sausages is messy, but to provide sausages for every breakfast table in America is grandiose. To realize his ambition Van Harrington plays fast and loose with conventional ethics, but unlike Frank Cowperwood he seeks a new ethics. As a superman his work will be justified by its creativeness, by its service to humanity.

A Life for a Life (1910). In certain other of his work Herrick betrays naturalistic tendencies, notably in *The Web of Life* (1900), where he considers the problem of social complexity and how it binds the life of men and women and determines their fate. But in *A Life for a Life* he surrenders wholly to the problem. His theme is how the predatory egoism of the profit-struggle may be cured, and he presents alternative solutions: syndicalism and Christianity. The cure lies in individual self-conquest—breaking through the web of "things as they are" and choosing life instead of power.

Herrick was on the threshold of naturalism. He felt the complexity of life and the determining force of that complexity; but he failed to achieve the attitude of objectivity.

3. Ernest Poole. *The Harbor* (1915). The culmination of the novel of naturalistic propaganda and the most widely read. A dramatic record of a changing industrial order, traced through three stages: (1) The old world of small competitive business that is dead; (2) The present world of corporation control; (3) The world of syndicalistic control that struggles to be born.

Against this changing world stands the young idealist troubled in his loyalties, who sets up different gods to worship: (1) The idol of art—aloofness from the mass struggle; (2) The idol of efficiency by the supermen who rule in trusteeship; (3) The idol of mass solidarity and workers' control—the conclusion that is on the dawn of realization: "The world for all the workers." *Conclusion.* The ferment of social thought, shot through with Marxianism, familiarized the American novelists with one doctrine important for the naturalist—the doctrine of economic determinism. In none of them did it pass over into a larger conception of philosophical determinism, and this sets the limitation to their naturalism. The common zeal for reform or revolution, moreover, kept them from objectivity. In none is there the calm detachment and the amoral presentation of material without which naturalism sinks into propaganda. Their position presupposes a large confidence in individual initiative—a confidence in the power of men to alter the world they live in. It is admirable, but it is not the way of the naturalists, who do not seek to change what they regard as an essentially unresponsive world that changes only after its own way.

JACK LONDON: THE NOVELIST OF THE PROLETARIAT*

Experienced the harsh contacts of a seasonal worker and tramp. Became a Marxian socialist and revolutionist, preaching the war of the classes in *The Iron Heel* (1908), *The Revolution* (1910), and other works. A man of strong vital energy with a philosophy shaped by Darwin, Spencer, and Nietzsche. Emphasizes a passionate will-to-power, a superman of swift and violent action.

The Call of the Wild (1903); a study in atavism, brilliant, poetic, set against a wild Alaska background. The resurgence of the primitive wolf-instincts in a domesticated dog.

The Sea Wolf (1904); the frankest statement in American literature of the unbridled will-to-power, egoistic, amoral. A malignant ferocity in a philosophical, herculean sea captain, whose body is destroyed by paresis, but whose malignancy is unconquered.

Martin Eden (1909); autobiographical. So compare *John Barleycorn* (1913). The former deals with his struggle to educate himself, to write, and to gain recognition. A background of his experience at the University of California. A profound contempt for *bourgeois* standards of life and thought. The note of revolution and the lapsing of the will-to-live.

London carries to the extreme the "elemental" of Norris, translating it into the primitive and abysmal. A potential naturalist in his amoral attitude and his underlying pessimism, but carried away by zeal of revolution. Lacks restraint and finish.

* From the syllabus.—*Publisher*.

UPTON SINCLAIR *

The most insistent and outspoken of the muckrakers. Began as a novelist, but his art submerged by propaganda—a profound suspicion of capitalism and all its ways.

The Jungle (1906); a story of the packing houses and the immigrant: the technique of "speeding up" and the labor scrap-heap. The social consequences of the profit principle—saving everything but the squeal of the hog and the health of the laborer.

King Coal (1917); a story of the Rockefeller coal fields in Colorado and the miners' union. Probably his most skillful story.

Numerous other titles, among them: *The Brass Check*, an examination of the American newspaper—the charge that these are the tools of plutocracy; *The Goose Step*, an examination of the American university—the charge that these serve wealth; *The Goslings*, an attack upon the public school as an agent of capitalism.

* From the syllabus.—*Publisher.*

THEODORE DREISER: CHIEF OF AMERICAN
NATURALISTS *

Against this background of eager ferment and various propaganda stands Theodore Dreiser, who is of this changing world and yet apart from it: the most detached and keenly observant of all our writers, a huge figure of ungainly proportions—a heavy-footed peasant with unslaked curiosity and a boundless pity, who is determined to examine critically "this animal called man" and portray him truthfully. He tramps across fields straight to his objective, messing sadly the neat little beds of American convention, peering into the secret places that are marked "Not Open To The Public," keeping nothing hidden, ashamed of nothing, apologizing for nothing. Not since Walt Whitman has there been another such frank and detached projection of reality, such insistence that the world shall stop and consider those facts which convention has politely agreed to ignore. Naturally a great hue and cry of the Pharisees has been raised against him. The respectable middle class will have none of this peasant directness and brutal truth. He has entered our *bourgeois* society "murmurous of morality" with an alien philosophy, which he must defend. At every moment he feels under the necessity of assisting the truth as he sees it, and instead of suffering his portrayal to stand on its own feet he props it up with argument and interminable debate. The artist suffers at the hands of the disputant.

The Man and his Philosophy. Marked by an immense and openeyed curiosity that ends in agnosticism. His anthropocentric conceptions:

I have lived now to my fortieth year and have seen a good deal of life. . . . But I am one of those curious persons who cannot make up their minds about anything. I read and read. . . . But I find that one history contradicts another, one philosopher drives out another. Essayists, in the main, point out flaws and paradoxes in the current conception of things, novelists, dramatists and biographers spread tales of endless disasters, or silly illusions concerning life, duty, opportunity and the like. And I sit here and read and read, when I have time, wondering.[1]

* Lecture notes.—*Publisher.*   [1] *Hey Rub-a-Dub-Dub*, New York, 1920, p. 1.

"Nothing is proved, all is permitted," he says in *The Titan*. Men will do what they think they can get away with. In briefest terms his philosophy may be phrased thus:

1. The world is without reason or meaning to us. Why we are here and to what end is unknowable.

2. Men are chemical compounds, existing in a world where they play about like water-flies, skipping restlessly and unintelligently as their legs drive them, whom the universe in its vast indifference suffers for a time.

3. Men divide into the strong and the weak; not the good and the bad. The will to power, the desire for pleasure, drive men on their courses. What restrains? Moral codes and social conventions, often useful, often harmful.

A metaphysical idealism will always tell him that it is better to preserve a cleanly balance, and the storms of circumstance will teach him a noble stoicism. Beyond this there is nothing which can reasonably be imposed upon the conscience of man.[2]

4. Hence the profound need of sympathy and mercy.

Let no one underestimate the need of pity. We live in a stony universe whose hard, brilliant forces rage fiercely. From the prowling hunger of the Hyrcan tiger to the concentric grip of Arcturus and Canopus there is the same ruthless, sightless disregard of the individual and the minor thing. Life moves in an ordered hierarchy of forces of which the lesser is as nothing to the greater . . . And in the midst of the rip of desperate things—in odd crannies and chance flaws between forces—there spring and blossom these small flowers of sentiment. Tenderness! Mercy! Affection! Sorrow! The Hindus worship an image of pain. And well they may. It is a classic amid the painless, the indifferent—Nirvana. Blessed are the merciful, for they shall receive mercy! No, no. Blessed are the merciful, for they create mercy. Of such is the kingdom of the ideal.[3]

His Attitude toward his Material. Dreiser possesses a vast and terrifying imagination. Like James Branch Cabell he broods over the plight of man in the universe. But he does not seek refuge in the ideal. He will confront things as they are. The very chemistry of decaying flesh fascinates him. It is a phenomenon of this impersonal and relentless universe. Compared with the realities of time and space and force—what is man and what are his puny efforts and ideals?

The damnable scheme of things which we call existence brings about conditions whereby whole masses suffer who have no cause to suffer, and

[2] *The Financier*, New York, c. 1912, p. 250.   [3]*Ibid.*, p. 409.

. . . whole masses joy who have no cause for joy. . . . We suffer for our temperaments, which we did not make, and for our weaknesses and lacks, which are no part of our willing or doing.[4]

His Objectivity. The larger view of life gives detachment. Only one who has emerged from the jungle can see the whole in broad perspective. In no other American writer, except Whitman, is such complete detachment achieved. His life is a long process of stripping away group illusions, of casting off group conventions. And for this the mass cannot forgive him, for the mass live in the strait-jacket of custom, thinking in no other terms than group or tribal terms, worshiping the communal idols, clinging to the tribal taboos. They cannot achieve individuality themselves and they hate Dreiser. It puts him outside the tribe, for the first law of the tribe is tribal-mindedness. Whoever is not of us is against us. Whoever questions the validity of the tribal sanctions is an enemy and must be destroyed. It is in vain that Dreiser asserts vehemently that he is telling the truth. Another version of the truth than the tribal version is not wanted.

The significance of Dreiser lies in the fact that he is an individual apart—one who has broken with the group and sits in judgment on the group sanctions. He is an anarchist who will be partisan to no taboos. This is a rare and perilous thing to do. He stands outside.

His Amoral Attitude. It is on this score that Dreiser stands condemned by our *bourgeois* censors. His amoral attitude is strangely metamorphosed into immorality. His indifference to the common preachments, his inability to accept Christian maxims, his refusal to do lip service to creeds—this is set down as evidence of viciousness, for *ipso facto* there can be no other moral standards than the tribal standards. What is Dreiser's justification? This, that in the physical universe he can discover no morality—no justice, mercy, pity, but everywhere great and indifferent force. And in society—in the instincts of men and in their hidden desires and secret acts—a disregard of conventional morality. Society is steeped in hypocrisy.

He saw no morals anywhere—nothing but moods, emotions, needs, greeds. People talked and talked, but they acted according to their necessities and desires.[5]

But in frankly revealing the hypocrisy of men Dreiser is no cynic. There is in him a profound morality—the morality of truth and pity

[4] *Ibid.,* p. 479.   [5] *The Financier*, p. 432.

and mercy. Let us not stone men for their sins but deal generously and kindly with them. What he protests against is superimposed codes. There is, for him, "in Nature, no such thing as the right to do, or the right not to do." [6]

But is there not social expediency? To which the individual for his own good should conform? Experience has taught men some excellent things.

His Work. Dreiser has given us full-length portraits of two women—Sister Carrie and Jennie Gerhardt—and of two men—Eugene Witla and Frank Cowperwood. These constitute his major contribution and on them his reputation rests.* In addition there is *Hey Rub-a-Dub-Dub,* a book of essays in which his philosophy is set forth, a naturalistic play, *The Hand of the Potter*—a study in pathology where the hand of the potter slipped—a book of travel, and some short stories. Of his four major characters the two women are passive and pliable, easily made victims of circumstance. Of the two men one—Eugene Witla—is weak, and the other—Frank Cowperwood—is the supreme example in American literature of the will to power.

The Financier and *The Titan.* A colossal study of the American business man, in two volumes of a total of 1332 pages. Compared with this all other studies are crude and unconvincing. Here the thing has been done once for all.

"These crude and greedy captains of finance had to be given some kind of literary embodiment, and Dreiser has hammered a raw epic out of their lives." [7]

Where did Dreiser get his intimate and detailed information concerning high finance? Where his knowledge of such a character? Out of his own powerful mind. Cowperwood a portrait of Charles Yerkes. Two periods: his Philadelphia life to 1873; his Chicago life to 1898. In both he molds circumstance to his advantage; in both he is caught by chance and fails.

The Man. Driven by three impulses: love of power, love of women, love of art. There is in him a unity of character and an inevitability of development that are overwhelming. Dreiser does not judge, apologize, praise, or condemn; he is content to permit the

[6] *Hey Rub-a-Dub-Dub,* p. 87.
* When this was written of course *The American Tragedy, A Book about Myself,* Dreiser's poems, *Moods Cadenced and Declaimed,* and his further books of travel had not been published.—*Publisher.*
[7] Randolph Bourne, *History of a Literary Radical,* p. 203.

character to develop. From first to last he is detached and objective. He presents Cowperwood as a magnificent physical and mental machine: a born fighter and leader, strong, alert, with a cool resourceful mind. A pronounced hardness that goes with strength —contempt for the weakling, impatience with the inefficient. In his sex passages there is no glamour of romance. They are direct and brutal—but more moral than glamorous. Nevertheless great personal charm—the magnetism of a virile mind and indomitable will. To men he is an inspiration, to women a fascination. And yet a frank egoist, self-centered, imperturbable.

The fate of the individualist: in pitting his will against life Cowperwood feared chance, which undid him in Philadelphia. But his very prevision, which carried him to triumph, brought his downfall. The many are stronger than the superman. And in the end, failure. Strength endures for so short a time and is so weak. Age, weakness, social forces—these undermine the strong. A vast irony. Cowperwood is punished not because he is evil but because he is a man.

Cowperwood's Philosophy. From his youth up life was a puzzle to him. Nothing was certain, for beyond and above all was a blind, irrational chance. Nevertheless within reasonable limits it was plain enough that strength and intelligence prevail. This lesson he first learned from the squib and the lobster, and it became his guiding principle. When chance had brought him within the shadow of the penitentiary, he summed it up:

It is a grim, bitter world we are all born into. . . . Who was to straighten out the matter of the unjust equipment with which most people began? Who was to give them strong minds in place of feeble ones, able bodies instead of wretched ones? Where were they to get pure-tendencies instead of impure ones, as the world looked on these things? . . . Some were sent into the world with a great lust and great ability for wealth like himself, a mind swift to see, a body strong to endure; and some were sent half equipped, almost shapeless and formless. . . . Strength and weakness—there lay the key, the answer.[8]

Stuart Sherman on Dreiser:

By eliminating distinctively human motives and making animal instincts the supreme factors in human life, Mr. Dreiser reduces the problem of the novelist to the lowest possible terms. . . . His philosophy quite excludes him from the field in which the great realist must work. He has deliberately rejected the novelist's supreme task—understanding and

[8] *The Financier,* p. 660.

presenting the development of character; he has chosen only to illustrate the unrestricted flow of temperament. He has evaded the enterprise of representing human conduct; he has confined himself to representation of animal behavior.[9]

And the two novels he says are "like a club sandwich composed of slices of business, alternating with erotic episodes." It is true, but the failure is one of art that does not merge them. What would Sherman have? Shall these impulses be eliminated from literature, or from human nature itself?

[9] Stuart P. Sherman, *On Contemporary Literature*, New York, 1923, p. 94. In the syllabus Professor Parrington says: "The most intelligent estimates of Dreiser are in Randolph Bourne, *History of a Literary Radical;* H. L. Mencken, *Prefaces;* and Carl Van Doren, *Contemporary American Novelists.* All other commentators are stupid."

SINCLAIR LEWIS: OUR OWN DIOGENES *

As the row of his pudgy orange-backed volumes lengthens on the shelf, it becomes evident that Sinclair Lewis is the bad boy of American letters whose thoughts are on bent-pins while the deacon is laboring in prayer. His irrepressible satire belongs to a new and irritatingly effective school. He has studied the technique of the realists, and under the beguiling pretense of telling the truth objectively and dispassionately, he insists on revealing to us unaccommodated man as a poor, bare, forked animal, who like Jurgen persists in thinking himself a monstrous clever fellow. He is maliciously severe on all respectable dignities. In his hands the noble *homo sapiens* of common repute is translated into an ignoble *homo libidinus et ventosissimus*—an unattractive animal that runs in herds, serves its belly, and has a taking way with the dams. The free-born American citizen, master of the earth and its destiny, is little flattered by the portrait he draws, and Mr. Lewis finds himself, in consequence, *persona non grata* in any convention of Elks or Rotarians.

The method he has chosen to adopt is a clever advance over the technique of the eighteenth century, when pricking balloons was the business of every wit. Those older satirists—nagging souls like Pope and bold bad fellows like Churchill—were mainly concerned to annoy their victims with pin-pricks. They were too completely the gentleman to grow chummy with base fellows whom they frankly despised; and in consequence they never discovered half the possibilities of the gentle art of satire. Sinclair Lewis is wiser than they were. He has learned that before one can effectively impale one's victim, one must know all his weaknesses and take him off his guard. So he ingratiatingly makes up to George F. Babbitt of Zenith, drinks chummily with him, swaps greasy jokes, learns all the hidden vanities and secret obscenities that slip out in the confidences of the cups, beguiles him into painting his own portrait in the manly midnight hours; and when the last garment that covers his nakedness is stripped off, the flashlight explodes and the

* Published as Number Five of *University of Washington Chapbooks*, 1927.— *Publisher.*

360

camera has caught the victim in every feature of his mean and vacuous reality.

No doubt it is an ungentlemanly thing to do—a calculating betrayal of trusting human nature done in the sacred name of art; and it is certain that the unhappy victim will hate the artist when he sees the developed print next morning. Yet the picture is extraordinarily lifelike. All the unlovely details of fat stomach and flabby muscles are sharply revealed. It is too late to put on one's clothes, and *homo sapiens* in the person of George F. Babbitt is revealed as a shambling, two-legged animal, for the world to laugh at. The method is immensely clever; it is the last word in the technique of despoiling one's victim of adventitious dignity, without which life becomes a mean, bleak affair; but it is scarcely charitable. To think well of oneself and to wish to impose that good opinion upon others, are common human weaknesses that every tailor blesses. Without clothes man is only a caricature of the godlike, and the artist who betrays our nakedness to our enemies is very far from a gentleman. The confidences of the cups must be held sacred, for if we cannot drink without fear of our babbling being reported, what becomes of goodfellowship?

But the charge of betraying goodfellowship leaves Sinclair Lewis unconcerned. His satire knows no compunctions. An irreverent soul, he dares the wrath not only of George F. Babbitt, but of the innumerable clubs to which Babbitt belongs. A buoyant scoffer, he does not permit even the organized wrath of the Chamber of Commerce to disturb his equanimity. He provokes respectable people on principle, and he has laid a devilish plan to work systematically through our sacred American decalogue, smashing one commandment after another. Already behind him is strewn a sorry wreckage of established creeds and authoritative slogans—a wreckage that delights the wicked and gives aid and comfort to all evil-wishers in our comfortable and excellent society. Not even a banker is sacred to him. Rotarians and Kiwanians, Billy Sundays and Billy Bryans, voluble Congressmen and silent Presidents, even our venerable Constitution itself, he scoffs at and makes merry over. And to add insult to injury, he prospers in his sins. His calculating wickedness returns him a fattening bank account. His impudent satires sell like bargain-counter silk stockings. We pay handsomely to see ourselves most unhandsomely depicted. If we would only take a lesson from the strategy of the heathen Chinese, we might boycott Mr. Lewis's wares and reduce him to the beggary that is more becoming to wickedness than a wanton prosperity. But a Christian people will not go to school to the heathen, and so Mr. Lewis prospers in his wickedness and waxes vulgarly rich.

Now what is the tremendous discovery that Sinclair Lewis makes so much of, and that we pay so great a price to learn? It is no other than this: that the goodly United States of America are peopled by a mighty herd, which like those earlier herds that rumbled about the plains, drives foolishly in whatever direction their noses point— a herd endowed with tremendous blind power, with big bull leaders, but with minds rarely above their bellies and their dams. In the mass and at their own romantic rating they are distinctly imposing —big-necked, red-blooded, lusty, with glossy coats got from rich feeding-grounds, and with a herd power that sweeps majestically onward in a cloud of dust of its own raising, veritable lords and masters of a continent. But considered more critically and resolved into individual members, they appear to the realist somewhat stupid, feeble in brain and will, stuffed with conceit of their own excellence, esteeming themselves the great end for which creation has been in travail, the finest handiwork of the Most High who spread the plains for their feeding-grounds: with a vast respect for totems and fetishes; purveyors and victims of the mysterious thing called Bunk, who valiantly horn to death any audacious heretic who may suggest that rumbling about the plains, filling their bellies, bellowing sacred slogans, and cornering the lushest grass, are scarcely adequate objectives for such immense power: a vast middleman herd, that dominates the continent, but cannot reduce it to order or decency.

Consider, suggests Mr. Lewis, what this rumbling herd signifies in the light of rational and humane ideals. What sort of custodians of civilization are these lumbering mobsters with their back-slappings and bellowings? What becomes of the good life in a society that flowers in Rotarian conventions? The banker has reduced America to the level of a banker's Utopia, and now bids us admire his handiwork. Other societies, aristocratic and feudal, honored the priest and knight and artist above the usurer and tradesman; other generations professed to serve truth and beauty and godliness in their daily lives; but the great American herd cares nothing for such things. In the name of democracy priest and knight and artist are turned lackeys to merchants and realtors, to men who would not recognize faith or chivalry or imagination if they met them on the golf course, and who understand democracy as little as they understand Christianity. In this land of material abundance the good life is reduced to being measured in commissions and percentages; civilization comes to flower in the broker; the mahogany desk is the altar at which we sacrifice in a land of triumphant materialism. "God help the country," said Fenimore Cooper, years ago when the herd was small, "that has only commercial towns for its capitals." "Such a country is past helping," retorts Sinclair Lewis. "God cannot help it, or the Devil. In the name of George F. Babbitt and Dr. Almus Pickerbaugh and the Reverend Elmer Gantry, what can be expected of such a country? A people that worships the great god Bunk shall have its reward!"

To prove his amiable thesis Mr. Lewis has been at enormous pains to gather his materials at their sources. He has taken upon himself to become a specialist in depicting the *genus Americanus*. He has loafed along Main Street, played poker in back rooms with wicked young men, drunk in respectable clubs, and exchanged hearty back-slappings with the sons of Rotary. He has devoted days to the smoking-compartments of Pullmans, garnering the ripest wisdom and choicest stories of traveling salesmen. He has listened to philosophic brokers discourse on ethics, studied political and constitutional theory with realtors, learned all about Bolshevism from presidents of Chambers of Commerce, been instructed in the elements of economics by Republican Congressmen, discovered the fallacies in Darwinian evolution from clerical fundamentalists and the superiority of Fascism over democracy from the greatest captains of industry. No field of American experience has escaped his minute investigation, no authority has eluded his catechizing. In the course of his studies he has come to master the lusty American language in its subtlest shades and manliest *nuances*, from the comic supplement to Dunn and Bradstreet, and he talks easily with Main Street in its own vernacular. His rich and copious vocabulary fills a commonplace scholar with envy, and his ebullient slang, his easy slovenliness of enunciation, inflict on the simple-minded user of the King's English a hopeless inferiority complex.

Thus amply equipped with all the resources of scholarship, he has written four learned treatises in exemplification of the thesis that the *genus Americanus* is cousin-german to the scoffing Mr. Mencken's lately discovered *boobus Americanus*. The introductory study, *Main Street*, provided a comprehensive background and setting for the full-length portraits he was to draw later. Gopher Prairie, situated in the heart of agricultural America—in Meredith Nicholson's Valley of Democracy where the old-fashioned, kindly, neighborly, wholesome, democratic virtues are presumed to thrive in a congenial habitat—becomes in his unsympathetic analysis a place that William Allen White would not recognize as his home town. Here, he tells us, is respectability made sluggish and sterile. Here is "slavery self-sought and self-defended." Here is "dullness made God." Here, diluted and spread over a vast territory, the spirit of Babbitt has erupted in cheap and pretentious county-seats, parasites on the producing hinterland over whose politics and credit and morals Main Street tradesmen have set up a strict custodianship—futile and complacent and drab, mere echoes of the greater cities that lie on the horizon and to which the sons of Main Street turn for light and guidance.

It is these greater cities that constitute the true capitals of our red-blooded Americans who proclaim themselves "the greatest race in the world"—fruitful centers from which radiates the philosophy of pep, punch, and progress for the upbuilding and enlightenment of the world. Of these centers the hustling and mighty Zenith is the wonder and admiration of all right-minded citizens; it is the brightest and bloomiest sunflower of the great American garden. And in Zenith dwells George F. Babbitt, realtor, Sinclair Lewis's full-length portrait of a hero sprung from the loins of America, the completest embodiment of the triumphant American genius that is conquering the earth. Babbitt as an upstanding he-member of the great herd is a marvel, the apotheosis of the regnant middle class, the finished product of our snappy civilization. Other lands, no doubt, have produced men accounted great. Plato and Saul of Tarsus, St. Francis and Leonardo, Pascal and Galileo and Hegel, were no doubt esteemed in their own times and by their own cities; but Zenith does not go in for out-of-date merchandise; it is up-to-the-minute and it specialized in George F. Babbitts. And so when the Reverend Elmer Gantry rises to influence in Gopher Prairie, he is called to Zenith as its spiritual counselor, and becomes the custodian of the Zenith moralities, the apostle of Zenith Bunk, the devotee of the Zenith Mumbo Jumbo. And through Zenith passes also Martin Arrowsmith the rebel, the perverse outlandish scientist who refuses to worship Mumbo

Jumbo, on his solitary way to discover reality in a world of Zenith chicanery. Babbitt, Gantry, Arrowsmith—these are the figures that Sinclair Lewis comes upon in his exploration of the land of the free and the home of the brave. A somewhat curious showing at the best.

So slashing an attack upon our common creed and practice has naturally aroused vigorous protest. Human nature does not like to have its idols assailed; even the devotees of Mumbo Jumbo will defend their god against the heretics; and Sinclair Lewis has become the target for many a shaft. The critics have pressed home their counter attack with ardor. They insist that he is suffering from an aggravated case of astigmatism, and that in consequence he does not see eye to eye with those of normal vision. The world is out of focus to him—askew in all its structural lines; and this distorted vision prompts those jaundiced opinions and malicious judgments in regard to the ideals cherished by our best citizens. He has deliberately cultivated a spleen that makes him dislike his neighbors because they are comfortable and contented. Diogenes railing at mankind gained a vast reputation, but it is a nice question if Diogenes was a useful citizen. What did he do to further the well-being of his community? How much time and money did he give to charity and the upbuilding of his city? For all his talking Mr. Lewis does not seem to know what the good life is. He rails at Babbitt for not being Plato, but does he understand the A B C of service? To take a homely figure: the family cow, standing knee-deep in June and chewing the cud of contentment, would excite his Diogenic scorn. As a fault-finder and knocker, Brindle is not the equal of Diogenes; but to criticize her mentality and manners, forgetful of the fact that from the contented chewing of a plentiful cud will come a plentiful supply of milk and cream and butter to sweeten the bread of life, is a somewhat sorry business. In her modest, democratic sphere she is devoted to service, and if there is a nobler function, Rotary humbly confesses it had not discovered it. One must not, of course, press too far the analogy between Brindle and Babbitt; the figure is useful only to suggest that even in the lowliest spheres Mr. Lewis completely fails to understand the fine ethical values that underlie and animate the common American life at which he rails. How, then, shall he understand them in the higher? Comfort and service are excellent things in themselves, and if they can be merged in everyday experience, surely the good life is in the way of achievement.

The point is of vast importance, for it is here that Diogenes Lewis, his critics assert, has totally misread the meaning and faith of America. Here in this prosperous land the union between comfort and service—or to put it in more dignified phrase, the synthesis of Hellenism and Hebraism—has been achieved in practice. A rich and abundant life, motivated by a fine sense of ethical responsibility and disciplined by a democratic public school, is, in sober fact, the distinguishing characteristic of America that sets our country apart from all other lands in western civilization. Call it a Babbitt warren if you will, nevertheless where else has the industrial revolution been brought so completely and happily under dominion to the democratic ideal, or been so ennobled by ethical values? Here it has scattered its wealth amongst the plain people with a bountiful hand, until the poorest family enjoys its nickel-plated plumbing, its flivver, its telephone, its radio, its movies, its funnies, and all the thousand aids to comfort and intelligence which a few generations ago were denied kings—the result of all which is a standard of living that our forefathers would have envied. Our Hellenism is, happily, not Greek. That, as every schoolboy in America knows, was established in slavery; whereas our modern Hellenism is established in democracy and ennobled by a sensitive social conscience. Here the master serves. The richest and greatest amongst us—our Judge Garys and Andrew Mellons— are servants of the nameless public, and dedicate their creative genius to the common democratic prosperity. Our Hellenism, in short, is engrafted on a sturdy Hebraic root and flowers in righteousness—in charity, in education, in free clinics and hospitals, in scientific foundations, in great public libraries, in all the vast gifts that wealth freely offers to the cause of social amelioration. The Puritan strain is fortunately still the American strain, and we owe much to those excellent origins that Mr. Lewis scoffs at without understanding. Comfort and service—Hellenism and Hebraism: if this is not the good life, where shall one find it? In Bolshevik Russia? After all Diogenes Lewis is no more important—or useful —than the gad-fly that Brindle brushes from her glossy sides as she chews her cud. What gad-fly ever produced butter?

If Sinclair Lewis is unimpressed by such arguments it is because he is quite disillusioned with the current ideal of material progress. His dreams do not find their satisfaction in good roads and cheap gasoline. He would seem to be an incorrigible idealist who has been bred up on the vigorous Utopianisms of the late nineteenth century. In the golden days before the deluge he had gone blithely to school to all the current idealisms that flourished in the land—to Jeffersonian democracy and to Marxian socialism; and in the well-stocked pharmacopoeias of hopeful young liberals he professed to discover specifics for all our social ills. But the war destroyed his faith in nostrums and removed his Utopia to a dim and foggy future. He has not yet traveled so far in disillusion as Mr. Cabell, who has seen fit to dwarf man to the compass of a flea on the epidermis of earth; nor has he achieved the irony—or the technique—of Clarence Darrow, who suggests casually: "Of course I know that Confucius was as great a philosopher as Billy Sunday, and that as a thinker Buddha was the equal of Billy Bryan. But still all orthodox people know that Confucius and Buddha were spurious and the Billy brothers genuine." He has not even achieved the smug satisfaction of the psychologists who impose their preposterous intelligence tests on simple folk and triumphantly discover morons in respectable neighbors. Some lingering faith in our poor human nature he still clings to. In the great American mass that human nature is certainly foolish and unlovely enough. It is too often blown up with flatulence, corroded with lust, on familiar terms with chicanery and lying; it openly delights in hocus-pocus and discovers its miracle-workers in its Comstocks and Aimee Semple McPhersons. But for all its pitiful flabbiness human nature is not wholly bad, nor is man so helpless a creature of circumstance as the cynics would have us believe. There are other and greater gods than Mumbo Jumbo worshiped in America, worthier things than hocus-pocus; and in rare moments even Babbitt dimly perceives that the feet of his idol are clay. There are Martin Arrowsmiths as well as Elmer Gantrys, and human nature, if it will, can pull itself out of the trap. Bad social machinery makes bad men. Put the banker in the scullery instead of the drawing-room; exalt the test-tube and deflate the cash register; rid society of the dictatorship of the middle class; and the artist and the scientist will erect in America a civilization that may become what civilization was in earlier days, a thing to be respected. For all his modernity and the disillusion learned from Pullman-car philosophers, Sinclair Lewis is still an echo of Jean Jacques and the golden hopes of the Enlightenment—thin and far off, no doubt, but still an authentic echo.

Whether we like Mr. Lewis's technique or not, whether we agree with his indictment of middle-class ideals or dissent from it, his writings are suggestive documents symptomatic of a dissatisfied generation given over to disillusion. The optimistic dreams of middle-class capitalism are not so golden as they seemed to us before the war; and these pudgy novels are slashing attacks on a world that in mouthing empty shibboleths is only whistling to keep up its courage. The faith of America is dead. These brisk pages are filled with the doings of automata—not living men but the simulacra of men, done with astonishing verisimilitude, speaking an amazingly realistic language, professing a surprising lifelikeness; yet nevertheless only shells from which the life has departed, without faith or hope or creative energy, not even aware that they are dead.

It is this consciousness of sketching in a morgue that differentiates Mr. Lewis from the earlier satirists of middle-class America, who in the hopeful years before the war were busily engaged in rebuilding the American temple. The preceding generation—earnest souls like Robert Herrick and Jack London and Upton Sinclair—were as well aware of the shortcomings of our industrial order as Sinclair Lewis, and hated them as vigorously. From the days of Emerson and George Ripley, of Carlyle and Ruskin, capitalistic society had been persistently subjected to sharp and devastating analysis; its drabness and regimentation, its sterility and emptiness and joylessness, had been pointed out by many pens. The Victorians long ago discovered that no generous or humane civilization was to be expected from the hands of Plugson of Undershot—that the banker conceiving of human felicity in terms of eight per cent. is a mean and shabby fellow in comparison with St. Francis or Michelangelo. Long before Sherwood Anderson, William Morris had observed that the workman no longer sings in the factory as in other days he sang over his tool, and concluded that the creation of beauty is more important for human happiness than figuring profits from mass production.

But those earlier analysts were dealing with causes of which they could only forecast the ultimate consequences, whereas Sinclair Lewis is dealing with effects. Plugson of Undershot is now the universal dictator. Before the war there was still life and hope in western civilization; it was not yet reduced to being a common Babbitt warren, with its Billy Sundays and Almus Pickerbaughs, its artists and editors and scientists, on the Plugson pay-roll. What emerges from the drab pages of Sinclair Lewis that is suggestive is the authoritative pronouncement that the effects forecast by the earlier critics have become in our day the regnant order of things. Babbitt is the son of Plugson of Undershot, and Babbitt is a walking corpse who refuses to be put decently away to make room for living men. An empty soul, he is the symbol of our common emptiness. Historically he marks the final passing in America of the civilization that came from the fruitful loins of the eighteenth century. For a hundred and fifty years western civilization had sustained its hopes on the rich nourishment provided by the great age of the Enlightenment. Faith in the excellence of man, in the law of progress, in the ultimate reign of justice, in the conquest of nature, in the finality and sufficiency of democracy, faith in short in the excellence of life, was the great driving force in those earlier, simpler days. It was a noble dream—that dream of the Enlightenment —but it was slowly dissipated by an encompassing materialism that came likewise out of the eighteenth century. Faith in machinery came to supersede faith in man; the Industrial Revolution submerged the hopes of the French Revolution. And now we have fallen so low that our faith in justice, progress, the potentialities of human nature, the excellence of democracy, is stricken with pernicious anemia, and even faith in the machine is dying. Only science remains to take the place of the old romantic creed, and science with its psychology and physics is fast reducing man to a complex bundle of glands, at the mercy of a mechanistic universe. Babbitt, to be sure, has not yet discovered the predicament he is in, but Martin Arrowsmith knows; and while Babbitt is whistling somewhat futilely, Arrowsmith is hard at work in the laboratory seeking a new philosophy to take the place of the old. The outlook is not promising, but until a new faith emerges from the test-tube Sinclair Lewis will wander in the fogs of disillusion.

But enough of such crape-hanging at a time when our best minds are engaged in the great work of stabilizing prosperity. What are test-tubes in comparison with the infallible statistics patriotically disseminated by the National City Bank? To parade such heresies in the face of the progressive American public is enough to damn any man, genius or not. We want no carpers or cynics in our congenial membership. We must all get together to put across the drive for a bigger and richer and better America; and so, reluctantly, despite the fact that in many ways he is a good fellow, we blackball Sinclair Lewis.

SHERWOOD ANDERSON: A PSYCHOLOGICAL
NATURALIST *

Unlike our earlier naturalists in handling of material and dramatic interests. Concerned with inner life rather than outer, with hidden drives rather than environment. Accepts the main criteria of naturalism: determinism, distortion, pessimism. A lean and sparing writer whose symbolisms are obscure and puzzling. A single theme: the disastrous effect of frustrations and repressions that create grotesques. Due to (1) Crude, narrow environment that drives to strange aberrations; (2) Repressed instincts that break forth in abnormal action. The consequence a black loneliness—the hunger of fellowship and its denial. Limited in scope to episodic crises—hence his better stories short. Many failures: *Marching Men; Windy McPherson's Son; Poor White* (1920); *Many Marriages* (1923)—a clumsy account of a Babbitt gone on a psychological spree; *Horses and Men* (1923)—some more Grotesques; see in particular "A Chicago Hamlet."

Winesburg, Ohio (1918). A prose *Spoon River Anthology*, with an excellent collection of grotesques. Sharp vignettes; lonely, thwarted lives, "confused and disconcerted by the facts of life." A background of earlier America, crude and ugly, that drives to religious fanaticism in Steve Bentley; to passionate rebellion in Kate Swift; to bitter irony in Ray Pearson. Note the deterministic conclusion of "The Untold Lie"—"Tricked, by Gad, that's what I was; tricked by life and made a fool of"; and the pessimism: . . . "he shouted a protest against his life, against all life, against everything that makes life ugly."

The Triumph of the Egg (1921). A strange and difficult book with its subtle symbolisms. The theme is the common hunger for romance and fellowship that confuses itself with sex and is unsatisfied. Suggested in prefatory poem: "I have a wonderful story to tell but know no way to tell it."

1. *The Egg.* An epitome of his philosophy of grotesques. The egg breeds life that is futile, and life reproduces the egg. A morbid disgust that would bottle the egg, and the failure.

* The notes that follow are from the syllabus.—*Publisher.*

370

2. *Out of Nowhere Into Nothing.* Theme is the "white wonder of life"—what it is and the part it plays in shaping life; a sex illusion that in its mystic appeal to youth guarantees the perpetuation of the race. To age there is no "white wonder," but the life processes are dirty, and lead to final imprisonment in a common trap. Hence the "white wonder" is the supreme jest of nature, sardonic, beguiling, gathering its victims who eagerly run their predetermined course.

3. *Brothers.* A suggestion of the true "white wonder of life"— the brotherhood of man in a lonely world—"beyond words, beyond passion—the fellowship in living, the fellowship in life." But men cannot break through the walls of themselves to grasp it, and the dirt of the world destroys its beauty. "The whole story of mankind's loneliness, of the effort to reach out to unattainable beauty, tried to get itself expressed from the lips of a mumbling old man, crazed with loneliness." "We have different names but we are brothers." "Already I have written three hundred, four hundred thousand words. Are there no words that lead into life?" See conclusion of "The Man in the Brown Coat."

A Story Teller's Story (1924). An attempt to lay bare the emotional life of one seeking to be an artist in America; to plumb his own consciousness, to escape from a world he hates. Such escape comes from reaching down "through all the broken surface distractions of modern life to that old craft out of which culture springs." He must pull himself free from a deadening and devastating routine of an industrial society with its empty ambitions. And having found his craft he finds a recompense in life. "I sang as I worked, as in my boyhood I had often seen old craftsmen sing and as I had never heard men sing in factories. And for what I had written at such times I had been called unclean by men and women who had never known me, could have no personal reasons for thinking me unclean. Was I unclean? Were the hands that, for such brief periods of my life, had really served me, had they been unclean at such moments of service?" A stimulating and suggestive document of modern life.

The note of determinism in Anderson expressed in two images, the wall and escape—running to get away from what holds us fast. But in running away from the old self to find a new, we carry the old self with us. Anderson one of the three or four most important men now writing fiction in America. Compare with D. H. Lawrence.

A NEW ROMANCE

The new romance and the new naturalism both spring from a common root—hatred of the meanness and ugliness of modern life; but romance seeks to evade and forget what naturalism examines curiously. It is a defense mechanism against things as they are and springs from:

1. Disgust at the verisimilitude of naturalism that parades the crude ugliness of life as if it were the reality. The dream more important than the fact, for our real existence is within the imagination, removed from material futilities, where we may satisfy our hunger for beauty, for far-ranging adventure, for ideal existence.

2. The impulse to free creation. Real life overshadowed and darkened by a sense of impotence; men are flies caught in the web of circumstance. But in romance the will is unshackled and the free imagination plays with time and space, shaping fate to its liking in terms of beauty, dwelling in a world as we should like it to be. Romance hence is the ideal cosmos of the ego.

3. The spirit of youth that has brooded over life and refuses to abandon its dreams. The inevitable outcome irony, an undertone of sadness, a recognition of the pessimism against which it desires to be a defense. This the final note. So compare the *Eros et mors* of old romance. . . .*

* Cabell omitted, as there is a fuller discussion of him given.—*Publisher.*

1917–1924 *

Introduction: With the entry of America into the war came a sharp change in literary development. Regimentation due to war psychology destroyed the movement of social criticism which dominated fiction between 1903 and 1917. The liberal movement in economics and politics came to an abrupt end, and the problem novel ceased to be written. Almost overnight it became old-fashioned. The year 1918 sterile.[1] With the year 1919 began a new literary period. Three major movements:

1. A resurgence of naturalism, inspired by psychology rather than by economics, with a tendency to impressionism in handling: represented by Sherwood Anderson.

2. A new romanticism, seeking ideal beauty as a defense against reality and emerging in irony: represented by James Branch Cabell.

3. A new criticism: A revolt of the young intellectuals against the dominant middle class—its Puritanism, its Victorianism, its acquisitive ideals: represented by Sinclair Lewis.

I

THE SMALL TOWN IN FICTION

The first expression of the new literature. Chiefly a middle-western development—and a late phase of the literature of the local. A reaction from the "economic city," with its centralizing economics, which dominated the problem novel. Two antagonistic interpretations: (1) The romantic small town, or the theory of a kindly, democratic world; (2) The realistic small town, or the theory of a petty, competitive world.

I. *The Romantic Interpretation of the Small Town.* A hold-over from an earlier period. Derives from Riley; elaborated and defended by Meredith Nicholson, *The Valley of Democracy* (1918). According to this theory the middle-western village is: (1) A land of economic well-being, uncursed by poverty and unspoiled by wealth; (2) A land of "folksiness"—the village a great family in its

---

* From the syllabus.—*Publisher.*
[1] For a statement of the reaction of a young intellectual to the war, see Randolph Bourne, *Untimely Papers*, 1919.

373

neighborliness, friendliness, sympathy; (3) Primarily middle-class, and therefore characteristically American, wholesome, and human in spite of its prosaic shortcomings; (4) The home of American democracy, dominated by the spirit of equality, where men are measured by their native qualities.[2]

WILLIAM ALLEN WHITE: A SON OF THE MIDDLE BORDER

Product of middle-class, Puritan Kansas. Dominated by sentiment, believes in the essential fairness of men. Two major ideas: (1) Belief in the excellence of western village life; (2) Fear lest this life be submerged by industrialism. A romantic and political Progressive. Formulated his political theory in *The Old Order Changeth* (1910)—thesis, that America is changing from representative republicanism to democracy. The problem is to make business honest. Not an intellectual. His plots resemble Thackeray's— leisurely, gossipy, confidential asides, a large canvas, many figures, a long period of time. His attitude admirably expressed in *Emporia and New York* (1906).

At the Court of Boyville (1899). The romance of youth set against the background of the small town. A world of dreams and loveliness: adventures that await beyond the horizon; the glory of pigtails and overalls. The democracy of the vacant lot: rivalry in marbles and hand-springs—the leadership of the capable. Sincerer work than Tarkington's *Penrod*. Contrast with Garland's *Son of the Middle Border*, and Mark Twain's *Tom Sawyer*.

A Certain Rich Man (1909). His plunge into the problem novel. Theme: fear of the economic city that draws the villager into its web. A contrast between the two worlds and two social ideals—the friendly democracy of the older America threatened by economic centralization.

In the Heart of a Fool (1918). One of the last of the problem novels. Theme—the invasion of the small town by industrialism and the disintegration of village virtues. The story of an idealist who opposes the ends of Main Street and his destruction by the herd. A suggestion of Sinclair Lewis. The conclusion—the excellence of love and the foolishness of selfishness. The background characters, studies in the reaction of the older ideal to the new egoism.

[2] For a criticism of Nicholson, see Randolph Bourne, *The History of a Literary Radical*, p. 128.

BOOTH TARKINGTON: THE DEAN OF AMERICAN MIDDLE-CLASS LETTERS

Possesses the virtues of cleverness, optimism, humor, respectability. Honors all the Victorian taboos. Life is an agreeable experience—to the successful, hence it is well to rise. His chief theme, middle-class romance as exemplified in the "valley of democracy": courtship of nice young people through the agencies of parties and picnics. A skillful writer, with a light touch, but his art destroyed by love of popularity—a novel ends well that ends happily. A perennial sophomore, purveyor of comfortable literature to middle-class America.[3]

The Gentleman from Indiana (1899). A dramatization of the "good, dear people" theme. The college man who goes back to his people to live and work with them. A satisfying life results from merging individual life in the common village life. A flabby and somewhat saccharine philosophy.

Alice Adams (1921). The story of an instinctive actress and her competitive struggle for social position and a man. A clever, attractive, lovable girl defeated by her background—led into foolish little deceits to keep up appearances—victim of middle-class conventionality. Shabby parlors versus conservatories as settings for proposals. The Adams family has fallen behind their acquaintances in the business of rising in the world, and Alice sinks to a lower social scale. An overrated book.

The Midlander (1923). A contribution to booster literature and an unconscious satire on the emptiness of the middle-class mind. A real-estate venture and what came of it. The conception that "man is a wealth-and-comfort-producing machine." Supposed to be tragedy, but the tragedy lies in preferring the imported to the domestic article—choosing a New York girl instead of a local one. The suburb thrives, the automobile business goes forward, and the gods of getting on smile in the end.[4]

The other numerous titles of Tarkington signify nothing except to lovers of comfortable literature. The clever Hoosier has ceased to be an artist—the great failure in contemporary American fiction.

DOROTHY CANFIELD (FISHER)

A clever dramatizer of the obvious: believes in the Woman Triumphant, and discovers in the right education of children—particularly girls—the solution of all problems. Two main themes:

[3] See Mr. Cabell's criticism in *Beyond Life*, pp. 301–307.
[4] For a review see the *Nation*, March 19, 1924.

1. A protest against the demands of "social life." *The Squirrel Cage* (1912). A contribution to the problem novel. A William Morris suggestion of the sufficiency of handicraft as an escape from social demands. An arraignment of the American home where the father scarcely knows the children and the mother is shut away from the outside world.

The Bent Twig (1915). A study of university community life—the struggle between plain living and high thinking—of social pleasure and no thinking.

2. The defense of the village. The belief that community fellowship—a gathering to watch a century plant bloom—breeds an artistic spirit finer than old-world art and culture can offer. Especially a Vermont town is ideal for the proper bringing up of children. *The Brimming Cup* (1920). A story of the right bringing up of children. *Rough Hewn* (1922). The love of art and travel which leads inevitably to a Vermont town and marriage. *Raw Material* (1923). Sketches. The point of view given in "Paul Meyer"—the folly of thinking that a normal girl should prefer philology to matrimony.

II

THE REALISTIC SMALL TOWN AND THE NEW NATURALISM

The work of the younger intellectuals, more disciplined than the muckrakers, with wider culture and severer standards. Concerned for civilization, the things of the spirit, a free creative individualism, rather than political liberalism. A searching criticism of the triumphant middle class, its ideals and its habitat, the town and city; the repressive tyrannies of its herd mind; the futility of its materialism. Back of the novelists is a group of essayists, young critics of established ways: Van Wyck Brooks, Ludwig Lewisohn, Randolph Bourne, H. L. Mencken. They embody a reaction from: (1) The acquisitive ideal of a machine civilization. (2) "The great illusion of American civilization, the illusion of optimism"—the staple of middle-class business morale. (3) The sentimentalism of "comfortable literature," that evades reality and weakens the intellectual fiber. (4) The inhibitions of a Puritanism that has lost its sanctions. (5) The White-Tarkington doctrine of the "beautiful people" and "folksy village."

The movement began with Masters's *Spoon River Anthology*

(1915). An earlier work is E. W. Howe's *Story of a Country Town* (1883):—stark, grim, unrelieved, revealing the "smoldering discontent of an inarticulate frontier."

ZONA GALE—THE TRANSITION FROM ROMANCE TO REALISM

I. Friendship Village romance. *The Loves of Pelleas and Etarre* (1907). Everyone is helpful, everyone loves, or wants to, or is unhappy for lack of it. *Friendship Village* (1908). A world where there is no sorrow, or sickness, and where brotherly love rules. Of the "folksy" school.

II. The shift to realism. *Miss Lulu Bett* (1920). A homely village tragedy of the repressed soul that rebels under the irritation of domestic pin-pricks. Plebeian characters, thin, cheap, tiresome; set in a shoddy world and rubbing each other's nerves. Deacon Dwight a sadist; Miss Lulu a grotesque. Treated from the outside in contrast with Sherwood Anderson's method. *Faint Perfume* (1923). A glorification of martyrdom. The conviction that life is hard, and the excellence of the economy of pain. A partial return to the *Friendship Village* note, but like *Miss Lulu Bett* in the picture of a self-worshiping family.*

· · · · · · · ·

DONN BYRNE †

American born but Irish bred. His early work, *The Stranger's Banquet* (1919), half problem novel—industrialism—which offered little scope for the Celtic wistfulness in which he conceives romance to lie.

Messer Marco Polo (1921). The romance of distant times and places, of unfamiliar backgrounds and lovely worlds: medieval Venice and its pageantry; a far quest over burning sands; the loveliness of little Golden Bells at the court of Kubla Khan; the ardor of love that tangles itself in religion. A wistfulness and beauty of phrase that remind one of Synge's *Riders to the Sea.* The loveliest romance of recent years.[5]

The Wind That Bloweth (1922). A rich fabric—Gaelic folk; the woman of the boulevard; the white sun-baked road to Damascus;

* Sinclair Lewis omitted, as fuller material has been given.—*Publisher.*
† From the third section in the syllabus, which deals with "A New Romance."—*Publisher.*
[5] See Cabell's review of *Messer Marco Polo* in *Straws and Prayer-Books*, pp. 52–59. The writer's full name is Brian Oswald Donn-Byrne.

the fire of revolution; the crack of cordage as the ship rounds the Horn—a saga of the unquiet heart.

The Changeling (1923). Short stories of quaint places, forgotten people; the Bible and love of Ireland. Done with excellent craftsmanship.

Blind Raftery (1924). A tale of a blind harpist in Dean Swift's Ireland and of his wife, Hilaria, who sings the song of the women of the streets in Cadiz. Life teaches them a philosophy expressed by the harpist in these words: "We sit a little while by ourselves in an apart, dark place, and we learn truths, of how certain things one believes to be good are but vulgar selfish things, and how certain things the small think evil are but futile accidents. And we learn to be kind; such wisdom comes when we are dead. And those who have never died in life . . . are pleasant shallow people, soulless as seals."

ROBERT NATHAN

Began like Donn Byrne with a problem study—*Peter Kindred* (1919). A dual personality cut asunder and embodied in two characters: David the romantic fades out of the story, and Peter becomes a modern, absorbed in eugenics. A background of Phillips Exeter and Harvard.

Autumn (1921). An idyll of loneliness, with a commentary on materialism, done in simple, wistful language.

1. Mr. Jeminy, a village philosopher, disciple of Boëthius and St. Francis, half pagan and yet Christian. Troubled over the poverty of the world that does not amass "love, peace, the quiet of the heart, the work of one's hand."

2. A village background. Mr. Jeminy wished to teach the children the secret of happiness instead of the folly of plus and minus, and was turned out of his school. An echo of *Main Street* in its commentary on village narrowness, hardness, gossip. A frigid Puritanism that disapproves Mr. Jeminy for speaking disrespectfully of God and denies happiness to Mrs. Wicket who is under God's sentence of unhappiness.

3. A note of determinism. A world of grotesques—all are hemmed in and cramped, longing for fresh experience and strange adventures, all are unhappy. So Aaron Bade with his flute and his "awkward thoughts and clumsy feelings." Margaret Bade with her conviction, "Life is so much spilt milk"; Farmer Barly with his

commentary, "Folks are queer crotchets"; Anna Barly with her yearning for the "white wonder of life" and the trap. An indictment of New England for its destruction of natural happiness and the simple joy of life.

4. A profound irony. The end of Mr. Jeminy's hopefulness is disillusion. "Here within this circle of hills, is to be found faith, virtue, passion, and good sense. In this valley youth is not without courage, or age without wisdom." The outcome disproves this faith. Of his many pupils, "Not one is tidy of mind, or humble of heart. Not one has learned to be happy in poverty, or gentle in good fortune." Life as a whole is futile. The dead alone can ask God the meaning of life. "But for us, who remain, it has no meaning." The tale is Robert Frost done in prose—compare "Mending Wall."

The Puppet Master (1923). The most graceful fantasy in American literature. Papa Jonas, the puppet creator and master, watches the love of Annabelle Lee, a rag doll with shoe-button eyes, and Mr. Aristotle, a red-nosed, philosopher-clown puppet; and of Mary Holly and Christopher Lane, the poet. The theme is love— "Love is a man's soul: it does not grow like his hopes, it does not break like his heart. . . . But love goes by after a while." Papa Jonas is Mr. Jeminy, converted to the Stoic philosophy but lacking love. The note of determinism persists, but the Stoic attitude overcomes. "Yes," he said slowly, "one must make the best of what one has."

JOSEPH HERGESHEIMER: A SOPHISTICATED ROMANTIC

Began as a painter. After fourteen years' apprenticeship was accepted by the *Saturday Evening Post*, and began a career in popularity that rivals Tarkington's. Possesses the virtues and vices of the *Post* school. In earlier work a colorist, painting statuesques against artfully arranged backgrounds; a connoisseur of fabrics and poses and nature settings—nearly as "much concerned with the stuffs as with the stuff of life." In *Cytherea* the setting a sophisticated manipulation of the theme, as the hot Cuban night in Cobra with its naked primitive passions. A dabbler in psychology that develops into a crude Freudianism, particularly in *Cytherea*. Always a hint of artistic insincerity; something of a poseur yet a sensuous artist nature. His gorgeous prose style spotty and streaked by amazing crudeness.

The Three Black Pennys (1917). A study in the breaking out of willfulness in successive generations, set against a background of the history of iron-making in Pennsylvania. An elaboration of *Tubal Cain*. An anticlimax arranged for dramatic significance, suggesting the decay of romance in a hundred and fifty years of American industrial development. The first episode is Hergesheimer at his best. Howat Penny a study in moods that make him "angry at life"; but swept on by the will to possess. Ludowica Winscomb embodies a favorite theme—the suggestion of an older culture contrasted with the crude American reality. So compare Taou Yuen.

Linda Condon (1919). A study in the decay of surface beauty— an empty form caught in the web of a shallow mother and the demands of stronger natures, but preserved by lack of emotional concern. Handled skillfully, with a somewhat forced unity symbolized by Linda's straight black bang; but the story leaves one with a sense of unconcern for Linda and her fate. The ending melodramatic. Note Van Doren's curious comment—"nearly the most beautiful American novel since Hawthorne and Henry James."

Java Head (1919). The story of an exotic that languishes in an uncongenial habitat. A contrast in backgrounds: the romance of old Salem in the days of the clipper ship; the romance of a far older East that makes Salem seem raw and crude. Taou Yuen a decorative lay figure, with aristocratic suggestions beyond anything the West knows. The dramatic significance of opium, that hangs like a pall over the East and brings degeneration and death to Puritan Salem. The end with its cheap love adventure, a conscious satire on western life. Hergesheimer's best work. A romantic atmosphere got without archaic trappings of speech and manners; nevertheless makes much of costume.

Balisand (1924). A romance of a Virginia Federalist in the days of the Revolution and after. A rich background of plantation life, with a touch of somewhat cheap mysticism. Of the school of Washington rather than Jefferson. A better work than *The Bright Shawl* or *Cytherea*.

His other titles signify little. Yet see the *Saturday Evening Post* for a series of furniture stories. Characteristic of his concern for the "stuffs of life." See in particular, "Mahogany" (Vol. 195, no.

53, January, 1923); "Pewter" (Vol. 196, no. 23, January, 1924):
"Oak" (Vol. 196, no. 3, July, 1923).[6]

IV
CERTAIN OTHER WRITERS

EDITH WHARTON—THE GENTEEL TRADITION AND THE NEW PLUTOCRACY

A temperamental aristocrat, endowed with keen intelligence and ripe culture. Observes the ways of a wealthy society without culture and unconcerned with standards. A protest against the domination of the middle class. Mrs. Wharton isolated in America by her native aristocratic tastes. The older New York society without real distinction, bound by convention and with middle-class concern for respectability; the new society a vulgar plutocracy; outside both a pushing *nouveau-riche* class eager to climb. Hence she turns to the authentic aristocracy of Europe for satisfaction of her genteel tastes. In spirit she belongs to the *ancien régime*. The highest law of society is convention, but it must be noble, not vulgar.

The House of Mirth (1905). A story of New York's gilded society, and how it served one of its daughters. Lily Bart, trained for social leadership in a plutocracy, a finished and costly parasite, seeking a market for her beauty, yet restrained by instinctive refinement from seeing the game through. Lacking money she is caught in a web of convention and destroyed. In her world convention is the social law, and the tragedy flows from her inability to rise above it or to keep it wholly. The contrast between Selden and Trenor—the aristocrat and the plutocrat—characteristic of Mrs. Wharton.

Ethan Frome (1911). A dramatization of the "narrow house" theme—life held relentlessly in the grip of poverty and duty. A bleak and joyless existence that seeks escape and suffers lingering tragedy. Thereafter a stern isolation and iron repression. Mrs. Wharton's finest work.

The Custom of the Country (1915). A study of the social climber. The best of a series of novels satirizing the encroachments on New York exclusiveness by the rising plutocracy and its daughters. The western plutocracy of pork presumably more vulgar than the

[6] For a striking characterization of Hergesheimer, see *The Bookman*, May, 1922. For an appreciation, see Cabell, *Straws and Prayer-Books*, pp. 195-221.

eastern plutocracy of Wall Street, yet between them the older gentry crushed. So compare Boyesen, *Social Strugglers* (1893); Robert Grant, *Unleavened Bread* (1900). Undine Spragg, like Selma White, pushing, heartless, vulgar, showy, is set over against Ralph Marvell, a refined "dabbler with life"; Peter Van Degen, the "plunger"; and Elmer Moffatt, the self-made man. She embodies all that Mrs. Wharton most hates; all climbers are vulgar, she believes, both men and women.

The Age of Innocence (1920). A study of the older world of the eighteen-seventies. A loving yet satirical picture of a Pharisaic society, "wholly absorbed in barricading self against the unpleasant"; that lives secluded, protected by its taboos, and fears reality. A sterile world of clan conventions and negations; a decadent Victorianism. The Van der Luydens of Skuytercliff are of the same stuff as the Dagonets in *The Custom of the Country;* and the dilettante Newland Archer is another Ralph Marvell. Into this dead world enters Ellen Olenska with her vivid old-world experiences, who threatens to rebel, yet finally yields to the clan taboos. The book fades out like the lives of the Van der Luydens. An admirable work.

Old New York (1924). Four carefully done tales that sketch New York in the forties, fifties, sixties, and seventies. A return to her best manner, with the finish of *The Age of Innocence.*

Her other later work not important. *Glimpses of the Moon* (1922) inconsequential; and *A Son at the Front* (1923)—an attempt to document the reactions of an artist with a son in the army—only half successful.

Mrs. Wharton a finished artist who grasps her material firmly; an intellectual attitude, delighting in irony. Unaffected by the problem novel, and schools of naturalism or romanticism. Not a thinker like Cabell, whose irony springs from an imagination that contemplates man in his relation to cosmic forces, but an observer whose irony springs from noting the clash between men and social convention. The last of our literary aristocrats of the genteel tradition. Her attitude expressed in the words, "*Je suis venue trop tard dans un monde trop vulgaire.*"

WILLA CATHER: EPICS OF WOMEN

The Middle Border of Hamlin Garland seen through different eyes. She looks back lovingly to a pioneer West, as the cradle of heroic lives. An epic breadth of prairie spaces and industrious years, with a note of regret—*Optima dies prima fugit.* Against this background she sets her immigrant women, with their vigor and wealth of life, and considers how the West has dealt with them. Peasant heroines, with their strong natures hidden under queer speech and garb, set in a waste of wild red grass, bitter winters, burning summers, virgin soil and great loneliness. A long-ignored theme—the lot of the immigrant who has come on a desperate adventure—the struggle of their children with the soil. Compare *The Jungle,* for the industrial exploitation of the immigrant.

Has matured slowly. *The Troll Garden* (1905), and *Alexander's Bridge* (1910), are inconsequential. Her real work done late. Belongs to no school. Is neither naturalistic nor romantic. Is unconcerned with problems. Except for a single attack on the ugliness of the small western town—"The Sculptor's Funeral" in *The Troll Garden*—she ignores middle-class America and its Main Streets. An individual artist, sincere, capable; an excellent craftsman.

O Pioneers (1913). The story of Alexandra Bergson, a daughter of the Middle Border; calm, tenacious, capable; loving the soil and bringing it to abundant productiveness. The new world had brought out diverse qualities in the Swedish peasant family; the older brothers common, dull, vulgarized by Americanization; the younger brother suggestive of the better side of American opportunity. Alexandra the directing mind and controlling will. Over against her is set the Bohemian Marie Tovesky, childlike in her spontaneous enthusiasm. The tragic ending handled with great skill. Thrown about the whole, a harsh Nebraska countryside through changing periods. One who had not lived through similar experiences and loved the memory could not write so.

The Song of the Lark (1915). The story of Thea Kronberg, who by virtue of fierce energy and iron strength rises to triumph as an artist. There are no romantic stage-effects, only the passionate struggle of a tenacious will. Thea a peasant nature of vast solidity. The most convincing story of artist life written by an American. A changing background: the mean little Colorado town, the loneliness of Chicago, Europe, the great spaces of the Southwest.

My Ántonia (1918). The story of Ántonia Shimerda: an opulent peasant nature with strong mother instinct, thwarted by meager opportunities and vulgar environment. Her life runs a narrow round: the early pioneer experience with its loneliness and black tragedy; the town experience of the hired girl, who lives eagerly; the later life of a hard-working mother on a lonely farm. Ántonia "a rich mine of life like the founder of early races," loving, generous, eager, yet belonging to the soil. To vulgarize such natures by cramming them into a conventional mold, passes for Americanization—this the implied thesis.

One of Ours (1922). The story of Claude Wheeler, with strength imprisoned by a society that opens its opportunities to Main Street natures like Bayliss Wheeler. A suggestion of naturalism in the handling of the theme: Claude caught by the negative character Enid Royse because he fails to appreciate the complementary strength of Gladys Farmer—a true Cather woman, enmeshed in Gopher Prairie. A futile, ironical ending: better to die in battle than be destroyed by the pettiness of Gopher Prairie. The war atmosphere seems curiously old-fashioned.

The Lost Lady (1923). A change of theme. The story of Mrs. Forester, an embodiment of traditional feminine charm, quite superior to such incidents as age or loyalty—a type of woman outside Miss Cather's experience and understanding.*

V

SOME WAR BOOKS

The late war the first in our history that has produced an aftermath of searching criticism in fiction or drama. The romantic note dominant in all earlier accounts, particularly of the Revolution and the Rebellion. Such stories written by men who took no part in them. The Civil War produced only one book of realistic criticism, that was mutilated by the publisher to temper its cynicism, and that enjoyed no popularity—*The Recollections of a Private*, by Warren Goss. The late war is producing a considerable group, all realistic and critical; the romantic note has not yet appeared.

JOHN DOS PASSOS

Three Soldiers (1921). A naturalistic handling of war that serves as a commentary on *One of Ours*. The most notable American work on the theme since Stephen Crane's *The Red Badge of Courage*.

* See remarks on Miss Cather in the introduction to the text edition of Ole Rölvaag's *Giants in the Earth*, which follows these syllabus notes.—*Publisher*.

Similar in temper to Henri Barbusse, *Under Fire*, but dealing with the barracks and the drill field. Compare with Andreas Latzko, *Men in War*—impressionistic in handling. Dos Passos a young artist from the university, an idealist who enlists and is disillusioned. A study of the war machine and the effect of regimentation on different types of men—the contrast between army discipline and a lax individualism, and the disasters that may ensue from sudden change. Fuselli a low-grade character who wants to rise; Chrisfield a solid animal who becomes sullen; Andrews a highly nervous organism, to whom routine is killing. Coarse episodes set in a brilliant background: the glamour of militarism gone.

E. E. CUMMINGS

The Enormous Room (1922). A brilliant revelation of the tortures endured by an artist unjustly imprisoned in a French military prison. Supplements *Three Soldiers* in destroying the appeal of military glamour. An attack particularly on the common notion of heroic, chivalrous France.

THOMAS BOYD

Through the Wheat (1923). An impressionistic handling of the reactions of a normal American soldier, Private Hicks, to the war. The keynote is numbness—a deadly numbness which offers the sole defense of the normal mind against the horrors it confronts. Its matter-of-factness, detached point of view, and the ordinariness of the hero, set it apart from *Three Soldiers* and *The Enormous Room*. An excellent bit of impressionism.

LAURENCE STALLINGS

Plumes (1924). A story of war by one who has suffered mutilation from it. The theme—"If you are smashed badly . . . and if you have any intelligence you must remake a world to live in." A study of post-war disillusionment, naturalistically handled. So compare the play in which he collaborated—*What Price Glory?*

VI

YOUTH IN REVOLT—CERTAIN PURVEYORS OF THE HECTIC

A group of youthful poseurs at the mercy of undigested reactions to Nietzsche, Butler, Dadaism, Vorticism, Socialism; overbalanced by changes in American critical and creative standards, and in love with copious vocabularies and callow emotions. Given to satirizing the educational methods of *alma mater;* quick to espouse new causes; enthusiastic for revolt as a profession. A prolific movement which as yet has accomplished nothing seriously creative.

F. SCOTT FITZGERALD

This Side of Paradise (1921); *The Beautiful and the Damned* (1922). A bad boy who loves to smash things to show how naughty he is; a bright boy who loves to say smart things to show how clever he is. Precocious, ignorant—a short candle already burnt out.

STEPHEN VINCENT BENÉT AND FLOYD DELL

Benét: *Heavens and Earth* (1920); *The Beginning of Wisdom* (1921); *Young People's Pride* (1923); *Jean Hugenot* (1923). Floyd Dell: *Moon Calf* (1921); *Briary Bush* (1922); *Janet March* (1923).

Luminaries of the school which holds that the sufficient tests of intellectual emancipation are rolled hose, midnight discussions, black coffee, and the discarding of wedding rings. Floyd Dell the most serious and ablest of the group.

BEN HECHT

Eric Dorn (1921); *Gargoyles* (1922). An almost naturalistic distrust of formal education, love, and government, and an unsubstantiated belief in the efficacy of revolt in general and the romance of city streets in particular. A burnt-out rocket. His last books— *1001 Afternoons in Chicago* (1923) and *Florentine Dagger* (1924) worse than inconsequential.

OLE RÖLVAAG'S "GIANTS IN THE EARTH" *

THE dramatic contrast between Per Hansa, type of the natural
pioneer who sees the golden light of promise flooding the wind-
swept plains, and Beret, child of an old folk civilization who
hungers for the home ways and in whose heart the terror of loneliness gathers, penetrates to the deeper reality of life as it was
lived for three hundred years on the American frontier. It is not
a late or rare phenomenon; it is only late and rare in literature.
We have been used to viewing the frontier in broad and generous
perspective and have responded most sympathetically to the epic
note that runs through the tale of the conquest of the continent.
It is the great American romance that gives life and drama to
our history. It was this epic quality that de Tocqueville felt when
he discovered the poetry of America in the silent march of a race
toward the far-off Pacific, hewing its way triumphantly through
forests and mountains to arrive at its objective. But the emotional side, the final ledger of human values, we have too little
considered—the men and women broken by the frontier, the great
army of derelicts who failed and were laid away, like the Norse
immigrant lad, in forgotten graves. The cost of it all in human
happiness—the loneliness, the disappointments, the renunciations,
the severing of old ties and quitting of familiar places, the appalling
lack of those intangible cushions for the nerves that could not be
transported on horseback or in prairie schooners: these imponderables too often have been left out of the reckoning in our traditional romantic interpretation. But with the growth of a maturer
realism we are beginning to understand how great was the price
exacted by the frontier; and it is because *Giants in the Earth*, for
the first time in our fiction, evaluates adequately the settlement
in terms of emotion, because it penetrates to the secret inner life
of men and women who undertook the heavy work of subduing
the wilderness, that it is—quite apart from all artistic values—a
great historical document.

* Introduction to the text edition of Rölvaag's *Giants in the Earth*. Copyright
1929 by Harper and Brothers, by whose permission it is reprinted here.—*Publisher.*

If in one sense the conquest of the continent is the great American epic, in another sense it is the great American tragedy. The vastness of the unexplored reaches, the inhospitality of the wilderness, the want of human aid and comfort when disaster came, these were terrifying things to gentle souls whom fate had not roughhewn for pioneering. Fear must have been a familiar visitor to the heart of the pioneer woman, and for a hundred and fifty years this fear of the dark wilderness was one reason why the settlements clung to the more hospitable seaboard. There, at least, was an outlook toward the old home. But with the crossing of the Allegheny Mountains, following the Revolutionary War, the frontier spirit came into its own. A spirit of restlessness took possession of men, and the thin line of settlements advanced swiftly, overrunning the Inland Empire with its interminable forests and malarial swamps, sprawling rudely from the Great Lakes to the Gulf of Mexico. To subdue the land was no easy task. Upon the old and the weak the wilderness laid a ruthless hand, and even of the strength of the young it took heavy toll. Tragedy was always lurking at the door of the backwoods cabin. In Beveridge's *Life of Lincoln* there is a grim story of the hardships suffered by the Lincoln family in Indiana that leaves no room for romance—husband, wife, two children, and later an old couple, were forced to pig together all winter in a brush camp open on one side to the weather, with only a fire in front for cooking and heating—a mode of life below that of the Indian in his skin teepee. And then a mysterious disease fell upon them, virulent and fateful, and the old couple were taken from their cots on the ground and put away beneath the soil to find what rest they might there. That men should break and women go mad under such strain is no more than may be expected of human nature. Beret, the wife of Per Hansa, brooding in her sod-hut in Dakota, afraid of life and of her own thoughts, and turning for comfort to a dark religion, is a type of thousands of frontier women who—as the historian Ridpath said of his parents—"toiled and suffered and died that their children might inherit the promise."

Very likely we should have felt the tragedy of the frontier long ago if we had been as much concerned with inner experience as with outward act, if we had been psychologists as well as chroniclers. But we have been too prone to romanticize the objective reality and disguise slatternly ways with the garb of backwoods independence. The realistic eighteenth century made no such mistake. Such infrequent glimpses of the first frontier as we catch in our early literature suggest a swift descent into grossness as the settlements were left behind. In the *Journal of Madam Sarah Knight*, which dates from the opening years of the eighteenth century, are brief notes of what fell under her sharp eyes on a horseback trip from Boston to New York. The sketches she has penciled are far from bucolic. Certain of the figures that emerge casually from her pages are no other than decivilized grotesques—animal-like creatures for whom returning to a state of nature meant living filthily in mean huts, traveling back centuries toward the primitive ways of the cavemen. Of the emotional reactions of these early children of the wilderness Madam Knight tells us nothing; so casual an observer would have no opportunity to penetrate beneath the unlovely surface.

A quarter century later Colonel William Byrd, the first gentleman of Virginia, wrote his graphic *History of the Dividing Line*, an account of a boundary survey run between the colonies of Virginia and South Carolina. As the survey leaves the seacoast behind and approaches the frontier, the same characteristics appear that Madam Knight noted—a rough and surly independence, a dislike of established law and order, and a shiftless way of life that is content to subsist off the country. "Lubberland," Colonel Byrd called the Carolina backwoods where a new race of poor whites was springing up—a rude decivilized existence that bore heavily on the women and was heedless of the common amenities of social life. In *Letters from an American Farmer* (1773) written by St. John de Crèvecœur, a cultivated Norman who established himself in the colonies after serving in the French army under Montcalm, the same sharp judgment is passed on the frontier. Crèvecœur was of the romantic school of Rousseau and eloquent in praise of life lived close to nature, yet even he discovers the frontier to be a blot on colonial civilization, the abode of rude and lawless figures who precede by a decade the sober army of occupation.

In the eighteenth century the testimony is clear that the frontiersmen—or "borderers," as they were commonly called—were rough bumptious fellows who fled the settlements partly because of a dislike of ordered and seemly ways. The colonial gentry, men like the Rev. Timothy Dwight, held them in deep contempt and rejoiced when they quitted the settlements and plunged deep into the wilderness beyond the jurisdiction of church and state. Lawlessness, shiftlessness, a passion like Jurgen's to follow after their own wishes and their own desires, seem to have been the characteristics of these rude men and slatternly women, as the aristocratic eighteenth century judged them. That is very far from the whole story, to be sure. Our later historians have made clear that from this same leveling frontier issued the spirit of American democracy, and that from these rough individualists came the great movement of Jacksonianism that swept away the class distinctions of an earlier century. Accepting so much, and recognizing the part played by the frontier in shaping the institutions and the psychology of America, it remains true, nevertheless, that the lot of the backwoodsman was hard and the price he paid in civilization for his freedom was great. The sod house of the Dakota plains was only a late adaptation of the primitive huts that were strung along the earlier frontier. What loneliness filled the hearts of the drab women who made hoecakes and dressed deer skins, what rebellions at their lot stirred dumbly within them, no record remains to tell and no literature has cared to concern itself about.

It was not till the nineteenth century that authentic accounts of the frontier, written by men who had come out of it, began to appear, yet even then in too scant volume. In Longstreet's *Georgia Scenes*, Joseph G. Baldwin's *Flush Times of Alabama and Mississippi*, and Davy Crockett's *Autobiography*, the frontier is painted in homely colors that time cannot fade. Their brisk pages seem to have been dipped in the butternut dye-pot of the backwoods cabin. By far the most significant of them is the braggart but naïvely truthful narrative of the life of Cane-brake Davy who in his several removals followed the advancing frontier the length of the State of Tennessee. Davy would seem to have been the authentic backwoodsman, and the life of the individual may be taken as a description of the genus. Restless, assertive, unsocial, buoyantly optimistic and obsessed with the faith that better land lay farther west, cultivating a bumptious wit that was a defense mechanism against the meanness of daily life, he was only an improvident child who fled instinctively from civilization. As a full-length portrait of the Jacksonian leveler, in the days when the great social revolution was establishing the principles of an equalitarian democracy, the picture is of vast significance. But it is incomplete. Concerning the wife and daughters who were dragged at his heels in the successive removals, the narrative is silent. It is a man's tale, unenriched by the emotional experiences of a woman, and as such it tells only half the story of the frontier.

The *Autobiography* was the last pungent note of realism before the romantic revolution swept over American literature; and it was not till two generations later, when the war was over and the glories of the Gilded Age were fading, that the frontier came to realistic expression again in the works of Hamlin Garland. *Main-Travelled Roads*, the first chapter in the tale of the Middle Border, is a prologue to *Giants in the Earth*, telling the story of the prairie settlement in the idiom of the generation that undertook the great adventure. In these brief tales is compressed the harsh temper of the eighties, when the spirit of revolt was running like wildfire across the prairies and the Middle Border was arming for battle. For a decade or more the farmers' affairs had been out of kilter, and a note of discontent had begun to appear in fiction. Before Garland, western life had been dealt with by Edward Eggleston in *The Hoosier Schoolmaster* and *The Circuit Rider*, and more searchingly by Ed Howe in *The Story of a Country Town*—a drab commentary on life in Atchison, Kansas, in the early eighties. But it is in Joseph Kirkland's *Zury, The Meanest Man in Spring County* (1887), that a deep sense of the meanness of frontier life is first adequately felt. The harsh constrictions of pioneer existence tightened about Zury as a boy when his father was struggling with debt, turning a naturally generous nature into a skinflint mortgage grabber. He early learned that he must fight to survive, and as a result his life was shut up in a narrow round of sordid accumulation. It was the poverty of the frontier, in Kirkland's eyes, that was the great hardship.

Hamlin Garland's more adequate story of the Middle Border, beginning militantly with *Main-Travelled Roads* (1887–92) and flowering in the idyllic saga of the Garlands and McClintocks (1914), is a chronicle that grows more significant as the times it deals with draw further into the past. Throughout his interpretation run two dominant notes: the promise of future fulfillment when the prairies have been brought under the plow—the Per Hansa note of pioneer optimism; and then later, rising slowly into a ground swell, a note of discouragement suggesting the utter futility of a laborious existence. Underlying *Main-Travelled Roads* is a mood of bitterness that springs from a deep sense of failure—a mood that grew harsher with the economic depression of the Middle Border in the eighties. The harvest was not fulfilling the expectations of seed time, and the bow of promise was gone from the prairie fields. The figures of bitter men and despondent women fill his pages and darken the colors of his realism. It is the cost of it all that depresses him—the toll exacted of human happiness. These early studies of Garland's strike the first note of the tragedy of the frontier. Starkly objective, they are sociological sketches, the militant expression of a rebellious mood that had been deepening since the panic of 1873 burst the romantic bubble of frontier hopes. The history of two decades of economic maladjustment, with their Granger Populism, their passionate resentment at the favoritisms of government, their blind striking out at the plutocracy that was visibly rising amid the American democracy, is compressed within a few acrid tales that proposed to tell the plain truth about life on the Middle Border farm. *Main-Travelled Roads* is as complete an expression of the mood of the last years of the century—the outlook upon life, the economic and political problems, the objective treatment of materials —as *Giants in the Earth* is an expression of the vastly different outlook and mood of our own day.

For a generation before 1917, when the movement was brought to a sudden stop, the mind of America was deeply concerned with problems of sociology. The growing spirit of realism was absorbed in politics and economics and concerned itself little with subjective analysis. The intellectuals were busily examining the Constitution in the light of its economic origins and interpreting American history in the light of frontier experience. The novelists, reflecting the current interests, were fascinated by the phenomena of industrialism and were studying curiously the new race of captains of industry who were weaving a strange pattern of life for America. The city had already come to dwarf the country. Chicago bestrode the Middle Border like a colossus, and the novelists found material for their realism in the cut-throat ways of business men. Their stories—harsh and strident as the grinding wheels on the overhead "Loop"—were set against a background of sprawling cities hastening to grow big, where the battles of giants were fought and where the *milieu*—a vast network of impersonal forces—was more significant than the individual men and women who were borne onward in the stream of tendency to submerge or rise as chance determined. A note of stark determinism runs through much of the work; but it was a determinism of environing forces—the objective world of the machine—rather than of character, and in consequence the deeper concern of fiction was sociological, the understanding of this impersonal machine order and the subduing of it to democratic ends. In such a world the farmer and the problems of the Middle Border were become as old-fashioned as ox-carts.

Ten years later, when *Giants in the Earth* was published, such objective treatment of materials was no longer the vogue. Since the war a revolutionary shift of interest has taken place, a shift from the sociological to the psychological. It is no longer the world of objective fact that obtrudes as the significant reality, but the subtler world of emotional experience, the furtive inner life of impulse and desire that Sherwood Anderson probes so curiously. The change of theme was first marked, perhaps, by *Spoon River Anthology*, with its mordant sketches of stunted and thwarted lives that Mr. Masters professes to regard as the natural harvest of a sterile village life. *Spoon River Anthology* is bitter in its sardonic rebellion against the genial optimisms of the "Valley of Democracy." From the epic thrust of expansion issued, as its natural progeny, a race of abortive grotesques, starved figures which suggest to Mr. Masters the cost in human values of severing the ties of kin and kind and throwing aside like an old shoe the creative wealth of social experience. The soil of the frontier village is too thin for men and women to strike deep root and grow to generous stature.

Since the publication of *Spoon River Anthology*, concern for psychological values has pretty much taken possession of our literature. In the lovely pages of Willa Cather's *O Pioneers!* and *My Ántonia* there is revealed a warm sympathy with the emotional life of pioneer women and a poignant understanding of their bleak lot. But the analysis—as in Hamlin Garland's work—draws back from the threshold of final tragedy, pausing before it has penetrated to the hidden core of futility. The waste of all finer values exacted by the prairies is suggested by the queer figures of lonely immigrants who fade in the uncongenial environment, but it is not thrust into the foreground to dominate the scene. The vast stretches of the prairies are there—stern, inhospitable, breeding a dumb homesickness in alien hearts—where the red grass bends before the restless winds and the forces of nature are not easily tamed; but in the end the prairie is subdued and the scars it has laid on men's lives are forgotten. Since Willa Cather, others have dealt with the West—Ruth Suckow, Margaret Wilson, and Herbert Quick, to name a few—yet in none of their work is there the profound insight and imaginative grasp of the theme that gives to *Giants in the Earth* so great a sense of tragic reality.

In this creative return to the theme of the great American adventure the causes of human failure lie deeper than politics or economics. They are to be found in the impersonal forces of nature that are too powerful for the human will to cope with; and in the hidden weakness of fearful souls that cannot live when their roots have been pulled up from the congenial home soil. For all his titanic labors, Per Hansa, the viking, is struck down at last. There are few nobler passages in our fiction—the more telling for its restraint—than the final scene where, driven inexorably by circumstance, Per Hansa sets forth into the February blizzard to fetch a minister to the bedside of his stricken comrade. The note of determinism is there, subtle, pervasive. The Norns of his fathers had decreed that it should be so—in the urgings of the mystical Beret, in the dumb pleadings of the dying Hans Olsa and his broken-hearted wife. Per Hansa the strong, the capable one who never failed, who was cunning enough to outwit fate itself—Per Hansa would go out into the storm and return with the minister who would point the way to heaven to the troubled Hans Olsa. And so, driven by all the imperatives of fate, he sets out, skis on his feet and others at his back, to face the last great adventure. The blinding snow quickly wraps him about, the cold grips his heart, and Per Hansa is seen no more until on a soft May day, when the wheat is green in his fields and the corn is ready for planting, he is found seated by a haystack, his skis beside him and his face turned to the untrodden West. For all the heroic labors of Per Hansa, for all the tragic loneliness of Beret, the end is futility.

And Beret, the sick one, likewise is in the hands of the Norns. She had sinned through love of Per Hansa, and in the long brooding hours on the Dakota plains her mind gives way. She cannot rise to Per Hansa's delight in the newborn son. Peder Victorious— symbol of Per Hansa's buoyant faith—for her is only another evidence of sin. This dark land of Dakota is marked by God's displeasure, and life for her becomes a silent struggle of renunciation and atonement. A primitive Norse Calvinist, victimized by a brooding imagination that sees more devils than vast hell can hold, she dwells "on the border of utter darkness" where the forces of good and evil struggle for the human soul. Across the gloomy Puritanism of her nature fall the shadows of an older and darker faith, and in her nostalgia the old Northland superstitions merge with the somber Northland religion to her undoing. The tragedy of Beret works itself out in the tender corridors of her own heart and, as Professor Commager has suggested, it is as universal as the tragedy of Goethe's Margarethe. In his portrayal of the "sick soul" of Beret hungering for the far homeland the Norse artist has achieved a triumph. The epic conquest of the continent must be read in the light of women's sufferings as well as in that of men's endurance. In whichever light it is read, it becomes something far more suggestive than a drab tale of frontier poverty or a sordid tale of frontier exploitation; it becomes vital and significant as life itself.

Giants in the Earth is a great and beautiful book that suggests the wealth of human potentialities brought to America year after year by the peasant immigrants who pass through Ellis Island and scatter the length and breadth of the land. Written in Norwegian, and stemming from a rich old-world literary tradition, it is at the same time deeply and vitally American. The very atmosphere of the Dakota plains is in its pages, and it could have been written only by one to whom the background was a familiar scene. The artist has lived with these peasant folk; he is one of them, and he penetrates sympathetically to the simple kindly hearts hidden to alien eyes by the unfamiliar folk ways. To gather up and preserve in letters these diverse folk strains before they are submerged and lost in the common American *mores*, would seem to be a business that our fiction might undertake with profit.

Ole Edvart Rölvaag is himself a viking of the Per Hansa strain. Born of fisher folk, 22 April, 1876, on the island of Donna at the very edge of the Arctic circle, he took his name, following a common Norwegian custom, from the name of a cove on the shores of which he was brought up. It is a land barren except for the gorse and heather, and the long winter nights and the restless sea were certain to bring the imagination under their somber spell. At the age of fourteen, discouraged from further schooling by the family that contrasted him unfavorably with a brilliant brother, he turned fisherman, and for five years went off to the Lofoten Islands some two hundred miles away for the winter catches. Distrustful of the future, he made his great decision to come to America, landing in New York in 1896 with only a railway ticket to South Dakota. In the great West, still turmoiled by the agrarian upheaval of the nineties, he joined an uncle who had provided him transportation money, tried his hand at farming, worked at other jobs, and at the age of twenty-three, not having found himself, he turned once more to the formal business of schooling. In the fall of 1899 he entered Augustana College, a preparatory school in Canton, South Dakota. From there he went to St. Olaf College, Northfield, Minnesota, graduating in 1905 at the age of twenty-eight. After a year at the University of Oslo in Norway, he joined the staff of St. Olaf College, where he is now Professor of Norwegian Literature. In the larger sense, however, his education has been got from life, which he seems to have lived with a rich and daring intensity; and it is his own venturesome experience, certainly, that finds expression in the creative realism and brooding imagination of his work. Intellectually and artistically he is of the excellent old-world culture. How greatly his professional studies determined his literary technique only a competent Norwegian critic can judge; yet it is worth while comparing *Giants in the Earth* with Johan Bojer's *The Emigrants*—a work which, when announced as being in preparation, dramatically influenced his own novel.

THE SHORT STORY *

Introduction. With the ferment of the seventies and eighties a new school of literature, that was effectively a denial of the genteel tradition: it was effectively a popularization—a taking it out of the severe realm of the *Atlantic Monthly.* It was an appeal to the middle class. From Henry James to Hamlin Garland a steady shift from right to left. This implied:

1. A shift from genteel to homely material.

2. A shift to realism from the earlier sentimentality. This genteel tradition constantly cropping out anew—in Margaret Deland, in a changed form in Zona Gale. It has been strongest in New England—from Rose Terry Cooke through Sarah Orne Jewett to Mary Wilkins.

The short story commonly believed to be peculiarly representative of our genius—the stripping-away of the superfluous and the love of technical refinement. Derived from Poe and Hawthorne: both artists yet far removed from the tendencies which have controlled the development of the short story since.

Theme. The American short story has dealt largely with the two great themes of all romance, love and adventure. The form constitutes the great staple—is largely provided by women for women. The handling of this love theme reveals the inevitable shift from the genteel tradition to middle-class efficiency, and the spirit of the change is revealed in the changing dress of the heroine. In the seventies, crinoline, innumerable flounces of white muslin, lace parasols—no tan, no freckles, but a gentle pallor. Such dress and such heroines will exude sentiment. It will concern itself with atmosphere. Action brisk and efficient will appear unladylike, almost vulgar. What a change when the heroine clothes herself in a silk flour-sack—showing silk stockings, bare arms and neck—cultivating tan and freckles, bobbing her hair, going in for automobiles and golf and tennis! The older heroine dwelt in a world of sentiment without sex; the present-day heroine lives in a world of sex interest without sentiment. The more flounces in life and literature, the

---

* Lecture notes. This subject was not included in the contents, but contains some matter of interest.—*Publisher.*

397

less the animal is exposed. Hence action has superseded sentiment
—plot has superseded atmosphere. The hero becomes a Hart,
Schaffner and Marx young business man and the middle-class note
is struck loudly in the honk of the motor-car. The genteel tradition
is laid away with the flowers.

Major Influences during the Sixties. Through the fifties and
sixties literature uncertain and halting. The style largely set by
old-world fashions. Three in particular:

1. Influence of Charlotte and Emily Brontë. A sort of sentimental and mawkish passion. Stilted style, as in Harriet Beecher
Stowe. This fell in with the Irving note of the picturesque and was
exploited in *Godey's Lady's Book.*

2. Influence of Dickens. At its height in the fifties: an emphasis
upon the vulgar—plain and homely characters. Exploited in the
Atlantic by Lowell. So Rose Terry Cooke in *Miss Lucinda* (1861).

3. Influence of the French realistic movement: Balzac, Flaubert.
Only a faint beginning. Still a lot of romance stuff but given a local
color and garnished with humor.

Counter Tendencies. The inevitable development of the middle-
class city and the middle-class magazine, persistently affected by
certain throw-backs to an older American tradition. America is of
the city today, but day before yesterday it was still country, and in
the backgrounds of our minds is a country setting and love of simple people. Three main tendencies:

1. The discovery of the local. The picturesqueness of the strange
and remote in character, manners, speech. The charm of dialect
and interest in out-of-the-way places. This a reaction from too
much pavement and the rubbing-down of individual differences
from city contact. "Characters" are bred in isolated places. This
the dominant note in the short story from 1870 to 1900: to follow
it from Bret Harte on is almost to write a history of the short
story. It does not dominate the longer story. Constance Fenimore
Woolson.

2. The discovery of "human interest." The feeling that men in
the rough—with the bark on—may prove more interesting than
the products of an artificial civilization. This had been spread by
Dickens and by certain of the *Atlantic* writers.

3. The growing interest in realism. At first confused with the
commonplace—so Pattee in his comment on Rose Terry Cooke's
Miss Lucinda. A good deal of this earlier work is only another form

of romance—little affected by the rising French movement. Realism was to come slowly and late. All three of these made against the genteel tradition.

Henry James. His position peculiar. From his youth *déraciné*—his father hated American vulgarity, American journalism, and would not permit his son to take root. He grew up with an aristocratic conception of civilization—his sole interest lay in such civilization, and the manners of the polite society of that civilization. No other American has so hated and feared contamination from the vulgar. He was thus the last flower of the Genteel Tradition, transplanted to an environment more congenial. As the middle-class became more clamorous, he withdrew to the Continent, to England, where the older ideas still lingered. There in the spirit of the realist he wrote with refined art and persistent detachment—even to a punctilious and princely refinement. As Mr. Howells says, "To enjoy his work, to feel its rare excellence, both in conception and expression, is a brevet of intellectual good form."

His World. Always that of the spender, of assured position. His main interest lies in women; their refinement appeals to his refinement—no flappers or vulgarians but elegantly gowned women who never did the family washing. He is concerned with that which is dearest to the heart of aristocracy—standards of excellence. And in this he was true to his conception of civilization, for civilization begins after a competence has been assured. Those who are struggling to acquire have not the leisure, the inclination, for civilization. Hence *Daisy Miller* is a type of much of his work—the contrast between civilized Europe and uncivilized America, the one with standards of culture and manners and the other vulgarian. And his interest in American women results from the fact that they alone in America care for civilization and are painfully seeking to achieve it.

His Realism. The beginnings of the movement which has been called psychological realism, concerning itself with motives and processes of thought—the inner life. Developed by Bourget and far more fully by Dorothy Richardson in such a book as *Pilgrimage,* the inner life of Miriam Henderson in many volumes. Far removed from later psychological fiction founded on Freudian theory—as in D. H. Lawrence, Sherwood Anderson. Again the genteel tradition dealing with people who in the main have genteel impulses only. James held in horror this later naturalism—it was merely vulgarian.

The Spirit of the Local. Into this prim world with its incipient realism came the note of the Far West: Mark Twain and Bret Harte, who set a new style—the romantic, picturesque, human-interest story. This is a part of the Pike County idea of literature—a native rogue-tale but with touches of sentiment and shortened to effective form. This followed by Eggleston's *Hoosier Schoolmaster* (1871) and this in turn by the flood of local work of the eighties. The most notable the work of Charles Egbert Craddock, Joel Chandler Harris, Sarah Orne Jewett, and Mary Wilkins. The first discovered the hill people, the second discovered the Negro—his primitive folk-poetry. In the work of the last, a struggle between the genteel tradition and realism—and the final triumph of the latter.

A CHAPTER IN AMERICAN LIBERALISM *

Liberals whose hair is growing thin and the lines of whose figures are no longer what they were, are likely to find themselves today in the unhappy predicament of being treated as mourners at their own funerals. When they pluck up heart to assert that they are not yet authentic corpses, but living men with brains in their heads, they are pretty certain to be gently chided and led back to the comfortable armchair that befits senility. Their counsel is smiled at as the chatter of a belated post-Victorian generation that knew not Freud, and if they must go abroad they are bidden take the air in the garden where other old-fashioned plants—mostly of the family *Democratici*—are still preserved. It is not pleasant for them. It is hard to be dispossessed by one's own heirs, and especially hard when those heirs, in the cheerful ignorance of youth, forget to acknowledge any obligations to a hard-working generation that laid by a very substantial body of intellectual wealth, the income from which the heirs are spending without even a "Thank you." If therefore the middle-aged liberal occasionally grows irritable and indulges in caustic comment on the wisdom of talkative young men it may be set down as the prerogative of the armchair age and lightly forgiven.

Yet in sober fact there are the solidest reasons for such irritation. The younger liberals who love to tweak the nose of democracy are too much enamored of what they find in their own mirrors. They are indisputably clever, they are spouting geysers of smart and cynical talk, they have far outrun their fathers in the free handling of ancient tribal totems—but they are afflicted with the short perspective of youth that finds a vanishing-point at the end of its own nose. There is no past for them beyond yesterday. They are having so good a time playing with ideas that it does not occur to them to question the validity of their intellectual processes or to inquire into the origins of the ideas they have adopted so blithely. Gaily engaged in smashing *bourgeois* idols, the young intellectuals are too busy to realize that it was the older generation that pro-

* This was apparently not intended as the introduction to Part I of Book Three, but covers much of the ground indicated there.—*Publisher.*

401

vided them with a hammer and pointed out the idols to be smashed. It is the way of youth.

Middle-aged liberals—let it be said by way of defense—at least know their history. They were brought up in a great age of liberalism—an age worthy to stand beside the golden forties of last century—and they went to school to excellent teachers. Darwin, Spencer, Mill, Karl Marx, Haeckel, Taine, William James, Henry George, were masters of which no school in any age need feel ashamed; nor were such tutors and undermasters as Ruskin, William Morris, Matthew Arnold, Lester Ward, Walt Whitman, Henry Adams, to be dismissed as incompetent. To the solution of the vexing problems entailed by industrialism—in America as well as in Europe—was brought all the knowledge that had been accumulating for a century. It was a time of reëvaluations when much substantial thinking was done; when the flood of light that came with the doctrine of biological evolution lay brilliant on the intellectual landscape and the dullest mind caught some of the reflection. Few of the young scholars attended the lectures of Friedrich Nietzsche, and behavioristic psychology had not yet got into the curriculum; but Ladd and James were inquiring curiously into the mechanism of the brain, and animal psychology was preparing the way for the later Freudians. It was the end of an age perhaps, the rich afterglow of the Enlightenment, but the going down of the sun was marked by sunset skies that gave promise of other and greater dawns.

To have spent one's youth in such a school was a liberal education. The mind opened of its own will. Intellectual horizons were daily widening and the new perspectives ran out into cosmic spaces. The cold from those outer spaces had not yet chilled the enthusiasms that were a heritage from the Enlightenment, and the social idealism begotten by the democratic nature school still looked confidently to the future. They were ardent democrats—the young liberals of the nineties—and none doubted the finality or sufficiency of the democratic principle, any more than Mill or Spencer had doubted it. All their history and all their biology justified it, and the business of the times was to make it prevail in the sphere of economics as it prevailed in the realm of the political. The cure for the evils of democracy was held to be more democracy, and when industrialism had been brought under its sway—when America had become an economic democracy—a just and humane civilization would be on the threshold of possibility. To the achieve-ment of that great purpose the young liberals devoted themselves and the accomplishments of the next score of years were the work of their hands. Certain intellectuals had been democrats—Paine and Jefferson and Emerson and Thoreau and Whitman and Mel-ville—but they were few in comparison with the skeptical Whigs who professed democracy only to bind its hands. The Republican party had not been democratic since former days — and as Henry Adams said in 1880, it was accounted foolishness to believe in it in 1880. Autocracy was a toy to distract the voting man from the business of money-getting.

It was from such a school—richer in intellectual content, one might argue, than any the younger liberals have frequented—that the ferment of twenty years ago issued; a school dedicated to the ideals of the Enlightenment and bent on carrying through the un-fulfilled program of democracy. Democratic aspirations had been thwarted hitherto by the uncontrolled play of the acquisitive in-stinct; the immediate problem of democracy was the control of that instinct in the common interest. Economics had controlled the political state to its narrow and selfish advantage; it was for the political state to resume its sovereignty and extend its control over economics. So in the spirit of the Enlightenment the current lib-eralism dedicated itself to history and sociology, accepting as its immediate and particular business a reëxamination of the American past in order to forcast an ampler democratic future. It must trace the rise of political power in America in order to understand how that power had fallen into the unsocial hands of economics. The problem was difficult. American political history had been grossly distorted by partisan interpretation and political theory had been dissipated by an arid constitutionalism. The speculative thinker had long been dispossessed by the eulogist and the lawyer, both of whom had subsisted on a thin gruel of patriotic myths. Even the social historians, though dealing in materials rich in suggestion, had been diffident in the matter of interpretation, without which his-tory is no more than the dry bones of chronicle. Inheriting no ade-quate philosophy of historical evolution, the young school of his-torians must first provide themselves with one, in the light of which the American past should take on meaning, and the partisan struggles, hitherto meaningless, should fall into comprehensible patterns.

That necessary work was to engage them for years, but in the meanwhile, as critical realists, their immediate business was with facts and the interpretation of facts. John Fiske a few years before had essayed to interpret the rise of democracy in America by analogy from biological evolution, tracing the source of American democracy to the New England town meeting, which he explained as a resurgence of ancient Teutonic folk-ways. The theory was tenuous and it was not till Professor Turner drew attention to the creative influence of the frontier on American life that the historians were provided with a suggestive working hypothesis. Before that hypothesis could be adequately explored, however, and brought into just relations to a comprehensive philosophy of history, the rise of liberalism was well under way, marked by a rich ferment of thought that made the early years of the new century singularly stimulating. That ferment resulted from pouring into the vial of native experience the reagent of European theory—examining the ways of American industrialism in the light of continental socialism; and the result was an awakening of popular interest in social control of economics, a widespread desire to bring an expanding industrialism into subjection to a rational democratic program, that was to provide abundant fuel to the social unrest that had burst forth in sporadic flames for a generation. The great movement of liberalism that took possession of the American mind after the turn of the century—a movement not unworthy to be compared with the ferment of the eighteen forties—was the spontaneous reaction of an America still only half urbanized, still clinging to ideals and ways of an older simpler America, to an industrialism that was driving its plowshare through the length and breadth of the familiar scene, turning under the rude furrows what before had been growing familiarly there. It was the first reaction of America to the revolutionary change that followed upon the exhaustion of the frontier—an attempt to secure through the political state the freedoms that before had come from unpreempted opportunity.

For a quarter of a century following the great westward expansion of the late sixties America had been drifting heedlessly towards a different social order. The shambling frontier democracy that had sufficed an earlier time was visibly breaking down in presence of the imperious power of a centralizing capitalism. The railways were a dramatic embodiment of the new machine civilization that was running head on into a primitive social organism fashioned by the old domestic economy, and the disruptions and confusions were a warning that the country was in for vast changes. New masters, new ways. The rule of the captain of industry had come. The farmers had long been in ugly mood, but their great rebellion was put down in 1896, and never again could they hope to wrest sovereignty from capitalism. The formal adoption of the gold standard in 1900 served notice to the world that America had put away its democratic agrarianism, that a shambling Jacksonian individualism had had its day, and that henceforth the destiny of the country lay in the hands of its business men. Capitalism was master of the country and though for the present it was content to use the political machinery of democracy it was driving towards an objective that was the negation of democracy.

The immediate reaction to so broad a shift in the course of manifest destiny was a growing uneasiness amongst the middle class—small business and professional men—who looked with fear upon the program of the captains of industry. Industrialization brought its jars and upsets. The little fish did not enjoy being swallowed by the big, and as they watched the movement of economic centralization encroaching on the field of competition they saw the doors of opportunity closing to them. It was to this great body of *petite bourgeoisie* that members of the lesser intellectuals—journalists, sociologists, reformers—were to make appeal. The work was begun dramatically with the spectacularly advertised *Frenzied Finance*, written by Thomas W. Lawson, and appearing as a series in *McClure's Magazine* in 1903. The immense popular success of the venture proved that the fire was ready for the fat, and at once a host of volunteer writers fell to feeding the flames. The new ten-cent magazines provided the necessary vehicle of publicity, and enterprising editors were soon increasing their circulations with every issue. As it became evident how popular was the chord that had been struck, more competent workmen joined themselves to the group of journalists: novelists—a growing army of them—essayists, historians, political scientists, philosophers, a host of heavy-armed troops that moved forward in a frontal attack on the strongholds of the new plutocracy. Few writers in the years between 1903 and 1917 escaped being drawn into the movement—an incorrigible romantic perhaps, like the young James Branch Cabell, or a cool patrician like Edith Wharton; and with such popular novelists as Winston Churchill, Robert Herrick, Ernest Poole, David Graham Phillips, Upton Sinclair, and Jack London embellishing the rising liberalism with dramatic heroes and villains, and dressing their salads with the wickedness of Big Business; with such political leaders as Bob La Follette and Theodore Roosevelt and Woodrow Wilson beating up the remotest villages for recruits; with such scholars as Thorstein Veblen, Charles A. Beard, and John Dewey, and such lawyers as Louis Brandeis, Frank P. Walsh, and Samuel Untermyer, the movement gathered such momentum and quickened such a ferment as had not been known before in the lands since the days of the Abolition controversy. The mind and conscience of America were stirred to their lowest sluggish stratum, and a democratic renaissance was all aglow on the eastern horizon.

At the core it was a critical realistic movement that spread quietly amongst intellectuals, but the nebulous tail of the comet blazed across the sky for all to wonder at: and it was the tail rather than the core that aroused the greatest immediate interest. Lincoln Steffens, Charles Edward Russell, Ida Tarbell, Gustavus Myers, and Upton Sinclair were read eagerly because they dealt with themes that many were interested in—the political machine, watered stock, Standard Oil, the making of great fortunes, and the like—and they invested their exposures with the dramatic interest of a detective story. Up to 1910 it was largely a muckraking movement—to borrow President Roosevelt's picturesque phrase; a time of brisk housecleaning that searched out old cobwebs and disturbed the dust that lay thick on the antiquated furniture. The Gilded Age had been slovenly and such a housecleaning was long overdue. There was a vast amount of nosing about to discover bad smells, and to sensitive noses the bad smells seemed to be everywhere. Evidently some hidden cesspool was fouling American life, and as the inquisitive plumbers tested the household drains they came upon the source of infection—not one cesspool but many, under every city hall and beneath every state capitol—dug secretly by politicians in the pay of respectable business men. It was these cesspools that were poisoning the national household, and there would be no health in America till they were filled in and no others dug.

It was a dramatic discovery and when the corruption of American politics was laid on the threshold of business—like a bastard on the doorsteps of the father—a tremendous disturbance resulted. There was a great fluttering and clamor amongst the bats and owls, an ominous creaking of the machine as the wrenches were thrown into the well-oiled wheels, and a fierce sullen anger at the hue and cry set up. To many honest Americans the years between 1903 and 1910 were abusive and scurrilous beyond decency, years when no man and no business, however honorable, was safe from the pillory; when wholesale exposure had grown profitable to sensation-mongers, and great reputations were lynched by vigilantes and reputable corporations laid under indictment at the bar of public opinion. Respectable citizens did not like to have their goodly city held up to the world as "corrupt and contented"; they did not like to have their municipal housekeeping brought into public disrepute no matter how sluttish it might be. It was not pleasant for members of great families to read a cynical history of the origins of their fortunes, or for railway presidents seeking political favors to find on the newsstand a realistic account of the bad scandals that had smirched their roads. It was worse than unpleasant, it was hurtful to business. And so quietly, and as speedily as could be done decently, the movement was brought to a stop by pressure put on the magazines that lent themselves to such harmful disclosures. Then followed a campaign of education. Responding to judicious instruction, conducted in the columns of the most respectable newspapers, the American public was soon brought to understand that it was not the muck that was harmful, but the indiscretion of those who commented in print on the bad smells. It was reckoned a notable triumph for sober and patriotic good sense.

So after a few years of amazing activity the muckraking movement came to a stop. But not before it had done its work; not before the American middle class had been indoctrinated in the elementary principles of political realism and had rediscovered the social conscience lost since the days of the Civil War. Many a totem had been thrown down by the irreverent hands of the muckrakers, and many a fetish held up to ridicule, and plutocracy in America would not recover its peace of mind until at great cost the totems should be set up again and the fetishes reanointed with the oil of sanctity. The substantial result of the movement was the instruction it afforded in the close kinship between business and politics—a lesson greatly needed by a people long fed on romantic unrealities. It did not crystallize for the popular mind in the broad

principle of economic determinism; that remained for certain of
the intellectuals to apply to American experience. But with its
sordid object—service—it punished the flabby optimism of the
Gilded Age, with its object-lessons in business politics; it revealed
the hidden hand that was pulling the strings of the political puppets; it tarnished the gilding that had been carefully laid on our
callous exploitation, and it brought under common suspicion
the captain of industry who had risen as a national hero from the
muck of individualism. It was a sharp guerilla attack on the sacred
American System, but behind the thin skirmish-line lay a volunteer
army that was making ready to deploy for a general engagement
with plutocracy.

With the flood of light thrown upon the fundamental law by the
historians, the movement of liberalism passed quickly through successive phases of thought. After the first startled surprise it set
about the necessary business of acquainting the American people
with its findings in the confident belief that a democratic electorate
would speedily democratize the instrument. Of this first stage the
late Professor J. Allen Smith's *The Spirit of American Government*
(1907) was the most adequate expression, a work that greatly influenced the program of the rising Progressive Party. But changes
came swiftly and within half a dozen years the movement had
passed from political programs to economic, concerned not so
greatly with political democracy as with economic democracy. Of
this second phase Professor Beard's notable study, *An Economic
Interpretation of the Constitution* (1913), was the greatest intellectual achievement. Underlying this significant work was a philosophy of politics that set it sharply apart from preceding studies—
a philosophy that unsympathetic readers were quick to attribute
to Karl Marx, but that in reality derived from sources far earlier
and for Americans at least far more respectable. The current conception of the political state as determined in its form and activities
by economic groups is no modern Marxian perversion of political
theory; it goes back to Aristotle, it underlay the thinking of Harrington and Locke and the seventeenth-century English school, it
shaped the conclusions of Madison and Hamilton and John Adams,
it ran through all the discussions of the Constitutional Convention,
and it reappeared in the arguments of Webster and Calhoun. It
was the main-traveled road of political thought until a new highway
was laid out by French engineers, who, disliking the bog of eco-

nomics, surveyed another route by way of romantic equalitarianism. The logic of the engineers was excellent, but the drift of politics is little influenced by logic, and abstract equalitarianism proved to be poor material for highway construction. In divorcing political theory from contact with sobering reality it gave it over to a treacherous romanticism. In seeking to avoid the bog of economics it ran into an arid desert.

To get back once more on the main-traveled road, to put away all profitless romanticisms and turn realist, taking up again the method of economic interpretation unused in America since the days of Webster and Calhoun, became therefore the business of the second phase of liberalism to which Professor Beard applied himself. The earlier group of liberals were ill equipped to wage successful war against plutocracy. Immersed in the traditional equalitarian philosophy, they underestimated the strength of the enemies of democracy. They did not realize what legions of Swiss Guards property can summon to its defense. They were still romantic idealists tilting at windmills, and it was to bring them to a sobering sense of reality that *The Economic Interpretation of the Constitution* was written. If property is the master force in every society one cannot understand American institutional development until one has come to understand the part property played in shaping the fundamental law. Interpreted thus the myths that had gathered about the Constitution fell away of themselves and the document was revealed as English rather than French, the judicious expression of substantial eighteenth-century realism that accepted the property basis of political action, was skeptical of romantic idealisms, and was more careful to protect title-deeds to legal holdings than to claim unsurveyed principalities in Utopia. If therefore liberalism were to accomplish any substantial results it must approach its problems in the same realistic spirit, recognizing the masterful ambitions of property, recruiting democratic forces to overmaster the Swiss Guards, leveling the strongholds that property had erected within the organic law, and taking care that no new strongholds should rise. The problem confronting liberalism was the problem of the subjection of property to social justice.

Yet interesting as was the muckraking tail of the comet, far more significant was the core—the substantial body of knowledge gathered by the scholars and flung into the scale of public opinion. The realities of the American past had been covered deep with

layers of patriotic myths, provided in simpler days when the young
Republic, suffering from a natural inferiority complex, was building
up a defense against the acrid criticism of Tory Europe. Those
myths had long since served their purpose and had become a convenient refuge for the bats and owls of the night; it was time to strip
them away and apply to the past objective standards of scholarship, and to interpret it in the light of an adequate philosophy of
history. To this work, so essential to any intelligent understanding
of the American experiment, a group of historians and political
scientists turned with competent skill, and the solid results of their
labor remained after the popular ferment subsided, as a foundation
for later liberals to build on.

The journalistic muckrakers had demonstrated that America
was not in fact the equalitarian democracy it professed to be, and
the scholars supplemented their work by tracing to its historical
source the weakness of the democratic principle in governmental
practice. America had never been a democracy for the sufficient
reason that too many handicaps had been imposed upon the majority will. The democratic principle had been bound with withes
like Samson and had become a plaything for the Philistines. From
the beginning—the scholars discovered—democracy and property
had been at bitter odds; the struggle invaded the Constitutional
Convention, it gave form to the party alignment between Hamilton and Jefferson, Jackson and Clay, and then during the slavery
struggle, sinking underground like a lost river, it nevertheless had
determined party conflicts down to the present. In this ceaseless
conflict between the man and the dollar, between democracy and
property, the reasons for persistent triumph of property were
sought in the provisions of the organic law, and from a critical
study of the Constitution came a discovery that struck home like
a submarine torpedo—the discovery that the drift toward plutocracy was not a drift away from the spirit of the Constitution, but
an inevitable unfolding from its premises; that instead of having
been conceived by the fathers as a democratic instrument, it
had been conceived in a spirit designedly hostile to democracy;
that it was, in fact, a carefully formulated expression of eighteenth-
century property consciousness, erected as a defense against the
democratic spirit that had got out of hand during the Revolution,
and that the much-praised system of checks and balances was designed and intended for no other end than a check on the political

power of the majority—a power acutely feared by the property consciousness of the times.

It was a startling discovery that profoundly stirred the liberal mind of the early years of the century; yet the really surprising thing is that it should have come as a surprise. It is not easy to understand today why since Civil War days intelligent Americans should so strangely have confused the Declaration of Independence and the Constitution, and have come to accept them as complementary statements of the democratic purpose of America. Their unlikeness is unmistakable: the one a classical statement of French humanitarian democracy, the other an organic law designed to safeguard the minority under republican rule. The confusion must be charged in part to the lawyers who had taken over the custodianship of the Constitution, and in part to the florid romantic temper of the middle nineteenth century. When the fierce slavery struggle fell into the past, whatever honest realism had risen from the passions of the times was buried with the dead issue. The militant attacks on the Constitution so common in Abolitionist circles after 1835, and the criticism of the Declaration that was a part of the southern argument, were both forgotten, and with the Union reestablished by force of arms, the idealistic cult of the fundamental law entered on a second youth. In the blowsy Gilded Age the old myths walked the land again, wrapped in battle-torn flags and appealing to the blood shed on southern battlefields. It was not till the advent of a generation unblinded by the passions of civil war that the Constitution again was examined critically, and the earlier charge of the Abolitionists that it was designed to serve property rather than men, was heard once more. But this time with far greater weight of evidence behind it. As the historians dug amongst the contemporary records they came upon a mass of fact the Abolitionists had been unaware of. The evidence was written so plainly, in such explicit and incontrovertible words— not only in *Elliott's Debates*, but in the minutes of the several State Conventions, in contemporary letters and memoirs, in newspapers and pamphlets and polite literature—that it seemed incredible that honest men could have erred so greatly in confusing the Constitution with the Declaration.

With the clarification of its philosophy the inflowing waters of liberalism reached flood-tide; the movement would either recede or pass over into radicalism. On the whole it followed the latter

course, and the years immediately preceding 1917 were years when
American intellectuals were immersing themselves in European
collectivistic philosophies—in Marxianism, Fabianism, Syndicalism, Guild Socialism.   New leaders were rising, philosophical
analysts like Thorstein Veblen who were mordant critics of American economics. The influence of socialism was fast sweeping away
the last shreds of political and social romanticism that so long had
confused American thinking. The doctrine of economic determinism was spreading widely, and in the light of that doctrine the deep
significance of the industrial revolution was revealing itself for the
first time to thoughtful Americans. In its reaction to industrialism
America had reached the point Chartist England had reached in the
eighteen-forties and Marxian Germany in the eighteen-seventies.
That was before a mechanistic science had laid its heavy discouragements on the drafters of democratic programs. Accepting the principle of economic determinism, liberalism still clung to
its older democratic teleology, convinced that somehow economic
determinism would turn out to be a fairy godmother to the proletariat and that from the imperious drift of industrial expansion
must eventually issue social justice. Armed with this faith liberalism threw itself into the work of cleaning the Augean stables, and
its reward came in the achievements of President Wilson's first
administration.

Then the war intervened and the green fields shriveled in an
afternoon. With the cynicism that came with post-war days the
democratic liberalism of 1917 was thrown away like an empty
whiskey-flask. Clever young men began to make merry over democracy. It was preposterous, they said, to concern oneself about
social justice; nobody wants social justice. The first want of every
man, as John Adams remarked a hundred years ago, is his dinner,
and the second his girl. Out of the muck of the war had come a
great discovery—so it was reported—the discovery that psychology
as well as economics has its word to say on politics. From the
army intelligence tests the moron emerged as a singular commentary on our American democracy, and with the discovery of
the moron the democratic principle was in for a slashing attack.
Almost overnight an army of enemies was marshaled against it.
The eugenist with his isolated germ theory flouted the perfectional
psychology of John Locke, with its emphasis on environment as
the determining factor in social evolution—a psychology on which

the whole idealistic interpretation was founded; the beardless philosopher discovered Nietzsche and in his pages found the fit master of the moron—the biological aristocrat who is the flower that every civilization struggles to produce; the satirist discovered the flatulent reality that is middle-class America and was eager to thrust his jibes at the complacent denizens of the Valley of Democracy. Only the behaviorist, with his insistence on the plasticity of the new-born child, offers some shreds of comfort to the democrat; but he quickly takes them away again with his simplification of conduct to imperious drives that stamp men as primitive animals. If the mass—the raw materials of democracy—never rises much above sex appeals and belly needs, surely it is poor stuff to try to work up into an excellent civilization, and the dreams of the social idealist who forecasts a glorious democratic future are about as substantial as moonshine. It is a discouraging essay. Yet it is perhaps conceivable that our current philosophy—the brilliant coruscations of our younger intelligentsia—may indeed not prove to be the last word in social philosophy. Perhaps—is this lèse-majesté—when our youngest liberals have themselves come to the armchair age they will be smiled at in turn by sons who are still cleverer and who will find their wisdom as foolish as the wisdom of 1917 seems to them today. But that lies on the knees of the gods.

BIBLIOGRAPHY

[Professor Parrington left no bibliography apart from the works mentioned in the text. It has been possible to formulate one with some certainty by reference to his personal library, theses written under his supervision, and the record of the books he borrowed from the University of Washington Library. In the two earlier volumes the bibliography is rigidly selective. Needless to say, I have not presumed such knowledge of his intentions. All the pertinent material which it is known that he used is included.—E. H. EBY.]

BOOK I: PART I

I. THE AMERICAN SCENE. For history of the period see Allan Nevins, *The Emergence of Modern America, 1865–1878* (in the series *A History of American Life*, Vol. VIII, New York, 1927); E. P. Oberholtzer, *History of the United States since the Civil War* (3 vols., New York, 1917–1926); Frederick L. Paxson, *Recent History of the United States* (Boston and New York, c. 1921).

For economic backgrounds see Harold Underwood Faulkner, *American Economic History* (New York and London, 1924); Gustavus Meyers, *History of Great American Fortunes* (3 vols., Chicago, 1910); Robert Irving Warshaw, *Jay Gould: The Story of a Fortune* (New York, 1928); and for the part played by railroads see John P. Davis, *The Union Pacific Railway* (New York, 1894); C. E. Russell, *Stories of Great Railroads* (Chicago, 1912); and Charles Francis Adams, Jr., and Henry Adams, *Chapters of Erie and Other Essays* (Boston, 1871).

For political corruption see Don Carlos Seitz, *The Dreadful Decade* (Indianapolis, 1926); and Denis Tilden Lynch, *"Boss" Tweed: The Story of a Grim Generation* (New York, 1927).

For journalism see Allan Nevins, *The Evening Post: A Century of Journalism* (New York, c. 1922); and Frank M. O'Brien, *The Story of the Sun* (New York, c. 1918).

General Ulysses S. Grant, *Personal Memoirs* (2 vols., New York, 1885–1886). For biography see W. E. Woodward, *Meet General Grant* (New York, 1928).

Jay Cooke. See E. P. Oberholtzer, *Jay Cooke, Financier of the Civil War* (2 vols. Philadelphia, c. 1907).

Charles A. Dana, *Recollections of the Civil War* (New York, 1902); J. H. Wilson, *Life of Charles A. Dana* (New York, 1907).

II. THE CULTURE OF THE SEVENTIES. For valuable sidelights on culture in the decade see Constance Mayfield Rourke, *Trumpets of Jubilee* (New York, c. 1927); Paxton Hibben, *Henry Ward Beecher: An American Portrait* (New York, c. 1927); Horace Greeley, *Recollections of a Busy Life* (New York, 1868); James Parton, *The Life of Horace Greeley* (Boston, c. 1896); Lewis Mumford, *The Golden Day: A Study in American Experience and Culture* (New York, 1926); and his *Sticks and Stones, A Study of American Architecture and Civilization* (New York, c. 1924).

For history of literature see Fred Lewis Pattee, *A History of American Literature since 1870* (New York, 1915); his *Sidelights on American Literature*

415

(New York, 1922); his *The Development of the American Short Story* (New York and London, 1923); and Carl Van Doren, *The American Novel* (New York, 1921).

Thomas Bailey Aldrich, *Prose Works* (7 vols., Boston, 1897); *The Poems of Thomas Bailey Aldrich* (2 vols., Boston, c. 1907). For his life see Ferris Greenslet, *The Life of Thomas Bailey Aldrich* (Boston and New York, 1908).

Mrs. Elizabeth Stuart Ward (Phelps), *The Silent Partner* (Boston, c. 1899); *A Singular Life* (Boston and New York, 1899); *Chapters from a Life* (Boston and New York, 1896).

Sarah Orne Jewett, *A Country Doctor* (Boston and New York, c. 1884); *A Native of Winby and Other Tales* (Boston and New York, c. 1893); *Deephaven* (Boston and New York, 1894). *Tales of New England* (Boston and New York, 1894); *The Life of Nancy* (Boston and New York, 1895); *The Queen's Twin and Other Stories* (Boston and New York, 1899); *The Country of Pointed Firs* (Boston and New York, c. 1910). For her life see *The Letters of Sarah Orne Jewett* (Boston and New York, 1911).

Mrs. Mary E. (Wilkins) Freeman, *A Humble Romance, and Other Stories* (New York, 1887); *The New England Nun, and Other Stories* (New York, 1891); *The Pot of Gold, and Other Stories* (Boston, c. 1892); *Pembroke; a Novel* (New York, c. 1894); *People of Our Neighborhood* (New York, 1901); *The Portion of Labor* (New York, c. 1901). *Young Lucretia, and Other Stories* (New York, 1903); *By the Light of the Soul* (New York and London, 1907).

Walt Whitman, *Leaves of Grass* (Inclusive edition edited by Emory Holloway, Garden City, New York, 1927); *The Complete Prose Works of Walt Whitman* (New York, 1898); *The Half-breed and Other Stories* (New York, 1927); *Autobiographia: or, the Story of a Life* (New York, 1892); *The Gathering of Forces* (New York and London, 1920); and *The Uncollected Poetry and Prose of Walt Whitman* (2 vols., Garden City, New York, 1921). For Whitman's life see Horace Traubel, *With Walt Whitman in Camden* (3 vols., New York, 1908–1914); Emory Holloway, *Whitman* (New York, 1926); John Addington Symonds, *Walt Whitman: a Study* (London, 1893); Léon Bazalgette, *Walt Whitman, the Man and his Work* (Garden City, New York, 1920); John Burroughs, *Whitman: a Study* (Boston and New York, c. 1924); Bliss Perry, *Walt Whitman: his Life and Work* (Boston and New York, 1906); and J. Johnston, M. D., and J. W. Wallace, *Visits to Walt Whitman* (New York, 1918).

For critical studies of his work see Norman Foerster, *American Criticism,* pp. 157–222 (New York, 1928); Basil De Selincourt, *Walt Whitman; a Critical Study* (London, 1914); Horace Traubel (ed.), *In re Walt Whitman* (Philadelphia, 1893).

Samuel Langhorne Clemens (Mark Twain), *The Writings of Mark Twain* (25 vols., New York and London, c. 1910–1911); *The Mysterious Stranger, and Other Stories* (New York and London, 1922); *What is Man?* (New York, 1917).

For his life see *Mark Twain's Autobiography* (New York and London, 1924); Albert Bigelow Paine, *Mark Twain, a Biography* (3 vols. New York, c. 1912); Van Wyck Brooks, *The Ordeal of Mark Twain* (New York, c. 1920); W. D. Howells, *My Mark Twain* (New York, c. 1910).

III. CHANGING THEORY. For a general history of economic theory see, Charles Gide and Charles Rist, *A History of Economic Doctrines from the Time of the Physiocrats to the Present Day* (Authorized translation from the second revised and augumented edition of 1913, Boston, New York, Chicago,

1913); *The Trend of Economics* (Edited by R. G. Tugwell, New York, 1924).

For material covered in this section see Francis Wayland, *Elements of Political Economy* (New York, 1837); Henry Charles Carey, *Principles of Social Science* (3 vols., Philadelphia, 1858–1860); his *The Harmony of Interests: Agricultural, Manufacturing, and Commercial* (2nd ed., New York, 1852); and his *Miscellaneous Works* (Philadelphia, 1875). Francis A. Walker, *The Wages Question, a Treatise on Wages and the Wages Class* (New York, 1891); his *Land and Its Rent* (Boston, 1891); and his *Political Economy* (New York, 1888).

For a general treatment of political theories see William A. Dunning, *A History of Political Theories from Rousseau to Spencer* (New York, 1920); Charles E. Merriam, *History of American Political Theories* (New York, 1920); and his *American Political Ideas: Studies in the Development of American Political Thought, 1865–1917* (New York, 1920).

Theodore Dwight Woolsey, *Political Science: or, the State Theoretically and Practically Considered* (New York, 1900); and his *Communism and Socialism in Their History and Theory* (New York, 1894).

John W. Burgess. *Political Science and Comparative Constitutional Law* (2 vols., Boston and London, 1896–1898); and his *The Sanctity of the Law; Wherein Does It Consist?* (Boston and New York, c. 1927).

J. Allen Smith, *The Growth and Decadence of Constitutional Government* (New York, 1930) is an invaluable aid to those wishing to get Parrington's viewpoint in political theory.

Henry George, *The Writings of Henry George* (Memorial edition, 10 vols., New York, 1898–1900). See particularly *Progress and Poverty* (Vols. I and II), and Henry George, Jr., *The Life of Henry George* (Vol. X).

Henry D. Lloyd, *Wealth Against Commonwealth* (New York, c. 1894); *Lords of Industry* (New York and London, 1910); *Man the Social Creator* (New York, 1906); *Strike of Millionaires Against Miners, or the Story of Spring Valley, with an Open Letter to Millionaires* (Chicago, 1890). For his life see Caroline Augusta Lloyd, *Henry Demarest Lloyd, 1847–1903* (2 vols., New York and London, 1912). (Parrington had intended to discuss Lloyd.)

IV. THE BEGINNINGS OF CRITICISM. Wendell Phillips, *Speeches, Lectures, and Letters* (2 vols., Boston, 1891–1892). For his life see Carlos Martyn, *Wendell Phillips, the Agitator* (Revised ed., New York, 1890); and Charles Edward Russell, *The Story of Wendell Phillips* (Chicago, c. 1914).

George William Curtis, *Nile Notes of a Howadji* (New York, 1851); *Trumps* (New York, 1861); *Potiphar Papers* (New York, 1854); *Prue and I* (New York, n. d.); *Orations and Addresses* (3 vols., New York, 1894); *From the Easy Chair* (3 vols., New York, 1894–1902); *Early Letters of George William Curtis to John S. Dwight; Brook Farm and Concord* (New York, and London 1898). For his life see Edward Cary, *George William Curtis* (Boston and New York, 1894).

Edwin Lawrence Godkin, *Reflections and Comments, 1865–1895* (New York, 1895); *Unforseen Tendencies of Democracy* (Boston, 1893); *Problems of Modern Democracy; Political and Economic Essays* (Third ed., New York, 1898). For his life see, *The Life and Letters of Edwin Lawrence Godkin* (Ed. by Rollo Ogden, 2 vols., New York and London, 1907). See also Gustav Pollak, *The Nation, Fifty Years of American Idealism: the New York Nation, 1865–1915* (New York, 1915).

The political novel: Mark Twain and Charles Dudley Warner, *The Gilded Age* (2 vols., New York, 1873); Henry Adams, *Democracy* (New York,

1880); F. Marion Crawford, *An American Politician* (New York, 1884). See also Albion W. Tourgee, *A Fool's Errand* (New York, 1880).

The economic novel: John Hay, *The Bread-Winners* (New York, 1883); H. F. Keenan, *The Moneymakers* (New York, 1885).

The sociological novel: Hjalmar Hjorth Boyessen, *The Mammon of Unrighteousness* (New York, 1891); his *The Golden Calf* (New York, 1892); and his *Social Strugglers* (New York, 1893); Robert Grant, *Unleavened Bread* (New York, 1900); Samuel Merwin and H. K. Webster, *Calumet K* (New York, 1901); and their *Short Line War* (New York, 1899). Francis Churchill Williams, *J. Develin-Boss* (New York, 1901); Elliot Flower, *The Spoilsman* (Boston, 1903); Winston Churchill, *Coniston* (New York, 1907); and his *Mr. Crewe's Career* (New York, 1908); Will Payne, *Mr. Salt* (Boston and New York, 1903); and his *The Money Captain* (New York, 1898).

For general accounts see Carl Van Doren, *The American Novel* (New York, 1921); Fred Lewis Pattee, *A History of American Literature since 1870* (New York, 1915); John Curtis Underwood, *Literature and Insurgency* (New York, 1914); and W. D. Howells, *Criticism and Fiction* (New York, 1891).

For material dealing with Henry Adams and John Hay see William Roscoe Thayer, *The Life and Letters of John Hay* (2 vols., Boston and New York, c. 1915). See also the bibliography on Henry Adams, Part II, section II.

BOOK I: PART II

I. DISINTEGRATION AND REINTEGRATION. For a general survey of philosophical thought during the period see W. H. Hudson, *Philosophies Ancient and Modern* (London, 1908); Woodbridge Riley, *American Thought from Puritanism to Pragmatism* (New York, 1915); William Archibald Dunning, *A History of Political Theories from Rousseau to Spencer* (New York, 1920).

Condorcet, Isidore, August Marie François Xavier, *Ouvres* (Paris, 1847). See also *A General View of Positivism* (Translated by H. J. Bridges, London, c. 1908).

Herbert Spencer, *Works* (18 vols., New York, 1915); see also his *Illustrations of Universal Progress; a Series of Discussions* (New York, 1890).

Ernst Heinrich Haeckel, *The Riddle of the Universe at the Close of the Nineteenth Century* (New York and London, 1900); and his *History of Creation* (2 vols., New York, 1914).

John Fiske, *American Political Ideas, Viewed from the Standpoint of Universal History* (New York, 1899); *Darwinism and Other Essays* (New ed. rev. and enl., Boston, 1892); *The Destiny of Man, Viewed in the Light of his Origin* (18 ed., Boston and New York, 1892); *Essays Historical and Literary* (2 vols., New York and London, 1902); *Excursions of an Evolutionist* (Boston and New York, 1892); *The Idea of God as Affected by Modern Knowledge* (Boston and New York, 1892); *Life Everlasting* (Boston and New York, 1902); *Outlines of Cosmic Philosophy, Based on the Doctrine of Evolution, with Criticisms of the Positive Philosophy* (4 vols., Boston and New York, c. 1903); *Through Nature to God* (Boston and New York, 1899); *Unseen World and Other Essays* (11th ed., Boston, 1876). For his life see J. S. Clark, *Life and Letters of John Fiske* (2 vols., Boston, 1917); and Henry Holt, *Garrulities of an Octogenarian Editor, with Other Essays Somewhat Biographical and Autobiographical* (Boston and New York, 1923).

II. THE SKEPTICISMS OF THE HOUSE OF ADAMS. Henry Adams, *The Degredation of the Democratic Dogma* (New York, 1920); *Democracy, a Novel* (New

York, 1880); *The Education of Henry Adams* (New York, 1918); *History of the United States during the Administration of Jefferson and Madison* (9 vols., New York, 1890–1898); *John Randolph* (Boston, 1895); *Letters to a Niece and Prayer to the Virgin of Chartres; with a Niece's Memoirs by Mabel La Farge* (Boston and New York, 1920); *Life of Albert Gallatin* (Philadelphia, 1880); *Mont-Saint-Michel and Chartres* (Boston and New York, 1913).

Brooks Adams, *America's Economic Supremacy* (New York, 1900); *Law of Civilization and Decay: an Essay on History* (New York, 1895); *The New Empire* (New York, London, 1902); *The Theory of Social Revolutions* (New York, 1913).

Charles Francis Adams, Jr., and Henry Adams, *Chapters of Erie and Other Essays* (Boston, 1871); Charles Francis Adams, Jr., *Charles Francis Adams 1835–1915; an Autobiography* (Boston and New York, 1916). See also W. C. Ford, *A Cycle of Adams Letters, 1861–1865* (2 vols., Boston and New York, 1920).

III. VICTORIAN REALISM. For material in Parrington's introduction to Chapter III see Francis Marion Crawford, *The Novel: What It Is* (New York, 1908); and H. H. Boyessen, *Literary and Social Silhouettes* (New York, 1894).

Henry James, *The Novels and Tales of Henry James* (24 vols., New York, 1907–1909); *Views and Reviews* (Boston, 1908); *The Letters of Henry James* (2 vols., New York, 1920). For criticism and biography see Pelham Edgar, *Henry James, Man and Author* (Boston and New York, 1927); Rebecca West, *Henry James* (New York, c. 1916); Van Wyck Brooks, *The Pilgrimage of Henry James* (New York, 1925).

William Dean Howells, *A Hazard of New Fortunes* (New York, 1891); *A Modern Instance* (Boston and New York, 1881); *Through the Eye of the Needle* (New York and London, 1907); *A Traveler from Altruria* (New York, 1908); *The Rise of Silas Lapham* (Boston, c. 1912); *April Hopes* (New York, 1888); *Certain Delightful English Towns; with Glimpses of the Pleasant Country Between* (New York and London, 1906); *Indian Summer* (Boston, c. 1914); *Venetian Life* (19th ed., new and enl., Boston, c. 1907); *Criticism and Fiction* (New York, 1891); *Literary Friends and Acquaintance* (New York and London, 1901); *Literature and Life* (New York and London, 1902); *My Literary Passions* (New York, c. 1895). For his life see *Life in Letters of William Dean Howells* (2 vols., Garden City, N. Y., 1928); *Years of My Youth* (New York, c. 1916). For critical estimates see Delmar Gross Cooke, *William Dean Howells; a Critical Study* (New York, c. 1922); Oscar W. Firkins, *William Dean Howells* (Cambridge, Mass., 1924); Alexander Harvey, *William Dean Howells; a Study of the Achievement of a Literary Artist* (New York, 1917).

BOOK II: PART I

I. THE PLIGHT OF THE FARMER. For general surveys of the Agrarian movement see Solon Justus Buck, *The Granger Movement* (In *Harvard Historical Studies*, Vol. XIX, Cambridge, 1913); and his *The Agrarian Crusade* (New Haven, c. 1920); F. E. Haynes, *Third Party Movements since the Civil War* (Iowa City, Iowa, c. 1916); F. J. Turner, *The Frontier in American History* (New York, 1920).

For discussions of the currency see *Homo's Letters on a National Currency* (Washington, 1817); *Currency Explosions, their Cause and Cure* (New York, 1858); *Our Currency: Some of Its Evils, and the Remedies for Them* (By a Citizen of North Carolina, Raleigh, N. C., 1861); D. H. Robertson, *Money*

(New York, c. 1922); J. Lawrence Laughlin, *The Principles of Money*, (New York, 1911).

David Ames Wells, *Practical Economics; a Collection of Essays Respecting Certain of the Recent Economic Experiences of the United States* (New York, 1885); *Robinson Crusoe's Money* (New ed. New York, 1896); *The Cremation Theory of Specie Resumption* (New York, 1875); *Contraction of Legal Tender Notes vs. Repudiation and Disloyalty* (New York, 1876).

Eleazar Lord, *Credit, Currency and Banking* (New York, 1828); *A Letter on the National Currency* (New York, 1861); *Six Letters on the Necessity and Practicability of the National Currency, etc.* (New York, 1862); *National Currency: A Review of the National Banking Law* (New York, 1863).

Peter Cooper, *Ideas for a Science of Good Government* (New York, 1883); *The Political and Financial Opinions of Peter Cooper* (New York, 1877).

William Hope Harvey, *Coin's Financial School* (Chicago, c. 1894); and J. A. Woodburn, *The Life of Thaddeus Stevens* (Indianapolis, c. 1913.)

III. HAMLIN GARLAND AND THE MIDDLE BORDER. For studies of the Middle Border see D. A. Dondore, *The Prairie and the Making of Middle America: Four Centuries of Description* (Cedar Rapids, Iowa, 1926); Lucy Lockwood Hazard, *The Frontier in American Literature* (New York, 1927).

For early realism of the Middle Border see Harold Frederick, *Seth's Brother's Wife* (London, 1898); and Joseph Kirkland, *Zury: The Meanest Man in Spring County* (Boston and New York, 1887).

Hamlin Garland, *Back-Trailers from the Middle Border* (New York, 1928); *Boy Life on the Prairie* (Revised ed., New York and London, c. 1899); *The Captain of the Gray Horse Troop: a Novel* (New York, c. 1902); *Crumbling Idols* (Chicago, 1894); *A Daughter of the Middle Border* (New York, 1921); *The Eagle's Heart* (New York, 1900); *Jason Edwards, An Average Man* (New York, 1897); *Main-Travelled Roads* (New York, c. 1891); *Her Mountain Lover* (New York, 1901); *Prairie Folk* (New and rev. ed., New York, 1899); *Rose of Dutcher's Cooly* (New York, c. 1899); *A Son of the Middle Border* (New York, 1917); *A Spoil of Office* (New York, 1897); *Trailmakers of the Middle Border* (New York, 1926).

BOOK II: PART II

II. THE QUEST OF UTOPIA. Edward Bellamy, *The Duke of Stockbridge; a Romance of Shay's Rebellion* (New York and Boston, 1901); *Equality* (3d ed., New York, 1897); *Looking Backward, 2000–1887* (Boston, c. 1889); see also *The Nationalist, a Monthly Magazine* (Vols. 1–3, May, 1889, to April, 1891. Edited by H. W. Austin).

For general material see Allyn B. Forbes, *The Literary Quest for Utopia, 1880–1900* (Social Forces, Vol. VII, 1927, pp. 179–189). Lewis Mumford, *The Story of Utopias* (New York, c. 1922); J. O. Hertzler, *The History of Utopian Thought* (New York, 1923).

INDEX

421

Lightning Source UK Ltd.
Milton Keynes UK
UKOW030035240513

211153UK00006B/42/P